China's Financial Transition at a Crossroads

China's Financial Transition at a Crossroads

EDITED BY
CHARLES W. CALOMIRIS

Columbia University Press

NEW YORK

Columbia University Press
Publishers Since 1893
New York   Chichester, West Sussex
Copyright © 2007 Columbia University Press
All rights reserved

Library of Congress Cataloging-in-Publication Data
China's financial transition at a crossroads / edited by
Charles W. Calomiris.
p.   cm.
Collection of papers presented at joint Columbia-Tsinghua
University conferences in 2005 and 2006.
Includes bibliographical references and index.
ISBN 978-0-231-14192-5 (cloth : alk. paper)—
ISBN 978-0-231-51209-1 (e-book)
1. Finance—China—Congresses.   I. Calomiris, Charles W.
II. Title.
HG187.C6C438   2007
332.0951—dc22   2007010371

∞

Columbia University Press books are printed on permanent
and durable acid-free paper.
This book is printed on paper with recycled content.
Printed in the United States of America

c 10 9 8 7 6 5 4 3 2 1

CONTENTS

List of Acronyms   vii
Acknowledgments   ix

———

Introduction   1
   Charles W. Calomiris

1. China's Financial Markets: An Overview   23
   Lee Branstetter
   Comment: Xiaobo Lü   79

2. China's Banking Sector and Economic Growth   86
   Loren Brandt and Xiaodong Zhu
   Comment: Michael DeStefano   137

3. Understanding the Structure of Cross-Border
  Capital Flows: The Case of China   144
   Eswar Prasad and Shang-Jin Wei
   Comment: Daniel H. Rosen   193

4. Financial Openness and the Chinese Growth Experience   202
   Geert Bekaert, Campbell R. Harvey, and
   Christian Lundblad
   Comment: Mary Wadsworth Darby   281

5. The Effects of Stock Market Listing on the
  Financial Performance of Chinese Firms   290
   Fred Hu
   Comment: Ailsa Röell   307

6. China's Exchange Rate Regime: The Long and Short of It   314
   Barry Eichengreen
   Comment: Jialin Yu   343

7. China's Foreign Exchange Policy: What Will China Do?
   What Should China Do?   350
       Peter Garber, Robert J. Hodrick, John H. Makin,
       David Malpass, Frederic S. Mishkin, and Eswar Prasad

Appendix 1
Regional Estimates of New Deposit and Loan Shares,   379
and Nonperforming Loans
       Loren Brandt and Xiaodong Zhu

Appendix 2
Evolution of Capital Controls in China   383
       Eswar Prasad and Shang-Jin Wei

List of Contributors   405
Index   413

ACRONYMS

ABC	Agricultural Bank of China
ADR	American Depository Receipt
AMC	asset management company
BERI	Business Environment Risk Intelligence
BOC	Bank of China
BOJ	Bank of Japan
CBRC	China Banking Regulatory Commission
CCB	China Construction Bank
CFETS	China Foreign Exchange Trading System
CGB	Chinese government bond
CIRC	China Insurance Regulatory Commission
CITIC	China International Trust Investment Company
CMB	China Merchants Bank
CPI	Consumer Price Index
CSRC	China Securities Regulatory Commission
FDI	foreign direct investment
FFE	foreign-funded enterprise
FIE	foreign-invested enterprise
GCF	gross capital formation
GDP	gross domestic product
GNP	gross national product
HKSE	Hong Kong Stock Exchange
ICBC	Industrial and Commercial Bank of China
ICRG	International Country Risk Guide
IFC	International Finance Corporation
IFRS	international financial reporting standards
IMF	International Monetary Fund

IPO	initial public offering
JSB	joint-stock bank
MOFTEC	Ministry of Foreign Trade and Economic Cooperation
MSCI	Morgan Stanley Capital International
NBFI	nonbank financial institution
NDF	nondeliverable forward
NPL	nonperforming loan
NYSE	New York Stock Exchange
OECD	Organization for Economic Co-operation and Development
PBOC	People's Bank of China
PRC	People's Republic of China
QFII	qualified foreign institutional investor
RCC	rural credit cooperative
RCF	rural credit foundation
RMB	renminbi (currency of People's Republic of China)
ROE	return on equity
SAEC	State Administration of Exchange Control
SAFE	State Administration for Foreign Exchange
SASAC	State-owned Asset Supervision and Administration Commission
SCRES	State Committee for the Reform of Economic Structure
SDB	Shenzhen Development Bank
SEC	Securities and Exchange Commission
SGAEC	State General Administration of Exchange Control
SOCB	state-owned commercial bank
SOE	state-owned enterprise
TFP	total factor productivity
TIC	trust and investment corporation
TVE	township and village enterprise
UCC	urban credit cooperative
UNDP	United Nations Development Programme
VAT	value-added tax
WTO	World Trade Organization

ACKNOWLEDGMENTS

The production of this volume has been an unusually collaborative effort involving many people living in the United States and China, in a variety of occupations. Upon taking over as academic director of the Jerome A. Chazen Institute of International Business, I proposed that our first major project should focus on China's financial transition, that the project should involve practitioners and academics, and that it should be informed by discussions that would take place in both China and the United States. Dean Glenn Hubbard and Associate Dean Jace Schinderman offered their enthusiasm and encouragement from the very beginning, and the dean's office ensured the crucial financial support that made it possible to attract so many talented people to the project and to realize the successful completion of the volume.

From the start, Professor Lee Branstetter, formerly my colleague at Columbia Business School and now a professor at Carnegie Mellon University, and a contributor to the volume, played a key leadership role in identifying the best people to serve as authors and commentators, and helping to coordinate our efforts in both China and the United States. Lee's efforts were crucial in ensuring that the authors and commentators who contributed to the chapters in this volume would be both a diverse and a distinguished group.

To ensure that the perspectives of participants would be up-to-date and informed by financial experts living in China, we enlisted the help of a team of scholars and practitioners at Tsinghua University in Beijing, headed by Dr. Fred Hu, who holds an appointment both at Goldman Sachs and at Tsinghua University, and who is a contributor to this volume. In collaboration with Tsinghua University, we organized a private conference in Beijing in August of 2005 for the early presentation and discussion of the chapters in this volume. In addition to the authors, the other scholars and practitioners who kindly attended and offered advice to the authors included Professor Chong-En Bai of Tsinghua University; Dr. Steve Barnard of the International Monetary Fund; Dr. David Dollar of the World Bank; Dr. Fang Xinghae, vice president of the Shanghai Stock Exchange; Professor David Li of Tsinghua University; Dr. Shan Li of Bank of China International Holdings; Dr. Lin Shoukang, managing director of China International Capital Corporation; Mr. Jesse Wang, deputy general manager of Central Huijin Co.; Professor Yijiang Wang of Tsinghua University and the University of Minnesota; Dr. Wang Jun of the World Bank; Professor Chenggang Xu of the London School of Economics; and Dr. Yongding Yu, director of the Institute of World Economy.

Several months after the private conference in Beijing, Columbia Business School hosted a public conference in New York, at which the revised versions of the chapters were presented and the discussants presented their commentaries. Through the efforts of Associate Dean Jace Schinderman and the extraordinarily capable staff of the Chazen Institute, including Director Joshua Safier, Katrina Barnas, and Jennifer Tromba, the event attracted a large and diverse group of participants, including many of Columbia Business School's prominent alumni, faculty, students, and friends.

Myles Thompson of Columbia University Press attended the conference and was an enthusiastic advocate of the volume at the press. His hard work helped us to achieve the important task of publishing the work in a timely fashion—which, given the pace of reform in China, all agreed was essential. Marina Petrova and Sarah Failla of Columbia University Press assisted in that effort, and their dedication is much appreciated. I am also indebted to two anonymous referees who assisted the press and the editor by providing very useful criticisms.

My job as editor was made much easier than it otherwise would have been through the help of two assistants. Katrina Barnas at the Chazen Institute was charged with the task of keeping all the authors and commentators (and the editor) on track in meeting their respective deadlines, as well as coordinating the schedules and paperwork related to the conferences. She managed to do so cheerfully, patiently, and above all, skillfully. I am also indebted to Johannes Koeppe, a Ph.D. candidate at Columbia, who provided extremely helpful and careful last-minute technical assistance to the editor and the authors.

China's Financial Transition at a Crossroads

———

INTRODUCTION

Charles W. Calomiris

In 2005, as part of a new set of initiatives designed to foster greater and deeper communication between academics and practitioners, the Jerome A. Chazen Institute of International Business at Columbia Business School decided to sponsor a major project exploring current prospects for financial policy reforms in China. The goals of this project were (1) to provide a treatment of the trajectory of financial reform at this time—its recent past, current status, and likely future; (2) to undertake both a deep and comprehensive effort by including detailed, empirical analysis of each major area of recent reform (domestic banking sector reform, securities market listings of Chinese firms, capital inflows from abroad, and foreign exchange policy); (3) to include a variety of perspectives and techniques in that analysis—that is, those of academics, practitioners and policymakers—all of whom have unique and important perspectives on financial reform, and all of whom can benefit from a collective effort to take stock of China's financial policies and prospects and to promote further communication among them; and (4) to ensure that, while preserving the authentic voices and techniques of these various participants, we would also produce a written volume of essays that would be accessible to someone with an MBA level of training in finance and a basic knowledge of the Chinese economy.

This volume is the result of that effort. The chapters are designed to be used either as part of a comprehensive investigation of China's current reforms or as stand-alone contributions to specific areas of investigation. Unlike a monograph, this volume brings together the perspectives of many authors and commentators. Unlike the typical "conference volume," it does not merely collect existing papers, but rather is designed to address important related questions. The chapters taken as a whole provide an integrated vision of China's financial reforms and prospects.

In a fundamental sense, the subject of this book is the future of Chinese economic modernization. Without question, financial policy choices have become the primary areas of focus in the current debates about Chinese growth prospects. Those financial policy choices include the structure of laws and regulations affecting financial intermediaries (including commercial banks and investment banks), rules governing firms' access to public markets for funds, rules governing international capital flows, and foreign exchange policy. Up to this point, with respect to its financial and foreign exchange systems, China has made a great deal of progress in real growth despite its underdeveloped financial and foreign exchange systems. The growing consensus is that this is no longer possible. This consensus is fueling an ambitious and wide-ranging effort to reform the financial system, as well as the rules and policies governing capital flows and exchange rate determination.

With respect to the domestic financial system's role as an effective resource allocator, self-finance has been the primary engine of growth for Chinese entrepreneurs. Savings channeled through retained earnings or the savings of individual entrepreneurs and their associates have been the engine of private sector growth, not bank or securities market-intermediated finance. The banking system has yet to enter an era in which banks perform true arms-length credit transactions, based on the analysis of credit risk, subject to enforceable laws that define and protect the rights of creditors and debtors. Securities markets have begun to develop, but entry into these markets is restricted and performance has sometimes been lackluster.

Foreign investment has been largely confined to foreign direct investment (FDI) because of capital controls limiting the ability of firms to use other forms of foreign capital. The foreign exchange system had been founded on a long-maintained fixed exchange rate, and strict controls of foreign exchange transactions, which at least ostensibly limit transactions to those involving foreign trade or the expatriation of profits to foreign owners.

This system is beginning to change. When China joined the World Trade Organization (WTO), it agreed to a dramatic and rapid opening of its financial markets to foreign entrants. Significant portions of the state's stakes in the largest ("big four") banks are being sold to private holders. Banks' balance sheets have been improved by the state's absorption of loan losses. A host of new financial laws and regulations are now being promulgated and debated. The previously fixed exchange rate is being allowed to fluctuate within a narrowly defined band, the currency has appreciated slightly, and a gradual, long-term continuing appreciation is widely expected. Limits on the ownership of foreign assets by domestic residents have been relaxed somewhat, and forms of capital other than FDI have been growing in importance over time.

China has reached an important crossroads in the development of its financial and foreign exchange systems, in six important respects at once:

1. A crossroads for determining the future path of capital allocation, with important implications for growth and stability.

2. A crossroads for China's foreign exchange rate policy, which will be defined in terms of both the pace of any near-term currency appreciation and the new long-term regime that will be established for determining the extent of currency variability.

3. A crossroads for deciding how much and what type of international capital market transactions will be allowed, which is also closely related to the question of how changes in the foreign exchange rate will be managed.

4. A crossroads for the developing relationships between the Chinese government and foreign financial institutions, which will now play an increasing role in Chinese financial markets.

5. A crossroads for the political relationships between China and the United States, which could pose significant shocks to trade relationships, trade flows, and global capital inflows, given the political heat that has been generated in the United States regarding China's alleged "currency manipulation."

6. A crossroads for China's own internal political evolution, which may be more closely linked to financial reform than is immediately apparent.

A CROSSROADS FOR CAPITAL ALLOCATION, INVESTMENT, AND GROWTH

Among the various determinants of China's continuing economic growth, current efforts at banking sector reform stand alone in importance. Chinese growth rates have been impressive thus far, but we need to be cautious about the future. Future growth will be more dependent than ever on the success of financial sector reform, especially banking sector reform. Two cautionary notes are particularly relevant.

First, despite China's rapid growth in the past, statistics on gross domestic product (GDP) have exaggerated the true growth in value added in the Chinese economy (as compared to, say, growth rates for the United States) because GDP statistics mask the large amount of intentional value destruction inherent in investments in state-owned enterprises (SOEs), which are mainly financed by loans from state-owned banks. Loans are made to SOEs often with little or no hope of repayment. The SOEs' investments financed by the state-owned banks are a clear case of value-destroying expenditures—that is, capital investments that are worth less as productive capital (in terms of the expected cash flows that those investments will generate) than the amount invested in that capital.

The amount of value destruction from such investments occurs at the time the loans are made and the capital is purchased, but the net destruction of value is not reflected in GDP growth at that time. Rather, the increase in GDP is measured as the amount *spent* on investments, not the amount that the investments are worth. In the United States, a reasonable presumption prevails that because investment is part of a competitive market process, capital purchases are an accurate, reasonable indicator of value added from investment, and thus there is no need to adjust U.S. GDP statistics to better capture true value creation from investment. But that is not true for China's investments in SOEs. The amounts spent for these investments are substantially greater than the amount they are worth. If GDP were adjusted for this effect, the actual level of GDP would be lower in China than the measured level.

The value destruction from China's SOE investments does eventually show itself, though not in the form of a downward GDP adjustment. When the government ultimately provides the taxpayer funds necessary to absorb the loan losses in the state-owned banks that result from value-destroying investments, that amount reflects ex ante value destruction. The cost of the partial cleanup of bank balance sheets undertaken by the Chinese government in recent years has already been enormous.

These losses did not just represent bad luck, and they were not a surprise. Rather, one of the primary functions of the Chinese banks in the economy has been to purposely and predictably lose money on their loans by making loans to finance value-destroying investments.

Branstetter (note 71 of chapter 1) estimates the eventual cost of cleaning up past NPLs from SOE loans at roughly $500 billion. Continuing losses on new SOE loans could remain large. Brandt and Zhu's data in chapter 2 shows that more than half of the loans made to SOEs in the 1990s became nonperforming. Loss rates on those loans reached 90 percent. Annual lending to SOEs remains at roughly 15 percent of GNP. If half of those loans became nonperforming, and if loss rates on those NPLs reach two-thirds, the continuing annual value destruction from new loans to SOEs would be 5 percent of GNP.

If China is unable to reform its banking sector, and transform it into a vehicle for efficient allocation of capital, the potential implications for China are far-reaching. Those implications include major risks of (1) a reduction of growth; (2) a financial crisis; and (3) a fiscal crisis. The risk of a growth slowdown in the absence of financial reform follows from the law of diminishing returns and was evident in the 1990s for several other high-growth countries in East Asia (e.g., Korea). As development proceeds, "low-hanging" fruit is picked first. Cheap labor, together with unexploited obvious production opportunities, make the efficiency of capital allocation less relevant for the earliest wave of investments. As an economy becomes more developed, maintaining growth becomes more challenging, and the importance of efficient capital market allocation for maintaining growth consequently rises over time.

As the Asian crises of the 1990s illustrate, the poor-capital market allocation that results in a growing stock of bad bank loans does not just result in diminishing productivity growth, but also in a bankrupt financial system. The rising risk of bank insolvency can itself create an incentive for deposit and foreign capital flight, as was evident in the Asian financial crises. The cost of resolving bank insolvency, preventing or mitigating depositors' losses and subsidizing government-favored lending institutions, can be enormous. The fiscal consequences of absorbing losses in Korea, Thailand, and Indonesia were greater than 20 percent of GDP in each of the three economies. These fiscal shocks, and the need to "monetize" them, go a long way toward explaining the large depreciations of the currencies that attended those crises. For China, such a fiscal cost would be especially unwelcome, given the large anticipated fiscal burden that Chinese taxpayers will already have to bear to support retirees, which will grow significantly in the coming decades as the result of China's low birthrate.

Continuing the growth experience and avoiding a major financial crisis like the one that plagued other Asian countries in 1997 will depend crucially on improvements in the financial sector. China's growth over the past three decades has been driven by vast amounts of savings, which have financed massive capital accumulation. China's stunningly high savings rate has reached nearly half of GDP in recent years, which is high even for high-saving Asia. Savings are channeled to investment either through the reinvestment of earnings outside the formal financial sector (entrepreneurial savings, the pooling of funds among business associates) or through the intermediation of the banking sector, and to a much lesser extent, via securities markets. The large quantities of savings and investment have produced remarkable growth in China, but because the efficiency of capital investments has been low and declining over time, high savings is no longer enough to sustain rapid growth. In the long run China's high savings rate is not desirable; after all, consumption, not production, is the ultimate purpose of economic activity.

Looking forward, the most important question about banking reform is whether the banks will be able to stop making value-destroying loans to SOEs in the future. An optimistic view would emphasize the enlightened self-interest of the government and the big four banks (and their investors), who recognize the substantial social and private costs of failing to reform. The pessimists, however, point to the extreme difficulty from a domestic political perspective of eliminating the implied loan subsidies received by favored bank borrowers, including influential SOEs. Bank loan losses are the lifeblood of political patronage, as Minxin Pei (2006) cogently argues in his recent book, *China's Trapped Transition*. Eliminating loan losses means eliminating the existing system on which politicians and their constituents rely. Pei contends that, absent a political revolution, lending reform is not feasible as a matter of simple arithmetic. That pessimistic view of reform is buttressed by the lack of existing legal infrastructure and the lack of experience with the management of credit risk within the financial sector, both of which are important for developing an arms-length system of efficient intermediation.

If the risk of failure in banking reform is great, then the need for successful reform of securities markets is all the greater. In order to create a captive market for favored securities offerings, the Chinese government has rationed access to securities market offerings by "de-statizing" enterprises. But returns performance has been weak for those offerings, particularly for the less desirable offerings, which tend to be placed in the Shanghai and Shenzhen exchanges rather than in Hong Kong or other foreign markets. Many firms that offer shares in the Shanghai and Shenzhen exchanges have not resolved internal corporate governance problems, which are often related to the continuing large stakes in those firms owned by the government. This limits the ability of firms to pursue value maximization and makes those firms less attractive to investors.

Thus, from the standpoint of both successful banking sector reform and securities market reform it is crucial that the government come to grips with the problem of inefficient SOEs. These SOEs impose a fiscal burden, sap resources from capital markets, and limit the government's willingness to liberalize financial markets in order to give private sector firms a chance to raise funds competitively.

A CROSSROADS FOR FOREIGN EXCHANGE AND INTERNATIONAL CAPITAL FLOWS POLICIES

After many years of maintaining a fixed yuan–dollar exchange rate, the Chinese government is facing intense pressure to allow its exchange rate to appreciate and to let the exchange rate float (that is, allow its value to be determined by market supply and demand, with minimal government currency "interventions" involving government buying or selling of foreign currency). China has accumulated a vast reserve of over $1 trillion in U.S. Treasury securities and currency as the result of its persistent current account surplus, which is closely related to its undervalued exchange rate. Although an undervalued currency boosts exports, it raises the cost of imports. It also presents political problems for China to the extent that political leaders and interest groups in the United States and elsewhere use undervaluation of the yuan to justify attempts to roll back free trade agreements or place punitive tariffs on China.

China's leadership has also signaled that it sees a need to reform its exchange rate regime. The government seeks to reduce the country's reliance on exports as an engine of growth and sees an increasing future reliance on internal demand as another motor of growth. China's government also is beginning to reduce some restrictions on Chinese capital market inflows and outflows. All of these trends would be consistent with both an appreciation of the yuan and a movement toward a flexible exchange rate. A flexible exchange rate would facilitate the emergence of an autonomous domestic monetary policy regime (which may be desirable to manage domestic aggregate demand in an economy less reliant on export growth). As international financial economists have long recognized, a "trilemma" characterizes monetary, exchange rate, and capital markets policies. A government can choose any two of the following policies, but not all three: a fixed exchange rate, open capital markets, and a domestic monetary policy. Given China's movement over time toward more reliance on domestic demand as the engine of growth, and toward greater openness in international capital markets, greater currency flexibility may be a desirable evolution.

A CROSSROADS FOR CHINA'S RELATIONS WITH WALL STREET AND THE U.S. GOVERNMENT

Financial and exchange rate policy changes have important consequences for China's evolving relationship with the West, with respect to both important Wall Street firms and the U.S. government. Wall Street is making significant investments in China's big four banks. This is best seen as a "pay to play" move; Wall Street is willing to make very risky investments in China's big banks in return for the ability to partner with those banks and others to deliver a growing range of financial services to China's expanding domestic financial market. Wall Street has not always found China a hospitable location for new opportunities, as Morgan Stanley's unpleasant experience in the 1990s bears witness. The stakes are much higher this time. If, on the one hand, financial reform succeeds, and if Wall Street firms are permitted to enter profitable new areas (credit cards, insurance, asset management), the potential for mutually beneficial growth and the transfer of technology in the financial sector is enormous. On the other hand, a financial crisis, large losses for investors, and the failure to realize new opportunities in China could have a lasting negative effect on Wall Street's interest in investing in China.

The stakes are also high for U.S.-China government relations. If China continues to maintain an overvalued exchange rate, which seems likely for the near term, the rising chorus of protectionism in the United States may someday succeed in restricting trade. And if, either in reaction to that threat or due to China's own political exigencies, China fails to deliver on its WTO obligations, including the promised opening in financial services, an international political backlash in trade and finance could be significant. Given the size of China's current account surplus, any sudden change in trade flows could have important repercussions for global exchange rates, interest rates, and stock markets.

A CROSSROADS FOR CHINA'S POLITICAL EVOLUTION

Finally, returning to Pei's (2006) view of China's "trapped transition," financial sector reform could have important consequences for China's political development. Pei is pessimistic about successful financial reform because he sees the need to preserve political patronage as too strong a force to overcome. But he may be wrong. Another possibility is that the economic, and therefore, political forces favoring reform are so strong that they will result in a major transformation of Chinese politics. At the moment, this possibility seems a remote one, but the world is full of surprises. Revolutions are not always predicted.

THE CONTRIBUTIONS IN THIS VOLUME

With these important stakes in mind, this volume examines the phenomenon of Chinese financial and foreign exchange systems reform from a variety of important perspectives, and addresses the following important questions.

1. What has been the history of China's progress in the development of its financial system?

2. Why has China now reached a "decision point" regarding financial and exchange rate reform?

3. Why are these financial, exchange rate, and international capital market reforms important to the future of China's growth?

4. What specific reforms are necessary, and which of those necessary reforms are likely to be successful?

To address these questions, with the intention of producing a volume of authoritative contributions on Chinese financial policies and prospects, Columbia Business School's Jerome A. Chazen Institute of International Business invited top scholars and practitioners concerned with financial and foreign exchange reforms to participate in a research project, consisting of two conferences—one in the summer of 2005 at Tsinghua University in Beijing, and one at Columbia Business School in the spring of 2006. Their efforts culminated in this book. The contributors come from diverse backgrounds and include professors, Wall Street economists, a Goldman Sachs director based in China, IMF officials, and a rating agency analyst.

The first six chapters of the book contain detailed scholarly reviews, followed by commentaries by the Columbia conference discussants. Chapter 1 (by Lee Branstetter) begins with a broad overview of the history of financial sector development, regulation, and performance over the past three decades. Chapter 2 (by Loren Brandt and Xiaodong Zhu) focuses on the banking sector and discusses the progress, challenges, and prospects relating to current banking sector reform. Chapter 3 (by Eswar Prasad and Shang-Jin Wei) describes the role of foreign capital in China's development and describes and analyzes the changes in capital flows and controls over time. Prasad and Wei explore various explanations for China's composition of foreign capital and foreign exchange policies, particularly the factors shaping China's reliance on FDI as the primary form of foreign investment. Chapter 4 (by Geert Bekaert, Campbell R. Harvey, and Christian Lundblad) provides an international comparative perspective on the remarkable growth experience of China, and the contribution of its institutional environment to that experience. Chapter 5 (by Fred Hu) examines the experience of foreign-listed initial public offerings (IPOs) of Chinese SOEs, and derives implications from that experience for the desirability of further privatization and further stock market liberalization. Chapter 6 (by Barry Eichengreen) examines the question of exchange rate regime choice for China, focusing on the long-run desirability of flexibility, as well as the appropriate sequencing of reforms in foreign exchange policy, domestic banking reform, and capital market openness.

Chapter 7 presents a roundtable discussion by prominent economists, including some of the top China analysts on Wall Street, at the IMF, and in the academy. Here the focus is on the questions of how much China will appreciate its currency, and what the likely consequences of that policy will be within and outside China. Participants include Peter Garber, Robert Hodrick, John Makin, David Malpass, Frederic Mishkin, and Eswar Prasad.

CHAPTER 1: THE EVOLUTION OF CAPITAL MARKET POLICIES TO DATE

Lee Branstetter ("China's Financial Markets: An Overview") provides a brief history of the breathtaking evolution of Chinese financial markets since the onset of the reform period. He lays out the principal remaining shortcomings and economic challenges the Chinese financial system is likely to face over the next five years. The primary role of this chapter is to provide an integrated historical perspective on the co-evolution of the various parts of the Chinese financial system and policies, and their relationship to Chinese macroeconomic cycles and political developments.

Several themes emerge: the fast pace of reform; the substantial remaining unresolved problems, primarily related to the remaining dominance of state-owned banks, state ownership of bank borrowers and securities issuers, and limitations on private market competition for funding by banks and securities markets; the uneven progress over time; encouraging recent improvements in the institutional regulatory apparatus; the close relationship between investment and growth over the business cycle; and the fiscal costs of bank losses produced by boom-and-bust cycles in which loose credit to SOEs during booms produces large losses during contractions. This latter observation provides a cautionary perspective on the prospects for continuing losses in state-owned banks in the future.

Xiaobo Lü's discussion properly broadens the perspective on financial reform to consider the political context of Chinese economic reform. Lü stresses the important distinguishing features of the Chinese reform strategy: gradualism, state leadership in transforming the function and nature of institutions, and "de-statization" (rather than true privatization) as a means of controlling the transition process of reform. He argues that Chinese reforms, including those in the financial sector, must be judged as part of a comprehensive strategy of reform, which appears to have served China well, despite its inherent weaknesses. The financial sector is a weak spot in the reform process, but those weaknesses are part and parcel of an overall strategy that has been successful, since, thus far, financial sector weakness has not been an obstacle to growth. Lü concludes, however, that the time has come for financial reform to take center stage, since the success of the past may not hold true in the future: "Old approaches such as gradualism and de-statization have worked in the past, but they have also left behind unintended consequences and may not work any more."

CHAPTER 2: THE PROSPECTS FOR BANKING SECTOR REFORM

Brandt and Zhu's review of banking sector reform ("China's Banking Sector and Economic Growth") begins by emphasizing the crucial historical role of value-destroying loans to SOEs in redistributing income and maintaining the political and economic equilibrium during the economic reform process. They examine the recent clean-up in banks' balance sheets, which has been far-reaching, but they point to a substantial new risk of new nonperforming loans emerging, especially if growth slows.

Brandt and Zhu analyze the changing composition of bank loans, based on their unique data collection effort, which allows them to track the characteristics of bank borrowers over time. Brandt and Zhu note that an important process of "recentralization" of the banking system has occurred in the past decade, along with an increased concentration of lending to large firms in a few sectors, which they argue heightens the risk of loss because of less diversification in lending.

Michael DeStefano's commentary echoes and amplifies the reasons for skepticism about the prospects for successful banking sector reform. He sees bright spots in some lending niches, especially in consumer lending, but expresses doubt about the ability of Western bank investors to transform or effectively govern the Chinese banks in which they have invested. He places little confidence in regulators to change bank practices. He also sees continuing impediments to market processes that would otherwise encourage reform—namely, little competition, continuing links to SOEs, sectoral concentration in lending, and little involvement of banks in lending to the export sector or small businesses. DeStefano notes that the increasing maturity of loans (which Brandt and Zhu identify in their data) can present problems for credit quality by masking credit quality problems for long periods of time.

CHAPTER 3: CAPITAL FLOWS AND CAPITAL CONTROLS

Prasad and Wei ("Understanding the Structure of Cross-Border Capital Flows") offer an exhaustive survey of the evolution of capital controls in China. (Their appendix alone—see appendix 2—should be of great value to scholars and practitioners trying to navigate the complexities and changes over time in Chinese capital controls.) FDI has dominated Chinese capital inflows, a phenomenon that the authors point out has occurred *despite* many aspects of the Chinese economic environment that are normally inhospitable to FDI investors in comparative international studies (e.g., a high level of corruption). Most of China's FDI comes from other Asian economies. Prasad and Wei hypothesize that some of China's apparently surprising success in attracting FDI may be related to its relative stability during the Asian financial crises, as well as to the widespread perception that its high level of foreign reserves and capital controls policies made it less susceptible to a financial crisis.

Prasad and Wei point to limitations in the Dooley, Folkerts-Landau, and Garber (2004) model (see the further discussion of this model by Garber, Hodrick, and Malpass in chapter 7) that purports to explain high FDI, high exports, and currency undervaluation as part of a political-economic strategy to use undervaluation to attract FDI and to use reserve accumulation as a form of "collateralization" for repatriation by FDI investors. Prasad and Wei point out that this "mercantilist" story for the high levels of FDI investment "cannot be the entire story" since most of FDI inflows into China are from Asian countries that export to China.

Prasad and Wei offer an alternative view. They emphasize that China's weaknesses in its domestic financial system, the government's desire to attract foreign technology, and other factors probably work together to promote FDI investing as the most desirable means of external finance.

Prasad and Wei identify growth over time in the importance of non-FDI sources of capital inflows into China, especially the category "errors and omissions," which has switched in sign from a net capital outflow to a net inflow. They hypothesize that this change may reflect "hot money flows" that circumvent capital market controls, and reflect the capital importers' desire to take advantage of the yuan's undervaluation.

Daniel Rosen's commentary offers additional facts and interpretations regarding the changing patterns of FDI into China. He notes that a major change has been the growth of FDI into regions other than Guangdong Province, which reflects an increasing focus by FDI firms on production for the domestic Chinese market rather than production for export.

Rosen also points out that repatriations by FDI investors have been rising over time. Part of the motive for repatriation may relate to another point he emphasizes: the recent push to permit Chinese nationals to invest abroad. In April 2006, the People's Bank of China permitted limited access to foreign exchange for the purpose of making foreign investments. This is an important observation: despite the motivation for capital inflows as the result of undervaluation, there is also a diversification motive that results in outflows of currency.

This observation leads Rosen to another interesting conclusion: to the extent that China would increase permissible foreign investments by its nationals, this could act to reduce the undervaluation problem by increasing the domestic demand for dollars. And higher returns to savers from access to foreign investments could also reduce the level of domestic savings and increase import demand, further buttressing demand for dollars. Rosen makes the important point that undervaluation of the yuan is itself partly a consequence of foreign exchange policies, capital controls, and low returns to saving in the domestic financial system. Reforms that buttress opportunities for savers could have far-reaching effects on consumption and the equilibrium exchange rate. The extent of presumed yuan undervaluation is subject to change depending on the path of financial sector and capital markets reforms.

CHAPTER 4: THE IMPACT OF INSTITUTIONAL
FACTORS ON CHINA'S GROWTH

Bekaert, Harvey, and Lundblad ("Financial Openness and the Chinese Growth Experience") reflect on China's economic performance from the perspective of the experiences of a broad panel of countries. They formulate an econometric framework, using standard growth regressions to measure the impact of various factors on a country's growth and the volatility of that growth. In essence, they examine China's experience through the statistical mirror of what its characteristics would predict about its growth and growth variability based on a regression derived from other countries' experiences.

Interestingly, they find that China is a highly exceptional country, providing evidence to back up the often-heard statement that "China is different." According to Bekaert, Harvey, and Lundblad, China clearly is different from the observed regression mapping that relate country characteristics to growth experience derived from the data for other countries. China's extraordinary average growth and low-growth volatility cannot be explained by patterns observed from other countries.

But Bekaert, Harvey, and Lundblad also uncover some surprising aspects of the Chinese growth experience, which are likely to puzzle many "China hands." Consistent with Branstetter's discussion and conventional wisdom about China, they find that the large size of investment has been an important and predictable contributor to growth, but according to their model, trade and FDI per se have not been very important in explaining China's growth.

It is important to emphasize what these findings do *not* mean. Bekaert and his co-authors find that China's trade and FDI cannot explain China's growth if one assumes a relationship between trade and FDI, on the one hand, and growth, on the other hand, that is derived from the experiences of *other* countries. That does not mean that FDI and trade were not important for China's growth; it simply means that if they were important, they were important for reasons that were particular to the Chinese experience and that could not have been predicted based on the experiences of other countries. Other countries' experiences would lead one to underpredict Chinese growth, based on the amounts of trade and FDI observed in China. Indeed, Bekaert, Harvey, and Lundblad point out that "it is conceivable that [as a peculiar feature of the Chinese development experience] trade and FDI indirectly provided significant contributions to factor productivity."

There is a possible connection between the previous chapters in this volume and this interesting conclusion. Because of weaknesses in China's economic and financial system, and its comparatively low level of development and per capita GDP—which are reflected in weaknesses of the domestic financial system, the low level of domestic consumption demand, and the absence of alternative means to promote foreign investment or technology transfer in China—it may be that the impact of trade and FDI on Chinese growth was unusually high.

Bekaert and his co-authors note that China remains a poor country in terms of GDP per capita and that future progress is likely to be more dependent on efficient capital allocations than it has been in the past. They suggest that this likely implies a greater future reliance on capital market reforms and broader access to foreign capital. In several of their prior studies, they have shown a significant positive effect on emerging market countries from connecting to global capital markets.[1] In this chapter they suggest the existence of "threshold effects" relating domestic institutional quality to the ability to reap the advantages of access to foreign capital. This, in turn, suggests that "full capital account convertibility should probably be preceded by a sound institutional framework." This conclusion reinforces the view that now is the crucial moment to push forward financial reforms in China, to clear the way for increasingly necessary improvements in capital allocation and greater reliance on international capital markets in the future.

Mary Darby's commentary emphasizes the perception that she and other practitioners have shared that China's exceptionally high growth does reflect, in large part, its trade policies and its ability to access FDI. She notes that a standard practice in China, which is visible in its policies encouraging joint ventures between foreigners and domestic firms in the financial services sector, is to encourage joint ventures as a means of importing best practices. "Recently when China wanted to allow its banks, which have long been subject to a Glass-Steagall like separation of banking and securities, to enter the mutual fund distribution business, how did it do it?—by requiring that the banks partner with large foreign mutual fund complexes with improved investment management technology."

Darby also points to an encouraging development in the Chinese financial landscape that has not been addressed by other authors, namely, the prospects for the growth of institutional investors. She notes the recent emergence of many new initiatives in China to encourage the growth of institutional investors, which she believes "will add depth and liquidity to the equity markets and will improve prospects for the market to better absorb increased share supply resulting from the sale of state shares." She also states that China has recently announced that it will permit foreign institutional investors to purchase strategic stakes in listed companies. Darby argues that such concentrated block holdings could encourage improvements in the corporate governance of listed firms.

CHAPTER 5: THE EFFECTS OF STOCK MARKET LISTING ON THE FINANCIAL PERFORMANCE OF CHINESE FIRMS

Fred Hu begins this chapter by recognizing that most commentaries on partial privatizations of Chinese SOEs through IPOs have expressed disappointment with that experience. As he points out, however, much of that pessimistic analysis reflects the poor performance of the firms listed on the local Chinese stock exchanges (Shanghai and Shenzhen), rather than those that listed on Hong Kong and other foreign exchanges. Some of the largest and most important (partial) privatizations of SOEs occurred in Hong Kong and other foreign markets, and these firms are the subject of Hu's analysis.

Hu finds that the post-IPO earnings growth, efficiency, profitability, and dividend payout of SOEs listing on the Hong Kong and other foreign markets has been quite positive. Improved profitability, he adds, is all the more remarkable in light of the significant de-leveraging that has accompanied public listing. Improved performance is visible for all sectors with the exception of airlines. His sample of firms represents more than 90 percent of the market value of the Morgan Stanley Capital International (MSCI) China Index as of 2005.

Hu concludes that a combination of factors explain how IPOs contribute to improvements in firms' performance. First, privatization changes the ownership structure of the firm and gives managers greater control and stronger incentives to improve performance. Second, prior to the IPO, important restructuring occurs, which carves out the most valuable parts of the firm for the IPO. This process of streamlining businesses, cutting costs, and cleaning up balance sheets helps to boost the performance of the firm relative to its past. Third, Chinese firms that are listed on international markets have to face strict disclosure standards and the discipline of market scrutiny, which further encourages good performance.

Hu states that "the widely held view that firms listed in China's domestic stock market have failed to live up to expectations should not be generalized to include overseas listed Chinese firms. . . . It also highlights the importance of reforming China's nascent domestic stock market so that it can play the role of efficiently allocating capital and fostering world class Chinese companies." This last comment is especially relevant because it appears that the Chinese government will focus primarily on the domestic market as the outlet for future IPOs.

Ailsa Röell's commentary raises some reservations about how much the performance improvements of the firms analyzed by Hu can tell us about either the actual improvements that have taken place to date for foreign-listed firms as a whole, or the likely improvements that would come from a more widespread use of IPOs as a privatization device. She makes five criticisms. First, the best SOEs in China tend to be selected for IPOs in foreign markets. Lower-quality firms are directed to the local markets where valuation multiples tend to be much higher, owing to the scarcity of offerings. This alleged selectivity bias implies that foreign-listed firms may not be representative of Chinese SOEs generally, thus implying that greater use of foreign listings for other firms might not deliver the same positive results measured by Hu.

Second, Hu does not control for potential survivorship bias, including in his analysis only those firms that survived until 2005. Firms that were delisted or that fell in value so much that they were no longer covered by Goldman Sachs are excluded from his sample. Thus, the average performance results of the sample will tend to exaggerate the performance improvements of all firms listing abroad.

Third, Hu sometimes uses forecasts of accounting information when the actual accounting data are not available. Although his Goldman Sachs forecasts tend to be more conservative than the average consensus forecasts, it is possible that they are still overly optimistic.

Fourth, Röell worries that earnings may be manipulated by management.

Fifth, Röell argues that dividend payments may reflect flows of profits from sources other than the cash flows of the privatized SOE.

These criticisms point to the need for further research to measure the importance of these potential distortions before one can be sure either that the entire sample of foreign IPOs have performed well on average or that prospective IPOs would also be likely to perform well. Nevertheless, Hu's chapter provides an important set of facts about the performance improvements that have occurred in an important segment of the Chinese

IPO market. He shows that, at least for a large fraction of foreign-listed Chinese IPOs, performance improvements have been large.

CHAPTER 6: THE DESIRABILITY OF EXCHANGE RATE FLEXIBILITY AND REFORM SEQUENCING

Barry Eichengreen ("China's Exchange Rate Regime") considers Chinese foreign exchange policy options from a long-term perspective. He analyzes the desirability of moving toward a more flexible foreign exchange rate and examines the necessary accompanying reforms to such a policy and their sequencing. He focuses primarily on the question of the desirability of a flexible exchange rate *regime* rather than on the appropriate level of the exchange rate or the appropriate near-term pace of revaluation.

Eichengreen summarizes his view of the received wisdom of the theoretical and empirical economics literature on the question of the desirability of exchange rate flexibility: "countries subject to distinctive business-cycle conditions ('asymmetric shocks') will want a more flexible exchange rate, since they can both afford and will wish to tailor monetary policy to domestic conditions. In contrast, relatively open economies with weak financial systems will want a less flexible [exchange] rate." From this perspective, China's exchange rate regime choice does not appear clear cut. Eichengreen notes that, on the one hand, China's large size and rapid development and transformation subject it to distinctive business cycle conditions. On the other hand, it has a large export sector and a weak banking system. But Eichengreen argues that these considerations point in an unambiguous direction for future reform: over time, exchange rate flexibility will likely become increasingly desirable for China.

Given that judgment, Eichengreen also considers the importance of adopting the proper sequence of complementary reforms. He argues that there should be a co-evolution of capital account opening and increasing exchange rate flexibility. The increased flexibility of the exchange rate should not await the development of deep markets for hedging exchange rate risk, since those markets will only develop over time in response to the needs created by greater flexibility.

Eichengreen recognizes that moving to a regime of greater exchange rate flexibility may complicate the job of prudential bank regulators, which he says makes it necessary for bank regulators to "issue guidelines for strengthening the banks' internal risk policies and procedures," and establish adequate procedures to monitor foreign exchange exposure.

From the perspective of these arguments for the desirability of greater flexibility, Eichengreen finds that policy actions thus far have not allowed greater flexibility; rather, they have simply set the exchange rate at a different level, with an expectation of continuing appreciation. Eichengreen also constructs a model to estimate the composition of the currency basket on which the managed exchange rate is based. He finds that it is still, in essence, a dollar peg. Eichengreen also contends that the maintenance of a narrow band for the exchange rate is a missed opportunity. Now is the time to widen the band, before market developments and changes in policy make the band a binding constraint.

As a lesson for China, Eichengreen considers Japan's exchange rate policy in the 1970s, when it faced a similar situation to China's present-day situation (an undervalued currency and an economy with a substantial dependency on exports). One significant lesson of the Japanese experience was that the appreciation of the yen in the years 1971 through 1973 did not result in significant adverse macroeconomic consequences. Japan successfully managed domestic demand during the revaluation to mitigate the macroeconomic consequences of revaluation.

Jialin Yu's commentary on Eichengreen's chapter considers one of the arguments sometimes made by proponents of China's more rapid movement toward exchange rate flexibility. Some economists argue that a regime characterized by undervaluation may invite short-term, "hot money" capital inflows, which some regard as undesirable and destabilizing influences. Hot money flows are possible in China, despite capital controls, because companies are able to circumvent controls through under- or over-invoicing of imports or exports (see also chapter 3's discussion of "errors and omissions" in the balance of payments).

Yu points out, however, that if the government's commitment to maintaining undervaluation over time is credible, as is arguably the case in China today, then there is no motivation for short-term hot money flows, since there is no opportunity for short-term profit. Yu analyzes market expectations of exchange rate policy using evidence from forward exchange markets in China, and finds that a one-way bet against the gradually appreciating exchange rate peg maintained by the government is not an attractive speculative opportunity.

CHAPTER 7: ROUNDTABLE ON FOREIGN EXCHANGE POLICY AND ITS CONSEQUENCES IN THE NEAR TERM

Peter Garber begins chapter 7's roundtable discussion ("China's Foreign Exchange Policy") with a summary of the Dooley, Folkerts-Landau, and Garber (2004) view of China's foreign exchange, FDI, and reserves strategy, which Prasad and Wei discussed in their chapter. Garber regards China's policy choice as a natural one for an excess-labor-supply economy, which sees export-led growth as the means to successfully transition from poverty to prosperity. He argues, therefore, that China will choose to change course only once excess labor is absorbed, allowing its currency to appreciate substantially and reversing its reliance on export-led growth and reserve accumulation.

Robert Hodrick reviews the historical Bretton Woods system as a way to cast light on the Dooley, Folkerts-Landau, and Garber (2004) model of China's foreign exchange policy. Under the Bretton Woods system, there was a similar long-term undervaluation of currencies relative to the dollar. The key difference, he argues, is that China's undervaluation is a voluntary action, whereas dollar overvaluation under Bretton Woods was the result of U.S. policy.

Hodrick agrees with Garber's explanation of the logic behind Chinese foreign exchange policy. He also notes that the acquisition of reserves, which are held in the form of U.S. Treasury securities, appears to have had a significant negative effect on long-term rates, which implies a benefit for the United States.

John Makin agrees that there is likely to be a protracted period of undervaluation, and he, like Hodrick, draws attention to the consequences for asset markets. Makin considers what consequences a sustained period of undervaluation of Asian currencies will have for the global economy. Makin, like Hodrick, points to important effects in the treasury market. Makin also argues that the effects on treasuries and other asset prices are likely to fuel inflation, which will, in turn, spur a monetary policy tightening that will eventually result in a substantial decline of asset prices.

David Malpass reinforces the view, shared by other roundtable participants, that China will maintain its policy of gradual appreciation, and he, like Jialin Yu, points to the evidence from forward markets showing that market participants share that view. He takes exception, however, to the view that China's foreign exchange policy is designed to subsidize exports. Like Prasad and Wei, in chapter 3, he notes that this story does not fit all the facts. In particular, China maintained its currency peg in 1998 when its currency was *over*valued. A better explanation of Chinese policy, he argues, is that China has been maintaining a stable long-run exchange rate as a means of achieving exchange rate stability for reasons other than export subsidization, a policy that he regards as quite successful.

Frederic Mishkin approaches China's undervaluation from the perspective of U.S. policymakers. He concurs with Dooley, Folkerts-Landau, and Garber (2004) that China may be pursuing a sensible development strategy. Furthermore, he argues that successful Chinese development is important as a means of alleviating world poverty and should therefore be welcomed by U.S. policymakers. He continues that China's policy has other tangible benefits for the United States, including the low prices of imported goods in the United States.

Eswar Prasad agrees that China is likely to maintain its gradually appreciating peg for some time, but he points to the important costs of this policy from the standpoint of the Chinese financial system's development, which commentators that favor undervaluation often ignore. The accumulation of foreign reserves in the Chinese financial system encourages the continuation of regulations that maintain artificially low lending and deposit interest rates in China, which limit depositors' returns and subsidize inefficient borrowers.

Prasad also worries that, as capital controls become increasingly ineffectual over time, they may become increasingly risky. He proposes that China should consider a movement toward exchange rate flexibility, combined with an inflation targeting policy to guide its monetary authority. He recommends that the Chinese government consider adopting this policy sooner rather than later; the best time to make such a policy change, he says, is in an environment of relative stability and growth rather than in reaction to a crisis.

CONCLUSION

These seven chapters taken together provide unique, timely, and detailed perspectives on one of the most important questions of the next decade: Will China succeed in implementing the crucial financial sector and foreign exchange reforms that financial service providers, practitioners, academics, and its government recognize as likely to be important ingredients for continuing rapid growth? The answer to this question is important in determining China's ability to transform itself from an immature economy characterized by extremely high savings, export-led growth, limited access to foreign capital, and an allocatively inefficient capital market to a mature economy characterized by higher consumption, efficient capital allocation, a globally integrated financial system, and an autonomous monetary policy. But the stakes are high not just for China, but for the growth and stability of the global economy, whose prospects have become increasingly intertwined with China's.

The perspectives of the participants in this volume are balanced and point to potential pitfalls at least as much as arguments for optimism. Reform, after all, is a political process, which makes it inherently difficult to predict, and China's remarkable recent history is a special case of development, whose path is hard to predict based on the experience of other countries. Our project will be deemed a success if we have helped practitioners and policymakers understand and manage some of the risks that await them as they travel the path of reform.

NOTE

1. This perspective disagrees with the more skeptical findings of Prasad et al. (2003), which is mentioned in chapter 3. This apparent disagreement seems to be largely attributable to the way liberalization is defined. When the definition of financial openness focuses on equity market liberalizations (as in the studies by Bekaert, Harvey, and Lundblad, and others), or specific removals of barriers to bank entry, there is little ambiguity about the positive effects of liberalization. For relevant reviews, see Calomiris (2005) and Forbes (2007).

REFERENCES

Calomiris, Charles W. 2005. "Capital Flows, Financial Crises, and Public Policy." In *Globalization: What's New*, ed. Michael Weinstein, 36–76. New York: Columbia University Press.

Dooley, Michael, David Folkerts-Landau, and Peter Garber. 2004. "Direct Investment, Rising Real Wages and the Absorption of Excess Labor in the Periphery." NBER Working Paper No. 10626 (July).

Forbes, Kristin J. 2007. "The Microeconomic Evidence on Capital Controls: No Free Lunch." In *Capital Controls and Capital Flows in Emerging Economies: Policies, Practices and Consequences*, ed. Sebastian Edwards. Chicago: University of Chicago Press.

Pei, Minxin. 2006. *China's Trapped Transition*. Cambridge, MA: Harvard University Press.

Prasad, Eswar, Kenneth Rogoff, Shang-Jin Wei, and Ayham Kose. 2003. "The Effects of Financial Globalization on Developing Countries: Some Empirical Evidence." IMF Occasional Paper No. 220.

CHAPTER 1

China's Financial Markets: An Overview

Lee Branstetter

INTRODUCTION

This chapter provides an historical overview of the development of Chinese capital markets since the onset of the reform period. This important subject has attracted the attention of some of the best scholars working on China over the last 20 years. There is a vast literature for the reader to learn from and build upon. No attempt will be made here to be complete or comprehensive in covering even the major English-language contributions to this literature, much less the enormous volume of work published by mainland Chinese scholars in Chinese.

Instead, the goal is to provide the reader with a basic understanding of the key economic, regulatory, and market developments that have shaped the evolution of China's financial markets up to the present. Whereas the other chapters in this volume focus to a significant extent on China's financial future, one must begin with a clear understanding of the recent past. Given the space constraints, the coverage will necessarily be selective, focusing primarily on banks and equity markets.

In presenting this material, three main themes will be repeatedly emphasized. The first is the centrality of the state in the intermediation of

In writing this historical overview, I have benefited immensely from reading the careful book-length studies of Stephen Green (2003), Yasheng Huang (2003), Nicholas Lardy (1998, 2002), Kellee Tsai (2002), and Carl Walter and Fraser Howie (2003). I have also learned a great deal from discussions with Michael DeStefano, Fred Hu, Wei Jiang, Jack Langlois, Nicholas Lardy, David Li, Shan Li, Xiaobo Lu, Neng Wang, and Shang-Jin Wei. Any errors or inaccuracies are solely my responsibility. Renminbi figures are converted to dollars at the market exchange rates prevailing in March 2006, and may therefore differ from the conversions that appear in the original sources.

capital in the Chinese economy, which has persisted to the present day.[1] Chinese financial markets are dominated by banks, and the banking sector has been and continues to be dominated by state-owned banks, which, until very recently, have concentrated their lending on state-owned enterprises (SOEs). The equity markets have largely consisted of state-owned firms in which the state and its agents have retained a controlling, usually majority, interest. China's dynamic non-state sector, especially its private firms, has been heavily discriminated against in the allocation of capital. Bond markets are dominated by issues of Chinese government bonds, and the right to issue fixed income securities has been tightly restricted.

This situation contrasts sharply with the general trajectory of Chinese economic reform since 1978.[2] At the dawn of the reform period, the prices of nearly all goods and services were set administratively; by the mid-1990s, more than 94 percent of all prices were set by the market. Foreign trade in the late 1970s was highly restricted and monopolized by 12 state-owned trading companies; by the late 1990s, foreign-invested enterprises accounted for more than 55 percent of China's imports and exports, and gross values of import and export flows were equivalent to 75 percent of gross domestic product (GDP). Industrial output was dominated by SOEs in 1978; this fraction has fallen substantially. Chinese labor "markets" were once characterized by lifetime employment, administratively set wages, strictly limited interfirm and geographic mobility, and a cradle-to-grave intrafirm welfare state. Today, Chinese labor markets function much more freely. China's dynamic private firms can increasingly compete freely in the product market and the labor market—but access to capital, while it is improving, remains restricted. The increasing reliance on the market mechanism that is such a visible and striking feature of other aspects of modern Chinese economic life is much less evident in the financial sector.

The second related theme is that reform of Chinese financial markets has been inextricably bound up with the state's efforts to reform and improve the efficiency of its SOEs, while retaining a large degree of ultimate control over them. When this goal proved elusive in the 1990s, the government accepted the need to downsize and privatize a large component of the SOE sector, but the state has consistently reaffirmed, at least rhetorically, its commitment to control the "commanding heights" of the economy by continuing to support (and direct) the largest and most important SOEs, including the most important components of the financial sector.

From a Western perspective, the goal of retaining ultimate state control may conflict with the goal of pursuing maximum efficiency. This conflict may continue to limit the success of ongoing government efforts to improve the functioning of the country's capital markets.

The third main theme is the context of macroeconomic instability in which Chinese financial markets have evolved.[3] This can be illustrated by figure 1.1. The top graph shows the investment to GDP ratio since the early years of the reform period. The bottom graph shows real GDP growth according to the official statistics, which have been the subject of some criticism in recent years. Although real GDP growth has remained consistently positive throughout this period, the growth rate has experienced pronounced fluctuations that are closely related to rapid increases in investment relative to GDP.

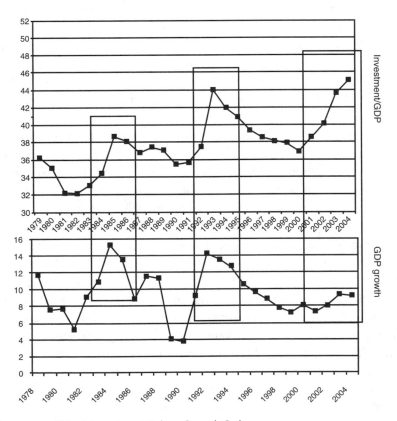

Figure 1.1   China's Investment-Driven Growth Cycles

Sources: Goldstein and Lardy (2004); National Bureau of Statistics.

China has already been through two investment-driven boom-and-bust cycles. The first, in the 1980s, was generated by an investment boom that led to serious macroeconomic imbalances, including rapid inflation, as well as the creation of excess capacity across a range of industrial sectors. The state had to sharply curtail bank lending, bringing investment back down to a sustainable level, but the result was a pronounced slowdown in macroeconomic growth. The second cycle came in the early 1990s. Deng Xiaoping's endorsement of continued economic reform during his famous "journey to the South"[4] touched off another investment boom even more dramatic than the one in the mid-1980s, financed principally by rapidly expanding bank loans. Once again, macroeconomic imbalances, including accelerating inflation, quickly became evident, and the authorities had to curtail bank lending, using a mix of sharp interest rate increases and administrative controls on the volume of lending. In the aftermath of this austerity regime, GDP growth slowed markedly and signs of excess capacity began to appear. Thomas Rawski (2001) has suggested that the combined effects of this slowdown, together with the onset of the Asian financial crisis in 1997, actually caused growth in the period from 1998 through 2000 to decline to considerably lower levels than the official GDP statistics suggest. Goldstein and Lardy (2004) estimate that roughly 40 percent of the loans extended during the early 1990s investment boom became nonperforming in the period of slower growth that followed.

The Chinese economy entered its third investment-driven boom in the early years of the current decade. Starting in 2002, bank lending and fixed asset investment began growing sharply relative to GDP. By 2004, the investment/GDP ratio had reached roughly 50 percent, an all-time high in recent decades.[5] Despite a slowdown in fixed asset investment growth in 2004, the ratio of fixed asset investment to GDP for 2005 remained close to 50 percent.[6] Over the past three years, real GDP growth has accelerated in response to the surge in investment, albeit to a lesser extent than in the past.[7] As in earlier investment-driven booms, government officials have decried the creation of excess capacity, particularly in certain industrial sectors, and the authorities have imposed stringent limits on lending and investment. While there is no sign yet of any significant deceleration in real GDP growth, some concern has arisen that economic growth will decelerate over the next several years, as the overhang of excess investment is slowly absorbed.[8]

A number of market observers have pointed out, correctly, that the current investment boom has been financed, to a greater extent than in the past, by enterprises' own retained earnings. Net external financing, most of it through bank loans, has only accounted for about 30 percent of enterprise investment in the current cycle, as opposed to 40–60 percent of investment in the investment boom of the 1990s. As a consequence, the inevitable slowdown may pose less of a risk to the banking system than the slowdown of the mid- to late 1990s.[9] That being said, even proponents of this view concede that the current investment rate is likely to be unsustainably high, and enterprises that have overextended themselves may be unable to pay off their bank loans. This will probably trigger another substantial increase in the level of nonperforming loans (NPLs) in the banking system.[10] A slowdown in corporate earnings and aggregate demand may complicate efforts to improve the functioning of the equity market. This macroeconomic context is critical as one considers the trajectory of financial reform over the next few years.

CHINA'S BANKING SYSTEM

Chinese financial markets are dominated by banks to an extent that stands out even in Asia, with its history of bank-dominated financial markets. Chinese domestic equity and bond markets continue to play a relatively small role in the intermediation of financial capital to businesses in contemporary China. In 2003, lending by Chinese banks, as measured by total growth in loans outstanding, totaled 2.99 trillion renminbi (RMB). The total amount of funds raised on domestic capital markets, not including Chinese treasury debt or financial policy bonds, was less than 116 billion RMB—that is, *less than 4 percent of the increase in loans outstanding.* The sum of initial public offerings, secondary offerings, rights issues, and the sale of convertible bonds on domestic equity markets amounted to less than 82 billion RMB. Net funds raised by nonfinancial corporations through corporate bonds issuance was less than 34 billion RMB.[11]

Most other East Asian economies have traditionally had bank-dominated financial systems, but in many of those countries, the role of banks, at least in relative terms, has shrunk as domestic capital markets have developed and expanded. There is no sign of such a general trend in China, as can be seen in figure 1.2.[12]

For this reason, any discussion of Chinese financial markets, their history, and their evolution, will have to begin with a discussion of the banking

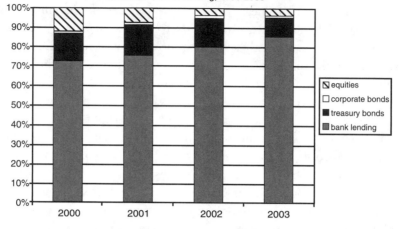

Figure 1.2   Sources of New Funds

Source: People's Bank of China.

system. I will begin by briefly reviewing the structural transformation of the Chinese banking system from a Soviet-style monobank on the eve of the reform period to the present.

FROM MONOBANK TO A BANKING SYSTEM — REFORMS OF THE 1980S

In the early years of the People's Republic of China (PRC), the private and quasi-private banks of the Republican era were either closed down or folded into state-owned financial institutions. By the dawn of the reform period, in 1978, China nominally possessed three separate state-owned banks, but in reality there was only one: the People's Bank of China (PBOC), which simultaneously served as the chief lending institution and the nation's central bank.[13] The PBOC regulated the money supply, set interest rates, managed the PRC's foreign exchange, and supervised the rest of the financial system. In addition, through a nationwide network of over 15,000 branches, subbranches, and offices, it controlled roughly 80 percent of all deposits and was the source of over 90 percent of all loans by financial institutions.[14]

The Bank of China (BOC) was effectively a subsidiary of the PBOC and specialized in handling foreign exchange transactions, working closely with the state-owned trading companies. The China Construction Bank (CCB), created by the PRC in 1954, operated as a branch of the Ministry of Finance, disbursing funds to approved investment projects that were part of the state economic plan; the funds came from the state budget. In reality, it was not a bank at all. There was a network of rural credit cooperatives, but their primary purpose was to mobilize rural savings—they did relatively little lending.[15]

In fact, the pre-reform banking system did relatively little lending in a modern economic sense. Household savings was very low relative to GDP. National savings were high but came primarily from the operating surplus of the state-owned industrial sector. This surplus was reinvested primarily through state budget allocations rather than lending per se. It is perhaps only a slight exaggeration to conclude that in the pre-reform era China lacked not only capital markets but also a banking system.[16]

Starting in 1979, the monobank began to evolve into a banking system with an increasingly complex and heterogeneous set of institutions. The Agricultural Bank of China (ABC) was reestablished with a mandate to focus on deposit and lending activity in rural areas, as part of the government's broad strategy to improve the agricultural sector. In the same year, the State Council brought the Bank of China out from under the authority of the PBOC and expanded its business scope in order to support China's rapidly expanding trade and foreign investment. Finally, the Construction Bank was elevated to similar status and allowed to take deposits and engage in lending activity rather than simply disbursing government funds.[17]

In 1983, the council decided to convert the PBOC into a central bank more on the lines of international standards. Over the next two years, the PBOC began to take on these normal central banking functions. However, the policy directives of the PBOC were subject to approval by the State Council—the PBOC has not had, nor does it have today, the kind of legally mandated independence granted to the U.S. Federal Reserve, the Bank of England, or the Bank of Japan.[18]

The former commercial banking functions of the PBOC, including its vast network of offices and its enormous loan portfolio, were transformed into an independent lending entity, the Industrial and Commercial Bank of China (ICBC), which upon establishment in 1984 was (and remains) the single largest bank on the mainland. Together, the big four state-owned banks—the BOC, the ABC, the ICBC, and the CCB—continue to dominate China's financial system, accounting for 55 percent of all assets in the financial system as of the end of 2003 and roughly half of all new lending in recent years.[19]

As these institutions were taking shape, revolutionary changes and rapid growth in the rural Chinese economy, mostly reflecting the rapid de-collectivization of agriculture, led to an explosion of household savings. In the absence of alternatives, much of this flow of new savings found its way into the banking system. Income growth and high savings rates persisted throughout the 1980s, providing the nascent banks with an ample supply of new funds.[20] Bank deposits grew nearly 25 percent per year from 1985 to 1990.[21]

INCREASING COMPETITION AND COMPLEXITY

In the early years of the reform era, the big four operated with mandates that were, for the most part, nonoverlapping. The BOC managed transactions associated with foreign trade, the ABC concentrated its activity in rural areas, the ICBC lent to state-owned industrial enterprises, and the CCB financed new infrastructure and other investment projects. However, starting in the mid-1980s, the boundaries of their business models began to blur, new financial institutions arose, and competition began to increase. For example, the Bank of China lost its monopoly on foreign currency transactions as other state-owned banks moved into this market.[22]

Perhaps more significantly, there were two main waves of new bank creation, the first occurring in the mid- to late 1980s and the second in the early to mid-1990s. These gave birth to banks that today account for about 14 percent of all bank assets. These banks are legally organized as shareholding companies, and many are listed on China's A-share domestic stock market. The composition of shareholders reflects multiple entities, including foreign financial institutions. In most cases, however, a majority or plurality of outstanding shares are held by government entities, including SOEs, and governmental authorities continue to exercise considerable influence over senior executive appointments and other high-level decisions.[23] Yet these institutions were generally not subject to the sort of policy-lending directives that distorted much of the lending of the big four through the late 1990s.[24]

On the other hand, direct competition with the big four has been limited inasmuch as these banks collectively possess much smaller branch networks than their big four rivals. The PBOC has to approve the establishment of new bank branches. By year-end 1994, the central bank had allowed the non-state banks to set up 130 branches, 98 subbranches, and 724 offices below subbranch level. In contrast, the big four possessed 138,081 offices below the subbranch level.[25] It seems clear that the pace of reform reflected the government's desire to retain direct control over capital allocation by ensuring the continued dominance of the financial institutions it directly supervised.[26]

Starting in the mid-1980s, there was also a proliferation of nonbank financial institutions, including leasing companies, trust and investment companies, and the internal financial arms of major state-owned conglomerate groups.[27] Urban credit cooperatives predated this period, but began their rapid expansion then. In the 1990s, mergers of these cooperatives in over one hundred cities created what has become the third tier of the modern banking system: city commercial banks. These institutions collectively accounted for about 5 percent of financial system assets by mid-year 2005.[28]

Despite the emergence of an increasingly wide range of players, the big four retained their dominance of financial assets and lending throughout the reform period, and their share of both remained as high as 70 percent as late as the mid-1990s. Furthermore, the business model consisted of taking deposits from households and lending to SOEs. At the end of 1995, the outstanding borrowing of SOEs from banks was 83 percent of all loans outstanding. Consumer credit remained very underdeveloped, and direct lending by state banks to private firms remained extremely limited.[29]

The concentration of lending in the state-owned sector reflected, in part, the degree to which the big four were constrained in their lending decisions by the policy directives of government at various levels. Official statistics do not provide clear indicators of the fraction of loans that were made on the basis of policy directives rather than commercial considerations, but estimates run as high as 40 percent for the banking sector as a whole.[30] More qualitative assessments suggest that 70 percent of the lending made by the big four to SOEs was "policy-based," with little consideration for commercial merit.[31] Through the mid-1990s, the big four were also constrained to follow annual credit quotas from the State Planning Commission that dictated the aggregate level of total lending and the geographic breakdown across provinces.[32]

This led to a distinctive pattern in the geographic distribution of Chinese bank lending that is clearly evident in the official statistics. Provinces in which SOEs accounted for a particularly large share of industrial output, such as Jilin, Inner Mongolia, and Heilongjiang provinces, were characterized by high "loan-to-deposit" ratios. Bank deposits grew rapidly in coastal provinces where private firms, foreign-funded enterprises, and township and village enterprises (TVEs) were expanding their share of industrial output. However, branch banks in these provinces were not constrained by high lending quotas, because of the limited amount of SOE activity. Instead, these banks tended to place a large portion of their funds on deposit with the central bank. The central bank then re-lent these funds to branch banks in the provinces in which SOEs tended to dominate local industrial activity, which were thus characterized by a high ratio of loans to deposits. The central bank also engaged in lending through its own branches in those provinces. Regression analysis by Boyreau-Debray and Wei (2005) suggests that official policy allocated capital away from the country's most productive regions and toward some of its least productive regions.[33]

Defenders of China's economic record have suggested a political rationale for this pattern of capital allocation and for the relatively slow pace of reform in China's financial sector more generally.[34] While economically inefficient on the face of it, preferential allocation of capital to SOEs might have been politically necessary in order to maintain broad-based support within the system for continuing economic reform. Had the SOE sector been forced to shrink too quickly or change too drastically, the momentum of reform might have been drastically undermined.[35] The truth of this assertion is obviously difficult to assess—we do not observe the counterfactual world in which a different pattern of allocation of capital obtained. Nevertheless, it is reasonable to think that pressure to compensate vested interests was an important factor in explaining the pattern of allocation of bank lending.

In addition to mandated credit quotas, the banks had to contend with regulated interest rates on both deposits and loans. Official interest rates appear to have been consistently set far below market-clearing rates. This is particularly evident during the periods of high inflation that occurred in the late 1980s and early to mid-1990s. The rate of increase in producer prices for industrial goods peaked in 1989 at 19 percent and again in 1993 at a scalding 24 percent, which far outstripped the nominal interest rate on working capital loans of 11.34 percent and 10.98 percent, respectively.[36] Strongly negative real interest rates exacerbated excess demand for capital and arguably induced excess investment on the part of firms with access to bank loans. The degree to which official rates deviate from a hypothetical market-clearing rate is less clear outside of these inflationary periods, but indirect evidence is provided by press accounts of the many illegal private banks that have sprung up throughout China to provide financing to the private entrepreneurs that were largely excluded from the formal financial system until the late 1990s. Tsai (2002) cites Chinese press accounts of interest rates in the informal financial sector running 30 to 100 percent higher than the official bank rate.[37]

Chinese commentators have pointed to a political explanation for the persistence of financial repression in China in the 1980s and 1990s. Li (2001) and Bai et al. (1999, 2001) have argued that these policies amounted to a flat tax on bank deposits and that, given the institutional constraints of the government's taxation system during the reform period, a partial reliance on this tax was actually optimal.[38] At the same time, these authors acknowledge the longer-run costs of financial repression and the need to move to a more market-directed financial system.

Political interference in the operations of the major banks was not limited to the lending quota and interest rate regulation that favored borrowers. Until the PBOC began to aggressively reassert control over its vast network of local offices in the mid-1990s, the provincial branches of the PBOC tended to be more responsive to the political directions of provincial governments than they were to the PBOC central headquarters in Beijing. This reflected the political realities of the appointment process— selection of the top officials in provincial PBOC branches was controlled by provincial party officials, not the central office of the PBOC. Because the local representatives of the agent of the state charged with overseeing the banking system tended to follow the dictates of local officials, it is not surprising that the provincial branches of the big four banks tended to do the same. The organizational structure of the PBOC was reformed in the mid-1990s at the instigation of Zhu Rongji, with the aim of reasserting central control.[39] The goal appears to have been largely successful, but local government influence over lending decisions continues to affect the efficiency of banking in China.[40]

The final dimension of government interference was confiscatory taxation of the banks. China's largest banks have been required to pay significant taxes on their gross income. Through the end of 1996, China's major lending institutions were compelled to pay the central government taxes equal to 5.5 percent of gross income as well as additional business income taxes on their operating income. Lardy (1998) has shown that this was equivalent to a business income tax rate of 73–84 percent in the mid-1990s for the largest banks. Perhaps it is not surprising that about one-sixth of central government revenue in the mid-1990s came from taxes on the big four banks. In the late 1990s, business income taxes on banks were reduced, but the tax on gross income was increased to 8 percent. This has been reduced since then, but taxes on gross income remain a significant barrier to profitable bank operations.[41]

The Ministry of Finance's disproportionate reliance on tax revenue from the banks in the 1990s created some interesting conflicts of interest from a regulatory perspective. The ministry has been reluctant to allow banks to make provisions for NPLs that would have the impact of reducing operating income and, thus, revenue for the state. As increasingly effective revenue collection and continuing economic growth allowed government revenues to increase substantially faster than GDP, the fiscal rationale for this kind of policy began to ebb.[42]

Over the course of the late 1980s and early to mid-1990s, the combined impact of these interventions took their toll on the health of the Chinese banking system as a whole and the big four banks in particular. Bank capital shrank as a fraction of assets, NPLs accumulated in the system at an increasing rate, and the margin on corporate lending diminished. By the mid-1990s, it was becoming increasingly clear that major reform of the financial system was required. The central government began to accept the fact that SOE reform had not succeeded, and the consensus at senior levels shifted in favor of privatizing and downsizing firms in that sector.[43] Press accounts suggest that the early stages of the East Asian economic crisis unfolding in neighboring countries helped convince the senior leadership that quick, decisive action was needed.

But it was also clear that bank reform could not take place in a vacuum. It had to be integrated with further reform of the state-owned sector. The dilemma facing the central government in the mid-1990s can be easily summarized. Despite rapid growth in the non-state economy, the government still relied heavily on the state sector for tax revenues; it relied on the investments of state firms to meet its industrial policy and development objectives; and it relied on state firms to provide what welfare state existed in Chinese cities.[44] Keeping the state sector alive in a liberalizing, marketizing, increasingly competitive economy required increasing infusions of capital from the banks, and this was the ultimate source of the banks' problems. Cutting off the state-owned firms without developing alternative sources of revenue, however, could precipitate a fiscal crisis, and cutting off state firms without first creating some kind of social safety net for the workers that would be inevitably displaced would invite social chaos. All of these nettlesome problems had to be tackled at once.

FROM POLICY-LENDING TO A COMMERCIAL CREDIT CULTURE—REFORMS SINCE 1994

Even before the shock of the Asian financial crisis, major steps toward reform were already being undertaken. We can divide these reforms into those directly focused on the banking sector and complementary reforms that we will only note briefly, referring the reader to more comprehensive treatments elsewhere in the literature. We will deal with the latter reforms first.

The central government instituted fundamental tax reform in the mid-1990s, making a value-added tax (VAT) the centerpiece of central government revenue collection. It took several years for the state revenue authority to effectively implement this system, but starting in the late 1990s, government revenue began growing as a percentage of GDP, after falling for the first 12 years of the reform era. This provided the government with a steadily increasing degree of financial independence from the SOE sector.[45]

Next, the government began taking steps to create a safety net in urban China that was increasingly independent of the SOE sector. Perhaps the most important component of this safety net is something that is not normally associated with those in the West: housing. Even in the late 1990s, a huge fraction of residential housing units in Chinese cities were owned by SOEs and provided to SOE employees at highly subsidized rates. Over the latter half of the 1990s, the urban housing stock was progressively privatized, and an active urban real estate market began to develop.

This allowed the state to take a harder line with chronically loss-making SOEs. Huge numbers of them were either shut down or forcibly converted into other categories of enterprises, with the state largely leaving them to their own devices.[46] Manufacturing employment in the state-owned sector fell by two-thirds over the course of the late 1990s.[47] Unofficial estimates of employment in the Northeastern provinces especially dependent on the SOE sector skyrocketed.

At roughly the same time that the government was cutting down the size of the state sector, it was taking important and expensive steps to strengthen the banking system, particularly the big four. First, the state created three new financial institutions that would henceforth be responsible for making loans in support of the state's policy objectives: the Agricultural Development Bank, the China Development Bank, and the Export-Import Bank. In principle, these institutions would pursue the "policy-lending" objectives of the government, allowing the state-owned commercial banks to refocus their lending on purely commercial lines.[48]

Second, the central government recapitalized the state-owned commercial banks. In 1998, the government injected RMB 270 billion ($34 billion) into the four major banks, directly boosting their capital reserves. Then, the government established four asset management companies (AMCs), each of which was paired with a major bank. The AMCs took RMB 1.4 trillion ($175 billion) in NPLs off the books of the four largest banks and an additional RMB 100 billion off the books of the China Development Bank.[49] The banks received interest-bearing bonds from the AMCs equal to the *face value* of the transferred loans (about 20 percent of their gross loan book), substantially strengthening their balance sheets.

Third, the banks were forced to adopt more stringent accounting standards, which made it progressively harder for them to conceal their bad loans. Starting in 1998, banks were no longer allowed to accrue unpaid interest on outstanding loans and count it as income.[50] At the same time, the formal lending quota system was abolished, providing the banks with more freedom in their allocation of capital. Senior bank managers were put on notice that a reduction in the NPLs to asset ratio was absolutely necessary, and they were encouraged to pursue aggressive targets for this reduction.[51] Banks were allowed, and even encouraged, to lend to consumers on a large scale. Some shareholding banks were allowed to undertake initial public offerings (IPOs), and the government made it clear that it intended to sell a stake in the stronger major banks when conditions were appropriate.

THE MIXED SUCCESS OF BANKING REFORM

In the period immediately following this bank reform through 2002, a number of positive signs emerged suggesting that attempts to instill a more commercially-oriented credit culture in the banking system were bearing fruit. First, the big four banks collectively made a major effort at internal reorganization, which included closing surplus and unprofitable branches; by 2002, they had collectively closed more than a third of their offices. Second, measured NPLs in the banking system declined, even as more stringent reporting requirements, at least on the part of the four major banks, were adopted. Third, the number of loans grew at a moderate pace, suggesting that the rapid, indiscriminate lending of the mid-1990s had been replaced by a greater degree of prudence. During the investment boom from 1992 through 1994, the growth in the stock of outstanding loans relative to GDP rose from about 12.5 percent in 1989 to a peak of 19 percent in 1993. From 1998 to 2001, this measure increased at a steady pace of about 15 percent or less, well below the extreme levels of the investment boom years. Fourth, there was a dramatic increase in lending to households, mostly to finance mortgages and auto purchases. The share of new lending to households increased from 1.1 percent in 1998 to an average of 20.2 percent from 1999 through 2002.[52] This implies that the share of lending to SOEs fell substantially.

Other economic indicators suggested that the allocation of capital became more efficient in the aftermath of these reforms. Throughout the 1990s, it was well known that the banking system was propping up SOE production of goods for which there was little demand. One could see evidence of this in the national accounts. In modern national accounting systems, inventory unsold at the end of the year is technically counted as investment, and its value is added to the GDP aggregate. However, in most industrialized economies, firms take care not to produce goods that customers will not buy, and unsold inventories usually account for less than 1 percent of GDP. From 1992 to 1997, unsold inventories accounted for 5.3 percent of Chinese GDP, on average, providing powerful evidence of the wasteful allocation of capital in China. From 1998 to 2003, this dropped to about 1 percent.[53]

TWO STEPS FORWARD, ONE STEP BACK

From the perspective of early 2006, it is apparent that while much progress has been made, much work remains in terms of reforming China's banks. First, it seems clear that the creation of the policy banks has not completely eliminated the burden of policy-lending from the state-owned commercial banks. Consider the way that the policy banks are funded: these institutions issue long-term bonds that are mostly purchased, on terms favorable to them, by the state-owned commercial banks. The level of issuance has increased sharply over recent years.[54] The banks clearly believe that policy bank bonds are backed by the state and that there is no meaningful risk of policy bank bond default, but the simple fact is that policy-lending continues to use the financial resources of the state-owned banks, albeit indirectly.

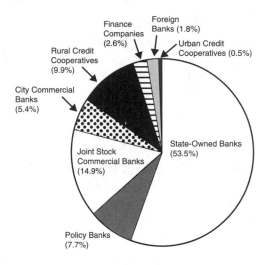

Figure 1.3   Composition of the Banking Sector in 2004

Source: OECD (2005). Note that this graph reports the distribution of assets within banks and finance companies only. Assets in insurance companies and fund management and securities companies are excluded. Trust and investment companies are counted together with finance companies.

Figure 1.3 illustrates the distribution of assets in the banking system across organizational categories. By 2004, the big four banks' collective share of banking sector assets had declined to 53.5 percent from levels of greater than 70 percent in the mid-1990s. But the policy banks accounted for another 7.7 percent of banking sector assets, suggesting that the total fraction of banking system resources controlled by institutions under direct state control remained above 60 percent.

Second, political factors likely continue to influence the lending of the state-owned banks. An interesting perspective on this was provided by a widely cited interview in *Caijing* Magazine given in April 2005 by Guo Shuping, recently appointed chairman of China Construction Bank, and Xie Ping, the head of Central Huijin Investment, which now holds shares in CCB on behalf of the state since the bank's conversion to a shareholding enterprise. Both individuals called for a reduction in the role of Communist Party committees in the operations of financial institutions. Mr. Guo acknowledged that the Party Committee had dominated bank governance to the point of debating individual loan decisions under his predecessor, whereas the board of directors, which was vested by CCB's corporate charter with ultimate authority, had played almost no role. Mr. Xie criticized the almost total control over senior appointments maintained by the party's organization department. Mr. Guo suggested that the conflict between the board and the Communist Party Committee would be eliminated under his stewardship. In addition to being chairman, he is also the party secretary, and he comes to CCB after serving as a senior administrator with the foreign exchange regulatory agency.[55]

Influence over senior appointments extends to the "joint-stock" banks in the second tier, as illustrated by a 2003 interview Ma Weihua, then CEO of Shenzhen-based China Merchants Bank (CMB), gave in the *China Economic Quarterly*. Mr. Ma was a graduate of the Communist Party School, a 20-year veteran of government service, and was head of a provincial branch of the PBOC before coming to CMB. At the time of the interview, he was also a delegate to the National People's Congress.[56]

Third, the lending restraint shown by the banks in the immediate post-reform period broke down in late 2002, helping power the investment surge depicted in figure 1.1. In 2003, the stock of loans outstanding expanded by nearly RMB 3 trillion. The increase in loans outstanding relative to GDP rose to 25 percent, well above the previous peak in the investment boom from 1993 through 1994. PBOC governor Zhou Xiaochuan and China Banking Regulatory Commission (CBRC) Chairman Liu Mingkang began trying to slow the growth rate of lending as early as mid-2003, and growth in lending has come down over the course of 2004 and 2005. Inflationary pressures that appeared to be building in the economy are moderating. Consumer Price Index (CPI) inflation has fallen substantially from its high of 5 percent in mid-2004, and the corporate goods price index has fallen from a high of over 9 percent to a roughly 5 percent rate of annual increase. However, the level of lending has reached such stratospheric levels that the investment to GDP ratio remains extremely high by historical standards.[57]

The manner in which lending growth was curtailed also suggests that reform has had its limits. In modern market economies, central banks will typically respond to a lending boom by raising the cost of capital, leaving it to the private market to sort out which projects to fund as the cost of funds increases. Interest rates were increased 27 basis points in late 2004, but this left short-term lending rates—at roughly 5.6 percent—lower in real terms than they had been in 2002. By late 2004, the corporate goods price index was increasing at more than 9 percent per year.[58] In other words, real interest rates were negative, just as they became in the lending boom from 1992 through 1994. Instead of substantially raising interest rates, the authorities sought to bring lending under control by simply ordering banks to stop lending, particularly to certain industrial sectors, regardless of the underlying quality of investment projects a particular bank might be considering. In terms of preventing inflationary pressures from building, this has evidently worked. On the other hand, government direction of lending by administrative fiat is not supposed to be the direction in which China's increasingly market-driven financial system is heading.

As of early 2006, growth remains robust, and it is as yet quite hard to determine what fraction of loans extended during the lending boom may become nonperforming. PBOC statistics suggest that growth in lending during the credit boom from 2002 through 2004 was concentrated not in the largest state banks, but in the other segments of the banking system, including the joint-stock commercial banks. Some warning signals have emerged in the financial press. In February 2004, China Minsheng Banking Corporation was hit with a fraud scandal. By June, China's bank regulator was publicly warning of deterioration in the solvency of the second tier of the banking sector.[59] Shenzhen Development Bank, effectively acquired by American private equity firm Newbridge Capital Management in a landmark deal in 2004, was criticized for deficiencies in risk management and bad loan accounting.[60] Rapid growth in loan portfolios—50 percent per year at the height of the credit boom—has generated the risk of a new flood of bad loans that could emerge as the economy slows.[61] In October 2004, sources at the China Banking Regulatory Commission indicated that the default rate on more than U.S. $23 billion worth of auto loans extended since 2002 already exceeds 50 percent.[62]

The fourth point of caution in the efficacy of bank reform is the asset management companies themselves. As noted, the four state-owned asset management companies purchased RMB 1.4 trillion of NPLs from the state-owned banks at face value. This purchase was financed by the issuance of RMB 820 billion in bonds and the assumption of roughly RMB 600 billion in existing central bank loans to the state-owned banks. The AMCs do not issue regular periodic reports on their financial position, so it has been difficult to determine the extent to which their recoveries on NPLs have been in excess of their costs.[63] As Lardy (2005) suggests, this recovery rate, net of operating costs, is probably less than 10 percent of the face value of the loans. The transfer of NPLs from the balance sheets of the state-owned banks was clearly necessary, but these calculations suggest that the ultimate cost to the Chinese taxpayer will be quite high.

The regulatory authorities are clearly aware of these issues, and efforts at reform have accelerated over the last two years. The locus of reform effort shifted with the creation of the CBRC in 2003; this commission took over the role of bank regulation that had been the responsibility of the PBOC. In December, CBRC Chairman Liu Minkang announced that the big four banks were now free to seek foreign "strategic shareholders"—something that had only been allowed in the lower tiers of the banking system. The CBRC also pushed through a regulatory change allowing banks to issue subordinated debt in order to strengthen their capital base.

In early 2004, the CBRC issued a new set of capital adequacy standards that will apply to all segments of the banking system, except for policy banks and rural credit cooperatives. These regulations require all commercial banks to meet an 8 percent capital adequacy ratio by January 1, 2007. Banks are also required to change the risk-weighting of their assets in a way that eliminates most of the discounting of risk that had been applied to loans to SOEs. By 2006, banks must have set aside provisions equal to 80 percent of their nonperforming loans, using a five-tier classification scheme that is much closer to international standards than the traditional four-tier system.[64] The stronger banks have been aggressively writing off NPLs, and nearly all major banks are seeking to raise capital through equity issues, sales of stakes to "strategic investors," and issues of subordinated debt. Industry observers also expect that this new regulatory regime will force banks to be much more selective in lending—expansion of assets can only take place when capital also grows.

The CBRC has also proactively sought to fundamentally reform China's largest banks, starting with the relatively healthier BOC and CCB. Both banks have been pushed to institute sweeping reforms of internal management, restructure the credit approval process, and make major investments in new IT systems. The Bank of China received a U.S. $22.5 billion capital injection from the government in December 2003 and was allowed to transfer another U.S. $19 billion of NPLs to Cinda Asset Management Company in June 2004 at a price that was probably higher than the fair value of the loans. In August 2004, the BOC became a shareholding company under Chinese law. CCB also received a U.S. $22.5 billion capital injection in December 2003 and sold roughly U.S. $17 billion in NPLs to Cinda Asset Management in June 2004. In September 2004, it became a shareholding company. In recognition of the improvement in financial health engendered by these changes, Standard & Poor's raised the bond ratings of BOC and CCB to investment grade.[65] Both banks have issued large amounts of subordinated debt to strengthen their capital bases, and both received substantial investments by foreign financial institutions in the banks prior to their international IPOs. CCB sold stakes to Bank of America, and Temasek, the investment arm of the government of Singapore. Bank of China received substantial investments from the Royal Bank of Scotland, Merrill Lynch, Temasek, and the Li Ka-Shing Foundation.[66] Global equity markets appear to have provided a strong endorsement to the government's reform strategy: CCB raised U.S. $9.2 billion in its November 2005 IPO, successfully selling new shares at the top of the indicative price range.

Despite this market success, recent news stories suggest that the ongoing management reforms at the large state-owned banks remain a work in progress.[67] A BOC subbranch manager in Harbin fled the country after stealing as much as $125 million in customer accounts at the end of 2004. This was followed by the announcement in April 2005 that the Beijing branch had lost $81 million in a major mortgage fraud.[68] These scandals followed the dismissal of the CEO of BOC's Hong Kong branch for approving loans to individuals later convicted of securities fraud.[69] A much larger scandal, involving a scheme to steal nearly $1 billion from the Industrial and Commercial Bank of China, emerged in January 2005, amid government announcements that nearly 80 officials, including senior ICBC executives, were involved in the plot.[70]

Presuming that ongoing management reform and the influence of foreign "strategic investors" do succeed in fundamentally altering the way the state-owned banks work, it will still require an enormous injection of capital from the state to bring the much weaker ICBC and ABC up to the levels of financial health that the government has helped BOC and CCB obtain over the last two years. Standard & Poor's has estimated that it could take up to U.S. $197 billion to clean up these two financial institutions.[71] This makes no allowance for bad debt elsewhere in the financial system. Analysts believe that there are extremely high levels of NPLs in the rural credit cooperatives and that these would constitute an additional burden to the state.[72]

China is in the fortunate position, however, of having rapid economic growth, steadily rising revenues relative to GDP, abundant foreign exchange reserves, and a relatively modest ratio of government debt to GDP.

It seems clear that China has the financial resources to clean up its banking system, and the current reform effort has taken a number of important steps in the right direction.[73] The institutional foundations of a sustainable, more market-driven banking system appear to be taking shape in China today. But we are not there yet.

EQUITY, DEBT, AND INSURANCE MARKETS

THE DEBATE OVER EQUITY MARKETS IN THE 1980S

Long before the central government formally established the current equity exchanges in Shanghai and Shenzhen in the early 1990s, there was widespread small-scale experimentation with equity issuance and trading. This history is described at length by Walter and Howie (2003). Agricultural collective enterprises began issuing financial instruments referred to as shares, although they were actually something more like a fixed income security. In the interests of promoting development and growth in a countryside that had been starved of investment for decades, the government formally approved this practice. Perhaps not surprisingly, enterprising factory managers, public officials, and private entrepreneurs began informally financing their ventures through issuance of equity shares. A Shanghai-based factory called Shanghai Feile Acoustics is given credit as being the first Chinese enterprise to issue common stock–like securities to the general public, back in 1984, long before the establishment of a national legal framework governing securities issuance or a formal, legally sanctioned stock exchange. While large numbers of share-issuing enterprises had sprung up by the mid-1980s, this phenomenon remained a spontaneous, small-scale response to the general problem of capital scarcity and excess demand for investment funds. At that time, the development of an organized equity market in China was not a major focus for the central government.[74]

That was about to change. At the same time that China's equity finance pioneers were experimenting with share issuance, a debate was growing within the Chinese government as to the future path of SOE reform. Reformers were beginning to advocate the "corporatization" of SOEs as the ultimate—indeed the only—solution to the problems of China's SOEs. In a strikingly radical and prescient internal government policy paper in 1983, two young government economists suggested that SOEs be reorganized as joint-stock corporations and that a substantial equity stake be sold to outside investors, including foreigners. This proposal was publicly circulated in 1985 as a front-page essay in the nation's most widely circulated economics newspaper, *Jingji Ribao*.[75]

The authors, Wu Jiaxiang, a 30-year-old official in the Theory Department of the Central Department of Propaganda, and Jin Linzuo, a 27-year-old official in the State Commission for Economic Structure Reform, began their argument by emphasizing the inefficiency of the allocation of capital in China. Central planners controlled much of this allocation, but they were simply unable to determine which firms could use these resources most efficiently, and there was no effective way in contemporary China for the private savings of households to fund especially productive firms.

Wu and Jin argued that these inefficiencies were made even more intractable by the absence of well-defined property rights that separated the firm from the state. Investment decisions were necessarily clouded by bureaucratic and political objectives that compromised their economic efficiency. Government-appointed managers identified more strongly with the ministries they came from than the firms they governed. The authors laid out a plan for solving this problem by legally separating firms from the state—one that appears to have served as an inspiration for the later "privatization" of SOEs.

In the initial step, the firms' assets would be evaluated and shares would be issued to the supervising agency or, as was often the case, multiple supervising agencies. Ownership of shares would empower the governmental bodies that had supervised the firm in the past to appoint representatives to a board of directors, which, in turn, would appoint professional managers—not government cadres—to run the company on behalf of its shareholders. Eventually, Wu and Jin advocated that the shares held by the governing agencies be transferred to state holding companies, which would manage the firms according to purely commercial criteria. This second stage would sever the political connection between regulating agency and private firm that might otherwise distort the actions of both firm and agency. At the same time, the majority stakes held by the state holding companies would preserve state ownership and ultimate state control.

The final stage would allow large SOEs to issue shares to private investors on domestic and international stock exchanges. This would allow productive, progressive SOEs to attract sufficient capital from private investors to enable them to emerge as world-class competitors. Clearly, however, issuance of shares on domestic exchanges would have other desirable

effects. The constant scrutiny provided by the equity market would monitor firm managers more effectively than the government ever could. Equity prices would be a constant, objective reflection of the effectiveness of
firm management, and their movements over time would help steer capital to the most productive firms.

EXPLOSIVE GROWTH OF EQUITY MARKETS IN THE 1990S

While central government officials were debating the theoretical merits of
selling shares in state companies to the public, the practice of doing so
was gathering momentum and increasing public interest, thanks to the
entrepreneurial effort of local governments. In 1986, the Shenzhen government established a set of local regulations known as the Shenzhen Provisions, which provided a legal basis for the corporatization of local SOEs
and other entities. Five SOEs offered shares to the public in 1987, including the Shenzhen Development Bank (SDB).[76] Generally, these initial offerings were poorly subscribed, owing in part to the lack of general
understanding about just what stocks were. The SDB raised public interest significantly a year after its IPO, when it paid its first dividend. The
SDB was quite generous to its investors, and the market value of its shares
soared on the informal over-the-counter exchanges. Suddenly, Chinese
investors had (re)discovered the truth that stocks can appreciate dramatically. Almost overnight, public interest in equity offerings soared.[77] What
had begun as a modest experiment was now becoming a national obses-
sion, at least in Southern China.

The events of June 1989 raised questions in the minds of many conservative government officials about the wisdom of establishing stock
exchanges, but frenetic black market trading in equity shares constituted a powerful argument in favor of establishing formal exchanges
that would bring this activity under stricter government control.[78] This
pragmatic realization combined with unceasing efforts on the part of
the governments of Shanghai (where Zhu Rongji had become mayor in
1988) and Shenzhen to obtain government approval for their exchanges.
In fact, the Shenzhen exchange actually began operations before formal
government approval had been obtained. The Shanghai exchange formally opened first, in December 1990; the Shenzhen exchange was approved in July 1991.[79]

The early years of the exchanges were quite dynamic, though cha-
otic. First, the official stock exchanges coexisted in the early years with

unauthorized trading in regional over-the-counter markets as well as two electronic exchanges, loosely modeled on the NASDAQ, which focused primarily on government bond trading but also engaged in the trading of shares. Second, the regulatory environment was marked by the absence of legal foundations for much of what was going on in the market, and there was uncertainty and ambiguity about which branch of the government was responsible for regulating it.

In 1992, after Deng's Southern Excursion, the State Committee for the Reform of Economic Structure (SCRES) issued the "Standard Opinion," which first set forth national guidelines for reorganizing state-owned companies as joint-stock enterprises that could list shares.[80] The Company Law was not issued until 1994, and, as Walter and Howie (2003) emphasize, it was less connected to the reality of Chinese equity markets than the Standard Opinion that it supposedly superseded. The reforms that converted the PBOC into the nation's central bank had also given it formal authority over the securities markets, but the evident need for a separate securities market regulator, along the lines of the American Securities Exchange Commission, led to the establishment of the China Securities Regulatory Commission (CSRC) in 1992. However, it took more than five years for the CSRC to acquire the resources and regulatory clout that would allow it to fulfill its mandate to effectively regulate China's securities markets. The matter was effectively settled by the 1999 implementation of the long-awaited Securities Law, which elevated the CSRC to ministerial status.[81]

As has been the case throughout China's reform period, market developments forged ahead of the regulatory regime that was supposedly governing the market. The absence of a clear legal basis for equity transactions did not prevent retail investors from wanting to earn quick profits. Memberships on the exchanges surged as eager newcomers piled into the market. Enthusiasm turned violent on August 10, 1992, when hundreds of thousands of would-be investors piled into Shenzhen to subscribe to a new listing. On the day of the offering, the official subscription forms ran out with suspicious speed, leading the frustrated investors to conclude that the subscription process had been corrupted by local PBOC officials. Violent riots broke out in the afternoon and evening. Order was quickly restored, but this event led directly to the establishment of the CSRC.[82]

The entrepreneurial spirit of Chinese managers (and that of their hired foreign investment bankers) was also on full display in October 1992, when Brilliance China Automotive became the first Chinese company to list on the New York Stock Exchange (NYSE)—something for which there was no established legal basis at the time.[83] Zhao Xiyou, chairman of Jinbei Automotive, was seeking to corner the Chinese market on luxury mini-buses, using technology acquired from Toyota. To finance his ambitious plans, he effectively sold an interest in his firm to a Bermuda-based holding company, Brilliance Automotive. Together with local and national politicians, who were brought into the deal, Mr. Zhao retained control of the Chinese enterprise through a nonprofit onshore Chinese foundation. The Bermuda holding company listed shares on the NYSE.[84] The company made its debut on the New York markets at a time when investor interest in China was surging and American investors had almost no avenues to buy into the "mainland China growth story." A billion dollars' worth of orders were placed for the $80 million share offering.[85] Brilliance's stock rose 117 percent within three months of listing. The unsanctioned experiment became a smashing success, prompting praise from none other than China's president, Jiang Zemin.[86] This success started a gold rush, as SOEs from around China sought to tap into global equity markets, which, in turn, were eager to increase their exposure to the world's fastest-growing economy.

Although some Chinese firms continued to use variations on the indirect, offshore structure pioneered by Brilliance Automotive, the Chinese government had already been negotiating with the Stock Exchange of Hong Kong regarding the possibility of listing Chinese SOEs. This more direct, officially sanctioned avenue to global markets was given its trial run in June 1993, when Tsingtao Beer undertook its Hong Kong IPO.[87] As with the Brilliance case, the success of this experiment did much to convince government officials that vast amounts of money could be raised by allowing Chinese SOEs to tap global equity markets. This triggered a burst of additional listings.

From their establishment in late 1990 through 1993, the domestic equity exchanges enjoyed robust demand from investors and rapidly rising equity prices. A sharp drop in the markets occurred following the August 10, 1992 riot in Shenzhen, but demand came roaring back a few months later. These sharp fluctuations reflected, in part, the underdeveloped state of the market. In 1992, there were only 40 listed stocks, so volatility was understandably high. The strong demand reflected, in part, the sizzling economic growth rates being recorded in mainland China in the early 1990s. Real GDP growth rates peaked at 14 percent in 1992 and declined only slightly in 1993. Unfortunately, the sharp acceleration in GDP growth triggered a burst of inflation. Consumer prices were rising slowly at rates in the low single digits in 1991. By 1993, the CPI was rising at 15 percent per year, and this accelerated in 1994 to nearly 25 percent per year. Fearing a hyperinflation and the social unrest this could trigger, the government began firmly applying the brakes in late 1993. Interest rates were sharply increased—the RMB deposit rate was quickly brought up to double-digit rates—and quantitative restrictions on new lending were firmly imposed throughout the economy. During this period of retrenchment, the government sought to limit IPOs and secondary stock offerings.

The harsh medicine worked, but it caused equity markets to drop sharply. Domestic equity indices collapsed, hit by both high interest rates and a slowing economy. The shares of Chinese companies listed in Hong Kong also fell as these internationally listed SOEs struggled with the domestic economic slowdown. By 1996, inflation had dropped back down into the single digits and the economy appeared to be stabilizing at lower rates of growth that were still extremely high by international standards. The central bank began reducing interest rates sharply, and this clearly helped boost demand for equities. The domestic markets enjoyed a spectacular surge in 1996. In addition, 218 companies listed shares on the domestic exchanges (as compared to 36 in 1995), and overseas listings also picked up.[88] In the run-up to the retrocession of Hong Kong to mainland sovereignty in mid-1997, there was also a sharp increase in unofficial overseas listings through offshore holding companies—the so-called Red Chip issues. Market observers have suggested that the final stages of this rally were marked by speculative excesses and that the government was actually seeking to slow the rate of price increase even in 1996.[89]

In any case, the market soon had to confront the onset of the Asian financial crisis in mid-1997. The Hong Kong economy and equity markets were strongly affected by this crisis, and Western investors' interest in Asian equities dropped off sharply, all of which had a rapid chilling effect on the official or unofficial use of Hong Kong to tap international equity markets. Indices of the stocks of Hong Kong–listed Chinese companies and indices of the unofficial Red Chip companies fell dramatically in late 1997. As the severity of the crisis became increasingly evident, the Chinese government responded by sharply cutting interest rates and substantially increasing deficit spending to stimulate economic growth. This action appears to have helped boost the equity markets, but issuance of new shares in both domestic and overseas markets dropped off sharply yet again.[90]

Exactly how well the Chinese economy performed in the aftermath of the Asian financial crisis has been the subject of a highly charged debate within the ranks of economists who follow the Chinese economy. As already noted, Thomas Rawski (2001) has argued that the official statistics in this period may substantially overstate true economic growth. He claims that there may have even been a brief period of negative GDP growth in the wake of the crisis. Other China experts dispute these claims, but a consensus has emerged that official GDP statistics probably overstate real growth in the immediate aftermath of the crisis. The official statistics suggest that GDP, retail sales, investment, and prices stopped declining in 1999 and began to stage a modest turnaround. To the extent that this reflects reality, it may provide the macroeconomic backdrop for the sharp run-up in equity markets from 1999 through 2001. China's listed companies tend to be concentrated in the more trade-dependent coastal provinces, and their local demand conditions were probably more robust than those of the overall economy. In any case, China's equity markets ended the century with a bang, enjoying robust appreciation from 1999 through 2001. Ten years after their establishment, the equity markets appeared to be a real success story for the regime. Over 10 years, share issuance had raised $129 billion for over 1,400 companies, and the total market capitalization of China's exchanges, *as conventionally measured*, made its equity markets the second largest in Asia after Japan.[91]

DECLINE SINCE 2001—WHY HAS THE MARKET FAILED TO REFLECT THE DYNAMISM OF THE ECONOMY?

Equity markets have declined fairly steadily since mid-2001. In 2003 and again in 2004, China's domestic equity markets were the world's most poorly performing major equity markets by a wide margin. The inexorable decline appeared to pause in 2005, and equity markets actually enjoyed a modest boost at the end of the year. Nevertheless, as of early 2006, Chinese equity markets had lost about half of their 2001 value, in spite of a sharp acceleration in real GDP growth. Figure 1.4 tracks equity prices on China's domestic (A-share) exchanges from August 1993 through early 2006. The top segment of the figure shows the indices in nominal terms, rebased so that August 1993 levels are equal to 100. The bottom graph tracks the Shanghai A-share index over time in both nominal and real terms, adjusting for inflation as measured by the CPI. The downturn since 2001 has been so severe that real returns in the Shanghai market since 1993 have been slightly negative. Total market capitalization has dropped even as hundreds of new firms have listed on the Shenzhen and Shanghai exchanges. Figure 1.5

A. Domestic Stock Market Equity Price Indices, August 1993=100

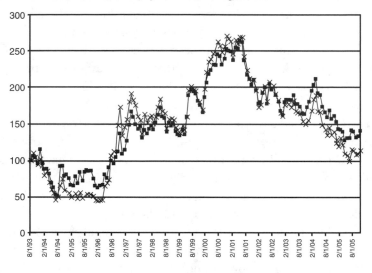

B. The Shanghai Equity Index, Adjusted for Inflation, August 1993=100

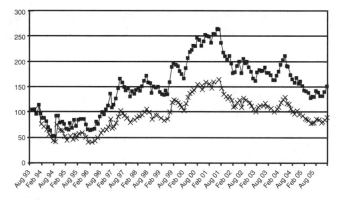

Figure 1.4   Domestic Equity Markets in Decline

Sources: Shanghai and Shenzhen Stock Exchanges; National Bureau of Statistics.

tracks equity indices for Chinese firms listed on the Hong Kong Stock Exchange and for the so-called Red Chip firms—Hong Kong companies whose true base of operations is the Chinese mainland. As of March 2006, both indices were well below the peak values set in the 1990s. Figure 1.6 tracks trends in equity issuance. Not surprisingly, equity issuance expands sharply in bull markets and contracts in bear markets. The volatility of overseas issuance is particularly pronounced.

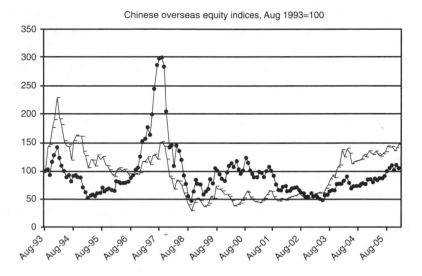

Chinese overseas equity indices, Aug 1993=100

Figure 1.5 Hong Kong China–Linked and Red Chip Equity Indices, August 1993=100

Source: Hong Kong Stock Exchange.

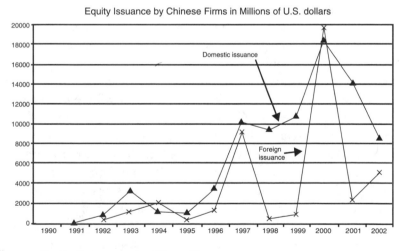

Equity Issuance by Chinese Firms in Millions of U.S. dollars

Figure 1.6 Equity Issuance by Chinese Firms

Source: Walter and Howie (2003).

The poor performance of China's equity markets contrasts sharply with the country's rapid economic growth. While China specialists may have suspected that the official GDP statistics overstated growth in the aftermath of the Asian financial crisis, most experts now believe that, if anything, official GDP statistics have understated real growth in recent years. If the official statistics are to be believed, the Chinese economy has expanded by more than 40 percent since 2001, and foreign direct investment (FDI) has soared, demonstrating the multinational corporations' intense interest in China's dynamic marketplace.

Why have China's equity markets failed to reflect the dynamism of the economy? First, access to public equity markets has been limited to the least dynamic sector of the economy: SOEs. Second, the state and state-controlled entities retain a majority stake in most publicly traded firms. These shares can be transferred under certain circumstances, but they are not traded in the marketplace. This vast overhang of nontraded shares continues to plague the market, and dealing with it constitutes one of the most serious challenges facing market regulators. Finally, the various arms of the state continue to interfere in the operations of many listed companies—a level of interference legally justified by the continuing high level of state ownership. This interference degrades the efficiency of investment decisions. The bottom line is that the ultimate separation of politics and enterprise management envisaged by Wu and Jin more than 20 years ago remains an elusive goal.

For most of their history, the official stock exchanges allowed only SOEs to list shares. The most dynamic sectors of the Chinese economy—private firms and the local subsidiaries of foreign multinationals—have been deliberately excluded from these markets, with a small number of exceptions. Allowing private firms and the local branches of foreign multinationals to compete freely for capital in the equity markets would dramatically reduce the amount of money local investors would willingly invest in the IPOs of SOEs. It would also probably lead to a sharp decline in the market capitalizations of existing SOEs, as investors would shift away from the incumbent firms, many of which have performed quite poorly, to the newly listing private organizations. The high price/ earnings ratios sustained in Chinese equity markets through 2001 largely reflected the limited investment choices available to domestic Chinese investors.

This brings us to the second point. The Chinese state faces a unique conflict of interest in that it is simultaneously the market regulator and the largest holder of equity. The 1992 Standard Opinion promulgated by SCRES laid out several classes of shares that were limited in terms of who could own them. First were the state shares, which for all intents and purposes have been nontradable and nontransferable. Second were legal person shares, which could not be held by individuals or traded directly on equity exchanges. These shares could be held by an organization with "legal person" status under Chinese law. This includes SOEs and other state-affiliated organizations; a large portion of legal person shares have historically been held by such organizations, but this status is not limited to them. Private domestic firms and even the Chinese subsidiaries of foreign firms can acquire this status and therefore hold these shares. The Standard Opinion allowed for the transfer of legal person shares subject to the approval of the exchange on which the underlying firm trades.

As of year-end 2005, roughly 70 percent of the shares in listed firms on China's domestic exchanges were either state shares or legal person shares. A large fraction of shares in the legal person shares category were held by organizations that were direct or indirect branches of the state.[92] The state, directly or indirectly, has retained a controlling interest in most firms via shares that could not be bought or sold in the marketplace. As historians of the market in China emphasize, this was deliberate: the state did not want to surrender control of its enterprises when shares were listed. Thus, as of year-end 2005, the tradable segment of the market was limited to about 30 percent of the shares. This tradable segment was itself divided into two distinct share classes—A shares that were still restricted to Chinese nationals and B shares that (until 2001) were restricted to foreign nationals. H shares, which were listed on overseas exchanges, constituted a third class of shares, but one entirely separate from China's domestic securities markets, in which Chinese citizens themselves could not generally invest due to China's capital controls.[93] While Chinese law indicated that these shares conferred equal rights and benefits on the holders, a casual inspection of share price data for listed companies indicated that, in 2002, H shares traded at a 42 to 88 percent discount relative to A shares in the same company.[94] While investment in B shares was prohibited for Chinese nationals, B shares typically traded at a roughly 80 percent discount to A shares in the same firm. After Chinese nationals were allowed to purchase these shares, the discount narrowed to 50 percent, but a discount remains even today.[95]

This raises fundamental questions of market valuation. There is no one answer to the question, what is a Chinese company worth—much less, what is the Chinese stock market worth? The typical answer quoted in the financial press takes the A-share market price and multiplies that by total shares outstanding, including the nontradable shares held by the state and by legal persons. This calculation, undertaken for the entire market, implied that China had the second largest equity market in Asia after Japan at year-end 2002, before the steep declines of 2003 and 2004 took their toll. However, if one valued only outstanding A shares at the A-share price (implicitly assigning a value of zero to other share classes), the market capitalization at the end of 2002 (before the steep market declines of 2003 and 2004) was only slightly larger than that of Malaysia.[96] Valuing all outstanding shares at the H-share price would yield yet a different value. For at least some of the reformers who argued for the establishment of equity markets, equity prices were meant to serve as a summary statistic of the performance of the firm, guiding capital to the most productive, best managed enterprises. Equity prices do not—and cannot—play this critical signaling role in the segmented markets of contemporary China. Correcting the current situation would seem to require the unification of these markets along with a dramatic increase in the "free float." This, in turn, would require the sell-off of a large component of the state's current direct and indirect shareholdings, which are locked up in nontradable state and legal person shares.[97]

In increasing numbers of cases legal person shares have exchanged hands, including cases in which legal person shares pass from an (often cash-strapped) state-affiliated organization to a private firm, allowing private interests to acquire effective control of a listed enterprise. At least 200 listed firms were believed to have been transferred to private control through these asset transfers as early as year-end 2003.[98] A transfer of legal person shares allowed Newbridge Capital, an American private equity firm, to implement its landmark acquisition of effective control over Shenzhen Development Bank.[99] However, these asset transfers take place without reference to the stock price on the A-share or B-share market. Often, the valuation of the legal person shares are made based on calculations of net asset value, and suggest a valuation that is only a fraction of that implied by the A-share market.[100] In the vast majority of cases, it appears that China's equity markets provide no input whatsoever into the prices at which these asset trades take place.

The fact that these asset trades are taking place at such a large discount to A-share prices illustrates another stark challenge confronting the regulators: the pressure for the state and its various arms and affiliated organizations to sell off their shareholdings. As the state has slowly come to terms with an increasingly important role for the private sector, it has become increasingly willing to sell off at least part of its stake in all but the most "essential" enterprises.[101] If it could do so at the price/earnings ratios that have historically prevailed in the A-share market, the potential windfall for the state would be enormous. Many of the financial challenges looming ahead, such as the recapitalization of the banking system and the looming pensions crisis, would pose much less of a challenge to the treasury if the state could simply sell off a chunk of its titanic equity portfolio.

Rumors that the state was planning such a sell-off to help shore up pension financing in 2001 helped end the bull market. Whenever this idea has resurfaced in policy debates, the market has dropped further. Knowledgeable observers suggest that one of the major factors behind the steady decline in equity prices since 2001 has been the market's anticipation that the state will eventually sell off a substantial portion of its holdings.

The major equity market development of 2005 was the government's push for listed firms to come up with a way of transforming illiquid state and legal person shares into fully tradable A shares. In the final quarter of 2005, at least 130 of the firms listed in Shanghai or Shenzhen had received formal approval from the government for these share transfer schemes.[102] Another 100 or so companies were waiting for approval, and many market participants expect that over the course of 2006 as many as 300 companies, collectively accounting for more than 60 percent of total domestic equity market capitalization, will go through with these transfers. The general pattern is already well established. To compensate existing A-share holders for the price impact of putting previously nontraded shares on the market, the largest holders of state and legal person shares gift a portion of their shares to the existing A-share holders. Generally, three bonus shares are provided for every 10 shares held. Occasionally, free puts or call warrants are transferred to existing shareholders in addition to or in place of new shares. The National Social Security Fund has admitted that it used large amounts of public funds to support the markets while the first set of firms undertook these share transfers. Financial support provided by the People's Bank of China to securities firms may have also played a role in supporting the market. Although it is unclear what role outright public support of the market has played, the equity markets have appeared to react fairly well to the implementation of this plan, even if the market capitalizations of some of the reforming firms have fallen. Additional price supports come from the restrictions placed on the erstwhile state and legal person shareholders. While they will now have a liquid asset, they are explicitly forbidden from dumping it on the market. They cannot sell more than 10 percent of the total share capital of the company over the next three years. The CSRC has also promised to limit domestic IPOs until a large enough number of sufficiently large companies have implemented their share transfer schemes. So far, the market appears to be reacting to these announcements with equanimity. In fact, domestic equity indices have enjoyed a modest boost.

This reform is a major step forward, and the oft-criticized Shang Fulin, chairman of the CSRC, deserves much credit for seeing it through. Once the majority of shares are tradable, the prospects for efficiency-enhancing mergers and acquisitions activity, consolidation, asset trading, and even the emergence of a limited market for corporate control would appear to be far more realistic. The functioning of the market could improve considerably.

Prospects will brighten further if the authorities relax their control over the access of currently unlisted private firms to the public equity markets. Even in a market in which most shares are tradable, investor appetite for a collection of poorly run SOEs is likely to be limited. The best way to bring more capital into the equity markets is to improve the quality of the firms on offer—but allowing private firms and foreign subsidiaries to list domestically would limit demand for the incumbent SOEs even further. Clearly, the state and its various branches want an opportunity to unwind their massive shareholdings first, before they improve the menu of options for Chinese individual investors.

The final barrier to improvement of the equity markets has to do with the pervasive influence of the state and its various arms in the investment decisions and other activities of leading enterprises in pillar industries. While the state is increasingly willing to divest itself of equity holdings in nonessential industries, even at the cost of a basic loss of control, it is not yet willing to let its national champions evolve without state "guidance." The Communist Party retains its control over senior executive appointments in the most important enterprises, depriving the corporate boards of one of their most important functions. These firms generally have party committees that vet—and sometimes reverse—the most important decisions of senior managers and the corporate board itself. It is hard to imagine the party relinquishing control of senior appointments or resisting the urge to meddle in major decisions. The separation of government and firm remains elusive for China's state-designated national champions.

In China's first ten years of operating equity markets, it would have been hard not to declare them a success. Despite deep-seated structural problems that, from a Western perspective, impaired their functioning as efficient asset markets, they nevertheless managed to raise large amounts of capital and provide reasonable returns to domestic investors. Over the last five years, as China's equity markets have steadily lost value in spite of a strong economy, and as the problems cloaked by share appreciation have increasingly come to fore, one might be tempted to declare the experiment a failure. The state's attempt to have its cake and eat it too would appear to have ended as most such attempts inevitably end. The state's efforts to ensure its control have also shielded firms from the consequences of their own underperformance, undermining investor demand. Equity prices have failed to play the role of improving capital allocation.

That judgment, too, may prove to be premature. China's falling equity indices have proved to be a public embarrassment for the regime, generating increasing pressure for fundamental reform of the system. Individual firms may be shielded from the consequences of their actions by state ownership, but the weaknesses of the fundamental approach to equity markets have been ruthlessly exposed. Although China's brokerages and auditing firms have failed to adequately inform investors, muckraking journals like *Caijing* have doggedly exposed these shortcomings. With the public encouragement of the CSRC, individual Chinese shareholders are now seeking redress by filing lawsuits in Chinese courts. By embarking on the path of *partial* privatization and being forced to confront its resounding failure, the regime may yet be compelled to move much further down the path to true privatization—a road that once would have been politically unthinkable.

BOND AND INSURANCE MARKETS

Whereas equity markets have gone through impressive cycles of boom and bust in China over the last 15 years, corporate bond markets have remained heavily suppressed, at least until very recently. The market for Chinese government bonds (CGBs) has grown substantially over the 1990s, as the central government stopped borrowing directly from the central bank and began borrowing from the financial system. The central government enthusiastically used fiscal pump-priming to jumpstart economic growth in the latter half of the 1990s, and it continues to run deficits today, even in the face of near-double-digit growth. The accumulation of large quantities of government debt in the financial system has led to pressure for partial deregulation of the government bond market, as it has in other Asian countries. As this happens, it reinforces the liquidity of the government bond market.

In striking contrast, issuance of corporate bonds remained well below the levels achieved in 1992 for more than a decade thereafter.[103] Many barriers to the further development of this market remain, the most important including laws that could protect the rights of arm's-length creditors. As China's banks and asset management companies have discovered, the de jure legal right to force a debtor into bankruptcy does not translate into a de facto right to acquire control over the debtor's assets.[104] The problems these organizations have encountered are likely to be magnified for private bondholders. After all, the largest banks and the asset management companies are SOEs; their acquisition of control over another SOE does not pose the same political challenge that would arise if a small group of private bondholders required control over the enterprise. The shaky finances of large numbers of SOEs imply that this scenario is all too plausible. A regime that has resisted true privatization in the equity markets may hesitate to embrace a back door to true privatization in the bond markets. In the absence of such legal protections, bonds acquire some of the risks of equities without their commensurate rewards.

A robust bond market would pose problems for the Chinese financial system along other dimensions. Until recently, commercial lending rates have been tightly regulated in China. A bond market would have undermined interest rate controls, since the effective interest rate is set by the marginal investor, not the state. The People's Bank of China partially deregulated commercial interest rates in late 2004. Commercial banks are now, in principle, free to charge rates higher than the rate set by the PBOC, but they have little practical experience in pricing risk into their lending rates.

Bond and equity market liberalization in Japan in the 1980s led to a rapid disintermediation of the banking sector. Blue-chip manufacturers were able to bypass commercial banks and go to domestic or foreign bond (or equity) markets to obtain the cheapest possible financing. As loan demand dropped but deposits continued to grow with the economy, Japanese banks found themselves with a loan portfolio that was increasingly concentrated in riskier sectors of the economy, such as real estate development. When the real estate downturn came, it essentially bankrupted what had been a healthy, profitable, and reasonably well-capitalized banking system.

It would be possible, if not exactly easy, to imagine a scenario in which robust bond markets and more functional equity markets pose the same threat to China's big four banks. Even in the absence of effective competition from the capital markets and in the presence of a rapidly growing economy, China's large banks have struggled to make profitable loans. One could envision a bond market-led disintermediation that simultaneously deprived the banks of their richest depositors and their most creditworthy corporate lending customers, leaving them with a portfolio full of NPLs and declining liquidity. A well-functioning bond market would also pose a threat to Chinese equity markets as they currently exist. From a retail investor's perspective, Chinese equity markets are extremely risky but have delivered meager returns over protracted periods. A functioning bond market that offered predictable returns well above the current (extremely low) RMB deposit rate would be heartily welcomed, and many investors might choose to allocate some of their equity holdings to bonds. These lessons have not been lost on financial market regulators, lending impetus to a "go slow" approach to bond market development.[105] It is telling that the one group of firms that have been given permission to issue bonds on a large scale in recent years are state-owned and joint-stock banks, insurance companies, and securities firms, seeking to issue subordinated debt in order to shore up their capital adequacy. For nonfinancial corporations, the right to issue bonds remains tightly restricted.

Unfortunately, the absence of a functioning bond market has enormous costs. Bond markets spread credit risk out among a large body of diversified investors. The current alternative in China—a high concentration of corporate lending and loan risk, in a small number of banks that all have the implicit backing of the state—carries costs that are becoming increasingly obvious. The absence of a functioning corporate bond market also deprives investors of a broad class of assets that can help them meet their own investment needs. American and European financial institutions have been almost endlessly inventive in their ability to create new bond-related and bond-like securities. The wealth of investment choices in these markets contrasts sharply with that of contemporary China, in which retail investors can place their funds into banks whose deposit rates have sometimes fallen below the rate of inflation, into secure, but low-yielding government debt, into highly risky (but underperforming) equity markets, or into real estate. It is easy to understand why, in this context, residential real estate investment has grown so rapidly that the government has felt compelled to take steps to deflate what many fear to be an emerging real estate bubble in cities like Shanghai.[106]

Households are not the only agents in the economy that suffer from this limited range of financial instruments. The insurance industry in China is growing rapidly as households increasingly look to the markets to provide the security once guaranteed by the work unit and, behind that, the state. Insurance companies profit by investing policyholder premiums effectively in order to build a level of wealth sufficient to meet their obligations to policyholders under a wide range of circumstances. This traditional business model is dramatically undermined in the Chinese context by the limited range of financial assets on offer. Locked out of the booming residential real estate market, at least officially, by prudential regulations, insurance companies are in some ways in an even less enviable position than households.[107]

The same could be said of China's pension system, such as it is. The demographic challenges confronting Western countries are by now well-known. The aging baby boom generation born after World War II will be replaced by a much less numerous cohort, placing strain on public sector pay-as-you-go pension systems owing to the declining ratio of workers to retirees. China's challenges in this regard are even more striking. Because of the stringent birth control policies adopted under Deng Xiaoping, China's population will age with breathtaking speed. By 2025, according to projections of the United Nations Development Programme (UNDP), China's median age will be higher than America's (39 for China versus 37.6 for the United States), and its population will be aging more rapidly than that of the United States.[108] China is not alone in this regard—the East Asian tigers and Japan will be in a similar position. The challenge for China 20 years hence is that it will have the age profile of a highly developed country but the income level of a developing country. In 2025, 13.4 percent of China's population will be 65 or older. When Japan crossed the 13.4 percent threshold, its per capita GDP was well over $20,000 per year. Even with robust economic growth, it is unlikely that China's per capita income will reach equivalent levels in real terms over the next 20 years.[109] Japan grew rich before it grew old. In China, the risk is that the country will, in the evocative phrase of Hong Kong pension expert Stuart Leckie (2005), "grow old before it gets rich."

While the pessimists' prognosis may not come about, the need to build wealth over the next generation lends some urgency to the debate in China over broadening and improving Chinese capital markets. In the pre-reform period, urban workers received a pension equal to 80 percent of their salary, and retirement age was set at a relatively early age, reflecting the short life expectancies that existed in the first decades of the People's Republic.[110] Over the course of the 1980s and 1990s, state-owned firms were increasingly squeezed by price reform and intensifying competition with the non-state sector. Some state firms found themselves with more pensioners than current employees and began to effectively default on their pension payments; the old system was clearly not sustainable. In 1997, the State Council formally adopted a three-pillar model consisting of a state pension funded by employer contributions that would provide a guaranteed benefit of only 20 percent of local average earnings, mandatory individual accounts (in which individuals contribute 8 percent and employers 3 percent), and optional private pensions for citizens who wished to invest more on their own, funded by individual contributions. Unfortunately, the state system is undermined by the unwillingness or inability of financially strapped firms to actually make their mandatory contributions. The individual account system has been subverted by provincial governments raiding these funds to pay current retirees. And all legs of the system have been constrained by regulations that require pension fund assets to be invested in low-return asset classes such as bank deposits and government bonds, generating returns of 2 to 3 percent per year.[111]

The traditional "pension system" in Chinese society has been the family, and even today an ethos of filial duty to care for aging parents remains reasonably well embedded in mainland culture. By 2025, however, nearly 300 million Chinese will be over 60, suggesting something approaching a one-to-one ratio between elderly parents and the children obliged to support them. A sizable fraction of this elderly population will have no living son on whom to rely for support.[112] A large fraction of the elderly population will therefore have to work, but herein lies another problem: much of the work available to these individuals is likely to be more physically taxing than it would be in richer countries, and some of these elderly workers may be poorly suited to these jobs.[113]

FOREIGN EXCHANGE AND CAPITAL CONTROLS

Prior to reform, the regime maintained an overvalued exchange rate in order to subsidize the import of capital goods that could not be produced domestically. Overvaluation led to excess demand for foreign exchange, necessitating an extensive system of rigid controls. Key elements of this control system included a 100 percent surrender requirement for exporters, tight limitations on the rights of individuals to hold foreign currency, and strict controls on the inflow or outflow of foreign capital.

Over the course of the reform period, all of these restrictions were relaxed. The official exchange rate was devalued in stages, from an official exchange rate of RMB 1.5 to the dollar in 1981 to 8.7 in 1994. Following a modest appreciation, the exchange rate was effectively fixed at RMB 8.3 to the dollar in 1995. The International Monetary Fund (IMF) estimates that the Chinese currency lost about 70 percent of its value against the dollar in real terms over this period, substantially enhancing the international competitiveness of China-based export operations. In addition to substantial real devaluation, Chinese exporters have been allowed to retain part of their foreign exchange earnings, individuals have been allowed to hold foreign exchange, and capital outflow requirements have been relaxed.[114]

By the mid-1990s, China was able to inform the IMF that it was in compliance with the conditions for current account convertibility. At the same time, however, the country maintained what were, in principle, tight controls on capital account transactions. The experience of the Asian financial crisis and the increasing official awareness that China's own banking system was fragile led top officials to conclude that maintaining these restrictions was essential until China's financial system could be substantially strengthened.

The general caution China's government has shown toward capital account transactions has not applied to FDI. Since the beginning of the reform period, China has shown increasing openness to foreign firms seeking to set up subsidiaries in the country. This pro-FDI stance has been extended to official encouragement (even government subsidization) of outward FDI by leading Chinese companies. Recent data suggest that the increasingly extensive international linkages forged by multinational corporations have helped open up a back door for unauthorized capital account transactions. In other words, regardless of official regulations, China already has an increasingly open capital account, albeit one that is only open to certain classes of investors. To the extent that the current structure of capital controls exists in order to buffer the economy from the instability of global capital markets, that buffering effect has already been somewhat compromised.

Barry Naughton has recently pointed out that the relative stability of FDI, as measured by actual capital deployment, and the current account surplus contrast sharply with pronounced volatility in other elements of aggregate statistics on China's balance of payments. Over the past eight years, from 1996 to 2004, these "other capital flows" have swung from a low of minus 8 percent of GDP to a positive 5 percent of GDP.[115] The level of change is reminiscent of the dramatic swings in capital flows seen in other Asian countries that had more officially open capital account regimes. These flows, especially the large and variable "errors and omissions" component, no doubt reflect unsanctioned capital movements. Money left the country on an enormous scale during the Asian financial crisis, and money returned on an equally enormous scale in the context of a domestic macroeconomic and real estate boom, as well as speculation about currency revaluation. China's outsized levels of exports and imports, relative to GDP, and the huge fraction of both that are mediated by multinationals, provide ample scope for the under- or overinvoicing of trade flows and related profit remittances. The capital mobility genie may be out of the bottle already.

THE CHALLENGES AHEAD

As part of its accession agreement to the World Trade Organization (WTO), China agreed to implement significant changes in its financial system, including "national treatment" of foreign financial firms in a number of product areas. Given the importance of banks in China's financial system, we will begin with an overview of the WTO-mandated liberalizations in that sector. Although foreign banks initially operated under a host of restrictions on the geographic scope of their operations, the customers they could transact with, and the types of business they could engage in, these restrictions have been progressively relaxed in line with gradual convergence to national treatment over five years mandated by the accession agreement. The principal restriction remaining on the operations of foreign banks is the requirement that they limit their RMB deposits to 50 percent of their foreign currency deposits. This limits their ability to engage in retail banking services on a large scale. This restriction is to be phased out over the course of the current year, at which point foreign banks will be subject only to the same rules and regulations that Chinese banks must follow. Given the many obvious advantages of foreign banks—particularly the absence of large levels of NPLs and superior financial technology—one might imagine that this liberalization would subject Chinese banks to an important source of new competition.[116]

Many experts, however, believe that expansion of the foreign banks is likely to be gradual for a number of reasons. Since foreign banks will be subject to China's international capital controls, it will not be possible to take Chinese deposits and invest or loan them offshore, eliminating one potential source of foreigners' comparative advantage. Furthermore, foreign banks will be subject to the same regulations that limit the ability of Chinese banks to directly engage in asset management, securities, or investment banking activities. While there appears to be some movement away from this segmentation of the financial markets, this shift is progressing slowly. Given these constraints, foreign banks will only want to grow their RMB deposit base as fast as they can find creditworthy firms and consumers to whom they can loan these funds.[117] In an environment characterized by extremely rapid change, highly imperfect information on the creditworthiness of borrowers, and the absence of a legal framework that gives a creditor the ability to foreclose the assets of a delinquent borrower, it is likely that foreign banks will wish to proceed with caution in building up their China businesses. The good news is that an immediate rush of deposits from domestic to foreign banks that could threaten the liquidity of the domestic banking system seems unlikely. The bad news is that the limited scale of foreign banking operations for the foreseeable future implies that the threat of competition from foreigners will also remain limited.

The insurance sector is also being opened up, and many of the important steps have already been taken. Foreign participation in life insurance is limited to 50 percent ownership in Sino-foreign joint ventures, but foreign insurance firms are already able to take majority positions in non-life insurance companies and operate anywhere in China.[118] Unfortunately, foreign insurers operating in China will be subject to the same capital controls, investment limitations, and rate regulations as domestic firms, which place stringent limits on their choices of assets in which to invest premium income. Until recently, Chinese insurers were largely limited to investing their funds in bank deposits, government debt, and a narrow range of other debt instruments. Approval to invest in domestic equity markets was only granted in 2005. In August 2004, Chinese insurers were allowed to invest a portion of their foreign exchange holdings in overseas debt markets, dramatically broadening the choice of assets but strictly limiting the amount of capital that could be invested offshore. In June 2005, insurers were allowed to invest, albeit in a very limited way, in overseas equities. For the time being, this investment is limited to the overseas shares of Chinese companies.[119]

Foreign entrants also have to contend with large, successful domestic incumbents that have built up massive sales forces, long-established branches, and popular products. Two well-known incumbents, China Life Insurance Company and Ping An Insurance Group, control more than 75 percent of the market for life insurance. The top four domestic firms controlled 95 percent of the market in life and non-life insurance at the end of 2003.[120] The incumbent firms have traditionally focused on the pursuit of market share rather than profitability. As in the commercial and retail banking sector, it is unlikely that foreigners will displace these dominant incumbents in the immediate future. On the other hand, the ability of foreign firms to offer group, health, pension, and corporate annuity products to sophisticated consumers and progressive firms creates a real zone of opportunity for leading firms with well-established China operations, such as AIG. Non-life insurance has been traditionally dominated by automobile insurance, but demand for other non-life insurance products is expected to accelerate as the market grows.

The leading Chinese firms have weak capital structures, by international standards. Prior to 1999, the firms sold life insurance policies that guaranteed high rates of return. When interest rates dropped sharply over the next several years, this created a serious problem of negative spreads. The firms' aggressive pursuit of market share has generated risks, and it is believed that non-life insurers particularly under-reserve given the risks they face.[121] As a consequence of more stringent oversight by the regulatory authorities, Chinese firms are seeking to shore up their capital bases through equity and subordinated bond issuance.

The rest of the financial services sector is expected to remain relatively closed, even after the phasing-in of all WTO-mandated liberalizations. For the indefinite future, foreign asset management companies will be restricted to minority positions in joint ventures, and foreign securities brokers and underwriters will be limited to one-third equity positions in joint ventures.[122] This has not prevented Goldman Sachs from acquiring de facto control of Goldman Sachs Gao Hua Securities Company with the option of raising its 33 percent stake, but it is unclear how many similar opportunities will exist in the immediate future.[123] On the one hand, this will give domestic companies opportunities to build skills and market positions in advance of any further opening. On the other hand, the competitive pressures foreign participants could exert will remain limited for the foreseeable future.

The securities industry in China could probably use this pressure, as domestic securities firms have been subject to withering criticism in the domestic and foreign press over the past few years.[124] Hu Shuli, of *Caijing* Magazine, offered the following perspective in 2003: "China has 131 brokerage firms, almost all of which are state-owned and most of their financial circumstances are not at all clear. . . . It is widely known that many securities firms are technically insolvent and depend for their survival on the unauthorized appropriation of clients' deposits, trust bonds, and other assets held in trust."[125] The government has tacitly admitted the truth of this situation by launching a two-year program of extending official loans and, in some cases, emergency cash injections, to bail out the brokerage firms. Like China's weak banks and insurance companies, brokerages are also being given the right to raise capital through bond issuance.[126]

CONCLUSION

As with other aspects of its economy, the transformation of China's financial markets over the course of the reform period has been breathtaking. In the late 1970s, China did not even have a banking system in the Western sense of the word. The legal framework that could undergird a modern financial system did not exist, nor were there regulatory agencies with the capacity to supervise such a system. Even the vocabulary needed to talk about such a system would have been alien to the Chinese entrepreneurs and officials who, in the decades since, have created China's financial system. Over the space of a quarter century, China has managed to build financial markets that, for all of their flaws, have still managed to function effectively enough to power one of economic history's great development successes. As Americans have been reminded by their own recent financial history, no country has a perfect capital market. Any assessment of the Chinese financial system has to begin by acknowledging the immense progress that has been made.

Only when one compares the speed and nature of reform of financial markets in China to the reform of other sectors of the economy does progress appear to be slow. As noted at the beginning of this chapter, a hallmark of the Chinese reform process has been the steady growth in importance of non-state actors and the increasing reliance on the market mechanism as a means of allocating resources. Whether one looks at Chinese industrial product markets, the determination of goods prices, or China's expanding foreign trade, one sees a rapid and pronounced relative decline of the role of the state and its enterprises as producer, price setter, and trader. In contrast, China's bank-dominated financial system remains dominated by enterprises under direct state control: the state-owned banks and policy banks collectively account for around 60 percent of banking system assets, even in 2005. Furthermore, even the banks that are least directly tied to the state in an organizational sense are still subject to its influence. Formal credit quotas have been replaced by what the PBOC calls "moral suasion to guide credit structure optimization."[127] The role of foreign firms—so visible and important throughout the modern Chinese economy in other sectors—remains quite limited and narrowly circumscribed in the financial sector, with little prospects for immediate change. Discrimination against private firms in the credit market persists, even as access to consumer credit has improved enormously.

The dominant hand of the state extends to Chinese equity markets. State control continues despite the "backdoor privatizations," in which a limited number of cash-strapped SOEs and other affiliates of the state sell their legal person shares. The domestic exchanges are dominated by these SOEs in which the state and its affiliated organizations retain a controlling—and often majority—stake. The access of firms to the primary equity markets remains tightly controlled and largely limited to SOEs. Party control of personnel appointments at key firms continues to obscure the boundaries between enterprises and the government, and interference in firm management by internal Communist Party committees remains pervasive. This general state of affairs extends to Chinese insurance companies and brokerages. Although China's WTO commitments require a substantial liberalization of this sector, financial markets will remain far more closed to foreigners and far more dominated by centrally controlled SOEs than is true of, say, international trade, where foreign-invested enterprises have become the dominant players and all indigenous firms now have trading rights. Bond issuance is largely limited to the government, its agencies, and the financial institutions it is attempting to strengthen; nonfinancial firms' lack of access to bond finance perpetuates their dependence on the banking sector.

Given the still-dominant role of SOEs in this sector, the pace and nature of reform remains closely tied to the government's strategy for reforming SOEs. Fortunately, this appears to be entering a new phase, opening up the prospects for an acceleration in the reform process that could allow for a serious diminution of the state's role.

Of the many critical factors that have enabled this shift in the reform process, one of the most important has been the ability of the regulatory agencies and the statutes they operate under to, in a sense, finally begin to catch up to market developments by the end of the 1990s. While the government played too large a role in Chinese financial markets, it consistently played too small a part as regulator, rule creator, and rule enforcer.[128] It was only at the end of the 1990s that the CSRC emerged as an agency with the technical expertise, legal authority, and political clout necessary to actually start bringing Chinese securities markets under control. The Securities Law itself was only passed in 1999. The China Banking Regulatory Commission (CBRC), which has emerged as the principal regulator of the banking system, was not created until 2003. It also took time for a generation of technocrats who really understood how capital markets work in the West to rise up into positions of power sufficiently strong to effect change in policy. While Chinese law lacks important elements that fully developed capital markets will need, the regulatory framework is now largely in place, and the key agencies are led by knowledgeable individuals who have a much clearer understanding of the necessary reforms ahead.

Under the influence of these leaders, the state has formally endorsed the notion that it will seek to retain a direct controlling interest in a relatively small number of firms. In March 2003, 196 huge enterprise groups supervised by the central government were placed under the ownership of the recently created State-owned Asset Supervision and Administration Commission (SASAC).[129] This organization will be the holding company originally envisaged by Wu and Jin back in the early 1980s; it will hold shares in these key enterprises on behalf of the state, but it will also provide a degree of separation of the firm from the regulating agencies.[130] These firms represent, in the government's view, the "commanding heights" of the industrial economy. Collectively, they accounted for more than half of state-owned assets at the end of 2002. True privatization of these key enterprises is not being considered, even if stakes in them are eventually sold. The government's priority with these firms will be to maximize efficiency, while retaining ultimate state control. As we have seen, history suggests that the government can pursue one or the other of these goals but not both.[131]

But for the remaining 159,000 state-owned and state-controlled enterprises in existence at the end of 2002, the state has accepted that it will eventually relinquish both formal ownership and actual control. Although the word "privatization" (siyouhua) does not show up in government documents, it seems clear that this will be the fate for the vast majority of smaller SOEs that have not yet been privatized or liquidated. The sell-off of these state assets to private interests promises to be one of the critical events in the history of Chinese capital markets.

The critical stage in this process will be the sale of currently nontradable legal person and state shares. As noted earlier, these shares constituted more than 70 percent of the total equity in mainland companies at the end of 2005. The government's clear willingness to press forward in its efforts to convert these into tradable shares, with the eventual goal of unwinding its shareholding in "nonessential" enterprises, has been the most significant equity market development of 2005. Indeed, it represents one of the most significant steps forward since the founding of China's domestic exchanges. The process of unwinding state shareholdings is likely to take some time; during that interval, state asset sales will take priority over the need for private firms to get access to public markets.

The less positive development is that the key enterprises over which the state will seek to retain ownership and control are collectively very large, accounting for just below 50 percent of the state's total assets. Notably, they will include the four largest banks. While the government seeks to sell significant stakes in the big four prior to IPO to foreign "strategic investors," and while it clearly plans to float shares on foreign exchanges, it is equally clear that the government has no intention of truly privatizing the banks. The party will retain control over executive appointments, and, for this reason alone, government policy priorities will get weighted heavily relative to shareholder value maximization. The government wishes to turn these enterprises into "national champions" that can compete globally. The realization of these ambitions is likely to require enormous amounts of capital. Because the government will retain control of the largest banks, it can ensure that these "champions" get the capital they need, even at the cost of crowding out private firms and limiting the returns the banks receive from their commercial lending business.

The commitment to the state-owned sector has narrowed considerably in scope, but it has not died. As long as designated "national champions" exist in which the government holds a majority interest, it will be difficult for the state to act as a neutral arbiter in maintaining a level playing field. Under China's WTO commitments, it will be difficult to keep out foreign competition in many industries—financial services being a notable exception. Foreign firms are likely to be able to compete with the state-owned national champions even if the latter have preferential access to subsidized capital. As usual, it will be the Chinese private sector that will pay the cost for the government's enduring commitment to maintain ownership and control of the commanding heights. This may continue to constrain the efficiency of capital allocation in the coming years.

POSTSCRIPT

Since this chapter was completed in March 2006, Chinese equity markets have appreciated by over 100 percent. The major indices have now surpassed their previous highs. This strong performance reflects, in part, the market reaction to the reform of state and legal person shareholding detailed in this chapter. These reforms have been implemented more quickly and more smoothly than expected. It also reflects the impact of faster than expected growth on corporate earnings over the last few years. The basic fact of the Chinese financial system is that it has a large stock of savings highly concentrated in low-yielding bank accounts and government bonds. The (re)emergence of China's equity market as an alternative investment offering the promise of high returns has clearly driven a substantial—though still limited—reallocation of savings into the equity markets, driving stock prices sharply higher. Robust share price appreciation has done much to shore up the portfolios of Chinese financial institutions that invest in the market. The challenges facing Chinese insurance companies and pension funds appear less daunting than they did in the early spring of 2006.

However, the recent public and private statements of government officials reflect the worry that the market has come too far, too fast. This author shares that concern. The potential for yet another boom-and-bust cycle in Chinese equity markets clearly exists. While China's financial market regulators clearly deserve the credit given to them in this chapter for accelerating the pace of market reform, serious issues remain. Corporate governance in China remains a work in progress. While state and legal person shares have been made tradable, they are being sold to private investors at a slow pace. The commitment to state ownership and control of the "commanding heights" of Chinese industry noted in this chapter has been regularly reiterated, even as reform has continued. It seems likely, given the problems that still exist, that Chinese financial markets will continue to offer a less than perfect reflection of the acknowledged dynamism of the economy for some time to come.

NOTES

1. A large fraction of corporate investment is financed out by retained earnings, such that one needs to make a distinction between the government's control over the intermediation of capital—which is still substantial—and the government's control over investment, which is considerably smaller.

2. This striking contrast has been emphasized by many other observers, including Lardy (2005).

3. By the unfortunate standards of many developing countries, of course, China's macroeconomic trajectory has been relatively stable in that sharp declines in real output and an outright collapse of the financial system have been avoided.

4. Deng Xiaoping's famous southern tour in 1992 marked a turning point in China's direction toward economic development. Deng visited Guangzhou, Shenzhen, Zhuhai, and Shanghai, and generated strong support for his reformist agenda and the importance of economic construction and openness.

5. The figure provides the ratio of total fixed asset investment to GDP, in RMB terms. The official estimate of capital formation as a percentage of GDP for 2004 is slightly lower, at 44 percent. At the end of 2005, Chinese statistical authorities announced major revisions of their estimates of the size of the Chinese economy and of the growth rates the economy has achieved over the last decade. The statistics cited in this chapter refer to the pre-revision estimates, unless otherwise indicated. The revision in GDP does not allow us to estimate by what percentage investment may also have been underestimated; revised investment/GDP ratio is therefore difficult to compute.

6. These estimates come from the *China Economic Quarterly* and are based on data published by the National Bureau of Statistics.

7. However, there is widespread speculation that real economic growth may actually *exceed* the official statistics, in contrast to the situation in the late 1990s.

8. See Goldstein and Lardy (2004).

9. Dr. Louis Kuijs, senior economist in the Beijing Office of the World Bank, has been an articulate proponent of this view. See his detailed discussion in the *China Economic Quarterly* Q3 (2005).

10. A leading official of the China Banking Regulatory Commission was quoted in the *China Economic Quarterly* Q4 (2005) as stating that he expected firms with outstanding loans equivalent to nearly RMB 200 billion to declare bankruptcy within three years.

11. The numbers in this paragraph are taken from Lardy (2005: 97–98).

12. I thank Barry Naughton for bringing these numbers to my attention.

13. See Dipchand, Zhang, and Ma (1994: 7–8).

14. Lardy (1998: 60–61).

15. See Dipchand, Zhang, and Ma (1994: 7–8, 19–20); Lardy (1998: 60–61).

16. Lardy (1998: 60–61).

17. Dipchand, Zhang, and Ma (1994: 20–21).

18. Lardy (1998: 63).

19. Dipchand, Zhang, and Ma (1994: 22–25); Lardy (1998: 63).

20. See Naughton (1995) for a detailed treatment of this reform and its financial consequences.

21. Dipchand, Zhang, and Ma (1994: 29).

22. Lardy (1998: 64–65).

23. Lardy (1998: 65–76); Lardy (2005: 99). Minsheng Bank and Shenzhen Development Bank are two banks widely considered to be "private," in that nongovernmental entities own a majority of shares.

24. Lardy (1998: 66).

25. Lardy (1998: 124–25). This enormous difference in the retail presence of the first and second tiers of the banking system has persisted to the present day, and has helped ensure continued dominance of the big four throughout the 1990s and into the current decade.

26. I would like to thank David Li for pointing out how leading government figures, such as Chen Yun, made the case for continuing state control of the financial sector.

27. Dipchand, Zhang, and Ma (1994: 29–30).

28. Statistics are taken from the Web site of the China Banking Regulatory Commission, "Total Assets and Liabilities as of June 30, 2005," http://www.cbrc.gov.cn/english.

29. Lardy (1998: 81–83).

30. See Lardy (1998: 86).

31. See Dipchand, Zhang, and Ma (1994: 41).

32. The formal annual credit quota was abolished in 1998, but the PBOC has continued to provide "guidance" to the banks on their lending activities.

33. See Boyreau-Debray and Wei (2005: 4–5, 16–19); Lardy (1998: 83–90).

34. See Lau, Qian, and Roland (2000) for a formal presentation of this argument.

35. I would like to thank David Li for stressing this point in conversations with the author.

36. Lardy (1998: 90).

37. Tsai (2002: 58).

38. Lardy has called this point into question as well as the earlier assertion that it was necessary to "compensate the losers" from financial reform through distortions in capital markets. Lardy suggests that the systematic underpricing of capital led to inappropriately capital-intensive production in SOEs. A more market-oriented system would have allowed for similar rates of growth with less foregone consumption and a higher rate of employment creation. See Lardy (1998: 184–86).

39. Brandt and Zhu, in their contribution to this volume, point out that recentralization of the financial sector actually limited the share of lending going to the non-state sector.

40. Lardy (1998: 90–91).

41. Lardy (1998: 170–72).

42. See Langlois (2001a: 1, 4–9).

43. Lardy (2002) shows that SOE profitability fell steadily throughout the 1990s.

44. See Naughton (1996: 287–95) for a detailed discussion of the triangular relationship between the state, the banks, and SOEs as of the mid-1990s. See Steinfeld (1998: 137–43) for a fascinating account of the array of welfare activities and social services provided by large SOEs in the steel industry to their workers.

45. See Naughton (1996: 291). Evidence of growing revenues is provided by recent issues of the *China Statistical Yearbook*. Government revenues grew from about 12 percent of GDP to roughly 17 percent over the last decade.

46. Some 14,000 firms were converted to joint-stock companies, which accounted for some of the measured reduction in the SOE workforce. The degree to which these enterprises were truly "reformed" may be called into question. Studwell (2003)

suggests that at least some of these firms probably continued to have preferential access to capital and to engage in inefficient production. He estimates that another 30,000 SOEs were sold to private parties or liquidated. However, there is little debate that a significant downsizing of the SOE sector occurred from 1999 to 2001.

47. See National Bureau of Statistics, *China Statistical Yearbook* (Beijing: China Statistics Press, 2000), 126.

48. Strictly speaking, the creation of the three policy banks preceded the most significant steps in SOE reform by a few years. The banks were created in 1994. See Lardy (1998: 176–80).

49. Standard & Poor's (2004).

50. See Lardy (2005: 101–2).

51. See Harner (2004: 42).

52. Many of the statistics in this paragraph are taken from Lardy (2005: 101–4).

53. See Kroeber (2004: 39).

54. Lardy (2005: 107).

55. See MacGregor (2005).

56. See "Best in Class: China Merchants Bank," *China Economic Quarterly* Q3 (2003).

57. Goldstein and Lardy (2004).

58. Goldstein and Lardy (2004).

59. See Kyne (2004).

60. See Sender (2004).

61. See Kyne (2004).

62. This allegation has been reported in a number of press outlets, including Studwell (2004) in the *Financial Times*.

63. Lardy (2005: 107–8).

64. This paragraph and the preceding one draw upon Harner (2004: 42–45).

65. Given the history of Standard & Poor's highly public criticism of the health of the Chinese banking sector over the last decade, this is significant.

66. The Industrial and Commercial Bank of China, though clearly not as far along in its "clean-up" process, has received substantial investments from Goldman Sachs and Allianz capital.

67. Bank executives associated with the big four banks have pointed out to me in private conversations the challenges involved in changing lending behavior throughout their far-flung networks of branches. One executive noted that more than one-third of the provincial heads in his bank did not have a college degree, much less training in modern credit-scoring methods. Some Chinese commentators, such as David Li, have suggested that the scale of the big four is so great that reform is impossible unless they are broken up into smaller organizations. Personal conversations with government officials suggest that this is unlikely to happen.

68. See Browne (2005b).

69. See Associated Press (2005b).

70. See Browne (2005a).

71. Standard & Poor's (2005b). Assuming it does cost $190 billion ($197 billion at current exchange rates) and that recovery rates of the AMCs continue to be very low

net of operation costs, this would bring the cumulative cost of fixing the banking system to date to over U.S. $500 billion.

72. The policy reports issued regularly by the PBOC make it clear that the rural credit cooperatives have been exempted from the tighter reporting, provisioning, and capital adequacy standards being imposed on the rest of the banking system. This fact implicitly suggests that compliance is simply infeasible given the accumulation of NPLs in this segment of the banking system.

73. See the fiscal sustainability calculations undertaken by Lardy (2005). He calculates a number of alternative scenarios regarding the size of the Chinese government's contingent liabilities related to NPLs in the banking system. Even in his worst-case scenario, the Chinese gross debt-to-GDP ratio never rises above 0.860, which is well below levels maintained today by advanced industrial countries such as Japan (1.4+). However, Lardy's calculations include no accounting for China's unfunded pension liabilities.

74. Walter and Howie (2003: 6).

75. This remarkable document was highlighted in the English-language literature by Steinfeld (1998: 132–37). The discussion in the following paragraphs closely follows Steinfeld's description.

76. Walter and Howie (2003: 24–25).

77. Walter and Howie (2003: 25).

78. Dipchand, Zhang, and Ma (1994: 161–63).

79. Walter and Howie (2003: 27–29).

80. Walter and Howie (2003: 72).

81. Walter and Howie (2003: 59–62).

82. Green (2003: 13–14).

83. The chief architect of the deal, Carl Walter, then with Credit Suisse First Boston, described the transaction as "an under-the-table deal, when there was no table." See Studwell (2003: 78).

84. Studwell (2003: 78).

85. Studwell (2003: 73).

86. Unfortunately, the story of this firm did not have a brilliant ending. The Stock Exchange of Hong Kong and the NYSE suspended trading in Brilliance shares in 2002 after a leading executive, Yang Rong, was forcibly removed from office. See Green (2003: 59).

87. Green (2003: 58).

88. Walter and Howie (2003: 21, table 6.1).

89. Green (2003: 22–23).

90. See Walter and Howie (2003: 207–18).

91. Green (2003: 26–28). Conventional measures assign the value implied by A-share prices to all the outstanding shares of Chinese listed firms, ignoring the reality that H shares and B shares have historically traded at a significant discount to the A-share prices, and that state and legal person shares have often changed hands at valuations implying an even steeper discount.

92. Green (2003: 119–21; 2004).

93. The "H" refers to Hong Kong, the foreign stock exchange most favored by Chinese firms seeking an overseas listing. However, like many others in the

literature, I use the term *H shares* to refer to the shares listed on any foreign stock exchange.

94. Walter and Howie (2003: 178–80). This discount has narrowed substantially in the last few years, but it still remains.

95. Green (2003: 55).

96. Walter and Howie (2003: 188–89).

97. This basic point has been eloquently stressed by Walter and Howie (2003: 175–206), which is the source from which the statistics in this paragraph are taken.

98. Green (2004).

99. See Sender (2003).

100. Walter and Howie (2003: 184–86).

101. Green (2004).

102. See Areddy (2005a).

103. Chinese banks were allowed to issue subordinated debt in order to strengthen their capital and meet government standards for capital adequacy. This touched off a sharp increase in subordinated bond issues in 2004. However, this does not appear to indicate a shift in policy regarding the issuance of bonds by nonfinancial corporations.

104. Reinforcing this point, Chinese commentators have pointed out that one reason for the slow pace of financial reform in China is the reliance of financial markets on these kinds of legal institutional foundations, which remain quite weak in China. I thank David Li for pointing this out to me.

105. Initial experiments in commercial paper issuance, allowed by the government, have been enthusiastically embraced by the market. However, press coverage has stressed the potential threat this financial instrument could pose to bank lending. See Areddy (2005b).

106. In June 2005, the central government required localities nationwide to levy a 5.5 percent tax on residential property sold less than two years after purchase. A number of restrictions were placed on real estate developers. This followed imposition of a similar tax in Shanghai, the country's hottest property market, in March. See Associated Press (2005a) and Areddy (2005c). As of March 2006, real estate market participants were noting price declines in some regions of metropolitan Shanghai on the order of 20 to 30 percent.

107. See Standard & Poor's (2004: 22). The government has taken a number of steps over the last three years to broaden the set of assets in which insurance companies can invest, but this remains a challenge for the industry.

108. See Eberstadt (2004: 9–10).

109. See Eberstadt (2004: 9).

110. See interview with Leckie (2005).

111. Leckie (2005).

112. See Eberstadt (2004: 10).

113. See Eberstadt (2004: 10).

114. Branstetter and Lardy (forthcoming).

115. Dong Fu of the Federal Reserve Bank of Dallas has also called attention to these features of the data. See Fu (2000).

116. See Langlois (2001b) for a summary of the WTO-mandated liberalizations for the financial sector.

117. See Lardy (2002) for a detailed discussion of the likely evolution of the banking sector after WTO-mandated liberalizations are phased in.

118. See Langlois (2001a). The life insurance industry has been about three times as big, measured by annual premiums paid, as the non-life insurance industry. See Standard & Poor's (2004).

119. See Browne (2004) and De Ramos (2005).

120. See Standard & Poor's (2004).

121. Standard & Poor's (2004).

122. See Langlois (2001b).

123. Rumors in the market indicate that the quid pro quo for this investment was that Goldman Sachs had to spend $60 million bailing out investors in an unrelated brokerage firm. See "A Marginalized Market," *Economist*, February 24, 2005.

124. The cover story of *Caijing* Magazine on October 5, 2000, stunned the markets by presenting incontrovertible evidence of stock price manipulation by 22 investment funds. Many other such exposes have followed in recent years. For a Western perspective, see Walter and Howie (2003: 139–74).

125. See Hu Shuli (2003).

126. See Areddy (2005a).

127. See China Monetary Policy Report, Quarter 2 (2004), official English translation, from the PBOC Web site.

128. This observation reflects the influence of the scholarship of Xiaobo Lu.

129. See Green (2004: 30–32).

130. A separate holding company, Central Huijin, will manage state shares in major financial institutions. This organization is headed by a former PBOC official, calling into question the true degree of separation between regulator and SOE.

131. See Clarke (2003: 27–30).

REFERENCES

Areddy, James. 2005a. "China's Tradable-Share Plan Remains Crucial to Markets." *Wall Street Journal Online.* July 25.

———. 2005b. "Nascent Chinese Market Proves Popular Source of Cheaper Funds." *Wall Street Journal Online.* September 29.

———. 2005c. "Property Sales in China Cool Ahead of New Tax." *Wall Street Journal Online.* May 26.

Associated Press. 2005a. "China to Curb Real Estate Prices." *Wall Street Journal Online.* May 12.

———. 2005b. "Regulators Order Bank of China to Investigate Suspected Fraud." *Wall Street Journal Online.* January 31.

Bai, Chong-En, David Lee, Yingyi Qian, and Yijang Wang. 1999. "Anonymous Banking and Financial Repression: How Did China's Reform Limit Government Predation Without Reducing Its Revenue?" CEPR Working Paper, London.

———. 2001. "Financial Repression and Optimal Taxation." *Economics Letters* 70(2): 245–51.

Boyreau-Debray, Genevieve and Shang-Jin Wei. 2005. "Pitfalls of a State-Dominated Financial System: The Case of China." NBER Working Paper No. 11214.

Branstetter, Lee and Nicholas Lardy. Forthcoming. "China's Embrace of Globalization." In *China's Great Economic Transition*, ed. Loren Brandt and Thomas G. Rawski. New York: Cambridge University Press.

Browne, Andrew. 2004. "China Opens Up Insurance Sector to Foreign Firms." *Wall Street Journal Online*. December 13.

———. 2005a. "China Arrests 69 in Case Tied to ICBC Scandal." *Wall Street Journal Online*. January 18.

———. 2005b. "New Loan Loss Mars the Veneer on Bank of China." *Wall Street Journal Online*. April 4.

Clarke, Donald. 2003. "Corporatization, Not Privatization." *China Economic Quarterly* Q3: 27–30.

De Ramos, Rita Raagas. 2005. "Beijing Allows Insurers to Buy Stocks Overseas." *Wall Street Journal Online*. June 20.

Dipchand, Cecil, Zhang Yichun, and Ma Mingjia. 1994. *The Chinese Financial System*. Westport, CT: Greenwood Press.

Eberstadt, Nicholas. 2004. "Power and Population in Asia." *Policy Review* (February): 9–10.

Fu, Dong. 2000. "Capital In and Out of China." *Southwest Economy* (March/April).

Goldstein, Morris and Nicholas Lardy. 2004. "What Kind of Landing for the Chinese Economy?" Institute of International Economics Policy Brief. PB04-7.

Green, Stephen. 2003. *China's Stockmarket: A Guide to Its Progress, Players and Prospects*. London: The Economist and Profile Books.

———. 2004. "Privatization: The Great State Sell-Down." *China Economic Quarterly* Q2: 30–32.

Harner, Stephen. 2004. "Bank Reform: Earthquake!" *China Economic Quarterly* Q3: 42–45.

Huang, Yasheng. 2003. *Selling China: Foreign Direct Investment During the Reform Era*. London: Cambridge University Press.

Hu Shuli. 2003. "Let There Be More Light." *China Economic Quarterly* Q3.

Kroeber, Arthur. 2004. "Growth: How Long Can It Last?" *China Economic Quarterly* Q4: 39–41.

Kyne, Pelim. 2004. "Smaller Lenders Lose Luster." *Wall Street Journal Online*. June 7.

Langlois, John. 2001a. "China's Financial System and the Private Sector." Unpublished manuscript.

———. 2001b. "The WTO and China's Financial System." *China Quarterly* 167 (September): 610–29.

Lardy, Nicholas. 1998. *China's Unfinished Economic Revolution*. Washington, DC: Brookings Institution Press.

———. 2002. *Integrating China Into the Global Economy*. Washington, DC: Brookings Institution Press.

———. 2005. "State-Owned Banks in China." In *The Future of State Financial Institutions,* ed. Gerard Caprio, Johnathan Feichter, Robert Litan, and Michael Pomerleano. Washington, DC: Brookings Institution Press.

Lau, Lawrence, Yingyi Qian, and Gerald Roland. "Reform Without Losers: An Interpretation of China's Dual-Track Approach to Transition." *Journal of Political Economy* 108(1): 120–43.

Leckie, Stuart. 2005. "China's Pension Crisis: Old and Broke." *China Economic Review* 15(3): 54–56.

Li, David D. 2001. "Beating the Trap of Financial Repression in China." *The CATO Journal* 21(1) (Spring/Summer).

MacGregor, Ronald. 2005. "China Bank Chiefs Hit at Communist Party Role." *Financial Times.* April 28.

Naughton, Barry. 1995. *Growing Out of the Plan: Chinese Economic Reform, 1978–1993.* New York: Cambridge University Press.

———. 1996. "China's Emergence and Prospects as a Trading Nation." *Brookings Papers on Economic Activity* 2: 273–343.

Organization for Economic Cooperation and Development (OECD). 2005. "Economic Survey of China 2005." http://www.oecd.org/document/.

Rawski, Thomas. 2001. "What's Happening to Chinese GDP Statistics?" *China Economic Review* 12(4): 347–54.

Rosen, Daniel. 1999. *Behind the Open Door: Foreign Enterprises in the Chinese Marketplace.* Washington, DC: Institute for International Economics.

Sender, Henny. 2004. "Newbridge Is Set to Take Control of China's SDB." *Wall Street Journal Online.* May 31.

Standard & Poor's. 2004. *China Financial Services Outlook 2004.* New York: Standard & Poor's.

———. 2005a. *Outlook for China's Banking Sector.* New York: Standard & Poor's.

———. 2005b. "Recapitalization of China's ICBC and ABC Could Cost U.S. $110 Billion and Up to U.S. $190 Billion." *Ratings Direct* (April).

Steinfeld, Edward. 1998. *Forging Reform in China: The Fate of State-Owned Industry.* Cambridge: Cambridge University Press.

Studwell, Joseph. 2003. *The China Dream: The Quest for the Last Great Untapped Market Left on Earth.* New York: Grove Press.

———. 2004. "China's Boom Has Led to Only Partial Change." *Financial Times.* April 4.

Tsai, Kellee. 2002. *Back-Alley Banking: Private Entrepreneurs in China.* Ithaca, NY: Cornell University Press.

Walter, Carl and Fraser Howie. 2003. *Privatizing China: The Stock Markets and Their Role in Corporate Reform.* Singapore: John Wiley & Sons.

COMMENT

Xiaobo Lü

One of the major political economic events in the last half of the twentieth century was the rapid economic growth in China. With a growth rate averaging roughly 9 percent annually, it is hardly disputable that China's economic growth has been the most remarkable world economic story in the last 20 years. However, reforms in the Chinese financial sector are far from a success. In fact, the financial sector has so lagged behind that some scholars suggest it is an "elephant mired in a swamp"—slowly moving ahead with great difficulty. Others call it the Achilles' heel of the Chinese reforms. If, for different reasons, there had been wavering and indecision on the need to speed up financial sector reforms, this is no longer the case. By the end of the 1990s, a consensus among Chinese policymakers had emerged that such reforms were imperative to the success of overall reforms. How have such successes been achieved? What lessons do the Chinese reforms—both in general and the financial sector in particular—offer? In this comment, I will offer some analysis of the Chinese financial market development in the larger context of reforms in China. The chapter by Lee Branstetter provides a comprehensive survey of the policy and institutional changes in the Chinese financial sector over the last two decades. His three main themes—the centrality of the state, the close relationship between financial and SOE reforms, and the changing macroeconomic environment of China's financial markets—provide a basis for my comments and analysis. I will draw upon his findings and arguments as well as other sources.

As part of the overall reforms in China, reforms in the financial sector have been characterized by the same traits and strategies as many other major reforms: state-led (rather than market-driven), gradualism (rather than "shock therapy"), and de-statization (rather than outright privatization). As an important part of the state sector and its main financing arm, Chinese banks and other financial institutions have been very closely tied to the SOE reforms, as Branstetter points out.

GRADUALISM

Financial sector reforms in China have followed a similar pattern to other major reforms—a gradualist, trial-and-error approach that tackled easy problems first and constantly adjusted. By doing so, the government tried to advance the modernization of the financial sector, making it more competitive and efficient while avoiding unwanted social and economic instability. Consider the evolution and change of the banking system. As Branstetter cogently describes, it has taken more than two decades and several major institutional reforms—from monobank to emergence of commercial banks, from creation of a central bank to opening up to non-state banks—for China to develop its banking sector. The pace of reform has been cautious—"crossing the river on one stepping stone at a time" to use a famous phrase by the late Deng Xiaoping, the architect of the Chinese reform. Facing the potential competition from overseas and private banks (as China's WTO commitment requires a further opening up of the financial market by the end of 2006), China has stepped up its financial market reform pace since 2001.

The development of the stock market is another illustration of how the attempt to balance economic reform and social stability often slowed down the pace of change. As Branstetter states, the equity market has seen volatility, chaos, and even violence, since its establishment in the early 1990s. In one case, in 2001 the government attempted to speed up the reform of the SOEs and the stock market by preparing to sell more holdings of the SOEs and other public institutions. Yet, to many individual stockholders this signaled the government's reduction of support for those SOEs. As a result, the stock market slumped, and there was widespread uncertainty about the future. In less than nine months, the government decided to rescind its policy to reduce state shares. The government's concerns were not just merely economic; they were also social and political. Individual stockholders, though relatively small in number, consisted of urban retirees whose livelihood depended greatly on the stock valuation. The dilemma that a reform regime often faces is how to balance the needs to drastically change existing inefficient institutions against the necessity to maintain stability and minimize consequential transition pains. In reforming the financial sector, Chinese leaders have faced the same dilemma. From the beginning, the equity market has served a critical role: help reform the SOEs. Many measures and institutions were implemented as a result of reacting to these problems.

A typical but innovative strategy in the gradualist approach with regard to Chinese reforms, is the so-called dual-track (*shuanggui zhi*)—the coexistence of two types of institutions as a transitional measure.[1] As in many other reforms, financial reformers also adopted this deliberate strategy in developing China's equity market, that is, the coexistence of two kinds of shares: tradable shares that individual investors can buy, and nontradable rights that state-owned enterprises and other legal persons hold. As Branstetter observes, by the end of 2005, the tradables only accounted for 30 percent of the shares. In fact, this may well be the last dual-track item in existence in China. A series of new measures were taken to convert nontradable rights to tradable shares in 2005. As a buffer to absorb the shock effect, the government restricted the sale of nontradables to tradable shares and preset trading thresholds for nontradables to be traded. It is too early to see if these measures will be effective in smoothly converting all nontradable rights and reducing the state holding in the equity market. So far, they have been relatively well received by the market.

Gradualism is also reflected in another unique character of the Chinese institutional reforms—the establishment of formal institutions often precede rules and regulations. In the United States, for example, any major institutional change would require that legislative statutes, court rulings, or administrative regulatory changes be established first. These statutes and rules would provide legal and regulatory basis for the formal institutions to be established. This approach, often found in mature democratic regimes, tends to guarantee predictable and stable procedures, reducing uncertainty. But the approach also lacks flexibility and can make change more difficult. The Chinese-style reform approach, particularly in the first two decades of the reform, tended to be more flexible and easy to amend and adjust. But it also has serious downsides: when rules and regulations lag behind formal institutions, often uncertainty, distortion, and even chaos result, as Branstetter notes. Although rules and regulations can be revised and fine-tuned to adjust to new situations, their effectiveness can also be reduced and diluted owing to frequent changes. Thus, this "institution first, rules second" approach often negatively affects the development and capacity of regulatory agencies, including the three major ones in the financial sector: the China Securities Regulatory Commission (CSRC), the China Banking Regulatory Commission (CBRC), and the China Insurance Regulatory Commission (CIRC). Fairly or unfairly, many blame the "regulatory lag" for problems in the Chinese financial sector. While Branstetter does refer to China's financial regulatory bodies in his analysis, the development and function of the regulatory system deserve more attention.

STATE-LED REFORMS

Unlike reforms in European and other Asian economies, where financial sector reforms have been driven mostly by financial crisis or private sector needs, China's financial reforms have been undertaken by the state's initiative. The state, attempting to establish more viable financial markets and to make state-owned banks more competitive, led the way to withdraw itself from excessive control, intervention, and regulation. Not only did the state launch and regulate the financial markets, it has also been a major player in expanding the marketplace. Indeed, this point is similar to Branstetter's theme of the centrality of the state in the intermediation of capital in the Chinese economy. But more than Branstetter, I would give the state greater credit for initiating and for trying to withdraw itself. I would also suggest that in the post–state-socialist transition, the state has inevitably led the reforms, owing to past dependency on the state (i.e., state socialism). To be sure, to say that the state has led the reforms by setting its goals, scopes, and pace does not mean that it is not also a source of problems. The dual role of player and referee, besides the piecemeal reforms typical of a gradualist approach, is blamed for investors' lack of confidence in China's financial markets, particularly the stock market. Many people are critical of the regulatory body, CSRC, for both having regulated too much (and thus stifling incentives for private firms and investors to be listed and invest in the stock market) and for having regulated too little and been ineffective in preventing widespread insider trading and manipulation of the market by large institutional stockholders. But in the process of transforming itself from an all-encompassing player-coach-referee in an uncompetitive game to a referee in a competitive game, the regulatory agencies are learning to function better.

State-led reforms reflect the reluctance of a regime determined not to give up all political and economic control, particularly with regard to important state-owned firms. Branstetter argues, correctly, that the state is committed to controlling the "commanding heights," including the most important components of the financial sector. Restructured banks will still face the challenge of governance. Many top officials continue to be appointed by the government. Branstetter sees the state's attempt not to relinquish total control over leadership as likely to run into conflict with the market. I would highlight an additional possible scenario for future reforms. In the gradualist, de-statization framework, Chinese reforms first tackled problems and changed institutions with relatively concentrated social interests. Tight authoritarian rule afforded these early reforms some maneuvering room. As reforms touch upon more and more core institutions and interests, and the social interests become more diverse and fragmented, it will become increasingly difficult for any major reform measures to be deliberated and implemented.

DE-STATIZATION

Instead of large-scale privatization of the state sector, since the beginning of the reforms China has adopted a deliberate policy of reducing the share of the state sector in the overall economy by what some scholars call a "growing out of the plan" strategy—in other words, maintaining the core industrial enterprises in the hands of the state while allowing the non-state sector to grow. The two differing concepts, *feiguoyouhua* (de-statization) and *siyouhua* (privatization), are not just semantics; rather, they reflect two different approaches to reforming a former state socialist economy. In China, the economy has been gradually de-statized without large-scale privatization of the state-owned firms over the last twenty some years. The financial sector is no exception, although it has moved at a much slower pace. The two may eventually converge once the state sector is no longer dominant in the economy and once the markets become more mature.

In banking reforms, the government has been determined to prevent large state-owned banks, particularly the big four, from failing. The four banks—the Bank of China (BOC), the China Construction Bank (CCB), the Industrial and Commerce Bank of China (ICBC), and the Agricultural Bank of China (ABC)—have received capital injections to restructure and prepare to receive foreign investments. They handle roughly 60 percent of all bank loans in China, a large portion of which have gone to SOEs. Chinese policymakers and scholars are debating whether the government should continue to inject capital to bail out state-owned banks.

Opponents argue that injecting further money into inefficient banks could create moral hazards, thus delaying and even distorting restructuring efforts. Advocates argue that the poor performance and high rate of NPLs[2] are caused by the state's own distortions and past institutional weaknesses. It is the government, they argue, that should take responsibility for helping the banks, and that only with the injection of public money can these banks survive and compete.

CONCLUSION

In discussing the development and reforms of the financial sector in China, it is apparent that these reforms are part of overall economic transition strategy in the post-Mao era. However, the financial reforms have clearly lagged behind other reforms, in part owing to the approaches the Chinese leaders adopted—gradualism, state-led reform, and de-statization. The financial sector, which has been regarded as an important component of the state sector, took a long time to implement reforms. Lee Branstetter has provided a detailed and convincing overview of the process of financial reform. His most important observation is that "[o]ver the space of a quarter of a century, China managed to build financial markets that—for all their flaws—have still managed to function effectively enough. . . . It is only when one compares the speed and nature of reform of financial markets in China to the reforms in other sectors of the economy that progress appears to be slow."

When we assess the success or failure of the financial reforms in China, we must view them with historical and comparative perspectives. As Branstetter reminds us, China has come a long way from its monobank, single-source-of-capital days in a relatively short span of time. Building market institutions requires time. Transforming the old *and* building new economic institutions takes even more time. When we criticize China's financial regulatory system as weak and rudimentary, we should not forget that it has taken nearly a century for a country like the United States to build up and improve its financial regulatory system. In the meantime, there should be no denial that financial sector reforms have been slow and overly cautious, sometimes because of noneconomic considerations. The financial markets are likely to be a bottleneck for China's future growth. The era of easier reforms is over. Now at every step of the way, reform policies will face tremendous difficulties. Old approaches such as gradualism and de-statization have worked in the past, but they have also left behind unintended consequences and may no longer work. Perhaps only by implementing more innovative and daring reform measures can China's financial sector, still dominated by state players, meet the challenges posed by the foreign competitors under WTO commitments, and more importantly, meet the challenges of financing China's continuing growth.

NOTES

1. The most illustrative example of this dual-track strategy is the price reform between the mid-1980s and the mid-1990s. In the beginning of this reform, the intention was to avoid high inflation and social unrest likely to be caused by a rapid lift of price control by the state. So the government allowed a noncontrolled, market-driven pricing mechanism to grow while maintaining the state-set pricing in more critical items. Eventually, all prices but a few strategic items were converted to a market-driven pricing mechanism. Although this measure resulted in successfully establishing market pricing without experiencing high inflation and social unrest in China, it also had some unintended consequences of causing widespread corruption and abuse by government officials.

2. One of the contentious points is the level of NPLs in the Chinese banks. As recently as May 11, 2006, the government criticized some estimates by overseas analysts as overly high. According to the official figures, the NPL rates at the big four are 5.41 percent (BOC), 3.84 percent (CCB), 4.69 percent (ICCB), and 2.37 percent (ABC) (see Xinhuanet.com, May 11, 2006).

CHAPTER 2

China's Banking Sector and Economic Growth

Loren Brandt and Xiaodong Zhu

Since 1994, China's banking system has undergone significant changes and reform. This chapter provides an assessment of these reforms, paying particular attention to their implications for economic growth and to any potential risks now facing the banking sector. The analysis is grounded in a brief examination of the role of the banking and financial systems prior to 1994.

At the risk of some simplification, four main conclusions emerge. First, prior to 1994, the Chinese government relied heavily on the financial system for redistributing income. Such a policy resulted in recurring inflation and instability in the growth process. A major success of the post-1994 banking reforms was a significant reduction in the government's use of the banking system for income redistribution purposes. This has allowed banks to curtail lending to many small and medium-sized state-owned enterprises (SOEs), which had been losing money and had relied on bank loans for their survival. It also allowed the central bank to maintain a tight monetary policy and thus keep inflation in check. As a consequence, the Chinese economy has experienced a much more stable growth process in the last decade than it did in the period before 1994.

Second, the reforms have succeeded in helping to clean up the loan portfolios of the state-owned commercial banks (SOCBs). This was done by transferring a large portion of their nonperforming loans (NPLs) to asset management companies (AMCs) and by injecting new capital to the SOCBs in the form of cash and government-backed debt securities. The transfers of NPLs contributed to the decline in the ratio of NPLs to total loans from over 50 percent in 1998 to 15 percent in 2004. However, a large portion of the decline in the NPL ratio was due to the rapid growth of new loans in recent years. Moreover, a majority of the new bank loans to SOEs have high potential risk. Because most of the new loans have long maturities, it will take several years before the potential problems show up on the banks' balance sheets. So, the rapid reduction in the NPL ratio for the SOCBs does not necessarily mean a significant reduction in these banks' portfolio risk.

An important negative effect of the post-1994 banking reforms is the significant recentralization of the banking system. This recentralization has helped to sustain lending to larger SOEs and shareholding companies, has reduced lending to small and medium enterprises, and has made bank lending less diversified. As a consequence, investment efficiency has declined in China in the last decade. Associated with the recentralization in the banking system, bank loans have become less diversified. The new loans have been concentrated on large firms (many of them state-owned) and in a few key sectors identified by the government.

Finally, with the concentration of loans to larger firms (many of them state-owned), the Chinese banks face risks similar to those that banks in Japan faced one and a half decades ago. First, increasing product market competition may imply that these large firms may become less profitable in the future and therefore loans to them will become riskier. Second, entry of foreign banks and capital market development may imply that better firms will find better sources of financing elsewhere, leaving the domestic banks with less profitable firms. Third, the concentration of lending by the banks among several key sectors also implies that the banks are highly exposed to sectoral shocks. All of these factors suggest that the strategy of concentrating loans on large firms is highly risky and may not be profitable in the long run.

The chapter is organized as follows. As a prelude to examining the post-1994 banking reforms, the first section briefly examines the workings of China's financial system up through the early 1990s. It explores the tension between ongoing decentralization in the financial system, and the redistributive role it was asked to play. The next two sections respectively review the major banking reforms since 1994 and discuss the fundamental goal of the reforms: recentralization in the financial system. Then we examine the consequences of the reforms, focusing on the changing role of the banks, regional dimensions and structure of bank lending, and finally, the behavior of nonperforming loans. The last section considers the implications of these changes looking forward.

CHINA'S PRE-1995 FINANCIAL SYSTEM

Banks dominated China's pre-1995 financial system. Especially important were the four state-owned banks: the Bank of China (BOC), the China Construction Bank (CCB), the Agricultural Bank of China (ABC), and the Industrial and Commercial Bank of China (ICBC), which were established in the late 1970s and early 1980s out of the former commercial divisions of the People's Bank of China (PBOC).[1] In addition, several other financial institutions emerged to play an important role intermediating the rapidly increasing pool of savings, including the rural credit cooperatives (RCCs) in the countryside, the urban credit cooperatives (UCCs) in the cities, and the trust and investment corporations (TICs).[2] Collectively, these institutions were referred to as nonbank financial institutions (NBFIs), and they held several features in common: (1) they were usually either locally controlled or owned; (2) their lending largely fell outside the government's credit plan; and (3) they often had links with the state-owned banks or financial institutions.[3]

Table 2.1   New Funds Raised by Source, 1987–2004 (billions of RMB)

Year	Enterprises, Equity Plus Debt	Government Debt	Loans, National Banks	Loans, Other Financial Institutions	Total New Funds Raised
1987		20.96	144.17	46.86	211.99
1988		24.91	151.88	42.87	219.66
1989		39.48	185.80	24.77	250.05
1990		32.82	275.73	56.33	364.87
1991	13.56	35.47	287.74	77.98	414.74
1992	46.68	54.54	357.17	141.35	599.73
1993	21.49	63.34	484.55	177.47	746.86
1994	4.96	39.20	598.01	173.51	815.68
1995	2.27	154.97	695.24	278.35	1130.83
1996	21.30	145.91	804.11	271.75	1243.07
1997	69.06	233.15	1188.28	187.85	1678.34
1998	82.07	396.99	912.46	248.54	1640.06
1999	99.51	411.69	875.37	195.65	1582.22
2000	161.00	344.03	1283.00	293.88	2081.91
2001	132.91	386.96	995.74	465.15	1980.77
2002	110.48	525.64	1318.80	779.80	2734.71
2003	117.76	570.47	1884.41	1087.32	3659.95
2004	116.27	555.14	1753.70	748.60	3173.70

Sources: Estimates of funds raised in debt and equity markets are based on new issues less any retirement, and are taken from the figures reported annually in *Zhongguo Jinrong Nianjian*. New loans by the national banks represent the change in year-end figures, adjusted for estimates of reported transfers of nonperforming loans.

Table 2.2   Percentage of New Funds Raised by Source, 1987–2004

Year	Enterprises, Equity Plus Debt	Government Debt	Loans, National Banks	Loans, Other Financial Institutions	Total, All Sources	Total as % of GDP	Gross Capital Formation as a % of GDP
1987	0.00	0.10	0.68	0.22	1.00	0.18	0.36
1988	0.00	0.11	0.69	0.20	1.00	0.15	0.37
1989	0.00	0.16	0.74	0.10	1.00	0.15	0.36
1990	0.00	0.09	0.76	0.15	1.00	0.20	0.35
1991	0.03	0.09	0.69	0.19	1.00	0.19	0.35
1992	0.08	0.09	0.60	0.24	1.00	0.23	0.36
1993	0.03	0.08	0.65	0.24	1.00	0.22	0.42
1994	0.01	0.05	0.73	0.21	1.00	0.17	0.40
1995	0.00	0.14	0.61	0.25	1.00	0.20	0.39
1996	0.02	0.12	0.65	0.22	1.00	0.19	0.38
1997	0.04	0.14	0.71	0.11	1.00	0.23	0.36
1998	0.05	0.24	0.56	0.15	1.00	0.21	0.35
1999	0.06	0.26	0.55	0.12	1.00	0.20	0.34
2000	0.08	0.17	0.62	0.14	1.00	0.24	0.33
2001	0.07	0.20	0.50	0.23	1.00	0.21	0.35
2002	0.04	0.19	0.48	0.29	1.00	0.26	0.34
2003	0.03	0.16	0.51	0.30	1.00	0.31	0.38
2004	0.04	0.17	0.55	0.24	1.00	0.23	0.40

Source: See table 2.1. GDP figures for years before 1993 are taken from *Zhongguo Tongji Nianjian*, 2005, p. 51. Estimates after 1993 are the revised GDP figures as reported by the National Bureau of Statistics in "Announcement on Revised Result About Historical Data of China's Gross Domestic Product," January 10, 2006.

NBFIs drew on their own resources, mainly deposits (or entrusted funds in the case of TICs), funds obtained through an emerging inter-bank market, as well as funds occasionally diverted from the state-owned banks that were looking for higher returns. Unlike the state-owned banks, the lending of the NBFIs was typically not governed by the national credit plan, which earmarked funds of the state-owned banks for state sector firms and projects. Less encumbered on the margin, and facing slightly tighter overall budget constraints, project returns mattered more to the NBFIs in the lending decisions.

We provide selective summary information on China's formal financial institutions in tables 2.1–2.4. Tables 2.1 and 2.2 provide a breakdown on new funds raised in each year since 1987 through the national banks, other financial institutions, the government debt market, and enterprise security (debt and equity) markets. In the pre-1994 period, the national banks included the PBOC, the four state-owned banks, plus the much smaller Bank of

Table 2.3   Increase in Deposits by Type of Financial Institutions, 1987–2004

Year	Total New Deposits (billion RMB)	National Banks (billion RMB)	Other Financial Institutions (billion RMB)	National Banks (% of total)	Other Financial Institutions (% of total)
1987	164.05	116.23	47.82	70.85	29.15
1988	130.56	90.88	39.68	69.61	30.39
1989	136.38	158.81	−22.43	116.45	−16.45
1990	322.64	263.10	59.54	81.55	18.45
1991	406.64	321.92	84.72	79.17	20.83
1992	538.90	402.70	136.20	74.73	25.27
1993	615.90	433.92	181.98	70.45	29.55
1994	1084.55	610.06	474.49	56.25	43.75
1995	1338.97	945.17	393.80	70.59	29.41
1996	1470.90	1081.07	389.83	73.50	26.50
1997	1381.91	1040.97	340.94	75.33	24.67
1998	1330.76	977.92	352.84	73.49	26.51
1999	1308.10	1019.13	288.97	77.91	22.09
2000	1502.55	1091.92	410.63	72.67	27.33
2001	1981.28	1302.68	678.601	65.75	34.25
2002	2730.02	1759.20	970.82	64.44	35.56
2003	3713.82	2344.18	1369.64	63.12	36.88
2004	3336.87	2119.80	1217.07	63.53	36.47

Source: Based on annual figures reported in *Zhongguo Jinrong Nianjian*, various years. After 2001, our estimates for the national banks continue to include the Bank of Communications, and the CITIC Bank. Tables 2.8 and 2.9 provide alternative estimates with them excluded from the national bank category.

Communications and the China International Trust Investment Company (CITIC) Bank, and postal savings. The category "Other financial institutions," on the other hand, consisted largely of the NBFIs we described above, and includes the RCCs, UCCs, TICs, finance companies, and leasing companies. We report the new funds that were raised in each year through each source, both in renminbi (RMB) (table 2.1), and as a percentage of total new funds raised (table 2.2). To help put these numbers in an overall perspective, in table 2.2 we also report total new intermediation in each year by these sources as a percentage of gross domestic product (GDP) and gross capital formation as a percentage of GDP.[4] Table 2.3, on the other hand, provides comparable data for new deposits in financial institutions. Table 2.4 presents a breakdown of the total assets in these same institutions.[5]

Several general observations can be made on the basis of these tables. First, the percentage of GDP that was intermediated by China's formal financial institutions in any one year was significant and consistently

Table 2.4a Assets in China's Financial Institutions (billions of RMB)

Year	PBOC	Policy Banks	SOCB (1)	SOCB(2)	JSB(1)	JSB(2)	UCB	UCC	RCB	RCC	TIC	TOTAL
1987	383.86	0.00	1509.14	1480.26	0.43	29.30		9.82		161.85	57.07	2122.17
1988	462.76	0.00	1936.45	1880.88	3.65	59.22		20.34		191.13	83.84	2698.17
1989	574.41	0.00	2266.66	2197.89	5.02	73.80		28.42		231.00	89.34	3194.85
1990	722.60	0.00	2888.89	2788.95	14.49	114.43		37.21		299.95	119.92	4083.06
1991	901.08	0.00	3714.10	3581.75	26.13	158.48		56.37		368.90	174.87	5241.45
1992	1016.86	0.00	4729.56	4539.75	48.93	238.74		110.47		487.40	249.35	6642.57
1993	1338.72	0.00	6052.09	5812.50	78.93	318.51		187.87		614.20	271.18	8542.99
1994	1758.82	93.35	7498.14	7122.45	166.84	542.53		214.85		505.33		10237.33
1995	2062.43	738.31	8004.67	7585.33	243.62	662.95	0.00	303.92		679.10		12032.05
1996	2646.68	1014.29	9261.26	8754.71	371.80	878.35	214.19	374.78		870.66		14753.66
1997	3141.32	1335.77	10111.91	9536.34	475.70	1051.27	371.11	498.94		1012.20		16946.95
1998	3126.77	1390.39	10277.74	9660.21	564.78	1182.31	494.18	560.63		1143.11		17557.60
1999	3534.98	1537.95	11330.25	10634.86	751.75	1447.14	550.00	630.15		1239.24		19574.31
2000	3900.15	1647.40	12238.25	11375.43	1032.42	1895.24	664.76	678.49		1393.06		21554.53
2001	4222.70	1752.24	13169.45	12207.66	1424.02	2385.80	873.04	128.70		1610.80		23180.94
2002	5110.76	1916.36	14750.09	13648.05	1891.53	2993.57	1166.14	119.23	30.54	2205.21		27189.86
2003	6200.41	2133.00	16816.06	15467.63	2468.36	3816.80	1465.37	148.72	38.48	2674.62		31945.03
2004	7865.53	2463.18	18732.17	17078.71	3043.76	4697.21	1693.80	179.98	85.40	3101.34		37165.16

Table 2.4b Assets in China's Financial Institutions (percent of total)

Year	PBOC	Policy Banks	SOCB (1)	SOCB(2)	JSB(1)	JSB(2)	UCB	UCC	RCB + RCC	TICs	
1987	18.09	0.00	71.11	69.75	0.02	1.38	0.00	0.46	7.63	2.69	100.00
1988	17.15	0.00	71.77	69.71	0.14	2.19	0.00	0.75	7.08	3.11	100.00
1989	17.98	0.00	70.95	68.79	0.16	2.31	0.00	0.89	7.23	2.80	100.00
1990	17.70	0.00	70.75	68.31	0.35	2.80	0.00	0.91	7.35	2.94	100.00
1991	17.19	0.00	70.86	68.34	0.50	3.02	0.00	1.08	7.04	3.34	100.00
1992	15.31	0.00	71.20	68.34	0.74	3.59	0.00	1.66	7.34	3.75	100.00
1993	15.67	0.00	70.84	68.04	0.92	3.73	0.00	2.20	7.19	3.17	100.00
1994	17.18	0.91	73.24	69.57	1.63	5.30	0.00	2.10	4.94	NA	100.00
1995	17.14	6.14	66.53	63.04	2.02	5.51	0.00	2.53	5.64	NA	100.00
1996	17.94	6.87	62.77	59.34	2.52	5.95	1.45	2.54	5.90	NA	100.00
1997	18.54	7.88	59.67	56.27	2.81	6.20	2.19	2.94	5.97	NA	100.00
1998	17.81	7.92	58.54	55.02	3.22	6.73	2.81	3.19	6.51	NA	100.00
1999	18.06	7.86	57.88	54.33	3.84	7.39	2.81	3.22	6.33	NA	100.00
2000	18.09	7.64	56.78	52.78	4.79	8.79	3.08	3.15	6.46	NA	100.00
2001	18.22	7.56	56.81	52.66	6.14	10.29	3.77	0.56	6.95	NA	100.00
2002	18.80	7.05	54.25	50.20	6.96	11.01	4.29	0.44	8.22	NA	100.00
2003	19.41	6.68	52.64	48.42	7.73	11.95	4.59	0.47	8.49	NA	100.00
2004	21.16	6.63	50.40	45.95	8.19	12.64	4.56	0.48	8.57	NA	100.00

1. Three main sources are used in the construction of the table including individual banks' balance sheets; relevant sections in the annual reports of these banks that review their business and operations; and consolidated balance sheets for financial institutions that are reported in *Zhongguo Jinrong Nianjian*.

2. Beginning in 2002, the consolidated balance sheets report "total assets." However, for 1994–2001, total assets are not reported as a separate item, and we add up relevant entries on the asset side. This likely underestimates total assets because of the omission of "other assets" and items that appear in the balance sheets beginning in 2002.

Sources for individual institutions:

PBOC: Taken from the table "balance sheet of monetary authority" as reported in *Zhongguo Jinrong Nianjian*.

Policy Banks: Calculated from the individual banks' balance sheets. Information for the China Development Bank is not available for 1995, and we interpolate using 1994 and 1996 values.

SOCB: Calculated from the individual banks' balance sheets.

JSB: Includes Bank of Communications, CITIC, Everbright, Huaxia, Minsheng, China Merchant, Shanghai Pudong Development, Guangdong Development, Shenzhen Development, Fujian Industrial, Hengfeng, and China Zheshang. For 2001–2004, estimates are taken from the section "Financial Supervision Review—Joint Stock Banks" as reported in *Zhongguo Jinrong Nianjian*. For earlier years, estimates are based on the balance sheets of the individual banks.

UCB: Asset totals are taken from estimates reported annually in *Zhongguo Jinrong Nianjian*.

UCC: Beginning in 2002, estimates are provided in the consolidated balance sheets of the UCCs as reported in *Zhongguo Jinrong Nianjian*. For 1994–2001, total assets are not reported as a separate item, and we add up relevant entries on the asset side of the consolidated balance sheet. This likely underestimates total assets because of the omission of "other assets" and items that appear in the balance sheets beginning in 2002. For 1987–1993, we use the estimate of total assets reported in the consolidated balance sheet for the UCCs for these years that appears in *Zhongguo Jinrong Nianjian*, 1994, p. 554.

RCB: Asset totals are taken from estimates reported annually in *Zhongguo Jinrong Nianjian*.

RCC: Same as the UCCs. For 1987–1993, see *Zhongguo Jinrong Nianjian*, 1994, p. 553.

TIC: Taken from Brandt and Zhu, 1994.

averaged in the vicinity of 20 to 25 percent. Second, with gross capital formation running between 35 and 40 percent of GDP, and China's net capital inflows modest during this period, our estimates suggest that more than half of China's pool of new savings each year was being intermediated by these sources.[6] Third, the national banks, largely the four state-owned banks, dominate formal intermediation, averaging almost three-quarters of new funds raised each year. However, prior to 1995 and in select years, the NBFIs were an important conduit for funds, especially to the non-state sector, in an increasingly decentralized economic environment. Fourth, prior to 1995, debt or equity markets played only a modest role, absorbing less than 10 percent of the total. Fifth, up through the early 1990s, and reflecting the rising saving rates in the economy and expanding role of these institutions, total assets in financial institutions increased as a ratio of GDP from 1.75 to 2.4.

LINKS WITH THE GROWTH DYNAMICS IN THE PRE-1995 ECONOMY

The behavior of China's financial institutions is pivotal to the growth dynamics we observe in the pre-1995 economy. China went through a recurring series of boom-bust or stop-go cycles that are captured in figure 2.1. Years of rapid growth were accompanied by accelerating rates of inflation. Important in explaining these dynamics is a tension between ongoing decentralization in China's financial system, which was conducive to the

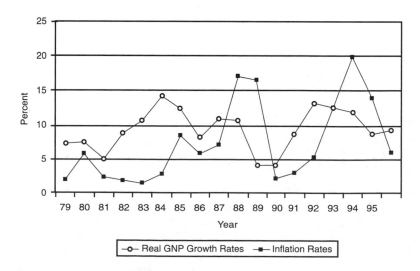

Figure 2.1   Inflation and GNP Growth in China

flow of financial resources to high-return investments and firms, and the redistributive role the financial system was asked to play in support of the state sector and certain regions. We will argue later that many of the reforms after 1994 were designed to resolve this fundamental dilemma.

Since the onset of economic reform in the late 1970s, China's non-state sector has been the key engine of economic growth. Initially, this sector largely consisted of collectively owned enterprises in the countryside (commonly referred to as township and village enterprises (TVEs) and the cities, but later the sector came to include (and to be dominated by) private enterprises and foreign-invested enterprises (FIEs). The non-state sector benefited significantly from market-liberalizing reforms that (1) removed barriers to entry in numerous sectors and (2) enabled access through emerging markets to key inputs and raw materials, which formerly had been allocated through the plan.[7] Between 1978 and 1994, for example, the non-state sectors' share of the gross value of industrial output increased from only 22 percent to 63 percent. Put slightly differently, the contribution of the SOEs to annual growth in industry fell from nearly 90 percent in 1978 to only 12 percent in 1994.[8]

Estimates suggest that the non-state sector enjoyed significantly higher total factor productivity (TFP) than the state sector on the order of 2 to 2.5:1.[9] But central to the growth in the non-state sector, and overall growth in the economy, was the level of investment in the non-state sector. We illustrate the strong positive relationship in China between the growth rate of non-state sector investment and gross national product (GNP) growth beginning in 1982 in figure 2.2. The two series track each other well through the peaks and troughs of China's early cyclical growth.

Despite its role as the engine of growth, the non-state sector was seriously constrained by the availability of credit from China's banks and the financial system more generally. In figure 2.3 we graph the growth rate of non-state sector investment and the growth rate of credits from China's financial system directed toward non-state sector investment. The two move in parallel, with years of rapid growth in non-state investment accompanied by increases in credit growth in the sector from the banking and financial system.

The constraints on credit access for China's non-state sector as well as the highly cyclical behavior of its access observed up through 1994 lies in its political economy. Banks, especially China's state-owned banks, were used to support a highly inefficient state enterprise sector and achieve regional goals (see below). In most years, 80 to 85 percent of all credit extended through the state-owned banks went to state-owned firms in the

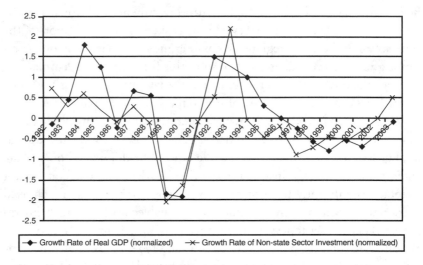

Figure 2.2   Growth and Non-state Sector Investment

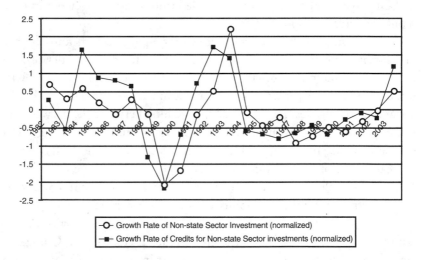

Figure 2.3   Access to Credit and Non-state Sector Investment

form of either working-capital or fixed investment loans. A slightly lower percentage of credit through the entire financial system went to the state sector. On an annual basis, the flow of resources through the financial system making its way to the state sector was as much as 15 to 20 percent of GNP.[10] With interest rates on deposits and loans heavily regulated, and the spread often negative, this represented a significant redistribution of resources from savers to borrowers, with the borrowers largely in the state sector.

The central government's use of the banking system to support the state sector reflected the Chinese government and Communist Party's deep commitment to workers and job growth in the largely urban state sector, and was necessitated by declining fiscal resources at the government's disposal. Between 1978 and 1994, the number of individuals working in urban state-owned units increased from 74.5 million to 112.1 million, or an increase of more than 50 percent.[11] Over the same period, however, government revenue as a percentage of GNP fell from 32 percent to less than 15 percent. The portion of this going to the central government rose through 1984, but then fell sharply, so that at its nadir, the central government controlled only slightly more than 3 percent of GNP.[12]

But financial resources did occasionally make their way to the non-state sector. As has been described elsewhere,[13] there was a marked cyclicality to non-state sector lending, facilitated by partial decentralization in the financial system. In most years, the credit plan was largely "indicative," and state-owned banks had some discretion in lending activity that enabled them to use their superior information on firms and project returns to allocate credit more efficiently. They used this discretion, however, to divert bank resources intended for the state sector under the credit plan to the non-state sector, in which project returns were typically higher. In doing so, they often exploited their links with the NBFIs. Combined with the lending by the NBFIs themselves, these resources helped to support the expansion in non-state sector investment we observe in some years in figure 2.3.

While the flow of resources to the more productive non-state sector was key to growth acceleration, it also left the state-owned banks without the financial resources they needed to fund the commitments outlined in the credit plan for the state sector working-capital and fixed investment needs. The only recourse for funding the ensuing gap was additional PBOC lending to the state-owned banks, which resulted in both an increase in the money supply and inflation. In late 1988 and early 1989, and then again in late 1992 and early 1993, for example, PBOC loans to the state-owned banks increased sharply and supported between 50 and 60 percent of the credit increase by the state-owned banks. By comparison, in early 1988 and 1994, the percentage was 10 percent.

Inevitably, concerns about accelerating inflation and possibly hyper-inflation required the central government to reassert full control over the allocation of credit by the financial institutions. This was usually done through the implementation of an "administrative credit plan," which imposed tight restrictions on the use and allocation of bank funds, and entailed significant recentralization in the financial system. In the pre-1995 reform period, retrenchment in the financial sector was carried out on three separate occasions: 1985, 1988 through 1989, and 1993.

Table 2.5 documents some of the selective policy measures that were taken in each of these episodes. Note the similarity. Restrictions on interbank lending, reduction in lending to TVEs and individuals, and re-implementation of binding credit quotas on the part of the state-owned banks were common. The effect in each case was to cut off the leakage of financial resources to the non-state sector, largely through the NBFIs, thereby preserving more resources within the banking system for the state sector. For example, between 1988 and 1989, the role of the TICs as a source of new funds fell from 11.04 to 1.56 percent, and between 1992 and 1993 from 8.88 to 5.49 percent.[14] At the macro level, retrenchment helped to reduce inflation by reducing the need for PBOC "re-lending" to the state-owned banks. However, this came at a cost: The reduction in non-state sector investment spending also resulted in sharp reductions in economic growth.

REGIONAL DIMENSIONS TO NATIONAL BANK LENDING

So far we have focused on the competition between the state and non-state sector in accessing financial resources under increasing decentralization in the pre-1995 period. There is also a marked regional dimension to banking behavior that is itself important to the story and the post-1994 reform: The banking system was also used to redistribute resources from the more rapidly growing coastal provinces to the interior. Between 1978 and 1994, the rate of growth of real GNP per capita in the six coastal provinces running from Shandong to Guangdong, including Shanghai, averaged over 12 percent per annum compared to 8–9 percent in the rest of the country. Typically, regional redistribution is the domain of fiscal policy and interregional fiscal transfers, but we need to recall the severe fiscal constraints facing the central government at this time. These constraints would not begin to be relaxed until the major fiscal reforms in

1994. Thus, the government resorted to the use of the financial system to achieve its regional objectives.

In table 2.6, drawing on provincial-level data on loans and deposits in the national banks, we provide a breakdown for select years of the regional shares of new loans and deposits. Estimates of the change in new loans divided by the change in new deposits reveal the same behavior but are not reported. The usual convention is to divide China into three regions, namely, eastern, central, and western. However, we break the eastern provinces into two: the six dynamic coastal provinces mentioned earlier and the remaining eastern provinces, giving us a total of four regions. Especially noticeable is the excess of new deposits over new loans in the six coastal provinces. In 1992, for example, the difference was more than 10 percent of all new deposits in the national banks (47.9 percent of deposits versus 37.7 percent of loans). Where did these resources go? They were directed to supporting loan growth in excess of deposit growth in the central and western regions. The western region's share of new loans was 18.4 percent compared to only 13.8 percent of new deposits. In the central provinces, the gap was 4.9 percent (18.4 percent versus 13.5 percent).

Some of this redistribution may have occurred within each of the state-owned banks, but it also likely occurred through PBOC regional lending (re-lending) operations to the state-banks, drawing on the required reserves of the NBFIs and increases in high-powered money.[15] The NBFIs faced higher reserve requirements than the state-owned banks, as suggested by figure 2.4, which graphs the loan-deposit ratios for all banks, and the national and nonnational banks, separately.[16] NBFIs were also more prominent in the faster growing regions of China. Policy-directed regional redistribution likely helped to counteract informal financial flows, as well as flows through the interbank market from the interior into the coastal provinces. These offsetting flows may help to explain a finding of highly segmented capital markets by Boyreau-Debray and Wei (2004) in the face of anecdotal evidence suggesting significant capital flows into the coastal regions.

The regional redistribution we describe is not entirely unrelated to the government's policy favoring the state sector. For historical reasons, and largely related to fixed investment spending during the 1960s and 1970s under the national policy to support the "Third Front,"[17] the state sector on the eve of economic reform was more prominent in the central and western provinces than it was in the coastal region.[18] This legacy has been a drag on growth and development in the interior as more

Table 2.5 Selected Policy Measures During Retrenchment Periods

Policy	1985	1988–1989	1993
1. Credit	—Mandatory credit controls imposed in fourth quarter with local leaders and department heads directly responsible. —No financing of fixed investment outside of the plan without State Council authorization. —Loans to TVEs and individuals reduced and controlled strictly within plan. —Recall of excessive specialized bank loans. —CCB brought under PBOC administration, and reserves set at 30%	—Mandatory cash and credit controls imposed in fourth quarter of 1988. —New credits for either working capital or fixed asset investment outside the plan required PBOC or SC authorization. —No new loans to TVEs or to individuals. —New loans to 10 types of projects prohibited. —Cash withdrawals by enterprises and other institutions restricted to levels of 8/1988. —Increase in reserve requirements of specialized banks.	—Mandatory credit controls for banks and NBFIs. —Specialized banks required to recall loans to NBFIs, and prohibited from lending to the NBFIs. —No new investment projects allowed.
2. Interest Rates	—Rates on deposits increased.	—Rates on short-term deposits increased and indexing on long-term deposits.	—Same as in 1988–1989.

3. Interbank market		—Restrictions on the use of the interbank market by TICs. —Other financial institutions prohibited from using the interbank market to finance fixed investment.	—NBFIs prohibited from using the interbank market.
4. NBFIs	—Increase in the percentage of deposits of RCCs held at ABC.	—Suspension of all new lending activity by TICs; TICs also required to deposit 2 billion RMB in PBOC.	—NBFIs included in the credit plan. —608 NBFIs shut down or suspended.
5. PBOC		—Recall of 25 billion RMB in short-term loans extended by PBOC branches in the first half of 1988.	—PBOC branches prohibited from short-term lending to banks. —Recall of PBOC loans to NBFIs. —Crackdown on illegal fund-raising activity. —Centralization of loan quota allocation, with quotas directly distributed to the specialized banks by the head office of the PBOC.

Sources: Qingbin Wang and Shengying Zhou, *Zhongguo Huobi Liutong de Huigu yu Zhanwang* (The Circulation of Money in China: Reflection and Outlook); Xinli Zheng, *Jingji Zhengce Fenxi: 1994–1995* (An Analysis of Macroeconomic Policy: 1994–1995); Shengying Zhou, *Zhongguo Huobi Zhengce Yanjiu* (Research on Chinese Monetary Policy); *Zhongguo Jinrong Nianjian* (Almanac of China's Finance and Banking), selected years.

Table 2.6   Regional Shares of New Loans and Deposits, Selected Years

	Region 1		Region 2		Region 3		Region 4	
	Loans	Deposits	Loans	Deposits	Loans	Deposits	Loans	Deposits
	Share of New Loans and Deposits: National Banks							
1987	25.3	31.1	39.8	36.5	19.0	17.0	16.0	15.4
1988	29.0	26.2	35.4	42.9	17.9	17.1	17.7	13.7
1992	25.4	24.8	37.7	47.7	18.4	13.5	18.4	13.8
1993	29.0	28.0	35.2	41.5	18.3	18.3	17.5	12.0
1997	27.0	29.2	38.3	43.3	16.1	11.9	18.6	15.6
1998	25.7	27.3	38.0	42.2	20.7	15.4	15.6	15.0
	Share of New Loans and Deposits: All Financial Institutions							
1997	23.4	24.2	39.7	47.3	18.3	13.1	18.6	15.4
1998	24.3	28.7	39.0	40.1	18.5	15.6	18.2	15.6
2002	21.5	27.2	52.9	52.0	13.7	13.3	12.7	11.4
2003	20.2	22.0	51.5	49.8	12.9	14.1	6.9	6.5

1. Based on figures reported by each province in *Zhongguo Jinrong Nianjian*, select years. Estimates for 2003 based on RMB and U.S. dollar loans and deposits. For all other years, RMB loans and deposits.
2. Region 1 includes Heilongjiang, Jilin, Liaoning, Hebei, Beijing, and Tianjin; region 2 includes Shandong, Jiangsu, Shanghai, Zhejiang, Fujian, and Guangdong; region 3 is made up of the central provinces of Shanxi, Jiangxi, Henan, Hunan, and Hubei; region 4 is the western provinces of Neimonggou, Chongqing, Sichuan, Guizhou, Guangxi, Yunnan, Tibet, Shaanxi, Gansu, Qinghai, Ningxia, and Xinjiang.

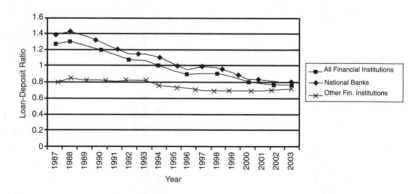

Figure 2.4   Loan Deposit Ratios by Type of Institution

resources have been consistently absorbed in the less productive state sector in these provinces, effectively crowding out the development of the non-state sector. In fact, we observe a sharp negative relationship between provincial growth rates between 1978 and 1995, and the size of the state sector in nonagriculture at the beginning of the reforms.[19] The coastal provinces have their natural "geographic" advantages and also enjoyed preferential national government policy in the 1980s and early 1990s with respect to FDI, but perhaps equally important in their success is the fact that they had smaller state sectors at the outset to protect and support.

ASSESSMENT OF THE PRE-1995 SYSTEM

China's financial institutions were occasionally able to direct credits to a more productive non-state sector. This feature of the pre-1995 financial system is often lost on observers. But this came at the expense of (1) occasional periods of high inflation and (2) mounting NPLs in the financial system. The inflation was related to the cyclical behavior of PBOC re-lending to the state-owned banks to support state interests, and not to the level of investment itself. The NPLs, on the other hand, can be linked to the weak governance structures and poorly defined ownership in the financial institutions; the policy-type lending carried out by the state-owned banks to support the state sector; and the very weak regulatory environment under which the NBFIs, especially the TICs, operated. Oversight and supervision were often minimal.[20] Problems of moral hazard were endemic and contributed to investment in projects that may have had higher average returns but that were often riskier. Good estimates of NPLs are not available for the early 1990s, but based on figures for a few years later (which we discuss below), more than half of the loan portfolio was likely nonperforming.

BANKING SECTOR REFORMS SINCE 1994

In the mid-1990s, fully aware of the need for a more efficient and healthier financial system, China embarked on a comprehensive reform of its banking sector, especially the state-owned banks. These reforms took on added urgency with the meltdown of the financial systems and the ensuing shocks to the real sectors of Indonesia, Thailand, and Korea during the Asian financial crisis in 1997. Significantly, the reforms in the financial sector were carried out simultaneously with a massive downsizing in the state enterprise sector itself, as well as major fiscal reform. By the end of 2004, the number of individuals working in the state sector had fallen from a peak of nearly 113 million in 1995 to 67 million.[21] As much as a third of all SOEs were privatized,[22] and countless other firms either went bankrupt or were merged with other firms. With respect to the fiscal system, a major recentralization occurred beginning with the Tax Reform of 1994, which significantly increased the percentage of fiscal revenue controlled by the center.[23]

In table 2.7, we provide a chronology of some of the major reforms in the banking system and the financial sector more generally. At the heart of the banking reform were several measures, including the establishment of three policy banks in 1994; the implementation of the Commercial Banking Law in 1995; the establishment of four asset management companies to handle the disposal of the specialized banks' NPLs; and the reform of the state-owned banks. The logic of the reform package is clear. The aim of the new policy banks, namely, the Import-Export Bank, the Agriculture Development Bank, and the China Development Bank, was to shift all policy lending formerly carried out by the state-owned banks to these institutions, thereby freeing up the state-owned banks to lend on a more commercial basis. Within the state-owned banks, nonperforming loans from earlier "policy-type" lending were to be transferred to four asset management companies, one for each of the four state-owned banks; the state-owned banks were to be recapitalized and converted to shareholding companies with the state as the controlling owner. The latter would open the door for the strategic "outside" investments, which have become very prominent the last few years. Combined, these reforms would free the banks from some of their past constraints and allow them to operate on a more commercial basis.

These reforms were complemented by several other important measures including the reorganization of the PBOC on a regional (from a largely provincial) basis beginning in 1999; a sharp reduction in the number of TICs that were allowed to operate and restrictions on the operations of those remaining; reform of the interbank market; conversion of the urban credit cooperatives to the urban commercial banks, with municipal governments often having controlling shares; the elimination of the RCFs (rural credit foundations); the shift of the RCCs from the supervision of the ABC to the PBOC; ongoing reform of the RCCs, including the setting up of Rural Credit Cooperative Unions, and the subsequent conversion of a small number of these into the rural commercial banks beginning in 2003; and the establishment of the China Banking Regulatory Commission (CBRC) in 2003.

Rather than provide a comprehensive assessment of these reforms, we wish to focus on one of the most important consequences: the overall centralization of the financial system.

Table 2.7 Chronology of New Policy Measures and Regulations for the Financial Sector

New regulation and regulatory authorities

1995

Enact People's Bank of China Law, Commercial Bank Law, Notes Act, and Insurance Law.

1998

Central Finance Work Committee established, the party authority in charge of the financial sector.

China Insurance Regulatory Commission established.

2003

China Banking Regulatory Commission established.

Central Huijin Investment Company established to help recapitalize CCB and BOC.

2004

5th Asset Management Company founded to deal with nonperforming assets of PBOC.

PBOC

1994

Three policy banks are established; policy and commercial financing to be separated in the financial system.

Implement *asset-liability ratio management,* and *asset risk management* in all commercial banks (other than state-owned banks), UCCs, and TICs.

1996

Decrease interest rates twice.

In 1995 and 1996, abolish the *credit ceiling control* for cooperative financial institutions and commercial banks other than the state-owned banks. For four state-owned commercial banks, implement *asset-liability ratio management* based on the credit ceiling control.

1997

Decrease interest rates on loans and deposits for a third time since 1996.

1998

Decrease required-reserve ratio from 13 to 8 percent.

Decrease interest rates and discount rates three times.

Monitoring responsibilities for security and insurance industries are separated from PBOC. China Securities Regulatory Commission made responsible for the supervision of the security industry, while China Insurance Regulatory Commission takes over supervision for the insurance industry.

PBOC abolishes the 32 provincial branches and establishes 9 cross-provincial regional branches; strengthens central bank's supervision independence and reduces unnecessary intervention of local governments.

Promulgate *Measures on Banning Illegal Financial Institutions and Illegal Financial Businesses.*

(continued)

Table 2.7 *continued*

PBOC (*continued*)

1999

Decrease interest rates for the seventh time since 1996.

Further decrease required-reserve ratio from 8 to 6 percent.

2002

Decrease interest rates for the eighth time since 1996. Since 1996, one-year loan interest rate decreased to 5.31 percent from 12.06 percent.

2004

Implement differential reserve ratio system. Reserve ratios for different financial institutions set to reflect capital adequacy ratios and asset quality.

Eliminate ceiling controls over commercial banks' loan interest rates. Loan interest rates for UCC and RCC can be adjusted 2.3 times above the designated benchmark rates; financial institutions are given discretion on pricing loans differently according to their risks and costs.

Lending behavior

1994

PBOC no longer directly loans to enterprises; Ministry of Finance can no longer borrow or overdraw from PBOC.

Fixed asset loans put under strict control; financial institutions prohibited from issuing fixed asset loans exceeding the administrative quota.

1995

Fixed asset loans remain under administrative plan; working-capital loans prohibited from financing fixed assets investment.

1996

Promulgate *General Lending Rules*, fundamental principles for all domestic commercial lending business.

Working-capital loans are directed to support SOE reforms; promulgate *Notice about Further Improving Financial Services to Large and Medium-Sized SOEs*.

Strengthen the bank-enterprise link; 300 SOEs selected to sign cooperation contracts with banks, providing stable financial services for the contracted SOEs.

Housing and auto loans are temporarily prohibited.

1997

Continued financial support for large and medium-sized SOEs; additional 212 SOEs selected as key support targets.

PBOC promulgates a notice in support of the profitable products of profit-losing SOEs.

PBOC promulgates *Provisional Measures on Syndicate Loans*, which is aimed to better service large and medium-sized SOEs and key construction projects.

1998

PBOC abolishes the administrative credit ceiling control over SOCBs.

Commercial banks can use funds at their own discretion after depositing required-reserves and purchasing policy bonds.

Table 2.7 *continued*

Lending behavior (*continued*)

Promulgate *Management Measures on Household Home Loans* and *Notice About Auto Loans* to encourage consumer lending to stimulate demand.

Support SOE development, promulgate supplementary notice on further support of the profitable products of profit-losing SOEs.

1999

Promulgate *Guidance on Individual Consumption Loans*; all commercial banks are allowed to carry out all consumption loan businesses.

Promulgate *Management Measures on Close-Ended Loans* to support profitable products of struggling SOEs and help them resume production.

PBOC re-lends a total of 41 billion RMB to UCC, RCC, and other joint-stock banks (JSBs) to support small and medium-sized enterprises; expand the range on loan rates for SMEs; promulgate *Guidance on Improving SME Financing.*

2000

PBOC promulgates *Guidance on the Management of Farmers-United-Collateral Loans by RCC*; requires RCC to increase credits for agricultural production.

Promulgate a notice to emphasize the qualification requirements for the close-ended loans to unprofitable SOEs.

2001

Supervise and guide the development of individual consumption market, promulgate *Notice About Standardizing Housing Financial Services, Notice About Standardizing Household Housing Loans Management,* and *Notice About the Prohibition of Individual Consumption Loans for Non-specified Usage.*

2002

Guide and channel credit intermediation with emphasis on infrastructure projects.

Enact the *Small and Medium-Sized Enterprises Advancement Act*; PBOC extends 20 billion RMB re-lending to urban commercial banks to support SMEs.

2003

Promulgate two notices in 2002 and 2003 to guide and monitor the development of the real estate market, emphasizing risk management in housing loans.

2004

PBOC and China Banking Regulatory Commission promulgate *Management Measures on Automobile Loans.*

AMC

1999

Four asset management companies are established to dispose of and manage the nonperforming loans of national banks and to facilitate debt-equity swap with the SOEs in support of SOE reforms.

2000

State Economic and Trade Commission recommends 601 large and medium-sized SOEs for debt-equity swap; 580 of them are approved by the AMCs with denominated debt value of 405 billion RMB.

(continued)

Table 2.7 *continued*

SOCB

1996, 1997

Reform the SOCB's branch distributional structure; abolish and consolidate 5506 and 5300 local branches and offices in 1996 and 1997, respectively.

1998

Ministry of Finance issues 270 billion special government bonds in order to supplement four SOCBs' bank capital.

Establish *Authorized Credit Extending System* in 4 SOCBs; the credit extending rights for all branches are determined by their operational ability and business achievement.

1999

Finish adjustment of the SOCB's branch distributional structure; redundant and unprofitable local branches are closed down.

2000

Establish nonperforming loans responsibility system; person in charge of local branches responsible for decreasing NPLs.

Strengthen credit approval procedure; must go through four stages, including assessment by loan business department, risk management department, and risk management committee, with final approval by person in charge of local branch.

2003

State Council decides to use U.S. $45 billion foreign exchange reserves to recapitalize CCB and BOC, initiating the joint-stock reform of SOCBs.

2004

BOC and CCB are recapitalized and incorporated as limited corporations.

Joint-stock banks

2003

Encourage JSB to supplement bank capital by allowing them to list domestically, and by increasing the limit on the share of foreign capital.

2004

Bank of Communication recapitalized, with HSBC becoming the second largest shareholder.

Zhejiang Commercial Bank approved to be recapitalized as a joint-stock bank with domestic private capital holding majority shares; it becomes the twelfth JSB in China.

Over half of JSBs have foreign capital shares.

7 JSBs are approved to issue subordinated securities to supplement capital.

UCC, UCB, RCC, RCB

1996

RCC administrative ties with ABC begin to be severed, a process completed in 1999.

1997

PBOC promulgates *Guidance on Establishment of Urban Commercial Banks*; to strengthen supervision of RCC, PBOC establishes *Bureau of Rural Cooperative Finance*.

Table 2.7 *continued*

<hr>

UCC, UCB, RCC, RCB (*continued*)

1998

PBOC sets up *Measures About Rectifying Urban Credit Cooperatives*; by the end of year, 21 UCCs are shut down.

1999

Shut down over 1,600 insolvent and high-risk UCCs and RCCs.

2000 and 2001

Start RCC reform experiment in Jiangsu Province in 2000; in 2001, Jiangsu Province Rural Credit Cooperative Union is established; also joint-stock Rural Commercial Banks are established in three cities in Jiangsu.

2002

Continue cleaning up of UCCs; through the closure, consolidation, and establishment of urban commercial banks, dispose of 766 and 195 UCCs in 2001 and 2002, respectively.

2004

In 2003 and 2004, reforms of UCC are extended to 21 provinces; by the end of 2004, there are seven rural commercial banks (RCBs).

NBFI

1995–1997

As part of the restructuring of the financial system, separation imposed between banking, securities, and trust industries; TICs are detached from their affiliated SOCBs; PBOC branch-owned security companies are separated from PBOC branches; security companies set up by commercial banks, credit cooperatives, TICs, insurance companies, finance companies, and leasing companies are separated from their owners.

1999

Promulgate *Measures on Rectifying Trust and Investment Companies*.

2000

Begin rectification of 239 TICs; 58 will be maintained, 67 consolidated, 18 restructured, and 96 shut down.

2001

Enact *Trust Law*.

Promulgate *Management Measures on Trust and Investment Companies*.

2004

Three automobile finance companies are established.

Promulgate *Management Measures on Automobile Finance Companies* and *Auto Loans Management Measures*.

Interbank market

1994

Before 1994, most interbank funds lent to NBFIs for investment in fixed assets, real estate, and stocks; PBOC promulgate *Provisional Measures on Credit Funds Management*, prescribing that interbank lending be restricted to 7-day and 7-day-to-4-month short-term loans. Banks cannot make loans to NBFI with maturities longer than 7 days.

(continued)

Table 2.7   *continued*

Interbank market (*continued*)

1996

Uniform national interbank market is established; PBOC abolishes the ceiling control over interbank lending rates, with rates to be market-determined.

PBOC carries out its first open-market operation.

1997

In June, PBOC abolishes commercial banks' debt security trading in security exchanges; instead, debt securities shall be traded in the interbank debt market.

1998

Policy banks initiate bond issuance in the interbank debt market.

1999

Security companies and RCCs are allowed to enter the interbank market for interbank lending and debt securities trading. Mutual fund companies are allowed access to interbank debt market for debt securities trading.

2002

Change participants' qualification system in the interbank debt market, from *authorization system* to *records system*; participants increase from 245 to 945.

2004

PBOC promulgates *Measures for Administration of the Issuance of Subordinated Bond by Commercial Banks;* BOC and CCB are allowed to issue 100 billion RMB subordinated bonds; in 2004 the two banks issued 66.07 billion RMB.

CENTRALIZATION WITHIN CHINA'S FINANCIAL SYSTEM

An important feature of many of the reforms was their role in facilitating a recentralization of overall authority in the financial system, thereby counteracting other powerful decentralizing tendencies in the economy. In this regard, they parallel the important fiscal system reforms in 1994, which significantly increased the percentage of fiscal resources under central government control.[24]

The PBOC reform, which reorganized the PBOC on a regional as opposed to a provincial or municipal basis, helped to reduce the influence of local governments on the branch lending of local state-owned banks. Previously, municipal or provincial-level offices of the PBOC had supervisory responsibility over local (including provincial-level) state-owned bank branch offices and were not entirely independent because of their ties to the local (provincial) government through the appointment system. This was complemented by an important reform in the *nomenklatura* system for local state-owned bank branch appointments, with appointments of branch managers now made higher up in the state-owned banks' hierarchy.

In principle, this would make local bank managers less beholden in their career concerns to local government officials and would better align their incentives with those of the banks' headquarters (which reflected the interests of the central government and the party). Seht (1999) argues that the conversion of the UCCs to urban commercial banks may have helped further this aim. As part of the UCC conversion, municipal governments became major shareholders in the new institutions. By giving them their "own" banks to manage, this effectively helped to reduce the influence of local officials in state-owned bank lending.

NBFIs, notably the TICs, on the other hand, were reformed in order to sever ties with the state-owned banks and were frequently shut down in the process. The number of TICs fell from nearly 350 in the early 1990s to less than 100. There was also reform in the interbank market to stem the horizontal flow of funds between institutions in favor of the vertical flow within the state-owned banks, that is, the four state-owned commercial banks plus the major joint-stock banks (JSBs). This ensured that most transfers of financial resources of local branches now occurred through the vertical deposit of surplus funds in the higher level branches of the same bank. Borrowing and lending was also limited to the short term.[25]

Finally, in the late 1990s, an apparent marked shift took place in the locus of new lending decisions within state-owned banks, with much more being done by each bank head office. In its assessment of major developments in the financial sector in 1997, for example, the *Jinrong Nianjian* (the *Almanac of China's Finance and Banking*) is replete with examples of this kind of behavior. For example, in 1997, the Construction Bank allocated more than half of its new deposits to the head office for management. The Industrial and Commerce Bank, on the other hand, seriously rescinded lending authority in all but 7 percent of its county level branches. At the same time, most of the new working-capital loans were also administered by the bank's head office. More recently, the 2004 annual report of the Bank of China noted the following:

> During 2004, a number of improvements were made to the "three-in-one" credit decision-making process. These include . . . centralization of approvals of new credit extensions to the Head Office and tier-one [provincial] branch headquarters. . . . In 2004, the Credit Review Committee in the Head Office convened 158 meetings and reviewed 656 credit proposals involving RMB 1,098.6 billion.

This recentralization in decision-making authority may have been motivated by the perceived weaknesses in the "capabilities" of local managers, including limited information on local firms, as well as problems of moral hazard and concerns that incentives of local managers were still not fully aligned with the objectives of the center. Recently, managers' capabilities have been increasingly highlighted, but incentive problems may be the true underlying reason for some of these measures.

CONSEQUENCES OF THE REFORMS

Micro-level bank data of the kind necessary to analyze bank behavior and identify fundamental shifts in behavior resulting from institutional reform are in very short supply.[26] The same is true of enterprise-level data, which can help reveal changes in bank behavior through an examination of firm access to credit, credit terms, and the hardness of the budget constraints. Short of that, we are left to rely on more aggregate data. We focus on several potentially important but imperfect indicators:

- The changing role of the banks, especially the state-owned banks, in the financial system
- Regional dimensions of bank lending behavior
- The structure of bank lending, including the percent going to the state-sector, term structure, and the sector breakdown
- The behavior of NPLs

As we will see, to date, the picture remains very mixed as to the effect of the banking reforms on the efficiency and overall health of bank portfolios.

THE EVOLVING ROLE OF THE BANKS IN THE FINANCIAL SYSTEM SINCE 1994

How important are the banks, and in particular, the state-owned national banks, in intermediating China's vast savings in the face of these reforms of the banking sector and the financial sector, more generally? We return to tables 2.1–2.4, focusing on the period since 1994. A few points of explanation are necessary relating to our estimates for the later years that bear on our interpretation.

First, in 2002 the Bank of Communications and the CITIC Bank were converted to JSBs and were thus reclassified as nonnational banks. For purposes of consistency with our earlier estimates, we usually include these two banks in the national bank category, which also includes the PBOC, the four state-owned commercial banks (SOCBs), the three new policy banks, and postal savings. Financial institutions outside the national banks (or "other financial institutions") consist of ten other JSBs; the urban commercial banks (formerly, the urban credit cooperatives) and a small number of remaining UCCs; the rural credit cooperatives and a few recently converted rural commercial banks; TICs, security corporations, and financial-leasing companies. Collectively, the JSBs (including the Bank of Communications and CITIC Bank) and the converted UCCs and RCCs are now usually designated as the "other commercial banks" (*chita shangye yinhang*) and make up the bulk of the group of lending institutions outside the national banks.

Second, the transfer of nonperforming assets of the state-owned banks after 1998 presents some difficulty in estimating new loans by these institutions, and thus their reported contribution to new funds raised by the nonfinancial sector. China's banking statistics typically report year-end loan figures and, much less frequently, new loans issued by financial institutions on an annual basis. If we did not have to worry about the transfer or write-off of NPLs, new loans would by definition equal the difference in the year-end loan stocks. Because of the transfers, in order to calculate the contribution of the national banks to total new funds raised each year, we take the difference between their reported year-end loans in any two years, and then adjust for any loans (largely nonperforming) that are reported to have been transferred or disposed of in that year. Not all of the assets that were transferred or disposed of were loans, however, and detailed breakdowns are sometimes not provided.[27] There are also small inconsistencies between Chinese sources in the amounts that are reported to have been transferred or disposed of. Both of these factors introduce some measurement error into the new loan figures for the SOCBs. We discuss NPL transfers more carefully later in the chapter; here we simply draw on these estimates in our calculations of the contributions of the state-owned banks to new funds that have been raised by the nonfinancial sector.

Third, since the late 1990s, the share of long-term investment in the portfolios of the SOCBs appears to have increased. The annual reports do not provide comprehensive information about these assets, but some of the increase is explicitly identified as AMC bonds and government bondholdings related to these banks' recapitalization. The rest (and, in fact, the majority) appears to consist of central government bondholdings, policy bank bonds, central bank notes, and quasigovernment bonds (*jun zhengfu zhaiquan*). The central bank notes are not to be confused with short-term notes related to open market operations. In terms of table 2.1, the increase in government bonds held by the SOCBs is part of any new government debt issue reported in column 2. Policy bank bonds, on the other hand, are likely being used to support the lending operations of the policy banks, which is included in lending by the national banks, or column 3. However, uses of SOCB funds to acquire central bank notes, quasigovernment bonds, and so on, are not likely captured in our estimates. Insofar as this is the case, table 2.2 may slightly overestimate (underestimate) any decline (rise) we observe in the role of the national banks in intermediation, a point to which we return later.

With these caveats in mind, we examine the period since 1994. In the last decade, China's financial institutions, including debt and equity markets, have remained as important in intermediating China's vast pool of savings as they were before. In most years, new funds raised from all of these sources averaged slightly more than 20 percent of GNP. In both 2002 and 2003, the percentage rose sharply, hitting 31 percent in 2003, before falling in 2004 to 23 percent. The majority of funds intermediated formally also continues to be through the banks. Combined, and with a few years exception, banks of all types consistently were the source of between 70 and 80 percent of new intermediation.

Among all of the banks, a noticeable shift has taken place, however. Up through 1997, the national banks were annually the source of between 65 and 70 percent of all new funds raised. Their role subsequently declined and fell to half of all new funds before rising slightly in 2004. This drop-off can be linked to several developments including the decline in PBOC re-lending to the state-owned banks, the transfer of the NPLs, recapitalization efforts, more rapid deposit growth outside the state-owned banks, and possibly a portfolio shift within the SOCBs. The annual flow between the PBOC and the state-owned banks was actually negative in the late 1990s after having been positive in most previous years. Even with this falloff, in 2004 the national banks still remained the source of half of all new credit that was being extended through these financial institutions.

Table 2.8   Detailed Breakdown of New Loan Sources, 1998–2004

	SOCB(1)	SOCB(2)	JSB(1)	JSB(2)	UCB + UCC	RCB + RCC	Total
1998	77.83	73.42	5.29	9.70	5.04	11.84	100.00
1999	78.10	74.22	8.35	12.24	4.35	9.19	100.00
2000	88.17	83.42	6.53	11.28	1.30	3.99	100.00
2001	69.69	64.53	15.10	20.25	5.34	9.88	100.00
2002	66.95	64.46	18.68	21.16	4.90	9.47	100.00
2003	66.16	61.14	17.08	22.10	6.55	10.21	100.00
2004	60.12	49.74	19.36	29.74	7.56	12.96	100.00

1. These estimates are based on the annual reports of the various banks. SOCB (1) (2) and JSB(1) (2) reflect alternative treatment of the Bank of Communications and CITIC Bank. Definition 1 includes the two banks with the national banks, and definition 2 includes them with the JSBs.
2. The officially reported numbers for the UCCs in both 2000 and 2001 appear to include the loans for the new UCBs as well. To avoid double-counting, we take the estimate for the UCCs as the estimate for both. In 2002, the loan data appear to be reported correctly.

Table 2.9   Detailed Breakdown of Increases in Deposits, 1998–2004

	SOCB(1)	SOCB(2)	JSB(1)	JSB(2)	UCB + UCC	RCB + RCC	
1999	76.01	73.45	10.11	12.67	4.39	9.49	100.00
2000	74.89	70.65	16.75	21.00	0.64	7.71	100.00
2001	64.79	58.80	18.56	24.55	5.40	11.24	100.00
2002	54.60	49.01	22.90	28.49	9.72	12.79	100.00
2003	61.79	55.46	17.49	23.81	9.02	11.70	100.00
2004	53.44	32.85	14.92	35.50	13.37	18.28	100.00

1. See notes 1 and 2 from table 2.8.
2. We do not report the estimates for 1998 because they are affected by a 35 percent reduction in the deposits of the Bank of Communications related to an accounting rule change.

Offsetting the decline in the role of the SOCBs in lending activity has been an expanded role of the remaining banks, especially the JSBs, and to a much lesser extent the urban commercial banks. In tables 2.8 and 2.9, we offer a slightly more disaggregated picture of loans and deposits by bank type for the years between 1998 and 2004. Our estimates include the state-owned commercial banks, the JSBs, the urban commercial banks plus the few remaining UCCs, and finally, the RCCs and rural commercial banks. Because of the recent conversion of the Bank of Communications and the CITIC Bank to JSBs, we report our estimates using two alternative definitions of state-owned banks: with the two banks included as national banks (SOCB(1)) and with the two banks excluded (SOCB(2)).

Between 1998 and 2004, and including the CITIC Bank and the Bank of Communications with the other JSBs, the share of the JSBs of total new loans rose significantly from only 9.70 percent to 29.74 percent. Some of this growth was initially offset by declining shares in both the UCCs and RCCs, but by 2004 both of these institutions had surpassed the contributions they made to new loans in 1998. As a result, loans by the national banks fell sharply from 73.42 percent in 1998 to 49.74 percent in 2004, or a decline of nearly a third. As for deposits, the share of the JSBs rose from 12.67 to 35.50 percent. Combined with the growth in the deposits in the UCBs and RCCs, we observe a sharp rise in the percentage of new deposits outside the state-owned commercial banks from 26.55 to 67.15 percent.

The government debt market, on the other hand, expanded through the late 1990s, as did the role of debt and equity markets, but then both fell after 2000. In the aftermath of the Asian financial crisis, and weakness in both domestic and international demand, the central government pursued expansionary fiscal policy that was deficit financed. In 2000, a quarter of all new funds raised were absorbed by government debt, but with economic recovery, this fell to 16–17 percent. The role of equity markets has also fallen, largely because of a downturn in the market and recurring government concerns over the impact of new issues on the values of existing shares.[28]

In summary, more than 20 percent of China's GNP annually continues to be intermediated by its formal financial markets. Even with their slight downsizing and increasing competition from the JSBs and urban commercial banks, the national banks continue to be intermediating between 12 and 15 percent of GNP annually.[29]

REGIONAL COMPOSITION OF LOANS AND DEPOSITS BY ALL FINANCIAL INSTITUTIONS

Our discussion of the pre-1994 financial system highlighted the redistributive aspects of the financial system in favor of the state sector and the more slowly growing regions. This transfer likely occurred through several channels and entailed drawing on the resources of financial institutions outside the national banks, the deposit-rich national banks in the coastal provinces, and the PBOC. The transfer through the PBOC drew on both the reserves of other financial institutions and their own resources, including high-powered money.

We return to table 2.6, focusing now on regional shares of bank loans for 2002 and 2003. These estimates are more comprehensive than our earlier estimates and are based on the loans and deposits of all lending institutions as opposed to only those of the national banks. We run into issues of comparability between periods because official sources no longer report figures for the national banks at the provincial level after 2000. For years before 1996, on the other hand, estimates covering all financial institutions are not provided. Only for 1997 and 1998 are we able to present estimates based on both sets of figures (all financial institutions and then separately for the national banks). A number of other data issues arise for the last few years that we have to deal with, which we discuss in more detail in appendix 1 at the end of this book.

Estimates of the regional shares of new loans and deposits for 2002 and 2003 seem to be pointing to an end, and at a minimum, a significant decline, in the regional redistribution through the banking system. This shift was occurring at the same time that we observe a further narrowing in the loan-deposit ratios across types of financial institutions (see figure 2.4). For the national banks, the loan-deposit ratio fell to 0.80 by 2003 compared to 0.70 for all other remaining financial institutions.

First, compared to the late 1980s and much of the 1990s, the six rapidly growing coastal provinces' (region 2) share of new loans increased relative to their share for deposits. We observe the exact opposite occurring in both the central and western regions. For example, in 2002 and 2003, region 2's share of new loans was now slightly higher than that for deposits. In both the central (region 3) and western (region 4) provinces, on the other hand, regional shares of new loans declined and fell in line with each region's share of deposits. In the remaining eastern provinces, however, the share of new deposits was significantly larger than that for loans in 2003, but the gap narrowed in 2003. Second, we observe an absolute increase in region 2's share of new loans and, to a lesser extent, deposits. Over the six-year period between 1997 and 2003, the share of new loans in the six coastal provinces increased between a quarter and a third. Deposits also rose in both 2002 and 2003. Paralleling this rise, the share of total new loans in the central provinces (region 3) and new loans and deposits in the west (region 4) fell sharply.

The increase in the share of new deposits and loans in the coastal provinces appears to have been through both the SOCBs, as well as the other banking institutions. We do not have province-level estimates of loans and deposits disaggregated between the national and nonnational banks for years after 2000; we only have the total. However, a regional break-down of new loans and deposits provided in the annual reports of three of the SOCBs for 2001, 2002, and 2003 confirms an increase in the share through the SOCBs going to the coastal provinces. Reinforcing this find-ing, the nonnational banks, especially the rapidly expanding JSBs, have been more prominent in the coastal provinces than in the interior. In 2000, for example, nonnational banks were the source of 25 percent of all new loans extended in the six coastal provinces compared to less than 15 percent in the remaining provinces. With the rapid growth in the JSBs in the last few years documented above, our expectation is that they have played an important role in the increase in the share of resources formally intermediated in the coastal provinces.

Data from a number of sources[30] are suggestive of significant regional differences in the efficiency and performance of financial institutions during the last decade, with those in coastal provinces typically faring better. This may reflect a combination of better governance structures and incentives in these institutions, superior human capital, less govern-ment interference, as well as better quality firms to lend to. The increase in the percentage of intermediation in the coastal provinces may be a product of some of these differences combined with a relaxation of con-straints on the regional flows of funds.

This marked regional shift in the distribution of resources in the finan-cial institutions, however, needs to be contrasted with the behavior of fixed investment. Although not all bank lending goes for fixed invest-ment, we expected the decline in the redistribution through the banking system to lead to an increase in the proportion of investment occurring in the coastal provinces. Table 2.10 provides the regional breakdown in the share of fixed investment. For each year, we report the percentage of total fixed investment in China that was carried out in each region. Since the early 1990s, aside from a slight reduction in the share of fixed investment in the six coastal provinces and an increase in the west, regional fixed in-vestment shares have been relatively constant. The increase in the west is consistent with the "Develop the West" policy dating from the late 1990s, which has funneled an enormous amount of resources into the region.

With less redistribution through the financial system, the contrasting behavior of fixed investment and institutional lending on a regional basis suggests that other channels of financing must now be playing a larger role in the noncoastal provinces. One possibility is the redistribution through the fiscal system orchestrated by the central government. Between 1994 and

Table 2.10   Proportion of Fixed Investment (FI) by Region

	Region 1 % of FI	Region 2 % of FI	Region 3 % of FI	Region 4 % of FI
1987	26.2	38.4	19.6	15.7
1988	25.6	40.4	18.7	15.3
1992	22.9	44.5	16.6	15.9
1993	22.0	47.4	15.7	14.9
1997	23.1	44.2	17.7	15.0
1998	22.9	43.2	17.6	16.3
2002	21.6	42.2	17.7	18.5
2003	20.3	44.1	17.4	18.2

NOTES: See table 2.6 for the definition of region. Fixed investment data are taken from *Zhongguo Tongji Nianjian*, various years.

2003, for example, central government transfers increased from 1.3 to 4.8 percent of GNP.[31]

The other possibility is the role of government or quasigovernment bond issues to finance regional infrastructure investment. Significantly, it appears that government-issued debt has become a much more important item in the portfolios of the four state-owned banks. As noted earlier, some of these holdings are related to the transfers of NPLs and recapitalization efforts of the SOCBs. These aside, there also appears to have been a significant increase in their holdings of debt instruments issued by the central government, the policy banks, the PBOC, as well as quasigovernment institutions. For the CCB, the BOC, and the ICBC, the increase in these holdings in 2002, 2003, and 2004 totaled 110, 290, and 508 billion RMB, respectively. Including ABC, the increases in 2003 and 2004 were 453 and 636 billion RMB, respectively. To help put these numbers in perspective, the increase in new loans by the four SOCBs in 2003 and 2004 were 1859 and 973 billion, respectively. This raises the possibility that the government is still using the resources of the state-owned banks to achieve redistributive goals, albeit indirectly through their holding of other financial instruments.

THE STRUCTURE OF BANK LENDING

State Versus Non-state

We do not have consistent data on the composition of bank loans by ownership. One of the biggest problems has to do with defining state-owned. Shareholding companies or even joint ventures (JVs) in which the state

Table 2.11   Composition of New Loans (percent)

Year	State Sector		Non-state Sector		Agriculture	Household	Total
	I	II	I	II			
1998	63	58	22	27	10	5	100
1999	64	58	23	29	3	10	100
2000	69	60	11	20	1	19	100
2001	53	41	19	31	6	21	100
2002	65	52	9	31	6	19	100
2003	67	57	14	22	5	14	100

NOTE: See text for definitions.

has significant interests, albeit minority, are often excluded in these estimates. These firms also tend to be larger on average than SOEs, which relates to the issue of lending by size of firms. Collectively owned enterprises, on the other hand, usually have significant local government ownership but are usually classified as non-state. To get at the issue of access to credit by non-state firms, we draw on data from a number of sources.

In table 2.11, we provide a breakdown for the period between 1998 and 2003 on the percentage of all new loans by the banking sector going to the state sector, the non-state sector, agriculture, and the household sector.[32] The non-state, nonagricultural, nonhousehold sector lending largely consists of lending to non-state firms for fixed investment, plus short-term lending identified as going to township enterprises, private enterprises, and JVs. We provide two estimates for lending to the non-state sector, identified as I and II, reflecting alternative treatment of fixed investment loans to shareholding companies. Definition I includes shareholding companies as part of the state sector, while II includes them in the non-state sector. Lending to the household sector, on the other hand, consists of mortgage lending and auto lending.

The important finding that emerges from table 2.11 is that lending to the state sector by financial institutions remains robust and continues to absorb as much as two-thirds, and at a minimum, well in excess of half, of all new annual lending by financial institutions. The percentage is similar to estimates for earlier years that we have made.[33] After 1999, if we include lending to shareholding companies as part of state sector lending, overall lending to the non-state, nonagricultural sector actually drops and is largely offset by the increase in lending to households. Under our alternative definition of the state sector, the decline is moderated slightly.

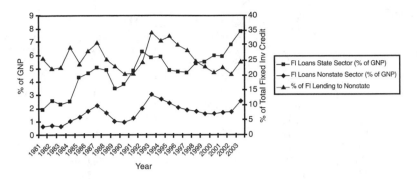

Figure 2.5   Access to Fixed Investment Credit

These data are complemented by figure 2.5, which focuses more narrowly on fixed investment lending. We report bank lending for fixed investment in the state and non-state sectors measured as a percentage of GNP and the share of fixed investment credit going to the non-state sector. There is an evident bias in favor of the state sector in the post-1994 period comparable to the pre-1994 period. The last decade, the non-state sector's share of fixed investment credit, has averaged roughly 25 percent, but over much of this period the share was actually falling. Only in 2003 do we see a significant increase. Also noteworthy is the sharp increase in credits for fixed investment spending in the state sector, which in 2003 was nearly 8 percent of GNP, compared to 2.5 percent in the non-state sector. Some of this increase is related to the changing term structure of bank lending, which we discuss in more detail in the next section.

Increasing constraints on non-state sector firms' access to new bank lending is corroborated by table 2.12 and figure 2.6, which captures the experience of firms at the township level and below for the period between 1990 and 2002. We graph new bank loans to these firms as a percentage of their fixed investment plus net additions to working capital. To help put these estimates in perspective, these firms employed slightly more than 130 million individuals in 2002 out of a total nonagricultural labor force of 500 million, and in the same year were the source of slightly less than a third of GDP. Through 1995, TVEs financed between 15 and 20 percent of their investment and net additions to working through bank loans. The shift after 1996 is very stark, with the percentage of financing coming from banks falling to less than 5 percent. In 2000 and 2002, it was actually negative. We do not have comparable data for later years for these

Table 2.12   Access to Credit by Enterprises at Township Level and Below

Year	Value-Added (bn RMB)	Employment (1000s)	Working Capital (bn RMB)	Fixed Investment (bn RMB)	Bank Loans Stock (bn RMB)	New Loans as % of FI+ΔWK
1990	250.43	92648	263.19	285.71	112.83	16.55
1991	297.21	96136	337.61	338.52	144.41	20.27
1992	448.53	106247	469.87	454.02	207.09	22.26
1993	800.68	123453	765.77	695.82	310.72	17.77
1994	1092.80	120175	1056.64	886.83	305.84	−0.89
1995	1459.52	128621	1449.30	1284.12	444.10	15.74
1996	1765.93	135083	1579.94	1492.43	532.65	18.95
1997	2074.03	130504	1796.71	1942.71	551.07	2.26
1998	2218.65	125366	2070.59	2156.65	579.61	4.18
1999	2488.26	127041	2248.41	2397.78	628.85	7.76
2000	2715.62	128196	2395.31	2622.36	628.21	−0.11
2001	2935.64	130856	2610.98	2905.16	650.26	2.90
2002	3238.58	132877	2809.94	3326.76	648.00	−0.25

Source: Zhongguo Tongji Nianjian, 2003, p. 450.

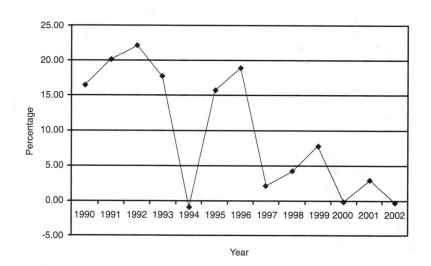

Figure 2.6   New Loans as a Percentage of Fixed Investment plus Change in Working Capital for Enterprise Township Level and Below

firms on value-added, working capital, fixed investment, and so on, but in 2003 lending to TVEs appears to have recovered slightly as the stock of bank loans increased by nearly 80 billion RMB, the largest single increase since 1996. In 2004, however, the increase fell to half of this amount, or 40 billion RMB.

In 2003, funds raised by the state sector through borrowing from financial institutions exclusive of funds raised through debt and equity markets was around 15 percent of GNP.[34] If we were to add to this (1) net new borrowing by the government and (2) funds raised by enterprises through the issue of debt and equity, which is dominated by state sector firms, the percentage of all funds raised domestically going to the state sector is nearer to 20 percent of GNP. A case can also be made that lending to the household sector, which increased as a percentage of the total more than fourfold between 1998 and 2001 before dropping the next two years, also is linked to state sector development and largely serves "state interests." First, auto lending reflects a major new policy in the last few years to help support the rapid expansion of the domestic auto industry, in which state (central and local) ownership is prominent. Mortgage lending, on the other hand, helps support local real estate development, in which local governments are heavily involved and are often dependent on as an important source of fiscal revenue through land sales.

This resiliency in lending to the state sector is occurring at the same time that the sector is getting smaller through privatization and enterprise restructuring, and the more rapid growth of non-state enterprises. These aggregate data are consistent with other information pointing to continued difficulty experienced by most private, and small and medium-sized firms in accessing credit,[35] despite occasional central government initiatives to redress it. The reforms do not appear to have ended an earlier bias in the financial sector in favor of the state sector.

Term Structure of Loans

There has also been a marked shift in the term structure of the loans extended by financial institutions. Beginning in 1997, we are able to provide a breakdown in the stock of loans between two loan categories—short term, and medium and long term. These two categories constitute more than 95 percent of all loans. A third category, "other loans" (*chita lei daikuan*) makes up the remainder, but we cannot break them down by maturity. In figure 2.7, we report the ratio of the stock of short-term to medium and long term loans for all financial institutions, and then separately for the national banks and all remaining financial institutions.

In 1997, a majority of all loans were short-term and were principally for working-capital purposes. This was especially true outside the national banks, with longer-term loans accounting for less than 10 percent of all short-term loans. In the national banks, the ratio was 0.28. Over the course of the last six years, the composition of the loan portfolio has

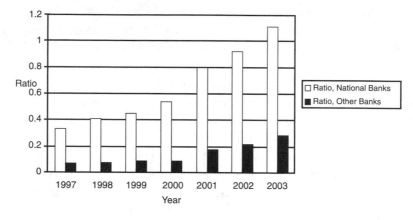

Figure 2.7   Ratio of Long- and Medium-Term Lending to Short-Term Lending

shifted heavily in favor of loans with longer term structure. The increase is especially pronounced in the national banks, with the size of medium- and long-term lending now exceeding that of short-term loans. We also observe an increase in other financial institutions, but in 2003 longer term loans were only 30 percent of short-term loans.

The increase in the ratio in the national banks reflects two developments: (1) an increase in the percentage of new loans that are longer term and (2) the transfer of largely short-term, NPLs to the AMCs. In both 1999 and 2000, for example, the national banks' stock of short-term loans actually declines. Longer-term loans are being extended to both the household and the enterprise sector. With respect to the household sector, loans are largely in the form of auto and mortgage lending. Loans to the enterprise sector include fixed investment lending as well as lending to state-owned corporations set up for purposes of public investment projects.

We are interested in the potential implications of this shift for the banks. Several observations can be made. Relative to the term structure of their deposits, the increase is probably not resulting in any big imbalance. More than half of the deposits of the national banks are identified as being either in savings or fixed-term deposits, with savings constituting the bulk of the two. In this regard, the term structures of assets and liabilities are converging. In addition, the increase in lending for longer term purposes may be slightly less than the numbers reported imply. Until recently, most of the lending by the state-owned banks was short-term and for working-capital purposes. However, firms diverted a hefty portion of these loans to finance longer-term investment, and this activity shows up in fixed investment financing under the category "self-raised funds." Some of the apparent shift in the term structure of lending is simply picking up the use to which the funds are actually being put.

The increase in long-term lending by the national banks raises potential issues with respect to their future NPLs. In the short run, these loans may be classified as current, but the medium- to long-run health of the banks' portfolio depends heavily on the quality of these investments and projects, and on their ability to generate returns sufficient to repay both interest and principle. The efficiency of fixed investment spending in China has been low and possibly falling,[36] and remains heavily influenced by government at all levels. In 2004, conservatively half of all fixed investment was by state or collectively owned units with ties to governments at all levels.[37] Moving forward, and with half of the portfolio in longer term investments, the behavior of NPLs in the national banks will be tied to how well these projects carried out by state-operated units pan out.

Sector Composition of Bank Loans

Drawing on their annual reports, we examine in more detail the portfolios of three of the SOCBs (BOC, CCB, and ICBC) plus seven JSBs.[38] Combined, these 10 institutions represent roughly two-thirds of the banking sector. Loan distributions in eight categories or sectors are reported: manufacturing, services, real estate, construction, energy, transportation, consumers, and others. We are interested in the underlying similarity of these portfolios and in the potential exposure of these banks to common aggregate shocks.

In table 2.13, we report for 2004 the loan distribution by sector for these banks. Immediately obvious is the marked similarity in the portfolios of these banks. The highest percentage of loans is consistently directed to manufacturing, followed by households, the service sector, and transportation. We do not report distributions for 2002 and 2003, but over time, there is a growing convergence in the sector composition of their loan portfolios. The average correlation of these weights increased from 0.69 in 2002 to 0.79 in 2003 and 0.85 in 2004. More specifically, the three SOCBs have reduced their loans in manufacturing and in the service sector, while the JSBs have increased their presence in these two sectors. All of these banks, on the other hand, have increased their lending to consumers, and almost all of them have increased the portion of loans that goes to the energy and transportation sectors.

Table 2.13 Loan Distribution by Sectors for Selected Banks in 2004 (percent)

	BOC	CCB	ICBC	BCOMM	CITIC	HuaXia	Merchant	Minsheng	Pudong	SDB
Manufacturing	29	18	32	30	25	26	16	27	30	26
Services	16	3	15	17	10	10	15	8	18	14
Real Estate	6	11	7	10	9	0	5	10	12	12
Construction	2	4	2	3	0	14	2	3	4	4
Energy	11	10	7	6	8	11	10	0	4	4
Transportation	9	11	11	7	7	11	16	7	6	11
Consumers	20	19	13	13	10	8	15	14	0*	0*
Others	7	25	13	13	31	21	20	31	27	30

NOTES: These estimates are based on the annual reports for each of the individual banks. For the Pudong Bank and the Shenzhen Development Bank (SDB), separate numbers for consumer loans are not available and are included in the "other" category.

The JSBs also report their ten largest borrowers in their annual reports. For all seven of the JSBs, at least five of the ten largest borrowers are in either real estate or highway construction. The remaining borrowers are mainly in the energy and telecommunication sectors. In other words, these banks' biggest customers are mostly in the sectors such as housing, infrastructure, energy, and telecommunication that have been "targeted" by the government as the key sectors. So, while the banks are no longer required to make policy loans, their lending behavior continues to be heavily influenced by the government's policy.

The Behavior of NPLs

The behavior of NPLs is not only an indication of the progress in banking reform, but also a bellwether for future problems. As outside observers are well aware, interpreting estimates of NPLs is tricky and filled with potentially significant measurement error. Drawing on annual reports of the various banks, reported estimates in *Jinrong Nianjian*, as well as reports provided by the CBRC, we have compiled "official" estimates of NPLs in both levels and measured as a percentage of the stock of loans of the various financial institutions. The reported estimates often reflect minor discrepancies, as well as the use of two alternative classification systems for nonperforming loans, which makes it harder to generate a consistent series spanning a longer period. The newer, five-loan-type system provides consistently higher estimates of the ratio of NPLs. However, even with problems of measurement error, important things can be learned from these estimates.

Table 2.14 provides estimates for the four state-owned commercial banks for most years since 1997. We report estimates on the basis of the old classification system for the years between 2000 and 2002, and then for the new classification system for the years 2001 through 2004. For 1998, we are also able to provide an estimate by using the percentage of NPLs in 2000 to estimate the stock, adding to it the transfer of NPLs in 1999 and 2000, and then normalizing this estimate by the stock of loans as of the end of 1998.[39] This procedure will overestimate the amount and percentage of NPLs in 1998 if some loans became nonperforming in 1999 and 2000.[40]

In 1998, at a minimum, more than half of the stock of loans in the four state-owned banks, or in the ballpark of 3–3.5 trillion RMB, was nonperforming on the basis of official estimates. The stock of NPLs is equal to roughly 40 percent of nominal GDP in 1998. NPLs were highest in the

Table 2.14   NPLs in SOCBs (in percent and billions of RMB)

Year	SOCBs(I)	SOCBs(II)	BOC(II)	ICBC(II)	ABC(II)	CCB(II)
		NPLs as a Percentage of Stock of Loans				
1998	52.10	60+				
1999						
2000	29.17		28.78	34.43		20.27
2001	25.36	30.54	27.51	29.78	38.62	19.35
2002	21.41	25.25	25.56	26.01	36.65	15.28
2003		19.74	19.49	21.84	30.73	8.6
2004		15.57	5.12	18.99	26.22	3.9
		NPLs, Stock (billion, RMB)				
1998	3255.36					
1999			605.46			
2000	1855.36		409.60	830.999	333.73	281.02
2001	1764.66	2155.24	436.02	791.989	635.83	291.39
2002	1702.32	2077.04	429.17	760.883	700.72	268.03
2003		1893.64	351.22	720.757	695.49	85.25
2004		1580.00	109.92	703.644	679.09	87.35

NOTES: For the state-owned banks as a group, we report two sets of estimates, based on the old four-loan type classification (I), and the new five-loan type (II). The estimate for the state-owned commercial banks in 1998 is equal to our estimate for 2000, plus the 1400 billion that was transferred in 1999 and 2000.

ABC and lowest in the CCB, and likely would have been even higher in the ABC had they not shifted some of their nonperforming loans to the RCCs when the two formally split in 1996, and the RCCs came under the supervision of the PBOC. Over the next six years, the ratio of the NPLs in the SOCBs fell to slightly more than 15 percent in 2004, with the most rapid progress observed in the BOC and CCB. As of the end of 2004, the NPL ratio in the BOC and CCB were 5.16 and 3.74 percent, compared to 19 and 27 percent in the ICBC and ABC, respectively.

In 2004, nearly 3.1 (2.5) trillion RMB in NPLs were either transferred or written off. To help put this statistic in perspective, the total stock of loans of the SOCBs at the end of 1998 was 6.25 trillion RMB. As of the end of 2004, the stock of loans in the SOCBs was 10.1 trillion, and in 2005, in excess of 11 trillion, both net of the transfer of NPLs. These estimates imply that even without any transfer of NPLs, the ratio of NPLs would have fallen by more than half simply because of the rapid growth in the stock of new loans in these institutions. In light of the amounts transferred between 1998 and 2004, the increase in new loans up through 2004 was on the order of magnitude 6.35 trillion RMB and nearly 7.5 trillion RMB through the end of 2005.[41] These estimates mean that more than two-thirds of the current loan portfolio likely consists of loans made since 1998.

This implies that the behavior of NPLs in the SOCBs has been tied heavily to the quality of the lending decisions since 1998. In fact, the currently reported estimates for NPLs imply that all new loans are performing. Reported increases in the "special mention" loans (i.e., loans that are current but whose future repayment is in question), as well as significantly higher alternative estimates of outside agencies of the NPL ratio, point to weaker portfolios than the official estimates might suggest.

How do these estimates compare to other financial institutions in China, notably, the rapidly growing JCBs, the UCBs, the remaining UCCs, and the RCCs? Drawing on table 2.15, we see that, on paper, the JCBs appear to be best and overall have the lowest ratio of NPLs. All other institutions also show a marked decline in the NPL ratio. In the case of the RCCs, we do not have an "absolute" for any one year; rather, we have only estimates relative to 2001, which imply a reduction in NPLs of nearly 20 percent between 2000 and 2003.[42] Most of this is related to the transfer of NPLs associated with the ongoing reform in the RCCs. As we observed in the case of the SOCBs, the rapid growth of new loans is the most important reason for the decline in the NPLs. For example, loans in 11 of the JCBs for which we have annual data increased from 0.52 trillion RMB in 1998 to 0.79 in

Table 2.15   Estimates of NPLs in Non-state-owned Banks

	JSB (I)	JSB (II)	UCB (I)	UCB (alt)	RCB (I)	RCB(II)	RCC	UCC
	NPLs as a Percentage of Stock of Loans							
1998			·					
1999								
2000	16.36		30.96				X+4.93	
2001	12.94		25.15	24.03			X	Y
2002	9.5	11.93	17.7		8.5		X−7.26	Y−7.98
2003		7.92	14.45		5.05		X−14.76	
2004		4.93	11.73			6.6		
	NPLs, Stock Estimates (Billion RMB)							
1998								
1999								
2000								
2001			107.08					
2002		202.46	104.87		1.24			
2003		187.7	116.40		1.04			
2004		142.28	106.10			3.22		

NOTES: JSB = joint-stock bank; UCB (RCB) = urban (rural) commercial bank; UCC (RCC) = urban (rural) credit cooperative.

2000 to 1.97 trillion in 2003. The first year for which we have an estimate of NPLs is 2000, when they were 16.36 percent. By 2003, this figure had fallen to 7.92 percent. In absolute terms the stock of NPLs increased slightly between 2000 and 2003, and the biggest reason for the fall in the ratio is the sharp increase in the stock of new loans. Once again, critical to the health of the portfolio is the quality of new loans made during the last few years.

Implications Looking Forward

With the decentralization of the financial system in the period 1978 to 1994, China's banks played an important role in helping to finance the nation's growth by getting resources to the more dynamic, non-state sector. During the same period, however, the tension between a partially decentralized banking system and the government's desire to use the banking system for redistributive purposes in favor of the state sector resulted in recurring inflation and mounting NPLs. These problems were exacerbated by a very weak regulatory environment, poorly defined ownership, and ineffective governance structures.

One of the main achievements of China's banking reforms since 1994 has been a significant reduction in the government's use of the banking system for explicitly redistributive purposes. This has allowed the banks to curtail lending to many money-losing small and medium-sized SOEs that were dependent on bank loans for their survival. It also allowed the central bank to maintain a tight monetary policy and therefore keep inflation under control.

The reforms have also been instrumental in helping to clean up the balance sheets of the state-owned commercial banks. This was accomplished by transferring a large portion of their NPLs to asset management companies and by injecting new capital to the SOCBs in the form of cash and government-backed debt securities. The transfer of NPLs contributed to the decline in the ratio of NPLs to total loans from over 50 percent in 1998 to 15.6 percent in 2004. However, a large portion of the decline in the NPL ratio is simply due to the rapid growth of new loans in recent years. Moreover, a majority of the new loans continue to be to the SOEs that carry high potential risk. Because most of the new loans have longer maturities, it may take several years before the potential problems show up on the banks' balance sheets. So, the rapid reduction in the NPL ratio for the SOCBs does not necessarily mean a significant reduction in these banks' portfolio risk.

At the same time, there has been significant recentralization in the banking system, which has made it harder for small and medium enterprises in the non-state sector to borrow money from banks. The percentage of new loans that went to non-state firms declined from 22 percent in 1998 to 14 percent in 2003. Since 1997, TVEs, which have been a major component of the non-state sector, have also experienced increasing difficulty in accessing credit through the formal financial sector. Associated with the recentralization in the banking system, bank loans have become less diversified. New loans have been concentrated on larger firms (many of them state-owned) and in a few key sectors identified by the government. While the government may have stopped using the banks to directly redistribute resources, it still exerts heavy influence on banks' lending behavior.

With the concentration of loans to large firms (many of them state-owned), the Chinese banks face similar risks that banks in Japan faced a decade and a half ago. In the 1980s Japan's banks were similar to the Chinese banks now in concentrating their lending on large domestic firms. Although such a strategy worked reasonably well in the decades of high economic growth of the 1960s and 1970s, its weakness was fully exposed during the 1980s and 1990s when Japan's large and better quality firms started to seek cheaper financing from capital markets. As a consequence, the Japanese banks were left with less profitable firms and the profitability of their loan portfolio deteriorated dramatically, resulting in the banking crisis in the 1990s.[43]

Chinese banks today may be facing similar risks to those that Japanese banks encountered. First, increasing domestic market integration and product market competition may contribute to lower profit margins in larger firms in the future, making their existing loans riskier. The television industry is a good example in which former market leaders are now fighting for their survival. In general, we are observing increasing turnover among firms in key sectors as a result of declining market barriers,[44] with firms in the interior now facing perhaps the greatest increase in market competition.

Second, entry of foreign banks, though modest to this point, means that domestic banks will face more competition in keeping good firms as their clients. Even in a mature economy like the United States, Calomiris and Carey (1994) find that on average foreign banks tend to deal exclusively with better-rated larger borrowers. Since information is less transparent for firms in China than in the United States, it is even more likely that foreign banks will concentrate their lending in China on larger and better quality firms.

Third, capital market development, including private equity and the corporate bond market, may imply that better firms will find better sources of direct financing in the capital market, leaving the domestic banks with less profitable firms. Some Chinese firms may also find lower cost sources of funds overseas.

Fourth, the concentration of lending by the banks among several key sectors also implies that the banks are highly exposed to sector shocks. For example, a reduction in the energy price or value of housing would have a large negative effect on the banks' portfolio. All of these factors suggest that the strategy of concentrating loans to large firms is highly risky and may not be profitable in the long run.

NOTES

1. These institutions were also commonly referred to as the "specialized" banks during this period.

2. Other NBFIs included finance corporations, insurance companies, security corporations, leasing corporations, and rural credit foundations (RCFs).

3. In 1994, for example, out of a total of 391 TICs in China, only 12 were under "central" administration, and the rest were under the administration of either the local branches of the state-owned banks or local governments. Up through 1996 RCCs were under the administration of local (township-level) branches of the Agricultural Bank of China. The RCFs, on the other hand, were under the local administrative supervision of the Ministry of Agriculture, usually at the township level.

4. In normalizing these estimates by GDP, we use the recently revised figures for nominal GDP for 1993 through 2004, which were released in January 2006 by the National Bureau of Statistics. The revision resulted in an increase in nominal GDP of 16.8 percent in 2004 and declining adjustments in earlier years. Most of the upward revision occurred in the tertiary sector, with a small downward adjustment in the secondary sector. It remains to be seen if estimates of gross capital formation will also be revised.

5. For the pre-1994 period, we do not have complete asset information for postal savings, security corporations, insurance companies, and finance companies, but we do have data for the TICs. For the post-1994 period, we are also without complete information on the assets of the TICs. Estimates reported by the Organisation for Economic Co-operation and Development (OECD 2005) put assets of these institutions at 10 percent or so of the total in 2003, but details on these estimates are not provided.

6. Informal financial institutions played an important role in intermediating the remainder. For a useful discussion of the role of informal finance in China, see Tsai (2002).

7. Naughton (1995).

8. Woo (2005).

9. Jefferson et al. (2000); Brandt, Hsieh, and Zhu (forthcoming).

10. This includes lending to the state sector through the banks and NBFI, funds raised by SOEs in debt or equity markets, and government borrowing, which largely went to support state sector activity.

11. *Zhongguo Tongji Nianjian* (2005: 120).

12. Bird and Wong (forthcoming).

13. Brandt and Zhu (2000).

14. Brandt and Zhu (1994).

15. Unfortunately, the PBOC does not provide a regional breakdown of their re-lending.

16. The lower loan-deposit ratios in the NBFIs may not fully reflect the "tax" on their deposits because of their use of interbank funds to support loan expansion. The diversion of funds through the interbank market also implies that the higher loan-deposit ratio of the state-owned banks may not reflect the full extent of PBOC re-lending.

17. The Third Front refers to China's development program carried out between 1964 and 1971 in the southwestern and western regions of the country. Its primary purpose was to create a self-sufficient industrial base that China could draw on in the event of war. See Naughton (1988).

18. Measured, for example, by the share of the gross value of industrial output produced by state-owned enterprises.

19. Brandt, Hsieh, and Zhu (forthcoming).

20. In fact, some NBFIs had direct ties with local PBOC offices, which in principle were supposed to oversee their behavior.

21. *Zhongguo Tongji Nianjian* (2005: 120).

22. Liu and Liu (2005).

23. Ball (1999); Bird and Wong (2005).

24. Bird and Wong (forthcoming).

25. Between 2001 and 2004, for example, seven-day lending increased from 71.4 to 91.1 percent of total interbank lending. In the last several years, the major lenders in the interbank market have been the SOCBs, and the major borrowers have been mutual funds. This may be either for liquidity reasons or as part of "repos" that enable the mutual funds to leverage their positions.

26. Several papers by one of the authors (Brandt and Li, 2003; Brandt, Li, and Roberts, 2005) have used branch-level data for the RCCs and ABCs to examine the effect of incentive structures on lending behavior and enterprise privatization decisions of local governments. Unfortunately, these data only capture bank behavior in the last half of the 1990s.

27. For example, in 2000, the Bank of China transferred 232.9 billion RMB in assets, which includes 173.6 billion in NPLs, 29.3 in performing assets, 18.3 in interest receivables, and 11.7 in other assets.

28. Poor performance has also affected the government in the ability to sell off its own shares of state-owned companies.

29. In light of our remarks above regarding the likely increase in long-term investment in the portfolios of the SOCBs, this may represent a lower bound.

30. Shih, Zhang, and Liu (2004); Brandt and Li (2003).

31. OECD (2005).

32. After 2003, statistical authorities no longer provided a breakdown of fixed investment by ownership, and so estimates for 2004 are not reported.

33. Brandt and Zhu (2000).

34. This is calculated as the product of: (total intermediation as a percentage of GNP)×(the percentage of intermediation through the national banks plus other financial institutions)×(percentage of new loans by these financial institutions going to the state sector).

35. OECD (2005).

36. Bai, Qian, and Zhu (2006).

37. In 2004, total fixed investment was 7.048 trillion RMB, of which 2.503 was by state-owned units, and 9.966 was by collectively owned units. This excludes 1.770 trillion by shareholding units, which often had a significant government component.

38. The annual report of the other SOCB, Agricultural Bank of China does not include detailed portfolio information.

39. Not all of the loans that were transferred were nonperforming, and so we might slightly overestimate the NPLs in 1998.

40. The stock of NPLs in 2000 is equal to the stock in 1998, less the transfer between 1998 and 2000, plus any loans that became nonperforming in 1999 and 2000. In principle, the only NPLs that were to be transferred were those extended prior to 1996.

41. For 2003: $10.1 - (6.25 - 2.5) = 6.35$.

42. Estimates based on surveys of RCCs in Sichuan, Shanxi, Jiangsu, and Zhejiang suggest that NPLs in 2000 were likely in the vicinity of 40 percent (Brandt, Park, and Wang, 2005).

43. See Hoshi and Kashyap (1999).

44. Brandt, Rawksi, and Sutton (forthcoming).

REFERENCES

Agricultural Bank of China. Various years. *Annual Report.*

Bahl, Roy. 1999. *Fiscal Policies in China: Taxation and Intergovernmental Fiscal Relations.* San Francisco, CA: 1990 Institute.

Bai, Chongen, Zhenjie Qian, and Xiaodong Zhu. 2006. *Recentralization and Declining Investment Efficiency in China: 1994–2004.* Mimeo. Beijing, China: Qinghua University.

Bank of China. Various years. *Annual Report.*

Bird, Richard and Christine Wong. Forthcoming. "China's Fiscal System: A Work in Progress." In *China's Great Economic Transformation,* ed. Loren Brandt and Thomas G. Rawski. New York: Cambridge University Press.

Boyreau-Debray, Genevieve and Shang-jin Wei. 2004. "Can China Grow Faster: A Diagnosis of the Fragmentation of the Domestic Capital Market." International Monetary Fund Working Paper WP/04/76.

Brandt, Loren, Changtai Hsieh, and Xiaodong Zhu. Forthcoming. "Growth and Structural Transformation in China." In *China's Great Economic Transformation*, ed. Loren Brandt and Thomas G. Rawski. New York: Cambridge University Press.

Brandt, Loren and Hongbin Li. 2003. "Bank Discrimination in Transition Economies: Ideology, Information, Incentives?" *Journal of Comparative Economics* 31(3): 387–413.

Brandt, Loren, Hongbin Li, and Joanne Roberts. 2005. "Banks and Enterprise Privatization in China." *Journal of Law, Economics and Organization* 21(2): 524–46.

Brandt, Loren, Albert Park, and Sangui Wang. 2005. "Are China's Financial Reforms Leaving the Poor Behind?" In *Financial Sector Reform in China*, ed. Yasheng Huang, Tony Saich, and Edward Steinfeld. Cambridge, MA: Harvard University Press.

Brandt, Loren, Thomas G. Rawski, and John Sutton. Forthcoming. "China's Industrial Development." In *China's Great Economic Transformation*, ed. Loren Brandt and Thomas G. Rawski. New York: Cambridge University Press.

Brandt, Loren and Xiaodong Zhu. 1994. *The Development of Non-bank Financial Institutions in China*. Mimeo. Toronto, Canada: University of Toronto.

———. 2000. "Redistribution in a Decentralizing Economy: Growth and Inflation in China." *Journal of Political Economy* 108(2): 422–39.

Calomiris, Charles W. and Mark Carey. 1994. "Loan Market Competition Between Foreign and U.S. Banks: Some Facts About Loans and Borrowers." In *The Declining Role of Banking*. Chicago: Federal Reserve Bank of Chicago.

China Construction Bank. Various years. *Annual Report.*

Hoshi, Takeo and Anil Kashyap. 1999. "The Japanese Banking Crisis: Where Did It Come from and How Will It End?" NBER Working Paper No. 7250.

Industrial and Commercial Bank of China. Various years. *Annual Report.*

Jefferson, Gary H., Thomas G. Rawski, Li Wang, and Yuxin Zheng. 2000. "Ownership, Productivity Change, and Financial Performance in Chinese Industry." *Journal of Comparative Economics* 28(4): 786–813.

Liu, Guy S. and Xianxuan Liu. 2005. *Research Report on the Survey of SOE's Ownership Transformation and Restructuring in China*. Mimeo. Beijing, China: Enterprise Research Institute Development Research Center, State Council.

Naughton, Barry. 1988. "The Third Front: Defense Industrialization in the Chinese Interior." *China Quarterly* 115: 351–86.

———. 1995. *Growing Out of the Plan: Chinese Economic Reform, 1978–1993*. New York: Cambridge University Press.

Organisation for Economic Co-operation and Development (OECD). 2005. *OECD Economic Surveys: China*. Paris: OECD Publications.

Seht, Kaja. 1999. *A Bank for Every Government: The Incorporation of Credit Cooperatives in the PRC*. Mimeo. Hanover, NH: Dartmouth College.

Shih, Victor, Qi Zhang, and Mingxing Liu. 2004. *Comparing the Performance of Chinese Banks: A Principal Component Approach*. Mimeo. Evanston, IL: Northwestern University.

Tsai, Kellee S. 2002. *Back-Alley Banking: Private Entrepreneurs in China*. Ithaca, NY: Cornell University Press.

Woo, Wing Thye. 2005. "China's Rural Enterprises in Crises: The Role of Inadequate Financial Intermediation." In *Financial Sector Reform in China*, ed. Yasheng Huang, Tony Saich, and Edward Steinfeld. Cambridge, MA: Harvard University Press.

Zhongguo Jinrong Nianjian (*Almanac of China's Finance and Banking*). Various years. Beijing: China Finance Publishing House.

Zhongguo Tongji Nianjian (*Statistical Yearbook of China*). Various years. Beijing: China Statistical Publishing House.

Michael DeStefano

Brandt and Zhu's discussion of China's banking sector contains a wealth of interesting and hard-to-find data. The research indicates that at least episodically the Chinese banking system has contributed to economic growth and that by implication it is therefore capable of doing so again. Its proposition is that changes that are occurring in Chinese banking are real and meaningful and that while there is much continuity with the past what is happening currently is largely positive. This perspective differs from the widely held view that the system is characterized by gross mismanagement and poor lending decisions that have contributed to the overall inefficiency of the Chinese economy, and that the system has not yet been transformed in ways that would make it an engine of sustainable economic growth. The traditionally held view is that the Chinese banking system is quite simple, with very few, but very large, banks that conduct unsophisticated operations. The banks are important as intermediaries in an economy, which is one of the most highly indebted in the world, with domestic credit to GDP of about 150 percent. This figure is a multiple of what it is in most emerging markets and is of a level that is generally seen only in highly developed economies. It is a leveraged economy in which the banks are the key players, given the lack of other means of intermediation.

The banks, as noted, conduct very basic operations: they take deposits, which they lend to borrowers. The deposits are gathered at "below-market" rates—that is, at rates that are consistently below the rate of inflation, as noted by Lee Branstetter in chapter 1 of this volume. The government, which plays a large role in setting rates, appears to have little motive to change this soon, and given the lack of competition, there is no realistic chance that market forces would bring about that change. The depositors are not going elsewhere since there is no place to go. They cannot send their deposits abroad seeking better rates, say to Hong Kong; they cannot place them with insurance companies, which do not generally exist; and there are no developed capital markets where individuals can buy bonds.

The banks then lend these deposits to certain borrowers, mostly to the state-owned sector and to agriculture. These loans, according to this paradigm, inevitably go bad, they are written off—at least at those banks subject to the reform process—and then the banks are recapitalized by the government. If this description is even remotely accurate, it follows that the banks do not perform the role that capitalist theory would assign to banks, that is, the efficient allocation of capital to those sectors that can best use the money. The high level of loan losses means that the banks are not contributing to sustainable efficient economic growth. In this view, the banks play a policy, not a commercial role. That is, they transfer resources from the nation's depositors to those areas where the government decides that the money should go. Who then benefits from this system? It is not the banks themselves. Margins in Chinese banking are very thin: there is not much difference between the rates at which they raise funds and the rates at which they lend. Accordingly, even leaving aside the need to provide for loans gone bad, the system is not especially profitable. Who then receives the benefit of the low deposit rates? Who receives a subsidy from the banking system?

The data presented in the chapter are quite extraordinary on the question of who receives the funds from the banking system because one would have expected more change in the composition of borrowers. Over the years, however, there has been little change at all. State-owned enterprises and agriculture remain the borrowers. I think that we can set aside the banking system's relation to the agricultural sector as a candidate for any kind of meaningful change. The Agricultural Bank of China, which has an extraordinarily high level of NPLs, is not likely going to be reformed any time soon. It would probably cost $100 billion to do so. The rural credit co-ops are in terrible shape, and while a small pilot program has been launched in one province, the government is not ready to tackle this problem. Nor is it likely that any resources that are currently going to agriculture will be terminated in the foreseeable future given the current state of rural China and current governmental policies.

Leaving aside the agricultural dimension, is there evidence that we are at an inflection point, that the banking system is becoming more commercial, and less policy driven, in its orientation? Without stating a definitive view, it would still be useful to examine where the system might be changing for the better, where it is the same, and where it might be getting worse.

POSSIBLE CHANGE

FOREIGN OWNERSHIP

Several large Western banks have made substantial investments recently into a few Chinese state-owned banks, which could presage change in these institutions. However, these foreign ownership interests are generally quite small and appear to be passive investments rather than strategic acquisitions. At most, the new owners are receiving one or two board seats, and none is sending large numbers of staff to help operate the banks. Nor can the investments be seen as ratification that lasting improvements have taken place at any of the target banks, since it is unlikely that the acquirers have performed any substantial due diligence on the banks. Moreover, Western banks do not have a very good track record when it comes to investing in emerging markets, as the Latin American woes of years ago attest. Moreover, even if the acquiring banks were to obtain operating control at some point in the future, it would take years, if not decades, for the foreign owners to effect substantial changes in the very large and unwieldy banks in which they have an ownership interest.

LENDING TO THE HOUSEHOLD SECTOR

Lending to consumers is a promising area, as the banks can focus on profitable customers, primarily through mortgage and car lending. Although this sector has been growing rapidly in recent years, it still comprises, as chapter 2 shows, a small fraction of the total portfolios of the large banks. This remains, however, an area of huge potential. While there is too limited a track record to reach conclusions about asset quality in this sector, some comfort may be taken from the experience of other banking systems in Asia. Here, the evidence is good that mortgage loans in particular have performed very well, and there is little reason to think that the experience in China would be materially different given the consumer's propensity to save and the ongoing scarcity of good housing. Provided that the householder remains employed, there should be little cause for concern over loans that are well underwritten and made to relatively affluent consumers.

REGULATION

In recent years the government has made a serious effort to strengthen regulation of the commercial banks, adopting prudential standards similar to those that prevail in developed banking systems. With an employment base of 25,000, including 15,000 examiners, if the regulatory body should fail in its mission, it will not be for want of resources. Disclosure norms have been established and are being enforced, and the regulator is convinced that bank asset quality reporting has improved markedly. Skills to monitor the incremental market risk in the system are being developed, and regulators are striving to be proactive in the surveillance of the system. Regulation, however, even in the most developed banking systems, cannot substitute for effective lending decisions, nor can it prevent fraud. Accordingly, while more effective regulation would be a welcome development, it cannot in itself ensure that the Chinese banking system will prosper. Nor does the system have the resources to clean up those parts of the system, such as the agricultural banks and rural co-ops, that have not yet been addressed by the government.

TRANSPARENCY AND GOVERNANCE

Despite continuing reports of fraud and financial malfeasance on a more than incidental basis, bank transparency has improved so that at least the external observer does have meaningful data on the condition of banks' portfolios. Moreover, although the banks have not yet adopted International Accounting Standards, they will soon do so, and this change is not expected to have a material impact on published financial statements. Management has also committed itself to improved governance standards, and the continuing reports of fraud may in part reflect the implementation of higher standards on managers. The principal Chinese banks, however, are very large, with a national presence, and have historically operated on a decentralized basis. It is difficult to know the extent to which improved governance norms have been pushed down throughout the organizations, but a degree of skepticism here would be in order, given the wide-ranging inefficiencies and fraud that characterize much of the economy.

REDISTRIBUTION

Brandt and Zhu examine the redistributionist effects that the banks have had, transferring wealth from the coastal regions to the interior, and argue that this form of redistribution has ended, at least for the nonagriculturally oriented banks. No one has claimed that the agricultural banks have ceased providing a subsidy to the rural regions, nor is any such development likely given present political realities. But it is not clear that even nonagricultural subsidization has ended.

THINGS THAT HAVE NOT CHANGED

NO COMPETITION

The highly concentrated Chinese banking system has had little competition, and there is little evidence of change in this basic structure. The state-owned banks still dominate, although a few of the JSBs have been growing and taking market share. The presence of foreign banks in a small way does not meaningfully change matters, and even with the proposed liberalization under the WTO it would take years, if not decades, for foreign banks to become meaningful presences in either deposit taking or lending. If change is to come, it would have to be administered change, not something that is brought about by market forces.

NO FEE INCOME

The Chinese banks' principal source of revenues is spread income on loans. The banks have little of the fee income from wealth management, custody, trading, and investment banking that characterizes banks in developed systems, since they provide few services other than deposit taking and lending. There is no evidence that this is changing, with banks continuing to emphasize their role as deposit takers and lenders.

LENDING TO THE STATE SECTOR

As the chapter makes clear, the bulk of loans are still being made to the state-owned sector, and especially to favored industries. Accordingly, if the banks are to contribute to growth, it will be due to the policy decisions made by the government, not because these favored industries are the ones that the market would favor. While the experience with this lending could very well be better than the loans made in the past to failing state enterprises, the banks would still be vulnerable if these sectors suffer during an economic slowdown.

NO FINANCING OF THE DYNAMIC EXPORT SECTOR OR SMALL BUSINESS

As in the past, the banks do not serve as incubators of small businesses, nor are they the principal financers of the dynamic export sector, which has been financed by private equity and retained earnings. If the banks are to contribute to sustainable growth, they will have to do so without the benefit of lending to the most dynamic part of the economy.

CHANGE FOR THE WORSE

LOANS HAVE LONGER TENURE

As the chapter shows, the tenure of loans in China has been getting longer as banks lend to favored sectors with demand for longer-term credit. While the short-term nature of loans made in the past was no guarantee of their lower-risk nature (since loans to failed enterprises could not in any case be called with any expectation that they would be repaid), the current longer-term lending trend may indicate greater risk. At the very least, long-term lending can mask credit deterioration since problems may not become evident until the loans become due.

INCREASING CONCENTRATION TO FEWER SECTORS

Either because of the banks' own decision-making process or because of government direction, or both, the chapter shows that lending is becoming increasingly concentrated to fewer sectors of the economy. This could facilitate growth if the sectors chosen are the best users of capital, or it could lead to problems if the chosen sectors experience difficulties. At any rate, loss of diversification by its very nature heightens the risk of the system and could lead to a replication of, for example, the Korean experience.

MORE MARKET RISK

As interest rates and currency are increasingly deregulated, the system will become characterized by increased market risk. Although this is not expected to happen rapidly, the banks themselves will have to learn how to deal with these risks since they have not had to do so in the past.

FEWER INSTITUTIONS

The chapter makes the point that the number of financial institutions has shrunk, and this trend is likely to continue. Rural cooperatives, for example, could very well be reorganized and consolidated. Although the decline in the number of domestic institutions may be offset eventually by the entry of foreign banks, for the time being the shrinkage in the number of banks will only decrease, not increase, the degree of competition, reinforcing other negative trends that characterize the system.

CONCLUSION

The Chinese banking system will remain the focus for those interested in assessing the future direction of the Chinese economy. While efforts have been made to introduce change in the system, as yet little convincing evidence has emerged that leads us to optimistic conclusions. Although the economy has shown an ability to grow dynamically for many years, the banking system cannot be credited with fostering sustainable growth, other than perhaps on an intermittent basis. Data should become available, however, over the intermediate term that will enable observers to draw more definitive conclusions on the success or failure of the recent efforts at change.

CHAPTER 3

Understanding the Structure of Cross-Border Capital Flows: The Case of China

Eswar Prasad and Shang-Jin Wei

INTRODUCTION

The 2 percent revaluation of the Chinese exchange rate on July 21, 2005 has generated what appears to be a disproportionate amount of interest around the world. In many ways, this attention has to do with China's massive buildup of foreign exchange reserves, its position as the world's largest destination for foreign direct investment (FDI), and its status as the third largest trading nation.

China's integration into the global economy started from a very low base but has been progressing steadily. Capital inflows, in particular, were minimal in the 1970s and 1980s, impeded by capital controls and the reluctance of international investors to undertake investment in a socialist economy with weak institutions and limited exposure to international trade. All of this changed in the early 1990s, when FDI inflows surged dramatically following the selective opening of China's capital account as well as the rapid trade expansion that, in conjunction with China's large labor pool, created opportunities for foreign investors. These inflows have remained strong ever since, even during the Asian crisis of the late 1990s.

The authors are grateful to Jahangir Aziz, Ray Brooks, Michael Dooley, Sebastian Edwards, Mark Wright, Yongding Yu, Tao Zhang, participants at various conferences and seminars, and especially Charles Calomiris, Daniel Rosen, and Qing Wang for helpful comments and suggestions; to members of the International Monetary Fund's (IMF) China team for related work from which we have drawn extensively; and to Ioana Hussiada for excellent research assistance. The views are those of the authors and do not necessarily represent those of the IMF. The authors alone are responsible for any possible errors.

Given China's status as a global economic power, characterizing the nature and determinants of its capital inflows is of considerable interest for analytical reasons as well as for understanding the implications for the regional and global allocation of capital. Our primary objective in this chapter is to provide a detailed descriptive analysis of the main aspects of capital inflows into China. Given the degree of interest in China and the relative paucity of data, we aim to provide a benchmark reference tool for other researchers by providing some critical perspectives on the numbers that we report.

The following section presents a detailed picture of the evolution of China's capital flows. China has both large inflows and large outflows in absolute dollar terms. Its inflows have generally been dominated by FDI, which, for an emerging market, constitutes a preferred form of inflows since FDI tends to be stable and associated with other benefits, such as transfers of technological and managerial expertise. An interesting aspect of these inflows is that, contrary to some popular perceptions, they come mainly from other advanced Asian countries that have net trade surpluses with China, rather than from the United States and Europe, which constitute China's main export markets. As for other types of inflows, China has limited its external debt to low levels, and until recently non-FDI private capital inflows have typically been quite limited. Its outflows are dominated by accumulation of official reserve assets and unrecorded private sector outflows (or capital flight).

In this chapter, we also examine the evolution of the balance of payments and consider the recent surge in the pace of accumulation of international reserves. A key finding is that, although current account surpluses and FDI have remained important contributors to reserve accumulation, the dramatic surge in the pace of reserve accumulation since 2001 is largely attributable to non-FDI capital inflows. We provide some analytical perspectives on the costs and benefits of holding a stock of reserves, which now amounts to nearly 40 percent of gross domestic product (GDP). In addition, considerable international attention has recently been focused on the currency composition of China's massive stock of international reserves (which is now second only to that of Japan). Despite data constraints, we attempt to shed some light on this issue, both by carefully examining a popular source of data for China's holding of U.S. securities and by calculating the potential balance-of-payments implications of reserve valuation effects associated with the depreciation of the U.S. dollar in recent years.

This chapter also discusses the broader composition of China's capital inflows in the context of the burgeoning literature on financial globalization. Notwithstanding the recent surge of non-FDI inflows, FDI remains historically the dominant source of inflows into China. The literature on the benefits and risks of financial globalization suggests that China may have benefited greatly in terms of improving the risk–return trade-offs by having its inflows tilted so much toward FDI.

Whether this composition of inflows is a result of enlightened policies, the structure of institutions, or plain luck is an intriguing question. We examine various hypotheses that have been offered to explain why China's inflows are so heavily tilted toward FDI. In this context, we provide a detailed description of China's capital account restrictions and how these restrictions have evolved over time. Although controls on non-FDI inflows as well as tax and other incentives appear to be proximate factors for explaining the FDI-heavy composition of inflows, other factors may also have contributed to this outcome. Disentangling the quantitative relevance of alternative hypotheses is not a straightforward task. Nonetheless, we argue that at least a few of the hypotheses—including some mercantilist-type arguments that have been advanced recently—are not consistent with the facts.

THE CHINESE PATTERN OF CROSS-BORDER FLOWS: AN INTERNATIONAL PERSPECTIVE

THE EVOLUTION OF CAPITAL INFLOWS

Gross capital inflows into China were minuscule before the early 1980s. After 1984, the "other investment" category, which includes bank lending, increased significantly and accounted for the largest share of total inflows during the 1980s (figure 3.1). FDI rose gradually from the early 1980s to early 1991 and then increased dramatically through the mid-1990s. During the 1990s, FDI accounted for the lion's share of inflows. Interestingly, FDI inflows were only marginally affected during the Asian crisis. Figure 3.2 provides some more detail on the evolution of the main components of the capital account, in terms of both gross outflows and inflows. Note that all components other than FDI show sharp increases in outflows in the period immediately after the Asian crisis, with the subsequent recovery in net inflows of these components taking two to three years to materialize. Recent data indicate that,

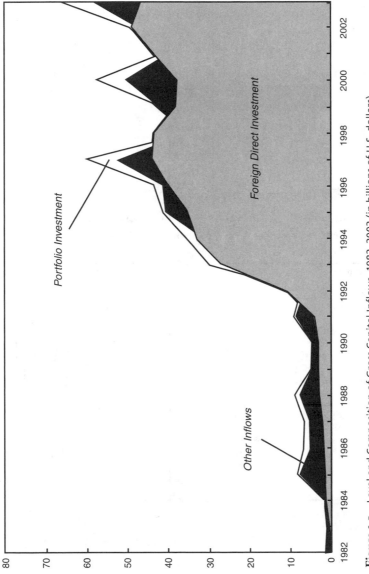

Figure 3.1 Level and Composition of Gross Capital Inflows, 1982–2003 (in billions of U.S. dollars)

147

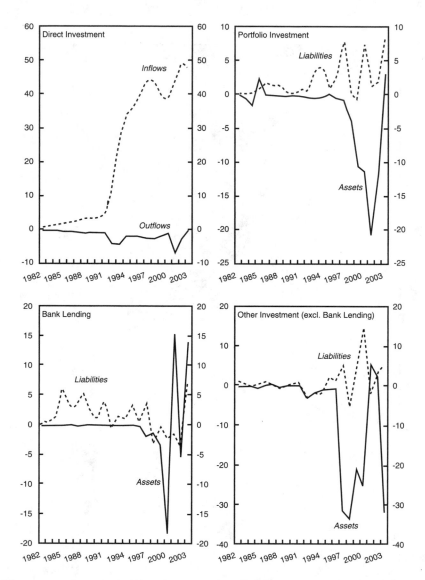

Figure 3.2 Gross Capital Flows by Component (in billions of U.S. dollars)

NOTE: Scales differ across the four panels of this figure.

Source: CEIC database.

after remaining in a range of around $50 billion from 2002 through 2003, gross FDI inflows increased to almost $61 billion in 2004.

From a cross-country perspective, China's net capital inflows are of course large in absolute magnitude but hardly remarkable relative to the size of the economy. Before the Asian crisis, many of the other "Asian tigers" had significantly larger inflows relative to their GDP (figure 3.3, top panel). What is striking, however, is that, except for Singapore, the share of FDI in total inflows is clearly the highest for China. Its total net inflows as a share of GDP rank among the highest across all emerging markets after the Asian crisis, especially since many of the Asian tigers were no longer the darlings of international investors (figure 3.3, bottom panel). While the net inflows dropped sharply across all emerging markets after the late 1990s, most of the inflows that did come into the emerging markets after 1999 took the form of FDI.

China's average net inflows, and the share of FDI in those inflows, look quite similar during the periods from 1990 through 1996 and from 1999 through 2003. Since FDI is clearly the main story in the context of China's capital inflows, we now turn to a more detailed examination of these flows.

FOREIGN DIRECT INVESTMENT

Over the past decade, China has accounted for about one-third of gross FDI flows to all emerging markets and about 60 percent of these flows to Asian emerging markets (figure 3.4, top panel). Even when we exclude flows from Hong Kong SAR (Special Administrative Region) to China from these calculations (on the extreme assumption that all of these flows represent "round-tripping"[1] of funds originating in China—this point is discussed further below), we find that China's share in these flows to emerging markets is substantial (figure 3.4, bottom panel). The shares spiked upward during the Asian crisis and, more recently, in 2002, when weaknesses in the global economy resulted in a slowdown in flows from industrial countries to most emerging markets other than China. With the pickup in flows to emerging markets in 2003, there has been a corresponding decline in China's share, even though flows to China remained essentially unchanged.

Where are China's FDI inflows coming from? Table 3.1 shows the share of utilized FDI by source country. Some aspects of the results are worth noting. First, the share of Hong Kong SAR has declined steadily over the

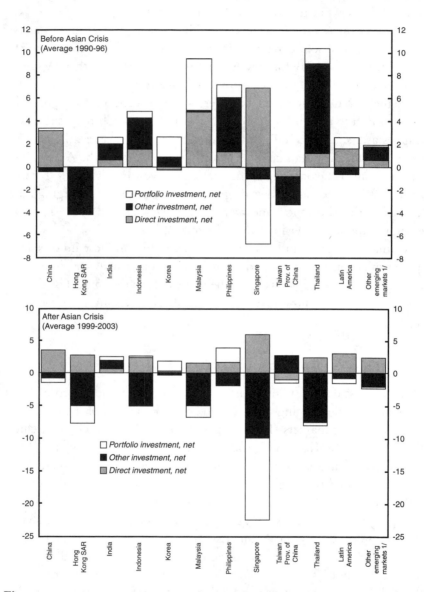

Figure 3.3 Asian Economies and Emerging Markets: Net Capital Flows (in percent of GDP)

1. Average for emerging markets in EMBI+ index, excluding Latin America and Asian countries.

Source: World Economic Outlook database.

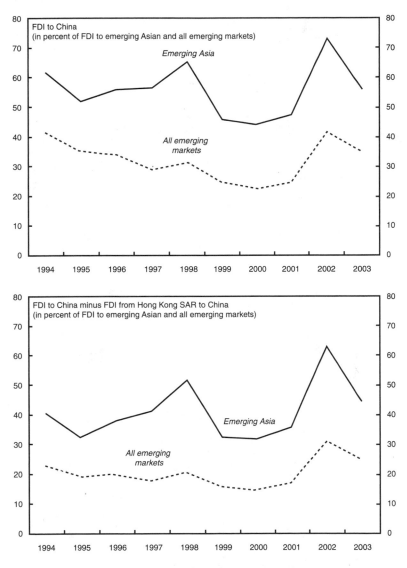

Figure 3.4   China's Share of FDI Inflows to Emerging Markets

NOTE: This figure uses data on gross FDI flows. The bottom panel excludes gross FDI flows to China originating from Hong Kong SAR from both the numerator and denominator of the two ratios shown.

Sources: World Economic Outlook Database, CEIC database, and authors' calculation.

Table 3.1 FDI Inflows by Source Country (percent share)

	1994	1995	1996	1997	1998	1999	2000	2001	2002	2003	2004	2005
Total	100	100	100	100	100	100	100	100	100	100	100	100
Hong Kong SAR	58.2	53.4	49.6	45.6	40.7	40.6	38.1	35.7	33.9	33.1	31.3	29.8
Virgin Islands	—	—	—	—	8.9	6.6	9.4	10.8	11.6	10.8	11.1	15.0
Japan	6.1	8.2	8.8	9.6	7.5	7.4	7.2	9.3	7.9	9.4	9.0	10.8
Korea	2.1	2.8	3.3	4.7	4.0	3.2	3.7	4.6	5.2	8.4	10.3	8.6
United States	7.4	8.2	8.2	7.2	8.6	10.5	10.8	9.5	10.3	7.8	6.5	5.1
European Union (15)	—	—	—	—	—	11.1	11.0	8.9	7.0	7.3	7.0	8.6
Taiwan Province of China	10.0	8.4	8.3	7.3	6.4	6.4	5.6	6.4	7.5	6.3	5.1	3.6
Singapore	3.5	4.9	5.4	5.8	7.5	6.6	5.3	4.6	4.4	3.8	3.3	3.7
Australia	0.6	0.6	0.5	0.7	0.6	0.0	0.8	0.7	0.7	1.1	1.1	1.1[1]
Western Samoa	—	—	—	—	0.3	0.5	0.7	1.1	1.7	1.8	1.9	2.2
Macao SAR	—	—	—	—	0.9	0.8	0.9	0.7	0.9	0.8	0.8	0.8[1]
Others	12.0	13.4	16.0	19.3	14.7	6.5	6.7	7.9	8.9	9.2	12.6	10.9

NOTES: This table is based on data for utilized (rather than contracted) FDI.
1. Data for these regions for 2004 and 2005 are not available, so the same share has been assumed as in 2003.

Sources: CEIC database and CEIC China database.

past decade, from 58 percent in 1994 to 30 percent in 2005. One concern that arises in interpreting FDI data for China is that a significant portion of these flows could potentially represent round-tripping to take advantage of preferential tax treatment of foreign investment relative to domestic investment. Much of this round-tripping is believed to take place through Hong Kong SAR. Although, on the one hand, it is difficult to estimate the extent of round-tripping, the declining share of Hong Kong SAR in total inflows at least suggests that the magnitude of round-tripping as a share of total FDI inflows may have been declining over time. On the other hand, the shares of small economies like the Virgin Islands and Western Samoa, which have increased over the past few years, could now be accounting for some of these round-tripping flows.[2]

Asian economies account for a substantial fraction of China's FDI inflows. For instance, over the period from 2001 through 2004, five Asian economies—Hong Kong SAR, Japan, Korea, Taiwan Province of China, and Singapore—together accounted for about 60 percent of FDI inflows. That a lot of China's FDI comes from these relatively advanced Asian economies suggests that these flows do bring the usual benefits associated with FDI, including transfers of technological and managerial expertise. The other interesting point to note is that—contrary to the widespread perception of large direct investment flows from Western industrial economies to China—the U.S. and European Union (EU) economies together accounted for only 15 percent of total inflows in 2003, and even that is down from a share of 22 percent from 1999 through 2000. Even if one were to assume that half of the reported FDI inflows from Hong Kong SAR are accounted for by round-tripping and that all of the share of the Virgin Islands in fact represents flows originating in the United States, the share of the United States and the EU in China's total FDI inflows would be about 30 percent, a large but hardly dominant share. Preliminary data for 2004 indicate that the share of Hong Kong SAR has declined by about 1.5 percent and that of the United States is down by 1 percent, whereas Korea's share has increased by over 2 percent.

To which parts and regions of China's economy are FDI inflows being directed? Table 3.2 shows that about two-thirds of these flows have been going into manufacturing, with real estate accounting for about another 10 percent. Within manufacturing, the largest identifiable share has consistently gone to electronics and communication equipment. The share of

Table 3.2   Utilized FDI by Sector (percent share)

	1998	1999	2000	2001	2002	2003	2004	2005 June
Primary sector	1.4	1.8	1.7	1.9	1.9	1.9	1.8	1.2
Extraction industries	1.3	1.4	1.4	1.7	1.1	0.6	0.9	0.5
Manufacturing	56.3	56.1	63.5	65.9	69.8	69.0	71.0	71.1
o/w Textile	3.4	3.4	3.4	4.1	5.6	4.1	3.3	3.4
Chemicals and raw materials	4.3	4.8	4.4	4.7	6.0	4.9	4.9	5.4
Medicine	0.8	1.7	1.3	1.3	1.7	1.4	1.1	0.8
Ordinary machinery	2.1	2.4	2.6	2.8	3.2	2.9	3.0	3.3
Special use equipment		1.3	1.3	1.7	2.5	2.3	3.0	3.0
Electronics and communication equipment	5.3	7.8	11.3	15.1	20.0	11.9	13.7	14.1
Utilities	6.8	9.2	5.5	4.8	2.6	2.4	1.9	3.2
Construction	4.5	2.3	2.2	1.7	1.3	1.1	1.3	0.7
Transport and telecommunication services	3.6	3.8	2.5	1.9	1.7	1.6	2.1	2.1
Distribution industries	2.6	2.4	2.1	2.5	1.8	2.1	1.2	1.5
Banking and finance		0.2	0.2	0.1	0.2	0.4	0.4	0.5
Real estate	14.1	13.9	11.4	11.0	10.7	9.8	9.8	8.8
Development and Operations	12.0	11.7	10.7	10.2	9.9	9.5	8.2	8.4
Social services	6.5	6.3	5.4	5.5	5.6	5.9	5.9	5.9[1]
Hotels	1.1	1.8	1.1	1.0	0.9	0.9	0.6	0.4
Health care, sports, and social welfare	0.2	0.4	0.3	0.3	0.2	0.2	0.1	0.0
Media and broadcasting	0.2	0.2	0.1	0.1	0.1	0.1	1.6	1.4
Scientific research services	0.1	0.3	0.1	0.3	0.4	0.5	0.5	0.6
Other	2.4	1.9	3.6	2.3	2.5	4.2	1.5	2.5

1. Assumed the same share as in 2003 as the definition of this category has changed.

Source: CEIC database.

manufacturing has risen by almost 15 percentage points since 1998, largely at the expense of the shares of utilities, construction, transport and telecommunication services, and real estate. Since the industries with declining FDI shares are largely focused on nontraded goods, the evolution of this pattern of FDI seems to be consistent with the notion that these inflows have been stimulated by China's increasing access (both actual and

Table 3.3   FDI Inflows Into China by Region (in percent of total FDI inflows)

	Average 1995– 2004	Average 1995– 1997	Average 2000– 2004	2004
Guangdong	24.2	27.0	21.2	16.5
Jiangsu	15.2	12.8	16.9	14.8
Shanghai	8.7	8.8	9.1	10.4
Fujian	8.1	9.9	6.4	3.2
Shandong	7.8	6.2	9.9	14.3
Beijing	3.9	3.4	3.9	4.2
Zhejiang	5.0	3.4	6.7	9.5
Tianjin	4.0	4.8	3.2	2.8
Liaoning	5.1	4.3	6.2	8.9
Hebei	1.9	2.0	1.5	1.2
Guangxi	1.3	1.8	0.8	0.5
Hubei	2.3	1.7	2.7	2.9
Hainan	1.3	2.1	0.8	0.2
Hunan	1.8	1.7	1.9	2.3
Jiangxi	1.4	0.8	2.0	3.4
Henan	1.2	1.4	1.0	0.7
Anhui	0.8	1.2	0.7	0.7
Sichuan	0.9	1.0	0.9	0.6
Heilongjiang	0.9	1.4	0.7	0.6
Jilin	0.7	1.0	0.5	0.3
Shaanxi	0.7	1.0	0.6	0.2
Chongqing	0.6	0.9	0.5	0.4
Shanxi	0.5	0.4	0.4	0.1
Inner Mongolia	0.5	0.2	0.7	0.6
Yunnan	0.3	0.3	0.2	0.2
Quizhou	0.1	0.1	0.1	0.1
Gansu	0.1	0.2	0.1	—
Qinghai	—	—	0.1	—
Ningxia	—	—	0.0	—
Xinjiang	—	0.0	0.0	—

Source: CEIC database.

anticipated) to world export markets following its accession to the World Trade Organization (WTO) in 2001.

The regional distribution of utilized FDI inflows within China has shown some changes over time (table 3.3). Guangdong Province has typically accounted for about one-quarter of FDI inflows, consistent with its proximity to Hong Kong SAR and its reputation as an exporting powerhouse, but its share fell by about 10 percent from 1995–1997 to 2004.

Table 3.4 Total Outward FDI (top 10 countries with the highest average percent share between 2001 and 2004)

	1995	1996	1997	1998	1999	2000	2001	2002	2003	2004	2005	Average (1995–2000)	Average (2001–2004)
Total Amount (U.S. $ mn)	110.0	290.0	200.0	260.0	590.0	551.0	785.0	2701.0	2850.0	5500.0	6920.0		
Hong Kong SAR	18.9	39.9	4.0	4.9	4.1	3.2	25.6	13.2	9.3	17.4		12.5	16.4
United States	22.0	2.0	0.0	9.9	13.7	4.2	6.8	5.6	4.0	2.6		8.6	4.7
Thailand	60.7	1.7	0.0	0.3	0.3	0.6	15.5	0.1	1.7	0.5		10.6	4.5
Republic of Korea	3.5	0.1	0.0	0.4	0.0	0.8	0.1	3.1	6.8	11.0		0.8	5.3
Vietnam	1.8	0.7	0.3	0.9	1.1	3.2	3.4	1.0	0.3	0.4		1.3	1.3
Australia	0.9	0.3	0.0	-0.1	0.3	1.8	1.3	1.8	1.2	4.2		0.5	2.1
Cambodia	0.0	7.9	6.1	2.3	5.6	3.1	4.4	0.2	1.2	1.8		4.2	1.9
Brazil	0.5	0.6	13.7	0.6	0.1	3.8	4.0	0.3	0.0	0.1		3.2	1.1
Russia	0.1	0.0	0.8	1.0	0.6	2.5	1.6	1.3	11.9	2.0		0.8	4.2
Yemen	0.0	0.0	0.0	0.0	0.0	2.0	2.7	0.0	0.0	0.4		0.3	0.8

Source: CEIC China database.

Another phenomenon of some interest is the increase in FDI outflows from China. As China has intensified its trade linkages with other Asian economies, anecdotal evidence suggests that its FDI outflows have increased significantly in recent years. The Chinese government has actively encouraged this phenomenon as part of its policy of gradual capital account liberalization. Since 2001, some steps have been taken each year to ease restrictions on FDI outflows (see appendix 2 at the end of this book). However, while FDI outflows undeniably rose almost ten-fold from the mid-1990s to 2003, the total outflows remain small, amounting to only about $3 billion in 2003 (table 3.4). Much of these outflows have indeed gone to other Asian economies, especially Hong Kong SAR. The United States has, over the past decade, accounted for about 8 percent of China's FDI outflows. More recently, the Chinese government has encouraged FDI outflows to countries in Asia and Latin America in order to ensure more reliable sources of raw materials (for instance, by purchasing mining operations) and upstream products for processing in China. Preliminary data for 2004 indicate that China's FDI outflows amounted to about $3.6 billion in 2004, with about half of this investment going to Latin America and 40 percent to other Asian countries.[3]

EXTERNAL DEBT

Unlike some other emerging markets, China has been quite cautious about taking on external debt (figure 3.5). It has engaged in little sovereign borrowing until very recently, and, as a matter of policy, it has discouraged enterprises from taking on external debt.[4] As a consequence, notwithstanding the significant increase in the absolute amount of external debt since the mid-1980s, the ratio of external debt to GDP has remained relatively stable at around 15 percent since the early 1990s.

Yet it is not just the level of external debt but also the maturity structure of this debt that has been shown to be associated with currency and financial crises. As discussed earlier, countries that have more short-term debt relative to long-term debt tend to be more susceptible to such crises. On this score, one noteworthy development is that the share of short-term debt in China's total external debt has risen significantly, from 9 percent in 2000 to over 45 percent in 2004 (figure 3.6 and table 3.5).[5] This level is close to the threshold that some studies have identified as posing a high risk of crises. However, this increase could appear

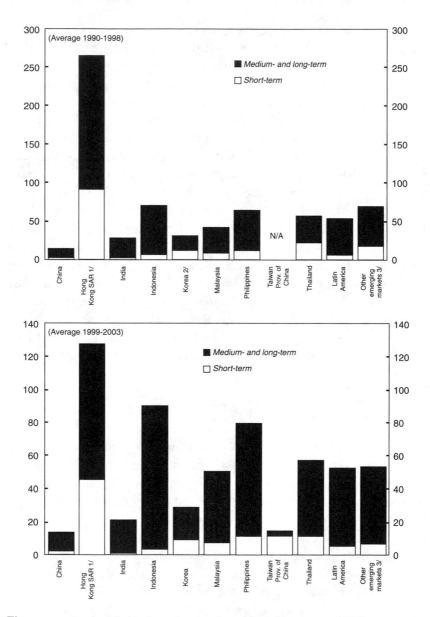

Figure 3.5 External Debt: Cross-Country Comparison (in percent of GDP)

1. Average for Hong Kong SAR consists of data between 1996 and 1998.
2. Average for Korea consists of data between 1994 and 1998.
3. Average for emerging markets in EMBI+ index, excluding Latin America and Asian countries.

Sources: World Economic Outlook Database, CEIC database, and joint BIS-OECD-IMF-WB statistics on external debt. Includes private sector debt.

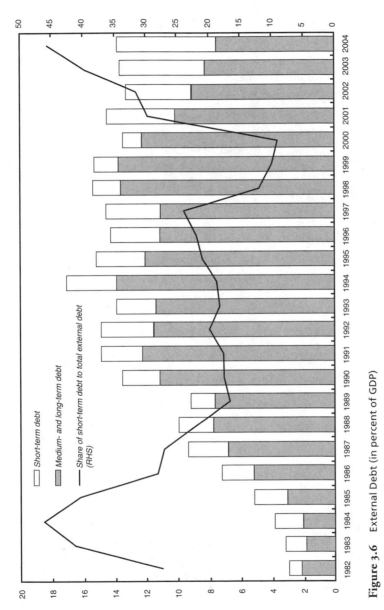

Figure 3.6 External Debt (in percent of GDP)

Sources: China, State Administration of Foreign Exchange (SAFE); World Bank, Global Development Finance database.

Legend:
□ Short-term debt
� Medium- and long-term debt
── Share of short-term debt to total external debt (RHS)

Table 3.5 External Debt

	1995	1996	1997	1998	1999	2000	2001	2002	2003	2004	2005
Total											
(in billions of U.S. dollars)	106.6	116.3	131.0	146.0	151.8	145.7	170.1	168.5	193.6	247.5	281.0
(in percent of GDP)	14.6	13.6	13.7	14.3	14.0	12.2	12.8	11.6	11.8	12.8	12.6
By Maturity											
(in percent of total debt)											
Short-term debt[1]	11.2	12.2	13.8	11.9	10.0	9.0	29.7	32.5	39.8	45.6	55.6
Medium and long-term debt	88.8	87.8	86.2	88.1	90.0	91.0	74.2	72.0	62.3	54.4	44.4
By Type											
(in percent of total debt)											
Registered external debt	—	—	—	—	—	—	87.3	84.6	81.1	79.7	67.7
Trade credit	—	—	—	—	—	—	12.7	15.4	18.9	20.3	32.3
Registered External Debt by Debtor[2]											
(in percent of registered external debt)											
Public and publicly guaranteed	29.2	28.8	27.5	28.5	31.2	33.6	33.5	34.8		18.4	17.3
Chinese-funded enterprises	11.0	10.6	10.2	10.6	9.7	9.3	7.6	6.9	4.9	3.3	2.4
Chinese-funded financial institutions	33.5	29.6	25.3	23.3	22.7	20.5	20.2	22.0	21.2	36.2	33.8[3]
Chinese-funded nonfinancial institutions	10.8	9.7	8.5	6.6	5.3	3.9	2.9	3.0	2.7	—	
Foreign-funded enterprises	2.1	3.2	5.3	6.3	—	—	23.7	22.9	24.1	24.5	26.6
Foreign-funded financial institutions	—					—	11.5	10.4	13.3	17.4	19.3[3]
Other		13.5	18.1	23.2	24.6	31.2	32.7	0.5	0.0	0.2	0.1	53.7

NOTES: Maturity structure is based on classification by residual maturity of outstanding debt.
1. Assumes original maturity through 2000 and remaining maturity from 2001 onwards.
2. Effective June 2004, loans from foreign governments that are assumed by policy banks were reclassified under debt of Chinese-funded financial institutions (rather than debt of government departments). Furthermore, in 2004, the outstanding external debt of government departments decreased, but that of Chinese-funded financial institutions increased by U.S. $18.7 billion. This accounts for the sharp shift in the shares of these two categories in 2004.
3. As of September 2005.

Sources: CEIC, Chinese authorities, and author's calculations.

more dramatic than warranted since this ratio appears to have bottomed in 2000. Furthermore, the surge in trade credits accounts for a significant part of the increase in the relative importance of short-term debt since 2001. Trade credits constituted 19 percent of total external debt in 2003, up from 13 percent in 2001 (table 3.5). The increase in trade credits accounted for about two-fifths of the total increase in outstanding external credit from 2001 to 2004.[6] While trade credits often have short maturities, they do not pose the same type of risks as other short-term borrowing since they tend to be closely linked to subsequent export receipts.

In short, while the stock of debt is in itself not a source of concern, the maturity structure and composition of this debt bear careful observation.[7]

CHINA'S CAPITAL OUTFLOWS[8]

RECENT DEVELOPMENTS IN CHINA'S INTERNATIONAL RESERVES

Examining the evolution of the balance of payments and the stock of international reserves provides a different perspective on China's capital flows. China's gross international reserves have risen sharply over the past decade, from well below $50 billion from 1990 through 1993 to $457 billion at the end of 2003, with almost a third of this buildup occurring in 2003, as shown in table 3.6.[9] This has left China with the second largest stock of international reserves in the world, behind Japan alone, amounting to about 32 percent of its nominal GDP at the end of 2003.

Gross reserves rose at an even faster pace in 2004 than in previous years, reaching $619 billion at the end of the year, according to official figures. However, in order to allow for comparability of stock levels in 2003 and 2004, we need to add in the $45 billion used for bank recapitalization at the end of 2003. (These adjusted figures are reported in table 3.6.) Thus, we arrive at an increase of $206 billion, or an average of about $17.2 billion a month, during 2004 (compared to $162 billion, or about $13.5 billion a month, during 2003). Since balance-of-payments data for 2004 are not yet available, the remainder of this section focuses on data through 2003.

Of the total increase of about $430 billion in reserves over the past decade, cumulative flows on the current account balance amount to about $216 billion, whereas flows on the capital account total $300 billion. The

Table 3.6   The Balance of Payments (in billions of U.S. dollars)

	1997	1998	1999	2000	2001	2002	2003	2004	2005
Gross international reserves	143.4	149.8	158.3	168.9	218.7	295.2	457.2[1]	663.9[1]	896.9[2]
Increase in international reserves	35.7	6.4	8.5	10.5	47.3	75.5	162.0[1]	206.7	233.0[2]
Current account balance	29.7	29.3	21.1	20.5	17.4	35.4	45.9	68.7	160.8
Merchandise trade balance	46.2	46.6	36.0	34.5	34.0	44.2	44.7	59.0	134.2
Capital account balance	23.0	−6.3	5.2	2.0	34.8	32.3	97.8	110.8	89.0
FDI, net	41.7	41.1	37.0	37.5	37.4	46.8	47.2	53.1	67.8
Errors and omissions, net	−17.0	−16.6	−17.8	−11.9	−4.9	7.8	18.4	27.0	−16.8
Non-FDI capital account balance (including errors and omissions)	−35.6	−64.0	−49.6	−47.4	−7.4	−6.7	69.0	84.9	4.4

1. Reserves data for 2003–2004 include the $45 billion used for bank recapitalization at the end of 2003. This amount is added to non-FDI capital inflows.
2. Reserves data for 2005 include the $45 billion used for bank recapitalization at the end of 2003, as well as additional $15 billion recapitalization in April 2005, $5 billion in September 2005 recap, and $6 billion foreign exchange swap. These amounts are added to non-FDI capital inflows.

Sources: CEIC, PBC, SAFE, and authors' calculations.

residual is given by cumulative errors and omissions, which amount to about minus $85 billion over this period.

It is instructive to examine the factors underlying changes in the pace of reserve accumulation over time. After registering relatively small changes over the period from 1985 through 1993, reserve accumulation rose sharply and averaged $30 billion a year over the period from 1994 through 1997. This was largely due to a strong capital account, which in turn reflected robust FDI inflows on the order of $30 to $40 billion a year. Interestingly, the errors and omissions category was significantly negative over this period (averaging about minus $15 billion a year). This finding suggests that unofficial capital outflows were occurring at the same time that significant FDI inflows were coming in through official channels.

Reserve accumulation then tapered off from 1998 through 2000, the years immediately following the Asian crisis. A sharp rise in outflows on other investment and large negative errors and omissions together offset much of the effects of continued robust FDI inflows and a strong current account, the latter reflecting an increase in the trade surplus.

Table 3.7   A Decomposition of the Recent Reserve Buildup (in billions of U.S. dollars)

	Average 1998–2000	Average 2001–2003	Change	Average 2001–2004	Change	Average 2001–2005	Change
	(1)	(2)	(2) – (1)	(3)	(3) – (1)	(4)	(4) – (1)
Foreign reserve increase	8.5	80.0	71.5	122.9	114.4	144.9	136.4
Current account balance	23.7	32.9	9.2	41.8	18.1	65.6	42.0
Capital account balance	0.3	40.0	39.7	68.9	68.6	72.9	72.6
FDI, net	38.5	43.8	5.3	46.1	7.6	50.5	11.9
Errors and omissions, net	−15.4	7.1	22.5	12.1	27.5	6.3	21.7
Non-FDI capital account balance (including errors and omissions)	−53.6	3.3	57.0	35.0	88.6	28.8	82.5

Sources: CEIC, PBC, and authors' calculations.

The subsequent sharp increase in reserves since 2001 is noteworthy, particularly because it was accompanied by a sustained export boom and the possibility—according to a number of observers and analysts—that the renminbi (RMB) may have become significantly undervalued over this period.[10] It is useful to compare the factors underlying the accumulation of reserves from 2001 through 2003 relative to that of the previous three-year period.

Table 3.7 shows that the average annual increase in foreign exchange reserves from 2001 through 2003 was an order of magnitude higher than from 1998 through 2000. The current account surplus was on average larger in the later period, but it does not account for much of the increase in the pace of reserve accumulation since 2001. Similarly, although FDI inflows are an important contributor to reserve accumulation, there is little evidence of a major increase in the pace of these inflows in the later period. The most significant increase is in non-FDI capital inflows (including errors and omissions), which swung from an average of minus $53.6 billion from 1998 through 2000 to $18.3 billion from 2001 through 2003, a turnaround of $72 billion on an annual basis. Errors and omissions, in particular, changed from an average of minus $15.4 billion in the first period to $7.1 billion in the second.

This decomposition is significant because it shows that much of the recent increase in the pace of reserve accumulation may be related to "hot money" rather than to a rising trade surplus or capital flows such as FDI, which are viewed as being driven by fundamentals. In fact, the merchandise

Table 3.8 Capital Flows Under the Financial Account (in billions of U.S. dollars)

	2000			2003			Change in Balance (2003 less 2000)	2004			Change in Balance (2004 less 2000)
	Balance	Credit	Debit	Balance	Credit	Debit		Balance	Credit	Debit	
Financial Account	2	92	90	98	220	122	96	156	343	188	154
Direct Investment	37	42	5	47	56	8	10	53	61	8	16
Inward	38	41	2	47	54	6	9	55	61	6	17
Outward	−1	1	2	0	2	2	1	−2	0	2	−1
Portfolio Investment	−4	8	12	11	12	1	15	20	20	1	24
Assets	−11	0	11	3	3	0	14	6	7	0	18
Equity Securities											
Debt Securities											
Liabilities	7	8	0	8	9	1	1	13	14	0	6
Equity Securities											
Debt Securities											
Other Investment	−32	42	74	39	152	113	71	83	262	179	114
Assets	−44	5	49	27	52	25	71	47	51	4	91
Trade Credit	−13	0	13	−1	0	1	11	−16	0	16	−3
Loans	−18	0	19	14	22	8		−10	0	10	9
Currency and Deposits	−6	1	7	−7	1	7	−1	20	21	1	26
Other Assets	−6	3	10	21	30	8	28	52	30	−22	59
Liabilities	12	37	25	12	100	88	0	36	211	175	24
Trade Credit	18	18	0	5	5	0	−14	19	19	0	0
Loans	−2	12	15	7	79	72	9	14	175	161	16
Currency and Deposits	0	0	0	1	9	8	1	2	15	13	2
Other Liabilities	−3	7	10	0	7	7	3	2	3	1	5

Source: CEIC database.

trade balance has been relatively stable in the range of $35 to $45 billion since 1997. The moderate increase in the average current account surplus is largely accounted for by the surge in net transfers.

To better understand recorded non-FDI capital inflows, we examine more detailed information from capital and financial account transactions. Table 3.8 shows how the main items changed from 2000 to 2003. Of the total increase of $96 billion in the capital and financial account over this period, the increases in net FDI inflows and net portfolio flows account for $10 billion and $15 billion, respectively. This leaves a substantial portion, about $71 billion, to be explained by other capital flows. The two biggest increases, adding up to about $60 billion, are in the categories of inward loans—representing offshore borrowing by Chinese households and firms—and other assets. This includes significant withdrawals of overseas lending by Chinese banks in order to meet rising domestic demand for foreign-currency-denominated loans. The general direction of all of these flows is consistent with expectations of an appreciation of the RMB during this period.

Similarly, the large switch in the errors and omissions category could be indicative of unrecorded capital flows into China, stimulated by the prospect of an appreciation of the RMB against the U.S. dollar. Such speculative pressures may have been exacerbated by the positive interest differential between China and the United States, which implies that investors may have seen a move into RMB-denominated instruments as essentially a one-way bet, and one without even an associated carrying cost.

This issue raises the prospect that, as long as the perception of an undervalued RMB persists—and unless the interest differential between China and the United States narrows further or shifts—these speculative inflows could continue. It should nevertheless be noted that, given the apparent one-way bet on the RMB the fact that these flows are not larger than they are suggests that capital controls may be at least partially effective.

In this context, we should investigate in more detail where the unrecorded flows are coming from, how much larger they could be in the absence of capital controls, and how much money may ultimately find its way around the capital controls. Anecdotal evidence suggests that the money inflow is primarily accounted for by a reversal of outflows from Chinese households and corporates that took place during the 1990s to evade taxes or to avoid losses associated with a possible depreciation of the RMB. It is

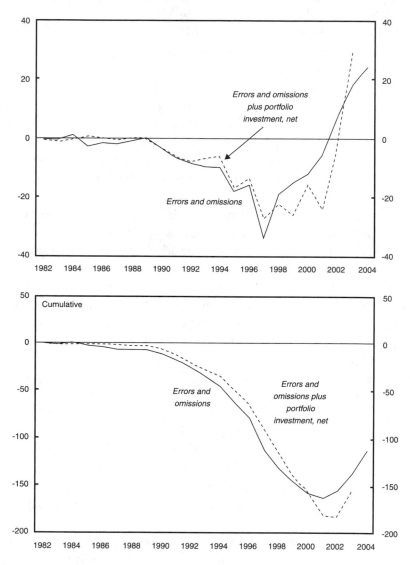

Figure 3.7 Errors and Omissions and Portfolio Investment, Net (in billions of U.S. dollars)

NOTE: Data for 2004 are preliminary (see notes to table 3.6).

Source: World Economic Outlook database.

difficult to give a precise answer to the question of how much such money is outside of China and could potentially come back into the country.

Here we take the simple approach of adding up errors and omissions and portfolio flows and labeling the total as "hot money" that could potentially switch directions within a short time horizon. Figure 3.7 shows the amount of such hot money flows over the past two decades.[11] The bottom panel of the figure shows that the cumulative amount of errors and omissions since the early 1990s is quite large, peaking at about $150 billion, and that the recent swing has reversed at best only a small part of this flow. Under this interpretation, significant amounts of further inflows are possible if a strong expectation of an appreciation of the RMB continues.

An alternative, and more benign, possibility is that the errors and omissions category may in part reflect an accounting issue.[12] China's officially reported holdings of foreign bonds are not marked to market in terms of exchange rate valuations, whereas the stock of international reserves on the People's Bank of China's (PBOC) balance sheet do reflect these currency valuation effects. This implies, for instance, that any changes in the dollar value of reserve holdings could end up in the balance of payments under the errors and omissions category.[13] In the absence of published data on the currency composition of foreign exchange reserves, it is widely believed that a substantial fraction of China's foreign exchange reserve holdings is in U.S. treasury bonds, with the remainder in government bonds denominated in euros and other currencies.[14] Given the recent large swings in the value of the U.S. dollar, however, even modest holdings of reserves in instruments denominated in other major currencies could have a significant quantitative effect on the dollar value of gross reserves.

Table 3.9 shows the effects of some simple simulations to illustrate how large these valuation effects could be. For instance, in panel 1, we assume that 80 percent of China's foreign reserve holdings are in U.S. dollar-denominated instruments, with the remainder in euro-denominated instruments. This calculation suggests that, in 2003, valuation changes in the stock of reserves could account for roughly $16 billion, representing about 85 percent of the errors and omissions amount for the year. In 2004, valuation changes could account for about $11 billion of unrecorded capital inflows, although, in the absence of full balance-of-payments data at this stage, one cannot tell how this fits into the broader picture. As a share of the total change in reserves, however, valuation effects were expected to

Table 3.9 Possible Effects of Valuation Changes on Reserves

Year	Foreign Exchange Reserves USD (bn)	Increase/Decrease in Reserves due to Foreign Exchange Rate Change			Errors & Omissions USD (bn)	Exchange Rates			
						USD/Euro		USD/Yen*100	
	USD (bn)	Euro	Yen	Total	USD (bn)	Beginning of Period	End of Period	Beginning of Period	End of Period
Assumed composition of reserves: 80% U.S. dollars and 20% euros									
2000	165.6	-2.4		-2.4	-11.9	1.00	0.93		
2001	212.2	-2.2		-2.2	-4.9	0.93	0.88		
2002	286.4	10.4		10.4	7.8	0.88	1.04		
2003	403.3	16.1		16.1	18.4	1.04	1.25		
2004	609.9	10.8		10.8	27.0	1.25	1.36		
2005	818.9	-21.3		-21.3	-16.8	1.36	1.18		
Assumed composition of reserves: 90% U.S. dollars and 10% euros									
2000	165.6	-1.2		-1.2	-11.9	1.00	0.93		
2001	212.2	-1.1		-1.1	-4.9	0.93	0.88		
2002	286.4	5.2		5.2	7.8	0.88	1.04		
2003	403.3	8.1		8.1	18.4	1.04	1.25		
2004	609.9	5.4		5.4	27.0	1.25	1.36		
2005	818.9	-10.6		-10.6	-16.8	1.36	1.18		
Assumed composition of reserves: 70% U.S. dollars, 20% euros, and 10% Japanese yen									
2000	165.6	-2.4	-1.8	-4.2	-11.9	1.00	0.93	0.98	0.87
2001	212.2	-2.2	-2.7	-4.9	-4.9	0.93	0.88	0.87	0.76
2002	286.4	10.4	2.9	13.3	7.8	0.88	1.04	0.76	0.84
2003	403.3	16.1	4.3	20.5	18.4	1.04	1.25	0.84	0.93
2004	609.9	10.8	2.7	13.5	27.0	1.25	1.36	0.93	0.97
2005	818.9	-21.3	-10.6	-31.9	-16.8	1.36	1.18	0.97	0.85

NOTES: Foreign exchange reserves shown in the second column are end-of-year stocks. In this table, we do not include the amounts used for bank recapitalization and bank swaps in the reserve stock numbers. In principle, any currency valuation changes on that amount should affect the balance sheets of the banks to whom those reserves were transferred. Thus, the currency valuation effects would matter for the net international investment position but not for official reserves.

Sources: IFS, CEIC, Datastream, and authors' calculations.

be a lot less important in 2004 than in 2003, both because the underlying exchange rate changes were smaller and because the change in reserves was larger in 2004.

The remaining panels of this table show how the results change under different assumptions about (1) the share of reserves held in U.S. dollar-denominated bonds and (2) the currencies (euro or yen) in which the remainder of the reserves is held. The results generally seem to confirm the possibility that errors and omissions in recent years may, to a significant extent, reflect currency valuation effects rather than unrecorded capital inflows. This issue clearly bears further investigation in the future.

IMPLICATIONS OF THE RECENT RESERVE BUILDUP

The fact that China's capital inflows over the past decade have been dominated by FDI is a positive outcome. As documented earlier, however, non-FDI capital inflows have accounted for much of the recent surge in the pace of reserve accumulation. This raises a question about whether, from China's domestic perspective, the continued rapid buildup of reserves is desirable.

The literature on the optimal level of reserves (see, e.g., Aizenman and Marion, 2004, and references therein) does not provide a clear-cut answer to this question. Possessing a large stock of reserves, especially for a country with a fixed exchange rate system, can be useful in helping that country stave off downward pressures on the exchange rate. The trade-off results from the fact that developing country reserves are typically held in treasury bonds denominated in hard currencies. The rate of return on these instruments is presumably lower than that which could be earned by physical capital investment within the developing country, which would typically have a scarcity of capital. In addition, the capital inflows that are reflected in reserve accumulation could increase liquidity in the banking system, creating potential problems in a weakly supervised banking system if banks have an incentive to relax their prudential standards in order to increase lending. Sterilization of capital inflows to avoid this outcome could generate fiscal costs because the rate of return on domestic sterilization instruments is typically higher than that earned on reserve holdings.

China, however, appears to be a special case in some respects. China's low (controlled) interest rates imply that, since its reserve holdings are believed to be held primarily in medium- and long-term industrial country

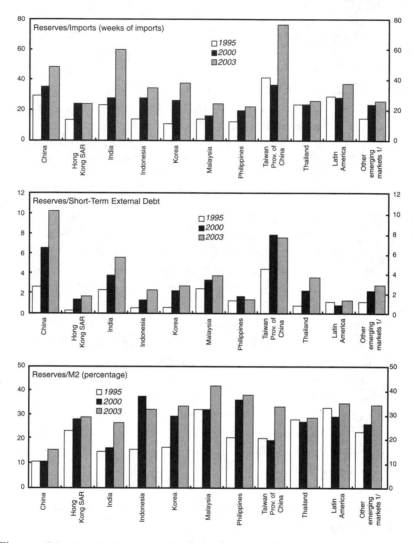

Figure 3.8   Reserve Adequacy Indicators

NOTES: In the top panel, end-of-year reserves are shown as a ratio to the number of weeks' worth of imports that year.

1. Average for emerging markets in EMBI+ index, excluding Latin America and Asian countries.

Sources: IFS, DOT, WEO, and Joint BIS/IMF/OECD/World Bank Statistics of External Debt.

treasury instruments and government agency bonds, there are in fact net marginal *benefits* to sterilization. These benefits, of course, are the result of domestic financial repression—with no effective competition for the state-owned banking sector—and capital controls.[15] With domestic investment rates of above 45 percent (supported mainly by domestic saving, which is an order of magnitude larger than FDI inflows), capital scarcity is apparently not a concern. Moreover, it is not obvious that the marginal return on investment is higher than the rate of return on reserve holdings, particularly in the likely scenario in which the allocation of capital remains the sole prerogative of an improving but still inefficient state banking system.[16]

Commonly used reserve adequacy indicators provide one way of assessing the insurance value provided by reserve holdings (figure 3.8).[17] China's reserve holdings provide comfortable coverage of its imports, more so than in most other emerging markets. The stock of reserves at the end of 2004 accounted for about 53 weeks' worth of imports in that year (and for about 43 weeks of the IMF's forecast of imports in 2005), significantly above the corresponding figures for most other emerging markets. In terms of reserve coverage of short-term external debt, China outperforms virtually every other emerging market, with its reserves amounting to more than ten times short-term external debt.[18] One area where China's position looks less favorable relative to other emerging markets is the reserve coverage of the monetary base, which is a useful indicator of reserve adequacy in the context of a currency peg. Reflecting the high degree of monetization of the Chinese economy (the ratio of M2 to GDP at year-end 2004 was about 1.9), reserves cover only about 20 percent of M2.

As a related matter, in addition to providing a buffer to stave off any future downward pressures on the fixed exchange rate, the high level of reserves has been cited as necessary to cushion the financial sector from external shocks. Reported nonperforming loans (NPLs) in the banking system amounted to about 30 percent of GDP in 2003 (see Prasad et al. 2004), similar in magnitude to the stock of reserves. This suggests that the present level of reserves could be used to finance a bailout of the banking system if the need should arise. Indeed, the recapitalization of two major state commercial banks at the end of 2003 using $45 billion of reserves indicates that the Chinese authorities intend to use reserve holdings to help strengthen the books of state banks. However, deficiencies in accounting practices and the reporting of NPLs could mean that their true level is higher than the reported numbers. Furthermore, the rapid expansion of credit during 2003 and the first half of 2004 that contributed to an investment boom could result in a new wave of problem loans in the future if the surge in investment results in excess capacity being built up in some sectors (Goldstein and Lardy 2004). This concern could justify maintaining a high level of reserves.[19]

One risk associated with maintaining a high level of reserves, however, is the vulnerability of the PBOC's balance sheet to changes in the industrial country treasury yield curve. An upward shift in the yield curve could significantly reduce the mark-to-market value of Chinese holdings of industrial country treasury instruments.[20] Similarly, an appreciation of the currency relative to, for example, the U.S. dollar could lead to a fall in the RMB value of dollar-denominated treasury bond holdings. Since the primary sterilization instrument in China—central bank bills—is denominated in RMB, the result could be a net capital loss in domestic currency terms. Interestingly, this suggests that, at least on this dimension, the costs of a move toward greater exchange rate flexibility (which, under present circumstances, is expected to lead to some appreciation of the RMB in the short run) could increase as the stock of reserves rises.[21] It could also increase the incentive to diversify out of dollar assets and into other hard currencies.

To summarize, there is no clear evidence that the buildup of reserves in China has significant direct sterilization costs, although it could have some efficiency costs and also expose the balance sheet of the PBOC to some exchange rate and capital risks, at least on a mark-to-market basis.

VIEWING CHINA'S CAPITAL FLOWS THROUGH THE PRISM OF THE LITERATURE ON FINANCIAL GLOBALIZATION[22]

It has long been an article of faith among most economists that international capital flows allow for a more efficient global allocation of capital. For capital-poor developing countries in particular, financial integration (with world capital markets) was seen as a key to moving onto a high-growth path. In addition, financial integration in theory provides enhanced possibilities for consumption smoothing through better sharing of income risk across countries. Those developing countries that subscribed to this logic by liberalizing their capital accounts starting in the mid-1980s—a group that has come to be known as the emerging markets—

captured a lion's share of the net capital flows from industrial to developing economies that took place over the subsequent decade. Capital account liberalization proved to be a mixed blessing, however, with many emerging markets suffering debilitating financial and balance-of-payments crises in the late 1990s. But do the crises by themselves imply that financial integration is not advisable for developing countries? A closer look at the evidence is in order.

FINANCIAL INTEGRATION AND GROWTH

In theory, capital inflows can help to raise economic growth in developing countries through both direct and indirect channels. Direct channels include augmentation of domestic savings, lower cost of capital, transfer of technology, and development of the domestic financial sector. Indirect channels include the inducements for better domestic policies offered by capital account openness and the promotion of specialization of production. Theory inexorably drives one to the conclusion that financial integration *must* be good for growth.

The empirical evidence paints a far more sobering picture, however. It is true that emerging markets as a group have posted much higher growth on average than other developing economies over the past two decades. Notwithstanding the painful crises that many of them experienced, these countries have done far better overall in terms of raising per capita incomes. However, this does not by itself imply a causal relationship. Indeed, while different studies show a considerable divergence of results, the weight of the evidence seems to point to the conclusion that it is difficult to find a strong and robust causal link once one controls for other factors that could affect growth.[23] There is an element of endogeneity here—financial integration could induce countries to have better macroeconomic policies and improve their institutions, but this effect would not be picked up in a regression framework. However, there is at best mixed evidence that financial integration induces a country to pursue better macroeconomic policies.[24] More research is needed on this question, but the bottom line is that it is difficult to make a prima facie case that financial integration provides a strong boost to growth in emerging markets.

FINANCIAL INTEGRATION AND VOLATILITY

With regard to volatility, economic theory strongly implies that access to financial markets—either at the household or national level—must be welfare enhancing from a consumption-smoothing perspective. As long as aggregate shocks (at the relevant level of aggregation) are not dominant in explaining variations in household or national income growth, financial markets should improve welfare by providing a mechanism that allows individual economic units to share their idiosyncratic income risk. Countries (and households) like to do this in order to smooth their consumption growth and reduce the otherwise necessarily close linkage of national consumption growth to national income growth and its intrinsic volatility. Although some countries may not be able to take full advantage of such risk-sharing opportunities (e.g., due to problems of monitoring and moral hazard), access to international financial markets should improve their welfare—in terms of reducing consumption volatility—at least marginally.

The reality for emerging markets is starkly different. Recent research suggests that, for these countries, the ratio of consumption growth volatility to output growth volatility increased on average in the 1990s, precisely during the key period of financial globalization.[25] Note that this result cannot simply be ascribed to the fact that some of these countries experienced crises during this period. In principle, a country should be able to do no worse than having its consumption growth be as volatile as its income growth. Formal regression analysis controlling for a variety of other determinants of volatility and growth suggests the existence of a nonlinearity in the relationship between the degree of financial integration and the relative volatility of consumption growth.[26]

An increase in financial integration from a low to a medium level tends to be associated with a rise in the relative volatility of consumption growth. At one end of the spectrum, countries with very limited access to international financial markets tend to experience consumption growth that is about as volatile as income growth.[27] At the other end, industrial countries, which tend to be highly integrated into global financial markets, are apparently able to take advantage of financial openness to effectively reduce their relative consumption growth volatility. For emerging markets, the problem is that international investors are willing to provide capital when times are good. These countries often lose access to international capital markets precisely when times are bad (see, e.g., Kaminsky,

Reinhart, and Végh 2004). Thus, sadly, it is precisely those countries that dip their toes into the waters of financial globalization that appear to be penalized by the procyclical nature of their access to world capital markets.

The situation appears bleak. Developing countries need external capital to grow. But is financial integration just "snake oil"—delivering at best weak growth effects and exposing countries to higher volatility? The answer, it turns out, depends on a number of factors.

THE COMPOSITION OF CAPITAL INFLOWS MATTERS

The literature shows that not only the degree of financial openness, but also the composition of capital inflows determines the quality of a developing country's experiences with globalization (see Prasad et al. 2003 for a survey and additional references for the points made here). For instance, FDI inflows, on the one hand, tend to be far less volatile than other types of inflows. In particular, FDI appears to be less subject to sharp reversals than other types of inflows, especially bank lending.[28] External debt, on the other hand, increases vulnerability to the risks of financial globalization. Specifically, debt crises are more likely to occur in countries where external debt is of relatively short maturity (see, e.g., Frankel and Rose 1996; Detragiache and Spilimbergo 2001).

The problem is that the composition of inflows as well as related matters such as the maturity structure of external debt are not entirely under the control of developing country governments. Countries with weak macroeconomic fundamentals are often forced to rely more on external debt and in the end have little choice but to borrow at short maturities. Financial integration can in fact aggravate the risks associated with weak macroeconomic policies. Access to world capital markets could lead to excessive borrowing that is channeled into unproductive government spending, ultimately increasing vulnerability to external shocks or changes in investor sentiment. In addition, lack of transparency has been shown to be associated with more herding behavior by international investors, which can destabilize financial markets in an emerging market economy. Furthermore, a high degree of corruption tends to adversely affect the composition of a country's inflows, making it more vulnerable to the risks of speculative attacks and contagion effects.

Thus, the apparently negative effects of globalization appear to be related to a particular kind of threshold effect. Only countries with good institutions and sound macroeconomic policies tend to have lower vulnerability to the risks associated with the initial phase of financial integration and are able to realize its full benefits.

THE RIGHT COMPOSITION OF INFLOWS FOR CHINA

From a number of different perspectives, China is a prototypical developing country that is best served by FDI rather than other types of inflows. In the context of the preceding discussion on the benefits and potential risks of financial globalization, the dominance of FDI in China's capital inflows implies that China has been able to control the risks and to achieve more of the promised benefits of financial integration than many other emerging markets that have taken a less cautious approach to capital account liberalization.

FDI may have served China well in other ways as well. Given China's low level of human capital and technical expertise, FDI could serve as a useful conduit for importing technical and managerial know-how.[29] Furthermore, the state-owned banking system is inefficient at allocating credit. This system has improved over time, particularly with the much-heralded end of the directed policy lending that these banks were forced to undertake until the late 1990s. However, most bank credit still goes to the public sector, especially since, with the controls on lending rates that existed until the end of October 2004, banks were not able to price-in the higher risk of lending to new and/or small firms in the private sector.[30] As the experiences of some of the Asian countries involved in the financial crisis of 1997 have shown, a weakly supervised banking system that is allowed to raise funds abroad and to channel them into the domestic economy can generate serious imbalances. Thus, restrictions on bank borrowing from abroad can serve a useful purpose.

With a fixed exchange rate, openness to other types of financial flows, which tend to be less stable and are subject to sudden stops or reversals, would be less advisable. For instance, external borrowing by banks could cause instability in exchange markets and would have at best dubious effects on growth. Substantial opening of the capital account would also be inadvisable in this context, suggesting that the sort of selective opening that China has pursued may have some advantages.[31]

WHAT EXPLAINS THE COMPOSITION
OF CHINA'S CAPITAL FLOWS?

Thus far we have highlighted two prominent features of China's cross-border capital flows: (1) its inflows are dominated by inward FDI and (2) its inflows are largely offset by correspondingly large outflows. In this section, we reflect on the underlying reasons for these patterns. Our bottom line is that the two features are better understood within a unified framework that takes into account a number of factors proposed *independently* in the literature. We begin the discussion by reviewing some arguments that focus solely on understanding the role of FDI in capital inflows.

With regard to inflows, China appears to have benefited from a pattern that is heavily oriented toward FDI. A key question is how China has attained such a composition of its inflows, one that many emerging markets aspire to but that few achieve. We need to present some context before addressing this question. Earlier work by Wei (2000c) suggests that the size of FDI inflows into China relative to the size of its GDP and other "natural" determinants is not unusually high. If anything, China seems to be an underperformer as a host of FDI from the world's five major source countries—Japan, Taiwan, Hong Kong, Singapore, and Korea. In more recent years, with the continued rise in FDI, China may have become a "normal" country in terms of its attractiveness as a destination for FDI.

One explanation for the composition of China's capital inflows is that it is the result of a pragmatic strategy that has been adjusted over time through trial and error. The pattern in the 1980s and early 1990s could well have reflected a combination of inertia and luck, with the post-1997 pattern reflecting the scare of the Asian financial crisis. Indeed, at the beginning of the reform period in the late 1970s and early 1980s, there were few capital inflows of any kind.

The early stage of reform sought to import only the type of foreign capital that was thought to help transmit technical and marketing know-how. Thus it was that the policy enunciated as "welcome to FDI, but no thank-you to foreign debt and portfolio flows" developed. Initially, export performance and foreign exchange balance requirements were imposed even on foreign-invested firms. The restrictions on FDI were relaxed step by step, together with certain "supranational treatment" (of incentives) for foreign-owned enterprises and joint ventures. Over time, the government also started to relax restrictions on foreign borrowing by corporations (and took steps to expand the B-, H-, and N-share markets). In the mid-1990s, the government declared that it intended to implement capital account convertibility by 2000.

The psychological effect of the subsequent Asian financial crisis may have been profound. Several countries that China had regarded as role models for its own development process (especially Korea) went into deep crises in a very short period of time. It was a common perception among policymakers in China that the swings in the non-FDI part of the international capital flows had played a crucial role in the process. In this sense, the Asian financial crisis caused the Chinese to rethink their approach to capital inflows. The idea of capital account liberalization disappeared by 2000, and in its place rose the notion that the higher the level of foreign exchange reserves the better in order to avoid painful crises.

INCENTIVES AND DISTORTIONS AFFECTING FDI

A more traditional explanation for the composition of China's capital inflows is that the unusually high share of FDI could reflect a simultaneous policy mix of discouraging foreign debt and foreign portfolio inflows as well as providing incentives for FDI.[32] Indeed, the existence of tax benefits for FDI has meant that, until recently, the playing field was in fact tilted in favor of foreign-funded firms. This was conceivably part of an enlightened policy choice, which included restricting other types of inflows using capital controls.

Since China promulgated laws governing foreign investment at the start of the reform, the government has offered generous tax treatment to foreign firms. In the first two years that a foreign-invested firm makes a profit, it is exempt from corporate income tax. In the subsequent three years, foreign companies are subject to an average corporate income tax of 15 percent, less than half the normal rate of 33 percent paid by Chinese companies.

This supranational treatment of foreign direct investment gives domestic entrepreneurs incentives to find ways to register their companies as "foreign" firms. Consider Xinghualian ("New China Union") conglomerate, whose business now includes automobile manufacturing, ceramics, wine-making, real estate, and natural gas services. It was founded in October 1990 by a Chinese national, Mr. Fu Jun, but it was registered as a Malaysian company, thus allowing it to enjoy all tax and other benefits in China accorded to foreign direct investment. Chinese authorities have full knowledge that this is really a Chinese company disguised as a foreign company. Mr. Fu, born in Yilin City, Hunan Province, in 1957, was once party secretary and director general of Yilin City's Foreign Trade Bureau. He is not an unknown commodity in his native Hunan Province. He has continued to assume various prominent positions, including offices in Hunan Province's Political Consultative Congress and All China Industry and Commerce Association. He has received several awards in recent years as well as press coverage, including a half-page story in the *Beijing Youth Daily* on December 6, 2005.[33] In many ways, the story of Mr. Fu and his business conglomerate is not unique. Numerous "foreign" companies from Hong Kong SAR are known to be Mainland Chinese firms in disguise (this practice, whereby Chinese entrepreneurs register their companies abroad but otherwise operate in China, is known as round-tripping). The exact number of such companies is not known, but they serve as one explanation of FDI in China.

Tax exemptions and reductions constitute only one aspect of government incentives favoring FDI. To capture these incentives more comprehensively and to place the Chinese FDI regime in a cross-country comparative context, we now make use of the description of the legal FDI regimes for 49 countries in 2000 constructed by Wei (2000b), who in turn relied on detailed, textual descriptions prepared by PricewaterhouseCoopers (PwC) in a series of country reports entitled "Doing Business and Investing in China" (or in whichever country may be the subject of the report). This series is written for multinational firms that intend to do business in a particular country. They are collected in one CD-ROM titled "Doing Business and Investing Worldwide" (PwC 2000). For each country, the relevant PwC country report covers a variety of legal and regulatory issues of interest to foreign investors, including restrictions on foreign investment and investors (typically chapter 5), investment incentives (typically chapter 4), and taxation of foreign corporations (typically chapter 16).

To convert the textual information in these reports into numerical codes, we read through the relevant chapters for all countries covered in the PwC series. PwC (2000) contains information on incentives for FDI in the following four categories:

1. Existence of special incentives to invest in certain industries or certain geographic areas.

2. Tax concessions specific to foreign firms (including tax holidays and tax rebates, but excluding tax concessions specifically designed for export promotion, which is in a separate category).

3. Cash grants, subsidized loans, reduced rent for land use, or other nontax concessions, specific to foreign firms.

4. Special promotion for exports (including existence of export processing zones and special economic zones).

For each category of incentives, we then created a dummy variable, which takes the value 1 if a particular type of incentive is present. An overall FDI incentives variable can then be constructed as the sum of these four dummies. This variable takes a value of 0 if there is no incentive in any of the categories and 4 if there are incentives in all of them.

Of the 49 countries for which one can obtain information, none has incentives in all four categories. The median number of incentives is 1 (mean=1.65). China is one of only three countries with incentives for FDI in three categories (the other two countries being Israel and Egypt). Therefore, based on this information, we might conclude that China offers more incentives to attract FDI than most countries in the world.

Legal incentives are not the only important considerations for international investors. To obtain a more complete picture, one also has to look at legal restrictions. The same PwC source also offers information, in a standardized format, on the presence or absence of restrictions in four areas:

1. Existence of foreign exchange control. (This may interfere with the ability of foreign firms to import intermediate inputs or repatriate profits abroad.)

2. Exclusion of foreign firms from certain strategic sectors (particularly national defense and mass media).

3. Exclusion of foreign firms from additional sectors that would otherwise be open in most developed countries.

4. Restrictions on foreign ownership (e.g., they may not be permitted 100 percent ownership).

We generated dummy variables for each category of restrictions and created an overall FDI restriction variable that is equal to the sum of those four dummies. This variable takes the value of 0 if there is no restriction in any category and 4 if there are restrictions in all of them.

The median number of restrictions is 1 (mean=1.69). Interestingly, China is one of only five countries in the sample (the others being Russia, Ukraine, Korea, and Taiwan) that place restrictions on FDI in all four categories. Different restrictions and incentives may have different effects on FDI, so they cannot be assigned equal weights. Notwithstanding this caveat, in terms of the overall legal regime, it is not obvious that China represents a particularly attractive FDI destination (as of 2000).[34]

So far we have been discussing explicit incentives and restrictions that are written into laws and regulations. Nonetheless, many other implicit incentives or restrictions are an important part of the overall investment climate in the mind of potential investors. For example, corruption and bureaucratic red tape raise business costs and are part of the implicit disincentives for investment. Statistical analyses by Wei (2000a, 2000b, 2000c) suggest that these costs are both economically and statistically significant.

To sum up, although Chinese laws and regulations offer many legal incentives to attract FDI, these incentives should be placed in the context of many implicit disincentives as well as explicit legal restrictions in order to form a more complete assessment of the overall investment climate.

A MERCANTILIST STORY

Another hypothesis offered to explain China's pattern of capital inflows is that the encouragement of FDI inflows is part of a mercantilist strategy to foster export-led growth, abetted by the maintenance of an undervalued exchange rate (see papers by Dooley, Folkerts-Landau, and Garber 2004a, 2004b; henceforth, DFG). The basic idea here is that, with a large pool of surplus labor and a banking system that is assumed to be irremediably inefficient, a more appropriate growth strategy for China is to use FDI to spur "good" investment in the export sector and to maintain an undervalued exchange rate in order to maintain export competitiveness. To support this equilibrium, China allows manufacturers in its export markets (the U.S. market in particular) to bring in FDI and take advantage of China's cheap labor to reap substantial profits. In this way, China seeks to build a constituency in the United States that will inhibit any U.S. action

Table 3.10 China's Purchases and Holdings of U.S. Financial Instruments (in billions of U.S. dollars)

| | | Panel A: Net Purchases of Securities in the U.S. | | | | | Panel B: Annual Flows | | | Panel C: End-of-Year Stocks | | |
| | | Long-Term Securities | | | | | | | | | | |
Year	Total	Treasury Bills	Treasury Bonds	Govt. Agency Bonds	Corporate Bonds & Stocks	Foreign Bonds & Stocks	Net Purchases of Securities (1)	Foreign Exchange Reserves (2)	Ratio (1)/(2)	Holdings of U.S. Treasury Securities (1)	Foreign Exchange Reserves (2)	Ratio (1)/(2)
1990	0.3	-0.2	0.3	0.0	0.0	0.2	0.3	5.5	0.06	—	11.1	—
1991	0.6	0.0	0.1	0.0	0.0	0.4	0.6	10.6	0.06	—	21.7	—
1992	5.3	0.3	3.4	0.5	0.7	0.4	5.3	-2.3	-2.32	—	19.4	—
1993	0.7	-0.1	0.5	0.6	0.1	-0.3	0.7	1.8	0.39	—	21.2	—
1994	16.1	3.7	12.2	0.5	0.1	-0.4	16.1	30.4	0.53	—	51.6	—
1995	14.8	13.7	0.7	0.9	0.0	-0.4	14.8	22.0	0.67	—	73.6	—
1996	14.6	-2.8	14.5	2.8	0.3	0.0	14.6	31.4	0.47	—	105.0	—
1997	2.1	-7.4	8.2	1.7	0.1	-0.4	2.1	34.9	0.06	—	139.9	—
1998	1.1	-4.1	2.6	0.9	0.0	1.7	1.1	5.1	0.21	—	145.0	—
1999	14.7	-2.7	8.2	8.3	0.7	0.1	14.7	9.7	1.51	—	154.7	—
2000	17.6	0.4	-4.0	18.8	0.7	1.6	17.6	10.9	1.61	60.3	165.6	0.36
2001	55.0	-0.9	19.1	26.0	6.7	4.1	55.0	46.6	1.18	78.6	212.2	0.37
2002	63.1	0.2	24.1	29.3	6.1	3.5	63.1	74.2	0.85	118.4	286.4	0.41
2003	68.4	0.3	30.1	29.4	4.5	4.0	68.4	161.8	0.42	157.7	448.3	0.35
2004	67.5	17.2	18.9	16.4	12.1	3.0	67.5	206.7	0.33	193.8	654.9	0.30

NOTES: The data in panel A are taken from the tables entitled "U.S. Banking Liabilities to Foreigners" and "U.S. Transactions with Foreigners in Long-Term Securities" on the U.S. Treasury Web site at http://www.treas.gov/tic/. Treasury bills have an original maturity of less than one year. Treasury bonds include marketable treasury and federal bank bonds and notes with an original maturity of one year or longer. Government agency bonds include the bonds of U.S. government corporations and federally-sponsored agencies. The stock data on holdings of U.S. Treasury securities (panel C) are taken from "Major Foreign Holders of U.S. Treasury Securities" on the U.S. Treasury Web site. Data on foreign exchange reserve increases in 2003 and corresponding stocks in 2003 and 2004 include the $45 billion used for bank recapitalization at the end of 2003. Note that the flow data on net purchases of treasury bills and treasury bonds in panel A cannot be fully reconciled with the estimated stock of treasury securities in panel C (e.g., for 2002 and 2003) because the stock data are re-benchmarked whenever a new survey is conducted.

Sources: Treasury International Capital System, CEIC, and authors' calculations.

to force China to change its exchange rate regime. In addition, China's purchases of U.S. government securities as a part of its reserve holdings (table 3.10) act as "collateral" or an insurance policy for foreign firms that invest in China. A major attraction of the DFG mercantilist story is its apparent ability to simultaneously explain the structure of inflows as dominated by FDIs and the structure of outflows as dominated by official reserve holdings.

While this approach is intriguing, it cannot be the entire story. For instance, most of the FDI inflows into China have come from countries that are exporting to China rather than importing from it (see the earlier discussion of the evolution of China's capital flows). Furthermore, it is worth noting that (1) China chose not to devalue from 1997 through 1998, even though that would have increased its exports; (2) the massive buildup of foreign exchange reserves is a relatively recent phenomenon; and (3) for much of the past two decades up to 2001, the Chinese currency was likely to be overvalued rather than undervalued according to the black market premium. Even if one were to accept the DFG approach as a sustainable one, the conceptual question that remains is whether it is the right approach. To take just one aspect, the sheer size of domestic saving (more than $500 billion a year) eclipses FDI (at about $45 to $50 billion a year, a smaller order of magnitude). Hence, writing off the domestic banking sector and focusing solely on FDI-led growth can hardly be regarded as a reasonable strategy. In short, although the DFG story is a seductive one and has many plausible elements, it does not appear to be a viable overall approach to fostering sustainable growth in China.[35]

INSTITUTIONS AND GOVERNANCE

A different possibility, suggested by the work of Yasheng Huang (2003), is that the dominant share of FDI in China's inflows over the past decade reflects deficiencies in domestic capital markets. In particular, private firms have faced discrimination relative to state-owned enterprises, both from the banking system (in terms of loan decisions by state-owned banks) and the equity market (in terms of approval of stock listings). As a result, private firms have taken advantage of pro-FDI policies in an unexpected way and have used foreign joint ventures as a way to acquire needed capital in order to undertake investment. Foreign investors have presumably been willing to go along because their Chinese partners compensate them appropriately in the form of profit shares, even in cases where the foreign investors offer no particular technological, managerial, or marketing know-how. If the Chinese financial system had no such discrimination in place, much of the foreign investment in the form of joint ventures might not have occurred. In this sense, the deficiency of the domestic financial system may have artificially raised the level of inward FDI.

This hypothesis is an interesting one and may well explain part of the inward FDI in the 1980s. However, there is some mismatch between this hypothesis and the data, especially in terms of the time-series patterns of FDI inflows. On the one hand, inward FDI has been increasing at a rapid rate—indeed, recent inflows over the period from 1998 through 2003 account for more than half of the cumulative stock of inward FDI. This hypothesis would require a financial system that is ever more discriminatory of private firms. On the other hand, domestic banks have become increasingly willing to make loans to non-state firms. Similarly, in the equity market, both the absolute number and the relative share of the non–state-owned firms in the two stock exchanges have been rising. Therefore, Huang's hypothesis is unlikely to be a major part of the explanation for the rapid rise in inward FDI in recent years.

Governance, which includes various aspects of public administration, is another potentially important determinant of the composition of inflows. Unlike other types of inflows, FDI that is used to build plants with joint ownership by Chinese entrepreneurs provides foreign investors with the best possibility of successfully negotiating the bureaucratic maze in China. However, this notion is somewhat at odds with recent literature that has examined the role of weak institutions (high level of corruption, lack of transparency, weak judicial system, etc.) in affecting the volume and patterns of capital inflows. Low levels of transparency typically tend to discourage international portfolio investment (Gelos and Wei 2005). Weak public governance—especially rampant insider trading—tends to exacerbate stock market volatility, further discouraging foreign portfolio inflows (Du and Wei 2004). High corruption also tends to discourage FDI (Wei 2000). Taken together, however, these factors are unlikely to explain the particular composition of the Chinese capital inflows, since weak public governance by itself should tilt the composition away from FDI and toward foreign debt (Wei and Wu 2002).

It is not easy to empirically disentangle the various hypotheses reviewed here explaining why China gets more FDI than other types of inflows. In our view, the nature of the capital controls regime and the incentives for FDI appear to have played a big part in encouraging FDI inflows. But the story is not quite that straightforward, for one would expect a counteracting effect from factors such as weak governance, legal restrictions on investment by foreigners, and poor legal infrastructure and property rights. Furthermore, it is useful to remember that the incentives for disguising other forms of inflows as FDI may have artificially inflated FDI inflow figures in order to get around capital account restrictions and to take advantage of tax and other policies favoring FDI.

A SYNTHESIS

In our view, no single factor discussed so far provides a satisfactory explanation for the large gross capital outflows, the large gross inflows, and the dominant role of FDI in inflows. One perhaps needs a synthetic explanation that emphasizes a combination of factors. The relative importance of the different factors may also change over time. We believe that a combination of an inefficient domestic financial system, a desire by the government to import technology, and a move by international investors to exploit China's regulatory peculiarities helps to define the structure of capital flows in the earlier days. A still inefficient financial system together with the scare evoked by the Asian financial crisis help to explain the more recent pattern of capital flows.

The Chinese financial system is inefficient in channeling domestic savings into productive domestic investments. The state domination of the financial system is the primary reason for the inefficiency (see Boyreau-Debray and Wei 2004). Recent papers (Caballero, Farhi, and Gourinchas 2005; Ju and Wei 2006) suggest that an inefficient financial system could coexist with and perhaps even encourage inward FDI. In a poor country with a low capital-to-labor ratio like China, one might think that marginal return to physical capital should be high. This is true and helps to explain part of the inward FDI.

Ju and Wei point out that the high marginal return to physical capital does not automatically translate into high returns to financial investors (or households on their savings); that would require efficient financial intermediation. The inefficiency in the Chinese financial system, together with controls on deposit interest rates, motivates Chinese households to move savings out of the domestic financial system into more efficient overseas financial systems. This capital flight can take many forms, including overinvoicing imports, underinvoicing exports, and other unrecorded flight routes that show up as "errors and omissions" in China's balance-of-payments statements. Precisely because of this inefficiency in the domestic financial system, foreign firms come into China with a greater volume because their funding does not rely on China's financial system and because more investment opportunities in China are left unexploited by domestic firms, owing to the financial constraint they face from the domestic financial system. In other words, inward FDI would have been smaller had the financial system been more efficient. The inefficient domestic financial system gives rise to two-way capital flows.[36]

Financial underdevelopment is only part of the story. The overall investment climate, including protection of property rights of foreign firms, has to be above some minimum threshold for foreign firms to be willing to come into China. In fact, most observers would agree that the protection of property rights has been improving steadily (and at a faster rate than the improvement in the domestic financial system) over the last three decades, which helps to explain the rapid growth in inward FDI.

Although China's progress in making financial sector reforms has been relatively slow, it has recently picked up its pace, partly in response to its obligations under the WTO accession agreement. Two of its large state-owned commercial banks (the Bank of Communication and the China Construction Bank) started listing on the Hong Kong Stock Exchange in 2005. Two others (the Bank of China and the China Industry and Commerce Bank) have also sold close to 20 percent of their shares to foreign "strategic investors" and are making preparations for overseas listing in 2006. Up to 25 cities in China were opened to foreign commercial banks by the end of 2005, meaning that they can compete with Chinese banks in these markets on local currency deposit and loan businesses. All of these changes should increase competition and improve the efficiency of the Chinese financial system. If our synthetic explanation for capital flows is correct, then, other things being equal, the upward momentum of FDI as a share of China's GDP will be moderated in the future and capital outflows as a share of GDP will also decline.

CONCLUDING REMARKS

In this chapter, we have provided an overview of developments in China's capital flows and analyzed the composition of these cross-border flows in the context of a rapidly burgeoning literature on financial globalization.

We have also examined a number of hypotheses for explaining China's success in attracting FDI inflows. Our view is that no single factor can account for all of the salient features of the patterns of capital flows in China. A combination of factors—a synthetic view—offers the best approach to explain the patterns. Understanding the reasons for China's success in tilting inflows toward FDI is important, especially as China continues its integration into world financial markets and becomes more exposed to the vagaries of these markets. China has thus far done well in managing the risks associated with financial globalization, but major challenges remain to ensure that continued integration with financial markets does not worsen the risk–return trade-off.

NOTES

1. Round-tripping is the practice whereby Chinese entrepreneurs register their companies abroad but otherwise operate in China.

2. A more likely possibility is that those could be flows from sources such as Japan, Taiwan Province of China, and the United States, which are channeled through such offshore financial centers in order to evade taxes in the source countries.

3. Official reports note that the cumulative amount of outward FDI as of the end of 2004 was $37 billion, which does not seem to match the annual data shown in this table. Based on anecdotal and other evidence, however, the upward trend in FDI outflows is incontrovertible even if the magnitudes may be suspect.

4. Enterprises are also discouraged from issuing corporate debt domestically. One possible explanation is the government's concern about a possible disintermediation following a liberalization of corporate debt regulation. Nonperforming loans in domestic state-owned banks are a major challenge facing the government, but the banks currently at least have captive deposit and lending bases. Once corporations are allowed to issue debt directly at home or abroad, the fear is that the domestic banks may lose some of the best borrowers and largest depositors, leaving them with a deteriorating portfolio.

5. The ratio of short-term external debt to GDP has risen from 1.2 to 5.5 percent over this period.

6. One cautionary note about the trade credit data in the external debt statistics is that they are partly estimated from data on imports. Consequently, they do not always match the balance-of-payments data on trade credits (discussed below), which are based on sample surveys. But the broad trends revealed by these two sources are similar.

7. The World Bank's 2003 *Global Development Finance Report* (pp. 136–39) indicates that, in recent years, about 70 percent of China's outstanding long-term external debt has been denominated in U.S. dollars and about 15 percent has been denominated in Japanese yen. Data on the currency composition of short-term external debt are not available in this report.

8. Some of the analysis in this section draws upon work done by members of the IMF's China team.

9. The figure for 2003 includes the $45 billion used to recapitalize two state commercial banks at the end of that year. Hence, the numbers reported in this table for foreign exchange reserve accumulation during 2003 and the level of gross official reserves at the end of 2003 are higher by $45 billion than the corresponding official figures. To understand the evolution of the capital account, it is relevant to include that figure in the calculations.

10. There is a considerable range of opinions about the degree of undervaluation of the RMB. IMF (2004) and Funke and Rahn (2005) conclude that there is no strong evidence that the RMB is substantially undervalued. In contrast, Goldstein (2004) and Frankel (2004) argue that the RMB may be undervalued by at least 25 to 30 percent. Market analysts have a similar broad range of views.

11. Capital flight through underinvoicing of exports or overinvoicing of imports may not show up in the errors and omissions or any other part of the balance-of-payments statistics. Net errors and omissions may also understate unrecorded capital flows to the extent that there are offsetting unrecorded flows on current and capital account transactions, or even among transactions within each of these categories. Gunter (2004) estimates that capital flight during the 1990s may have been greater than is suggested by such crude estimates.

12. The calculations below are based on unpublished work by Ray Brooks.

13. China does not report its international investment position, which would clarify this matter.

14. There has been a great deal of recent interest in the share of Chinese official reserve holdings accounted for by U.S. dollar-denominated instruments, particularly treasury bonds. The recent depreciation of the U.S. dollar has fueled speculation that China has been diversifying away from U.S. dollar bonds into other currencies. Appendix 2 provides a detailed analysis, including some cautionary notes, about one source of data that many analysts have used to examine this issue.

15. This suggests that there are implicit costs to these sterilization efforts. However, determining the incidence of these costs is not straightforward; much of these costs are presumably borne by depositors in the state banks. Recent data suggest that longer-term central bank bills (original maturity of one year or longer) have replaced short-term bills as the primary sterilization instrument used by the Chinese authorities. This change may have been driven by concerns about frequently rolling over the stock of short-term bills. In addition, purchases of shorter-term U.S. treasury instruments appear to have increased (see appendix 2). Thus, traditional sterilization costs also may soon start to come into play.

16. See Boyreau-Debray and Wei (2004) for evidence of low returns to lending by state banks.

17. The cross-country comparison in figure 3.8 shows data only through 2003. The discussion in this paragraph uses updated data for China through year-end 2004.

18. Figure 3.8 uses Bank for International Settlements (BIS) data on external debt that are, in principle, comparable across countries. Based on official Chinese data,

reserves amount to about six times the stock of short-term external debt, which is still above comparable ratios in almost all other emerging markets.

19. Preliminary indications are that the reported ratio of NPLs to GDP declined in 2004, but this may be partly attributable to the transfer of some NPLs off the books of state commercial banks.

20. One could argue that these notional capital losses in mark-to-market terms should not be of concern if the Chinese authorities intend to hold the bonds to maturity. This argument has validity only so long as the reserves do not need to be liquidated before maturity.

21. A related point is that if the accumulation of reserves continues apace, the potential capital loss from any appreciation would grow over time, suggesting that an earlier move toward exchange rate flexibility would be preferable from this narrow perspective (if such a move was regarded as being inevitable). In any event, we doubt whether this factor will significantly influence the timing of a move toward greater flexibility.

22. The discussion in this section draws on Prasad et al. (2003).

23. Prasad et al. (2003) provide an extensive survey of this literature.

24. Tytell and Wei (2004).

25. Kose, Prasad, and Terrones (2003).

26. In this subsection, the term *relative* volatility of consumption growth should always be taken to mean its volatility relative to that of income growth.

27. Even in a closed economy, the existence of investment opportunities should allow for some degree of intertemporal smoothing of national consumption.

28. See Wei (2001). The evidence that net FDI flows to emerging markets are less volatile than portfolio flows is weaker; see Dooley, Claessens, and Warner (1995); Wei (2001).

29. Borensztein, De Gregorio, and Lee (1995).

30. See Dunaway and Prasad (2004).

31. See Prasad, Rumbaugh, and Wang (2004).

32. Tseng and Zebregs (2002) discuss other factors that may have helped to attract FDI, such as market size, infrastructure, and the establishment of open economic zones, which have more liberal investment and trade regimes than other areas.

33. "New Thinking Inspired by the Success Stories of 2005 Double-Ten Personalities: Four Weapons Speed Up Strategic Innovations," *Beijing Youth Daily*, December 6, 2005, p. A18.

34. The regression analysis in Wei (2000b and 2001) suggests that these FDI incentives and restrictions variables explain part of the cross-country variation in inward FDI.

35. Roubini (2004) and Goldstein and Lardy (2005) present broader arguments against the DFG story.

36. See Wei (2006) for cross-country evidence on how an inefficient financial system may encourage inward FDI.

REFERENCES

Aizenman, Joshua and Nancy Marion. 2004. "International Reserve Holdings with Sovereign Risk and Costly Tax Collection." *The Economic Journal* 114 (July): 569–91.

Borensztein, Eduardo, José De Gregorio, and Jong-Wha Lee. 1998. "How Does Foreign Direct Investment Affect Growth?" *Journal of International Economics* 45 (June): 115–35.

Boyreau-Debray, Genevieve and Shang-Jin Wei. 2004. "Pitfalls of a State-Dominated Financial System: Evidence from China." CEPR Discussion Paper No. 4471. London: Centre for Economic Policy Research.

Caballero, Ricardo, Emmanuel Farhi, and Pierre-Olivier Gourinchas. 2005. "An Equilibrium Model of 'Global Imbalances' and Low Interest Rates." Working Paper. Cambridge, MA: MIT.

Detragiache, Enrica and Antonio Spilimbergo. 2001. "Crises and Liquidity—Evidence and Interpretation." IMF Working Paper 01/2. Washington, DC: International Monetary Fund.

Dooley, Michael P., Stijn Claessens, and Andrew Warner. 1995. "Portfolio Capital Flows: Hot or Cold?" *World Bank Economic Review* 9(1): 53–174.

Dooley, Michael P., David Folkerts-Landau, and Peter Garber. 2004a. "The Revived Bretton Woods System: The Effects of Periphery Intervention and Reserve Management on Interest Rates and Exchange Rates in Center Countries." NBER Working Paper No. 10332 (March). Cambridge, MA: National Bureau of Economic Research.

———. 2004b. "Direct Investment, Rising Real Wages and the Absorption of Excess Labor in the Periphery." NBER Working Paper No. 10626 (July). Cambridge, MA: National Bureau of Economic Research.

Du, Julan and Shang-Jin Wei. 2004. "Does Insider Trading Raise Market Volatility?" *The Economic Journal* 114(498): 916–42.

Dunaway, Steven and Eswar Prasad. 2004. "Interest Rate Liberalization in China." Op-ed article in *International Herald Tribune*, December 4.

Frankel, Jeffrey and Andrew Rose. 1996. "Currency Crashes in Emerging Markets: An Empirical Treatment." *Journal of International Economics* 41(3–4): 351–66.

Frankel, Jeffrey A. 2004. "On the Renminbi: The Choice Between Adjustment Under a Fixed Exchange Rate and Adjustment Under a Flexible Rate." Manuscript. Kennedy School of Government. Cambridge, MA: Harvard University.

Funke, Michael and Jörg Rahn. 2005. "Just How Undervalued Is the Chinese Renminbi." *The World Economy* 28(4): 465–89.

Gelos, Gaston R. and Shang-Jin Wei. 2005. "Transparency and International Portfolio Positions." *Journal of Finance* 60(6): 2987–3020.

Goldstein, Morris. 2004. "Adjusting China's Exchange Rate Policies." Institute for International Economics Working Paper 04/126. Washington, DC: Institute for International Economics.

Goldstein, Morris and Nicholas R. Lardy. 2004. "What Kind of Landing for the Chinese Economy?" Policy Briefs in International Economics No. PB04-7. Washington, DC: Institute for International Economics.

———. 2005. "China's Role in the Revived Bretton Woods System: A Case of Mistaken Identity." Institute for International Economics Working Paper 05/02. Washington, DC: Institute for International Economics.

Gunter, Frank R. 2004. "Capital Flight from China." *China Economic Review* 15: 63–85.

Hausmann, Ricardo and Eduardo Fernandez-Arias. 2000. "Foreign Direct Investment: Good Cholesterol?" IADB Working Paper No. 417. Washington, DC: Inter-American Development Bank.

Huang, Yasheng. 2003. *Selling China—Foreign Direct Investment During the Reform Era*. Cambridge: Cambridge University Press.

IMF. 2004. "People's Republic of China: Article IV Consultation—Staff Report." Washington, DC: International Monetary Fund. http://www.imf.org.

Ju, Jiangdong and Shang-Jin Wei. 2006. "A Solution to Two Paradoxes on International Capital Flows." NBER Working Paper No. 12668. Cambridge, MA: National Bureau of Economic Research.

Kaminsky, Graciela, Carmen Reinhart, and Carlos Végh. 2004. "When It Rains, It Pours: Procyclical Capital Flows and Macroeconomic Policies." In *NBER Macro Annual 2004*, ed. Mark Gertler and Ken Rogoff, 11–53. Cambridge, MA: National Bureau of Economic Research.

Kose, Ayhan M., Eswar S. Prasad, and Marco E. Terrones. 2003. "Financial Integration and Macroeconomic Volatility." *IMF Staff Papers* 50: 119–42.

Lane, Philip R. and Gian Maria Milesi-Ferretti. 2001. "The External Wealth of Nations: Measures of Foreign Assets and Liabilities for Industrial and Developing Nations." *Journal of International Economics* 55: 263–94.

Mody, Ashoka and Antu Panini Murshid. 2005. "Growing Up with Capital Flows." *Journal of International Economics* 65: 249–66.

Prasad, Eswar, ed. With contributions by Steven Barnett, Nicolas Blancher, Ray Brooks, Annalisa Fedelino, Tarhan Feyzioglu, Thomas Rumbaugh, Raju Jan Singh, and Tao Wang. 2004. *China's Growth and Integration Into the World Economy: Prospects and Challenges*. IMF Occasional Paper No. 232. Washington, DC: International Monetary Fund.

Prasad, Eswar, Kenneth Rogoff, Shang-Jin Wei, and M. Ayhan Kose. 2003. "The Effects of Financial Globalization on Developing Countries: Some Empirical Evidence." IMF Occasional Paper No. 220. Washington, DC: International Monetary Fund.

Prasad, Eswar, Thomas Rumbaugh, and Qing Wang. 2005. "Putting the Cart Before the Horse? Capital Account Liberalization and Exchange Rate Flexibility in China." IMF Policy Discussion Paper 05/1. Washington, DC: International Monetary Fund.

PricewaterhouseCoopers (PwC). 2000. "Doing Business and Investing Worldwide." CD-ROM.

Roubini, Nouriel. 2004. "BW2: Are We Back to a New Stable Bretton Woods Regime of Global Fixed Exchange Rates?" Nouriel Roubini's Global Economics Blog. October 8. http://www.roubiniglobal.com/archives/2004/10/are_we_back_to.html.

Tseng, Wanda and Harm Zebregs. 2002. "FDI in China: Lessons for Other Countries." IMF Policy Discussion Paper 02/3. Washington, DC: International Monetary Fund.

Tytell, Irina and Shang-Jin Wei. 2004. "Does Financial Globalization Induce Better Macroeconomic Policies?" Unpublished manuscript. Washington, DC: International Monetary Fund.

Wei, Shang-Jin. 2000a. "How Taxing Is Corruption on International Investors?" *Review of Economics and Statistics* 82(1): 1–11.

———. 2000b. "Local Corruption and Global Capital Flows." *Brookings Papers on Economic Activity* 2: 303–54.

———. 2000c. "Why Does China Attract So Little Foreign Direct Investment?" In *The Role of Foreign Direct Investment in East Asian Economic Development*, ed. Takatoshi Ito and Anne O. Krueger, 239–61. Chicago: University of Chicago Press.

———. 2001. "Domestic Crony Capitalism and International Fickle Capital: Is There a Connection?" *International Finance* 4(1): 15–45.

———. 2006. "Connecting Two Views on Financial Globalization: Can We Make Further Progress?" *Journal of Japanese and International Economics* 20(4): 459–81.

Wei, Shang-Jin and Yi Wu. 2002. "Negative Alchemy? Corruption, Composition of Capital Flows, and Currency Crises." In *Preventing Currency Crises in Emerging Markets*, ed. Sebastian Edwards and Jeffrey Frankel, 461–501. Chicago: University of Chicago Press.

Daniel H. Rosen

Prasad and Wei note that despite controlling the world's largest foreign exchange reserves (over $800 billion), China has a relatively small net capital inflow. Strong inbound FDI is countered by the modest outflow of portfolio investment and repatriated profits that are allowed under current restrictions on the capital account. China is *relatively* abundant in labor and scarce in capital; as a result, FDI sees higher rates of return in China compared to other markets. At the same time, weak domestic financial institutions and tightly controlled interest rates limit China's attractiveness for other forms of capital inflows, such as portfolio investment. Prasad and Wei describe this as the difference between returns to physical and financial capital. This is a useful way of understanding the nature of capital flows into and out of China and an appropriate way to organize my comments.

PHYSICAL CAPITAL: CHINA'S FDI STORY

Attracting a growing share of global FDI—from 1.7 percent in 1990 to 9.4 percent in 2004—China has become the envy of much of the developing world. Prasad and Wei dedicate much of their discussion to why China is a leading destination for FDI, the traditionally preferred form of inbound capital flows, including a review of the recent literature on the topic. They rightly discount the theory advanced by Dooley, Folkerts-Landau, and Garber that China has attracted FDI through a mercantilist strategy for export-led growth. Instead, Prasad and Wei ascribe China's FDI success to a confluence of factors, including a weak domestic financial system and relative domestic scarcity of capital. I largely agree with this explanation,

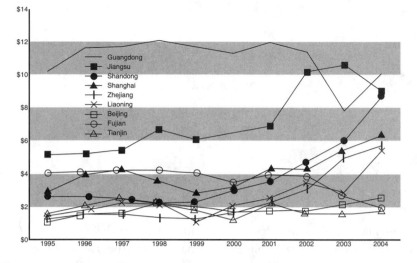

Figure 3.9   FDI by Province: Actual Utilized Investment, 1995–2004 (billions of U.S. dollars)

Source: CEIC.

although I think the authors miss some important aspects of the FDI story, some of which I will attempt to cover in this comment.

To fully understand the nature of FDI into China, it is necessary to recognize the difference between Guangdong Province, which has traditionally been an export platform, and the rest of China, where FDI has been more driven by interest in the domestic market. Until recently, Guangdong received the lion's share of FDI into China. As Prasad and Wei point out, over the past four years that has changed markedly. Figure 3.9 shows FDI inflows by province from 1995 to 2004. From 2001 onward, Guangdong has seen its share decline in comparison to the Yangtze River Delta provinces, especially Jiangsu, Zhejiang, and Shanghai.

Looking at what limited data are available on the variation in foreign-invested enterprises (FIEs) by region, we find that this trend has a significant bearing on the focus of FDI in China. Whereas FIEs in Guangdong are by and large net exporters, FIEs in the rest of China are more focused on the domestic market and have in fact traditionally been net importers (table 3.11). Although, as Prasad and Wei point out, the majority of FDI into China is directed into manufacturing, it is not

Table 3.11 Trade Balance for FIEs (net exports, millions of U.S. dollars)

Year	Guangdong	All but Guangdong
1996	402	−1,453
1997	4,044	−6,721
1998	7,403	−3,354
1999	5,478	−2,665
2000	7,010	−4,839
2001	10,046	−2,496
2002	10,668	−1,048
2003	16,070	−7,637
2004	17,003	−2,430

necessarily export-oriented, especially as more and more FDI is channeled outside Guangdong.

Even in Guangdong, the trade surplus may be overstated. Many analysts speculate that a substantial amount of the stated value of China's exports does not represent actual goods but, rather, overinvoicing by exporters and transfer payments between local operations and foreign affiliates. Tight controls on converting renminbi (RMB) to foreign currencies and speculation on exchange rate appreciation create an incentive to do both. A recent research note by Standard Chartered's Stephen Green estimates that $67 billion of China's $105 billion trade surplus in 2005 (based on Chinese figures) was really overinvoicing and transfer payments, used as a means of disguising profits and bringing additional foreign currency into the country.[1]

So if foreign enterprises are not investing in China simply as a platform to export back to their home markets, then what is attracting all that FDI? As Prasad and Wei point out, China's abundance of labor relative to capital translates into high returns on physical capital. Foreign firms invest in China because it is profitable to do so, even if the firm focuses entirely on the domestic market. This is borne out by the significant growth in repatriated profits over the past ten years, up to $30 billion annually (figure 3.10). It is not just the promise of a vast future market that attracts foreign capital to China; rather, it is the opportunity for profit right now.

China's labor abundance is necessary though not sufficient in explaining its large FDI inflows. India has a comparable-sized labor force with

Figure 3.10   Repatriated Profits: Billions of Dollars Sent Out of China by Foreign-Owned Investments in China

NOTE: Repatriated profits refer to payments abroad in respect of foreign-owned investments in the domestic economy, including interest, profit, and dividends, plus all forms of employee compensation.

Source: EIU.

lower average hourly wages, yet India's utilized FDI in 2005 was only $6.7 billion compared to over $60 billion for China. Policy toward foreign investment accounts for much of the difference. Prasad and Wei acknowledge that pro-FDI tax policies exist in China, but they caution that bureaucratic red tape and weakness in governance and in the legal system cancel out many of the positive effects. More important than the tax incentives, however, has been the degree to which China has opened the economy to FDI over the past 20 years. As in many developing countries, China initially permitted foreign investment only in special economic zones. But unlike smaller, more centrally administered countries, China was either unable to or uninterested in maintaining these restrictions. As the special economic zones prospered, local officials in other parts of the country began pressuring Beijing to allow foreign investment in their provinces. The resulting competition for foreign capital and technology has dramatically improved China's competitiveness and ability to attract FDI in a virtuous cycle.

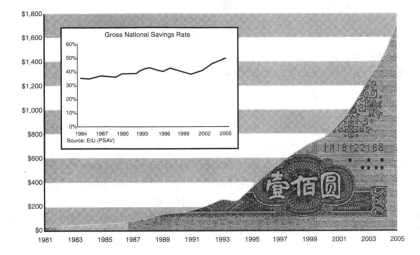

Figure 3.11   Super Savers: Total Savings Deposits, 1981–2005 (billions of U.S. dollars)
Sources: CEIC, CSA estimates.

Thus, China's FDI success is a combination of genuine comparative advantage in labor and a policy environment that promoted competition. If returns to physical capital are so good at home, what accounts for the outbound pressure on the capital account? As Prasad and Wei point out, a weak domestic banking system has meant that returns to financial capital have been significantly less attractive.

FINANCIAL CAPITAL: ROBBING CHINESE SAVERS

China is capital poor relative to labor, but it is not capital poor in absolute terms. Its 1.3 billion people save as much as 40 percent of their income, resulting in a financial system with over $1.9 trillion in household savings, in addition to $1.2 trillion in enterprise savings (figure 3.11). Because of tightly controlled interest rates and a closed capital account, however, China's savers have been forced to accept perhaps 2 percent returns on their savings. Prasad and Wei note in their essay that inefficient financial intermediation prevents savers from enjoying higher returns to financial capital. This has resulted in outbound capital flows wherever they are allowed for in the capital account. The authors argue that as the domestic financial system is opened to foreign competition and thus becomes more efficient, this already limited amount of capital flight will decline further, as the quality of returns domestically improves. They assume, however, that the capital account will remain closed for a considerable period. Recent events show this may not remain the case much longer.

Early on April 14, 2006 (oddly, just after midnight), the People's Bank of China (PBOC) released a public notice adjusting six foreign exchange policies. Each of the six policies makes it easier to transmit money out of China, mostly by opening some capital account flows. Every Chinese citizen will be able to buy up to $20,000 in foreign exchange *per year*, which they will soon be allowed to direct to foreign investments through qualified institutions. Mutual funds and securities companies will be able to invest abroad a quota of their *foreign exchange* holdings in China, whereas banks will be permitted to do this plus convert a quota of RMB into foreign exchange. Insurance companies are also admitted into the game, though they will be limited to investing in overseas fixed income securities (a less volatile, lower returning asset class). Meanwhile, back on the current account, converting RMB to foreign exchange to pay for foreign services (such as environmental remediation, asset management, design, and marketing) will be made much easier and may bolster the trade surplus in services that the United States already runs with China.

The *prospect* of significant exchange of RMB into dollars in order to invest Chinese savings abroad may change the thinking about the right exchange rate for the RMB and dollar. The actual effect that trading RMB and dollars will have on the market will, in the near term, be very small and not change any fundamentals; but the *psychological* effect of the prospect of $200 billion or more of RMB being cashed in for dollars over the next decade will temper currency speculators' thinking that RMB appreciation is a sure thing.

Estimates of RMB *undervaluation* in recent years generally suggested that 15 to 40 percent revaluation was called for, but all assumed a closed capital account. These estimates were debatable even under the assumption of a closed capital account. With the capital account partly open for capital outflows into the dollar, the euro, and the yen, the question of the RMB's long-term value is even less clear. Foreign views held by the IMF and G7 countries on the need for RMB revaluation do not seem to have softened, but the PBOC's moves have not had time to sink in yet.

These changes will have major implications for the domestic Chinese financial sector. Chinese households are in effect being robbed—or taxed, depending on which way you look at it—of the compounded interest they would enjoy in the United States or Europe. Given a higher return alternative, they will probably take it—up to the level permitted by quotas, of course. (Limits have not yet been set; there will be limits on outflows per institution, just as there are for foreign institutions that convert money *into* China to invest in China stocks.) This will put pressure on Chinese institutions to compete based on returns, as institutions do elsewhere, and to think harder about where they, in turn, lend money and how disciplined they are in recovering investments. Both of these notions—banks having to compete on returns and borrowers in the state sector having to pay a market price for their capital—are fairly radical for China.

In China, savings go into banks and are recycled as loans to state companies, but they can also flow into the struggling stock exchange, directly or via mutual funds. In 2006, as of the date of this writing, China's stock markets have seen 30 percent gains, and Shanghai brokers are feeling bullish and elated. But no Chinese fund manager can compare his 10-year record against Western average returns, and Chinese stock funds will experience enhanced pressure to raise returns. Chinese investment funds will have to demand better performance from China's listed companies. And if they cannot get this improved performance, they will have to maximize their options for investing in better governed companies elsewhere in the world.

A virtuous consequence of increased rates of return for savers is the wealth effect: over time, as they start to enjoy better capital gains on the savings they deposit, Chinese households will need to save less than the supposed 30 to 40 percent of disposable income they put aside now. (If capital gains are zero, then 40 percent savings rates are barely better than profligate; at a more reasonable 6 percent, 20 percent savings rates would be conservative.) This would mean a major boost for *consumption spending*, which is a holy grail for Beijing and Washington alike as they look for ways to relieve bilateral trade tensions.

These implications will play out starting now, but they will take years to be realized, even after the new measures are fully enacted. (Though announced, they will not come into force until the PBOC chooses, though the date for the first installment was set at May 1,

2006.) Implementation is contingent on stability in the Chinese financial sector, which is to say that these steps cannot lead to dangerous capital flight or they will be curtailed. But diversifying 10 percent of Chinese savings is imminently possible in the decade ahead (which presently means $300 billion-plus), and 20 percent is not out of keeping with regional patterns. More important than the end point of the changes is the strong signal about where China is going, which is what businesses and politicians must base their decisions on in the here and now. All signals point to deeper interdependence with the world economy and to broadening the scope and scale of economic reforms rather than slowing them.

Opening China's financial system to competition from mutual funds in New York may well do more for reform than opening domestic retail banking to foreign firms, as will happen at the end of 2006. In the long run, as returns on financial capital come closer to those on physical capital, the dramatic growth in FDI seen over the past few years will likely slow. On this point Prasad and Wei are correct. On the other side of the balance sheet, however, the slow pace of domestic reform coupled with moves to open the capital account means that outbound flows will pick up significantly in the near term.

CONCLUSION

China's lack of integration with global financial markets has served it well to this point, in terms of macroeconomic development. By opening to and encouraging FDI while limiting outbound capital flows, China has attracted an enviable amount of foreign investment (and accompanying technology), looking to take advantage of its comparative advantage in labor. China has been successful in becoming a global economic powerhouse while inoculating itself against the sometimes volatile global financial system.

Yet these choices have created microeconomic challenges that may hinder China's ability to climb the value ladder. The domestic financial system, shielded from international competition, is weak and inefficient. In labor-intensive industries, China excels, yet in industries where efficient allocation of capital is required, China is much less competitive. If China hopes to overcome what can be termed a "curse of labor," it must dramatically reform the way it handles investment. Opening up the capital account through the Qualified Domestic Institutional Investors program is a good start and will enable China to become a major source of FDI, not just a recipient.

NOTE

1. Stephen Green, "China's Trade: Bermuda Triangle, Accounting Issue or FX Flows?", *On the Ground in Asia*, April 13, 2006. Standard Chartered, Shanghai.

CHAPTER 4

Financial Openness and the Chinese Growth Experience

Geert Bekaert, Campbell R. Harvey, and Christian Lundblad

INTRODUCTION

If China's current rate of growth continues, the size of its economy will exceed that of the United States in only 12 years. Even if this projection is overly optimistic, China's growth track record has been remarkable, as can be seen in figure 4.1. Our chapter reflects on the Chinese growth experience from the perspective of an empirical multicountry model in the neoclassical tradition (see e.g., Barro 1997). That is, we link future growth to initial gross domestic product (GDP) per capita and a number of determinants of steady-state GDP, such as population growth, life expectancy, financial development, and the quality of institutions. We devote special attention to international openness. An extensive literature has documented the positive effects of trade openness on economic growth. China has progressively opened up its markets to trade and foreign direct investment (FDI) (see Branstetter and Lardy 2006, 2007 for a detailed account of this process), and we attempt to quantify the role of trade openness in the Chinese growth experience. China has also opened its capital markets to foreign investment, but this process is far from complete. Currently, a large debate is ongoing on the benefits of financial openness for growth (see, for instance, Prasad et al. 2003 for a summary article), which suggests that the growth effect is mixed. However, in this chapter we show, consistent with the results in Bekaert, Harvey, and Lundblad (2005) and Quinn and Toyoda (2003), that equity market openness and capital account openness are indeed associated with increased growth. Hence, China's efforts to open its capital account may further enhance growth.

Whatever the growth effect, many countries fear that opening their capital markets to foreign investors may have considerable costs in terms of real economic volatility. The crises many Southeast Asian countries underwent are often attributed to the capital market integration experience and the fact that China escaped the adverse growth consequences of the crises is seen as proof that capital controls may be beneficial (see the discussion in Forbes 2004). The current formal empirical investigations of the effects of financial openness on economic volatility do not yield a uniform picture: Kose, Prasad, and Torrones (2003) find that openness is associated with increased consumption to output volatility, whereas Bekaert, Harvey, and Lundblad (2006a) find mostly insignificant to negative effects.

In this chapter, we investigate the mean and volatility effects in a unified empirical framework developed in Bekaert, Harvey, and Lundblad (2006b). The framework also allows us to decompose the volatility experience of countries in their determinants. We estimate the system not only for GDP (output) growth but also for consumption growth. In standard representative agent models, average consumption growth and idiosyncratic consumption growth volatility would constitute the main determinants of a country's welfare.

It should be no surprise that the Chinese growth experience is difficult to capture by standard growth models and that, consequently, a benchmark model leads to a large and positive Chinese residual. We explore whether the Chinese growth puzzle can be attributed to the country receiving a high rate of foreign direct investment, low foreign debt, the high rate of domestic investment, or pure measurement problems, as suggested by, for example, Young (2003).

Our empirical framework measures average effects of financial openness, but there is much debate on whether China is "ready" for capital account openness (see, e.g., Prasad, Rumbaugh, and Wong 2005). It is quite conceivable that the effects of financial openness depend on local conditions and institutions. Prasad et al. (2003) and Bekaert, Harvey, and Lundblad (2006a) demonstrate the importance of such threshold effects. Therefore, we supplement our usual specification with a series of interaction variables to allow for heterogeneity in the openness impacts across countries. The interaction variables include measures of financial development, the role of government, the quality of institutions, and the investment climate.

The chapter, organized in seven sections, provides, respectively, some analysis of changes in the degree of financial openness through time as well as an assessment of financial development, political risk, and the quality of institutions in China; describes the data and provides some summary statistics; presents our econometric model, which explains both growth and volatility for a panel of countries; details our results on average growth; further explores the Chinese growth puzzle; summarizes our results on growth volatility; and studies the heterogeneity of the real effects of financial openness. Some concluding remarks are offered in the final section.

GROWTH DETERMINANTS AND CHINA

CHRONOLOGY AND SUMMARY DATA

Any examination of China's growth experience must start with a detailed examination of the country's history. Table 4.1 presents a chronology of important economic, political, and financial events over the past 25 years in China. While the Prasad and Wei chronology in appendix 2 focuses on important events related to the capital account in China, our chronology puts more focus on the equity market and broad macroeconomic events that affect financial development. We also pay special attention to regulatory events. The chronology is drawn from Bekaert and Harvey (2005) and details important events such as the dates when price fluctuation limits and stamp taxes changed, the formation of the China Securities Regulatory Commission (CSRC), and the introduction of A and B shares.

Figures 4.1–4.4 provide some summary analysis of China's growth experience. Figure 4.1 shows the time-series of real GDP and consumption growth. The growth rates are astounding. Since 1980, the lowest GDP growth rate has been 2.2 percent (in 2000). The average growth rate over this period is 7.8 percent. Consumption growth has averaged 7.0 percent; yet GDP growth and consumption have diverged in the last three years. During this period, consumption increased by only 1.7 percent per year, while GDP was increasing at a rate of 7.4 percent per year. This is also evident in figure 4.2, which shows the shares of the components of GDP. Consumption has dropped to only 40.4 percent of GDP. The comparable consumption ratio for the United States is 70.3 percent, and the average for all developing countries in 2003 is 68.3 percent. Investment in China is an extraordinary 44.3 percent of GDP. The U.S. investment ratio is 15.2 percent, and the average for developing countries is 21.5 percent. The share of investment to GDP in China is more than double the average for developing countries and almost three times the U.S. level. We show comparisons

Table 4.1 A Chronology of Economic, Political, and Financial Events in China

Date YYMMDD	Event
850314	Regulations governing the establishment of foreign joint ventures in Shanghai Province were relaxed.[IMF]
850315	China and India signed a three-year agreement to develop economic and trade relations; the accord provided for encouraging joint ventures, the creation of consultancy services, the exchange of economic, trade, and technical delegations, and participation.[IMF]
850326	The Foreign Economic Contract Law was adopted.[IMF]
850401	The Chinese Patent Law, enacted in 1984, came into effect. The Ministry of Petroleum and Industry announced that foreign oil companies would be allowed to participate in exploration and development of oil and gas reserves in nine provinces and one autonomous region.[IFC]
850402	The State Council introduced a regulation on the control of foreign banks and joint venture banks in special economic zones.[IMF]
850822	China approved establishment of the first foreign branch bank office in the country since 1949. Hong Kong and Shanghai Banking Corporation (a foreign commercial bank) announced a plan to begin branch operations in Shenzhen on October 5, 1985.[IMF]
851106	China and Libya signed a protocol aimed at consolidating bilateral cooperation between the two countries.[IMF]
851203	A joint venture bank was opened in Xiamen with the Panin Group of Hong Kong.[IMF]
870205	Provisional regulations were approved permitting financial institutions and enterprises with sources of foreign exchange income to guarantee foreign exchange obligations of other debtors.[IMF]
870827	Provisional regulations were issued on a new system requiring the timely registration of external borrowing with the State Administration of Exchange Control (SAEC).[IMF]
880413	The National People's Congress adopted a new Chinese-foreign cooperative joint ventures law.[IMF]
890214	All foreign commercial borrowing required the approval of the People's Bank of China (PBOC) and is to be channeled through one of ten domestic entities. The short-term debt of each entity may not exceed 20 percent of the entity's total debt, and short-term borrowing is to be used only for working-capital purposes.[IMF]
890306	The SAEC announced procedures governing Chinese direct investment abroad, which required government and SAEC approval, a deposit of 5 percent of the investment to secure repatriation of dividends and other income from the investment, and repatriation of earnings within six months.[IMF]
900404	The state would not nationalize joint ventures, simplified the approval procedures for new foreign investment enterprises, and extended the management rights of foreigners.[IMF]
900514	The Shanghai City Government announced plans for the development of the Pudong New Area, offering foreign joint ventures tax incentives similar to those available in the special economic zones.[IMF]

(continued)

Table 4.1 *continued*

Date YYMMDD	Event
900519	The State Council issued regulations for the sale and transfer of land-use rights in cities and towns to encourage foreign investors to plan long-term investment.[IMF]
901126	The Shanghai Securities Exchange reopened. It had been closed since December 8, 1941.[DT]
910409	The State Council adopted the Law Concerning the Income Tax of Foreign-Funded Enterprises and Foreign Enterprises and eliminated a 10 percent tax imposed on distributed profits remitted abroad by the foreign investors in foreign-funded enterprises.[IMF]
910426	The limit of daily price fluctuations increased from 0.5 percent to 1 percent.[GK]
910603	The stamp tax was decreased from 0.6 percent to 0.3 percent.[GK]
910926	"Regulations on Borrowing Overseas of Commercial Loans by Resident Institutions" and "Rules on Foreign Exchange Guarantee by Resident Institutions in China" were issued.[IMF]
910703	Shenzhen opened the country's second exchange.[DT]
9100	The "B" share came into existence. "B shares" can be owned by foreigners only, but they are afforded the same right of ownership as "A shares," which are reserved for Chinese nationals. In China, a share entitles the owner to a dividend distribution, but not to a right to influence the operations of the company.[CSRC]
9203	The policy on foreign trade and investment was further liberalized, opening a large number of island and border areas to such activities.[IMF]
920521	Free stock price was offered through free trading (less control of price formation). Shanghai index increased from 617 to 1266 on this day.[GK]
921026	China Securities Regulatory Commission begins.[GK]
9300	The Insider Trading Laws were introduced.[BD]
9305	Interim regulations were issued governing the activities of domestic investors, but there is no law explicitly covering the presence or activities of foreign firms. Foreign securities firms may establish representative offices, but they cannot establish local branches or subsidiaries. They can only purchase seats to broker "B" shares (denominated in renminbi [RMB] but must be purchased with foreign currency, issued by Chinese companies for sale exclusively to non-Chinese). Foreign firms cannot underwrite local securities issues or act as dealers or brokers in RMB-denominated securities.[DT]
930701	ADR effective date. (Company=SINOPEC SHANGHAI PETRO-CHEMICAL COMPANY LIMITED, Exchange=New York Stock Exchange).[BNY]
930806	A common order-driven market for A shares on Shanghai Stock Exchange was introduced. (Buy and sell orders compete for the best price. Throughout the trading session, customer orders are continuously matched according to price and time priorities.)[GK]

Table 4.1 *continued*

Date YYMMDD	Event
9400	The Chinese government converted four "specialized" banks into "commercial" banks by transferring their responsibilities for making noncommercial loans to three newly established "policy" bankings. The first PRC's central and commercial banking laws were passed to allow new, non-state-owned banks to set up business.[DT]
9400	The PBOC issued new supervisory guidelines requiring all banks to apply new credit control procedures designed to bring China in line with the risk-weighted capital adequacy established in the Basel Agreement. It also got approval to undertake a special U.S. $32 billion bond issue to re-capitalize the state-owned commercial banks and enable them to meet the 8 percent capital-adequacy ratio of the Basel Agreement.[DT]
940312	Announcement of the "Four No" rule. The chairman of the China Securities Regulatory Commission (CSRC) announced that RMB 5.5 billion new shares are not allowed to be traded on stock exchanges within half a year; the transaction tax for stocks would not be levied in 1994.[IFC]
940615	Illegal futures trading was prohibited.[GK]
9501	Real interest rates turned positive as inflation has been squeezed out of the economy.[DT]
950103	Initiate T+1 trading procedure. Stocks bought in one day could not be sold until the next day. This reduces intraday trading.[GK]
9503	Exports surged by 62 percent over last year, increasing trade surplus by $7 billion.[IFC]
950517	Futures trading stopped on treasury bonds due to CSRC concern that futures were attracting too much speculative money. On that day, the stock market surged 31 percent.[GK]
9505	The central bank increased the subsidy rate on bank deposits from 11.47 percent to 12.27 percent.[IFC]
950620	Commercial banks banned from entering stock or trust business.[GK]
9507	A new commercial bank law went into effect.[IFC]
9508	Inflation rate had decreased to 14.5 percent from 27 percent in October 1994.[IFC]
9511	China launched its first national interbank market linking 30 short-term credit offices across China into a single computer network.[IFC]
9603	China carried out three rounds of military exercise across the Taiwan Straits, clouding the relationship between two countries.[IFC]
9608	The government removed the authority of local city governments to manage the Shanghai and Shenzhen stock exchanges.[IFC]
9609	The Shanghai city government cut the income tax rate of Shanghai-based companies to 15 percent from 33 percent.[IFC]
960925	The regulation on External Guarantees Provided by Domestic Entities was passed, allowing for the provision of guarantees by authorized financial institutions and nonfinancial legal entities that have foreign exchange receipts.[IMF]
961003	Commissions for stock and fund transactions were decreased.[GK]

(continued)

Table 4.1 *continued*

Date YYMMDD	Event
9610	The CSRC issued a circular prohibiting Chinese from opening up stock trading accounts in the name of their work units.[IFC]
961114	Central Bank of China prohibits use of bank loans to invest in stocks.[GK]
961216	The CSRC tightened restrictions on Chinese residents opening B-share accounts, which are reserved for foreign investors. A new regulation that would limit the maximum daily change to 10 percent was imposed.[IFC]
970219	Paramount Chinese leader Deng Xiaoping died at age 92.[IFC]
9704	Government agreed to extend the preferential 15 percent corporate tax rate for 9 of 25 H-share stocks for another year.[IFC]
9705	The CSRC decided to retroactively boost the annual ceiling on new shares issued for 1996 by 50 percent. China's State Council opted to raise the stamp tax on stock trading to 0.5 percent from 0.4 percent.[IFC]
970606	Central Bank prohibited assets owned or controlled by banks from being used to purchase stocks.[GK]
970701	Hong Kong was handed over to China.[IFC]
9711	Securities Commission promulgated rules for establishing mutual funds.[IFC]
980101	Regulations for issuing bonds denominated in foreign currency by domestic institutions were issued. (Controls on credit operations) (1) The implementation bylaws of regulations for external guarantees by domestic institutions were issued. (2) Forward lines of credit with a maturity exceeding 90 days and less than 365 days have been included in the category of short-term credit, while those exceeding one year have been included in the category of medium- and long-term international commercial loans. (3) External borrowing regulations were changed. [IMF]
9802	Three-month interbank rates in Hong Kong drop to 7.143 percent, the lowest level since the previous October.[IFC]
9803	The Consumer Price Index fell 1.9 percent, marking the fifth straight monthly decline.[IFC]
9804	S&P revised Chinese foreign currency rating from stable to negative.[IFC]
9805	The government banned all activities of direct sales companies such as Amway and Avon.[SP]
980612	Weak Japanese yen forced Chinese exports to see its first decline in 22 months. The government cut the stock trading tax to 0.4 percent from 0.5 percent.[IFC]
9807	China cut bank lending rates on July 1 by 1.12 percent. The Japan Rating and Investment Information downgraded China's sovereign rating to A+ from AA−.[IFC]
9808	Catastrophic floods occurred along the Yangtze River, the country's worst since 1954. It was speculated that Beijing might devalue its currency because of a weaker Japanese yen and slower domestic growth.[IFC]
980820	(Controls on credit operations) Enterprises were barred from advance prepayment of debt. [IMF]

Table 4.1 *continued*

Date YYMMDD	Event
9809	The central bank ordered all companies to repatriate foreign currency held overseas without authorization by October 1. On September 7, the Hong Kong Stock Exchange instituted a "tick rule" for short-sellers.[IFC]
9810	China closed the 18-year-old GITIC (the Guangdong International Trust and Investment Corporation) on October 6, after the company missed an $8.75 million payment on a bond.[IFC]
9812	China's first securities law was passed on December 29. Under the laws, brokers are banned from using client funds to finance their own operations and foreigners may not buy A shares.[IFC]
9901	More than 70 companies in Shenzhen and at least 63 companies in Shanghai announced that they would report a net loss for 1998.[IFC]
9904	The government decided to allow cash-strapped brokerages to tap funds from the interbank market and state debt repurchase market. Measures that exempted foreign companies from 3 percent of local income tax were adopted by Beijing Municipal Government.[SP]
9905	The stamp duty on B-share trading was cut to 0.3 percent from 0.4 percent this month.[IFC]
9906	The PBOC announced it would cut rates on deposits by an average of 0.75 percent.[IFC]
9907	The tension in the Taiwan Straits was raised by a speech of President Lee Teng Hui that scrapped the "one China" policy.[IFC]
990715	(Controls on credit operations) Some controls on renminbi loans to foreign-funded enterprises under foreign exchange liens or guarantees were eased.[IMF]
990908	The CSRC allowed state-owned enterprises and all listed companies to issue shares and trade stocks.[GK]
9909	China planned to allow more banks and high-tech private firms to tap the stock market for financing.[IFC]
9910	The government imposed a 20 percent tax on bank deposit interest income and other market initiatives. Beijing allowed two state firms to sell state-owned shares and permitted certain share buybacks for Chinese B and H shares.[IFC]
9911	The Tracker Fund, representing part of the Hong Kong Special Administrative Region government's HK$208 billion (U.S. $27 billion) share portfolio, was listed. The Stock Exchange of Hong Kong launched the Growth Enterprise Market (GEM) for small-cap and high-tech firms, creating an outflow of foreign liquidity from the Mainland B-share market to the Hong Kong GEM market.[IFC]
200004	The CSRC allowed state and listed firms to purchase domestic IPOs without restrictions on the size of these stakes.[IFC]
200006	China Unicom Ltd. became the third-largest IPO in the world.[IFC]
200006	The Chinese government decided to delay the setup of a NASDAQ-style market for high-growth companies and announced the launch of its first mutual fund to be advised by foreign fund companies. Beijing formally approved the merger of the A-share markets of the Shanghai and Shenzhen exchanges.[IFC]

(continued)

Table 4.1 *continued*

Date YYMMDD	Event
200010	The government announced a planned interest rate reform and published regulations on the opening of the telecommunications sector. China Petroleum & Chemical Corp.'s IPO became the fifth largest in the world for the year.[IFC]
200100	The crackdown on share price manipulation by the China Securities Regulatory Commission rekindled investor concerns about China's volatile stock market.[IFC]
20010222	The opening of the B-share market to domestic investors boosted the markets. Domestic investors could only invest with existing foreign currency deposits.[IFC]
200105	China cut interest rates on its foreign currency deposits, following the United States' rate cuts.[IFC]
20010601	Domestic investors now invest in B shares with new foreign currency deposits.[PW]
200100	During the third quarter, the government cracked down on illegal bank loans to stock market speculators and its practice of selling shares to finance pension obligations.[IFC]
200108	China Mobile and China Unicom, the two leading telecommunications companies, saw share prices plunge on investor fears about market growth potential and profit margins.[IFC]
20010917	The World Trade Organization (WTO) successfully concluded negotiations on China's entry.[WTO]
20010919	Rules relaxed for purchasing foreign exchange for advance repayments of certain debt.[PW]
200110	The government suspended the sale of state-owned shares.[IFC]
20011116	Stamp tax decreased from 0.3 percent to 0.2 percent.[GK]
200112	New regulations were announced to tighten delisting rules. A major international rating agency upgraded China's sovereign rating.[IFC]
20011211	China's accession to the WTO included promises to open their markets to international competition.[WTO]
20020128	The regulations governing foreign banks and financial institutions were issued by the People's Bank of China and were to take effect on February 1, replacing the five sets of regulations in force since 1996.[IFC]
20020200	U.S. President George W. Bush visits, on the 30th anniversary of President Richard Nixon's visit to China (the first visit by a U.S. president).[IFC]
20020312	The government announced easing of restrictions limiting foreign investors to minority stakes in port infrastructure projects and approved foreign investment in urban pipeline projects for gas, heating, and water as part of the revised Industrial Catalogue for Foreign Investment, due to take effect on April 1, 2002.[WMA]
20020700	The United States said China was modernizing its military to make possible a forcible reunification with Taiwan. Beijing responded that its policy remained defensive.[IFC]
20021009	China let private and foreign investors buy controlling stakes in domestically listed firms for the first time.[IFC]
20021104	The authorities announced that foreign companies would be allowed to buy shares in listed Chinese companies.[IFC]

Table 4.1 *continued*

Date YYMMDD	Event
20021105	The CSRC and China's central bank (the PBOC) issued the Temporary Measures for Investment in Domestic Securities by Qualified Foreign Institutional Investors (the "QFII Regulation"), effective December 1, 2002. This monumental piece of legislation, for the first time in history, permitted foreign investors to directly invest and trade in publicly listed domestic securities. The historic regulation, released on the eve of the opening of the 16th Communist Party Congress, covers: (i) the eligibility standards of a Qualified Foreign Institutional Investor (a "QFII"), (ii) the foreign exchange aspect of the transactions, including the qualification and operation of the depositary banks and the management of the special QFII accounts at such banks, and (iii) control of the investment transactions per se.[RP]
20021105	Definition of Qualified Foreign Institutional Investor. (1) Funds (at least five years of operating history, more than U.S. $10 billion under management); (2) Insurance companies (at least 30 years of operating history, more than U.S. $10 billion under management); (3) Securities firms (at least 30 years of operating history, more than U.S. $10 billion under management); (4) Commercial banks (total assets ranked in top 100 globally and more than U.S. $10 billion under management).[RP]
20021115	Vice-President Hu Jintao was named head of the ruling Communist Party, replacing Jiang Zemin, the outgoing president. Jiang was reelected head of the influential Central Military Commission, which oversees the armed forces.[IFC]
20021203	China went back on its plan to allow foreign investors into the country's bond market as the registration process for QFIIs opened (December 2). QFIIs allowed to invest in A shares, subject to regulations.[IFC]
20021200	The seven-year RMB 60bn (U.S. $7.25bn) bond sale completed. The bond was oversubscribed by 22 times on generous terms offered by the Ministry of Finance.[WMA]
20030300	National People's Congress elected Hu Jintao as president. He replaced Jiang Zemin, who stepped down after 10 years in the post.[IFC]
20030311	A new rural land reform in China, extending land-use rights to 30 years, is expected to provide a significant boost to the rural economy by encouraging new investment and providing a source of capital.[IFC]
20030300	China and Hong Kong were hit by the pneumonia-like SARS virus, which was thought to have originated in Guangdong Province in November 2002. Strict quarantine measures were enforced to stop the disease from spreading.[WMA]
20030400	New rules on mergers and acquisitions were issued as China sought to facilitate mergers and acquisitions activity and boost inward investment.[WMA]
20030527	Two foreign brokers were granted the right to trade in RMB-denominated securities for the first time, marking a milestone in the development of China's capital market.[IFC]

(continued)

Table 4.1 *continued*

Date YYMMDD	Event
20030600	Sluice gates on Three Gorges Dam were closed to allow the reservoir to fill up. Construction of $25 billion project displaced almost one million people to make way for world's largest hydroelectric scheme.[BBC]
20030600	China India reached de facto agreement over status of Tibet and Sikkim in landmark cross-border trade agreement.[IFC]
20030600	Standard & Poor's estimated that Chinese banks needed U.S. $500bn bailout.[WMA]
20030700	Some 500,000 people marched in Hong Kong against Article 23, a controversial antisubversion bill. Two key Hong Kong government officials resigned. The government shelved the bill.[IFC]
20030800	The Chinese government announced reduction of the country's armed forces by 200,000 by 2005.[IFC]
20030900	Wu Bangguo, the Standing Committee chairman of the National People's Congress (NPC), confirmed that exchange rate policy would continue to focus on RMB stability, but asserted that a shift to market-based determination remained the government's ultimate goal.[IFC]
20031202	Authorities in China asserted no change in foreign exchange policy.
20040100	Ceiling for foreign investment in a Chinese bank was raised from 20 percent to 25 percent. Any single foreign bank's share was raised from 15 percent to 20 percent.[PW]
20040100	The Chinese government dipped into its U.S. $400bn foreign exchange reserves in order to recapitalize two of the big four state-owned banks, in a move to accelerate reform in the country's ailing financial sector.[WMA]
20040100	The World Bank's private sector division—the International Finance Corporation (IFC)—announced that it intended to double its investment in China, up to U.S. $500m by 2006.[IFC]
20040203	The country's State Council issued new investment guidelines for listed companies, clearing the way for greater capital investment and brokerage opportunities. The plan called for the establishment of a multilayered capital market system, consisting of a main board market and a secondary one for venture capital projects and corporate bond/futures products.[WMA]
20040200	The IFC arm of the World Bank confirmed that it had committed U.S. $2m to the Chinese mortgage market.[IFC]
2004	Qualified foreign institutional investors (QFIIs) were allowed to invest in A shares.[PW]
20040300	The U.S. government filed its first official suit against China under the auspices of the WTO, claiming that a tax on semiconductors gave domestic exporters unfair advantage. The suit underlined the United States' increasingly hard-line stance over bilateral trade, the inequities of which were embodied in the U.S. trade deficit with China, which ballooned to U.S. $124bn in 2003.[WMA]
20040426	Legislators rule out direct elections for Hong Kong leader in 2007.[IFC]

Table 4.1 *continued*

Date YYMMDD	Event
20040516	Liu Mingkang, head of the China Banking Regulatory Commission, said that China's banks should sue the firms and people whose bad debts were destabilizing the banking system.[IFC]
20040601	China's banking regulator ordered tighter scrutiny of bank lending as part of a government campaign against reckless investment.[IFC]
20040614	China's Premier Wen Jiabao stressed the need for local officials to implement policies designed to cool down China's overheating economy.[BBC]

Year	Regulations on Foreign Investors
1998	Restrictions: Foreign investors can only hold Class B shares. Investment amounts must be registered separately with each exchange. Holdings of more than 5 percent of total issued shares of a company must be reported to the People's Bank of China.
	Taxation: Rules on capital gains tax are being finalized. Dividends are untaxed. 0.3 percent stamp duty, 0.5 percent value transaction fee, 0.1 percent registration fee. $8 per transaction clearing fee with a custodian bank, and $4 without a custodian bank, $20 depository.
1999	Restrictions: Same. All settlements and income receipts are in U.S. dollars or Hong Kong dollars, without repatriation difficulty.
	Taxation: No capital gains tax. Dividend income is subject to 20 percent withholding tax applied at the registration company on the portion of dividends above the PBOC's (the central bank) one-year RMB certificate of deposit rate for the same period.[B]
2000	Restrictions: Requirements on foreign exchange balancing and domestic sales ratios were eliminated.
2001	Restrictions: Foreign-funded firms who wish to list on the Shanghai and Shenzhen stock exchanges must have operated in China for 3 years and give details of all foreign shareholders with more than 5 percent of the firm's stock.
	Taxation: 30 percent national corporate tax, 3 percent local corporate tax, 33 percent capital gains tax.
2002	Restrictions: (1)-Foreign bank branches must have at least U.S. $72.5 million in operating capital, and they will be able to conduct foreign and domestic currency business. Wholly foreign-owned banks and Sino-foreign joint venture banks must maintain a minimum registered capital of U.S. $120.8 million, 60 percent of which must be held in local currency and 40 percent in hard currencies. (2) Nonbank financial institutions, wholly foreign-owned and joint venture firms, are required to have a minimum registered capital of U.S. $84.6 million.

(continued)

Table 4.1   *continued*

Date YYMMDD	Event
2004	Qualified foreign institutional investors (QFIIs) are allowed to invest in A shares with the following conditions: (1) five years of investment experience and 30 years for insurance companies, plus they must manage at least $10 billion in assets and have no accounting irregularities over the past three years; (2) bank must be in top 100 of assets under management in world; (3) minimum paid-up capital for insurance company or a securities firm of $1 billion; (4) maximum ownership of any company listed in Shanghai or Shenzhen stock exchange is 10 percent and for any company it cannot exceed 20 percent; (5) QFIIs must use local banks and local securities firms. Special renminbi accounts must be set up; (6) closed-end QFIIs cannot remit capital until three years have passed from initial investment. Other QFIIs can remit capital after year. Closed-end QFIIs cannot remit more than 20 percent of capital at a time, and the minimum time between installments is one month. Other QFIIs also cannot remit more than 20 percent of the capital at any time. In this case, the minimum time between remittances is three months. In addition to these limits, there is a cap on total A-share purchases by QFIIs, which has severely limited foreign holdings (to less than $20 billion as of 2007).[PW]

References

B	Bridge, *The Bridge Handbook of World Stock, Derivative & Commodity Exchanges* (2000).
BBC	British Broadcasting System, UK edition.
BD	Utpal Bhattacharya and Hazem Daouk, "The World Price of Insider Trading," *Journal of Finance* 57(1) (2002): 75–108.
BNY	Bank of New York Web site, www.bankofny.com/.
CSRC	China Securities Regulatory Commission Web site, www.csrc.gov.cn.
DT	Department of Treasury, *National Treatment Study*.
GK	Lei Gao and Gerhard Kling, "Regulatory Changes and Market Liquidity in Chinese Stock Markets," *Emerging Markets Review* 7(2) (2006): 162–175.
IFC	International Finance Corporation, *Factbook* (various years).
IMF	International Monetary Fund, *Annual Report of Exchange Arrangements and Exchange Restrictions* (1980–2000).
PW	Eswar Prasad and Shang-Jin Wei, "Capital Flows into China" (2005).
RP	Roger Peng, "China Releases Temporary Measures for Investment," Morrison and Foerster, November 2002.
SP	Standard & Poor's Web site, www.standardandpoors.com/.
WMA	World Market Research Centre, *World Market Analysis*.
WTO	World Trade Organization, http://www.wto.org/English/thewto_ e/ countries_e/china_e.htm.

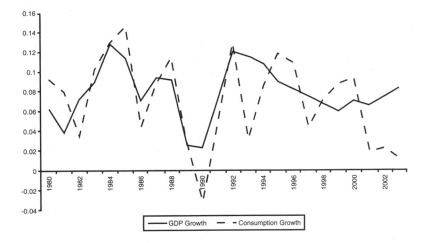

Figure 4.1   Macroeconomic Growth: China (real per capita U.S. dollars)

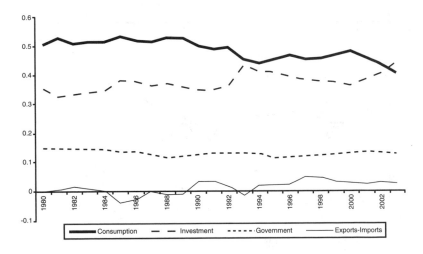

Figure 4.2   GDP Components: China

with other countries (grouped over developed and developing countries) in figure 4.3. Interestingly, exports minus imports comprises only 2.6 percent of GDP; consequently China runs, on average, a current account surplus. This is atypical for a developing country, as figure 4.3 demonstrates. China's huge investment level is mainly financed using domestic savings.

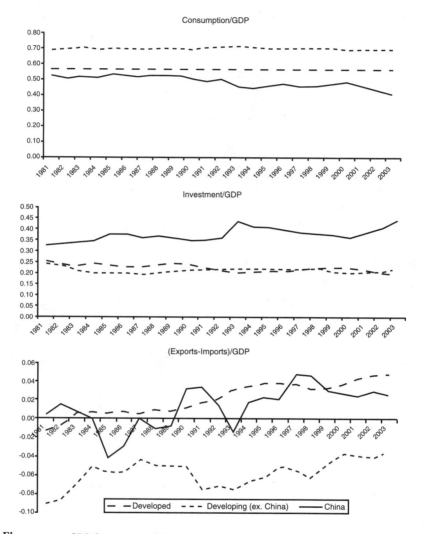

Figure 4.3   GDP Components: Comparison

China's high growth has not been associated with increased macroeconomic volatility (see figure 4.4). A rolling five-year standard deviation in China's GDP growth has dropped from a level of about 3 percent in the 1980s and 1990s to a level of 0.8 percent since 2000. Consumption growth volatility is higher but shows a similar pattern. In the 1980s, consumption growth volatility averaged 6.3 percent. The volatility decreased to 4.9 percent in the 1990s. Over the past four years, the volatility has decreased to 3.3 percent.

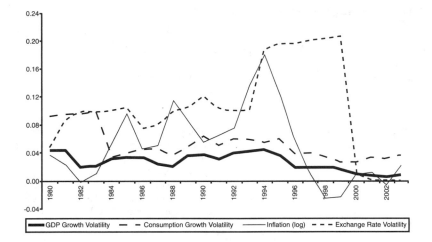

Figure 4.4   Macroeconomic Volatility: China (five-year rolling standard deviation)

DATA

Our multicountry macroeconomic and financial data, spanning the period from 1980 through 2003, are drawn from a number of sources detailed in table 4.2.[1] In our empirical exercises, we consider a broad cross section of countries. Unfortunately, measures of stock market development and the quality of institutions are available for only a limited set of countries. Our sample size is determined by data availability and ranges from 51 to 96 countries.

SUMMARY STATISTICS

We now examine some of the key variables and provide summary statistics. We consider developed markets as well as developing markets; regional averages across Asia, Africa, and Latin America; and the values for China. As a general warning sign, one difficulty our analysis faces is that quantitative measures do not always reflect the true regulatory constraints faced by economic agents operating in China. Before we examine a number of potentially important determinants of economic growth, let us use the numbers reported in table 4.3 to compare the Chinese growth experience with that of the rest of the world. Developed countries grow on average about 2 percent per year on a per capita basis, with about 2 percent volatility. Developing countries do not even generate 1 percent growth,

Table 4.2   Description of the Variables

Variable	Description
Gross domestic product (GDP) and its subcomponents	Real per capita GDP (and its components: consumption, investment, government expenditures, and exports less imports). Available for all countries from 1980 through 2003. *Source*: *World Bank Development Indicators* CD-ROM.
Capital Stock and Total Factor Productivity (TFP) Growth	We build per capita physical capital stocks over the 1980–2003 period using the method in King and Levine (1993). We derive an initial estimate of the capital stock, assuming each country is at its steady-state capital-output ratio at that time. Then, we use the aggregate real investment series and the perpetual inventory method with a depreciation rate of 7 percent to compute the capital stock in later years. TFP is calculated as the difference between the GDP growth rate and 0.3 times the capital stock growth rate, assuming a capital share of 0.3.

Measures of Openness

Quinn Capital account openness indicator	Quinn's capital account openness measure is also created from the text of the annual volume published by the International Monetary Fund (IMF), *Exchange Arrangements and Exchange Restrictions*. Rather than the indicator constructed by the IMF that takes a 1 if any restriction is in place, Quinn's openness measure is scored 0–4, in half-integer units, with 4 representing a fully open economy. The measure thus facilitates a more nuanced view of capital account openness and is available for 48 countries in our study. We transform the measure into a 0 to 1 scale.
Official equity market liberalization indicator	Corresponding to a date of formal regulatory change after which foreign investors officially have the opportunity to invest in domestic equity securities. Official liberalization dates are based on Bekaert and Harvey (2005), *A Chronology of Important Financial, Economic and Political Events in Emerging Markets*, http://www.duke.edu/~charvey/chronology.htm. This chronology is based on over 50 different source materials. A condensed version of the chronology, along with the selection of dates for a number of countries appears in Bekaert and Harvey (2000). We have extended their official liberalization dates to include Japan, New Zealand, and Spain. For the liberalizing countries, the associated official liberalization indicator takes a value of one when the equity market is officially liberalized and thereafter, and zero otherwise. For the remaining countries, fully segmented countries are assumed to have an indicator value of zero, and fully liberalized countries are assumed to have an indicator value of 1.

Table 4.2 *continued*

Variable	Description
Intensity equity market openness indicator	Following Bekaert (1995) and Edison and Warnock (2003), the intensity measure is based on the ratio of the market capitalization of the constituent firms comprising the IFC Investable index to those that comprise the IFC Global index for each country. The IFC Global index, subject to some exclusion restrictions, is designed to represent the overall market portfolio for each country, whereas the IFC Investable index is designed to represent a portfolio of domestic equities that are available to foreign investors. A ratio of one means that all of the stocks are available to foreign investors. Fully segmented countries have an intensity measure of zero, and fully liberalized countries have an intensity measure of one.
Initial GDP	Logarithm of real per capita GDP in 1980. Available for all countries. *Source*: *World Bank Development Indicators* CD-ROM.
Log life expectancy	Life expectancy at birth indicates the number of years a newborn infant would live if prevailing patterns of mortality at the time of its birth were to stay the same throughout its life. Available for all countries. *Source*: *World Bank Development Indicators* CD-ROM.
Population growth	Growth rate of total population which counts all residents regardless of legal status or citizenship. Available for all countries. *Source*: *World Bank Development Indicators* CD-ROM.
Trade/GDP	The trade dependency ratio is the sum of exports and imports of goods and services measured as a share of gross domestic product. Available for all countries. *Source*: *World Bank Development Indicators* CD-ROM.
Inflation	Inflation as measured by the log annual growth rate of the GDP implicit deflator. We use the CPI; if the GDP-deflator is not available. Available for all countries. *Source*: *World Bank Development Indicators* CD-ROM.
Private credit/GDP	Private credit divided by GDP. Credit to private sector refers to financial resources provided to the private sector, such as through loans, purchases of nonequity securities, and trade credits and other accounts receivable that establish a claim for repayment. Available for all countries. *Source*: *World Bank Development Indicators* CD-ROM. We also construct an *adjusted* private credit measure controlling for state ownership of the banking system. We interpolate the state ownership ratios provided by La Porta, Lopez de Silanes, and Shleifer (2002) for two years during our sample to the full sample, and create a new measure of banking development as official private credit to GDP times (1 − the ratio of state ownership).
Equity market turnover	The ratio of equity market value traded to the market capitalization. The data are available for 50 countries. *Source*: Standard & Poor's/International Finance Corporation's *Emerging Stock Markets Factbook*.

(continued)

Table 4.2 *continued*

Variable	Description
MCAP/GDP	The ratio of equity market capitalization to GDP. The data are available for 50 countries. *Source*: Standard & Poor's/International Finance Corporation's *Emerging Stock Markets Factbook*.
Economic risk rating	The value of the Political Risk Service (PRS) Group's economic risk indicator (which ranges between 0 and 50). The risk rating is a combination of 5 subcomponents: GDP levels and growth, respectively, inflation, balanced budgets, and the current account. The minimum number of points for each component is zero, while the maximum number of points depends on the fixed weight that component is given in the overall economics risk assessment.
Political risk rating	The value of the PRS Group's political risk indicator (which ranges between 0 and 100). The risk rating is a combination of 12 subcomponents (documented below). Overall, a political risk rating of 0.0 to 49.9 percent indicates a Very High Risk; 50.0 to 59.9 percent High Risk; 60.0 to 69.9 percent Moderate Risk; 70.0 to 79.9 percent Low Risk; and 80.0 percent or more Very Low Risk. The data are available for 75 countries from 1984 through 1997. For each country, we backfill the 1984 value to 1980. *Source*: Various issues of the *International Country Risk Guide*. There are 12 subcomponents to this index. We create four subindices: POL1 (Political Conditions), POL2 (Quality of Institutions), POL3 (Socioeconomic conditions), and POL4 (Conflict).
Political Conditions	The sum of International Country Risk Guide (ICRG) subcomponents: Military in Politics and Democratic Accountability
Military in Politics	ICRG political risk subcomponent (6 percent weight). The military is not elected by anyone. Therefore, its involvement in politics, even at a peripheral level, is a diminution of democratic accountability. However, it also has other significant implications. The military might, for example, become involved in government because of an actual or created internal or external threat. Such a situation would imply the distortion of government policy in order to meet this threat, for example by increasing the defense budget at the expense of other budget allocations. In some countries, the threat of military takeover can force an elected government to change policy or cause its replacement by another government more amenable to the military's wishes. A military takeover or threat may also represent a high risk if it is an indication that the government is unable to function effectively and that the country therefore has an uneasy environment for foreign businesses. A full-scale military regime poses the greatest risk.

Table 4.2 *continued*

Variable	Description
Democratic Accountability	ICRG political risk subcomponent (6 percent weight). This is a measure of how responsive government is to its people, on the basis that the less responsive it is, the more likely it is that the government will fall, peacefully in a democratic society, but possibly violently in a nondemocratic one. However, assessing democratic accountability is more complex than simply determining whether the country has free and fair elections. Even democratically elected governments, particularly those that are apparently popular, can delude themselves into thinking they know what is good for their people even when the people have made it abundantly clear that they do not approve of particular policies. Therefore, it is possible for an accountable democracy to have a lower score, that is, a higher risk, for this component than a less democratic form of government.
Quality of Institutions	The sum of ICRG subcomponents: Corruption, Law and Order, and Bureaucratic Quality.
Corruption	ICRG political risk subcomponent (6 percent weight). This is a measure of corruption within the political system. Such corruption distorts the economic and financial environment, reduces the efficiency of government and business by enabling people to assume positions of power through patronage rather than ability, and introduces an inherent instability into the political process. The most common form of corruption met directly by business is financial corruption in the form of demands for special payments and bribes connected with import and export licenses, exchange controls, tax assessments, police protection, or loans. Although the PRS measure takes such corruption into account, it is more concerned with actual or potential corruption in the form of excessive patronage, nepotism, job reservations, "favor-for-favors," secret party funding, and suspiciously close ties between politics and business. In PRS's view, these sorts of corruption pose risk to foreign business, potentially leading to popular discontent, unrealistic and inefficient controls on the state economy, and encourage the development of the black market.
Law and Order	ICRG political risk subcomponent (6 percent weight). PRS assesses Law and Order separately, with each subcomponent comprising zero to three points. The Law subcomponent is an assessment of the strength and impartiality of the legal system, while the Order subcomponent is an assessment of popular observance of the law. Thus, a country can enjoy a high rating (3.0) in terms of its judicial system but a low rating (1.0) if the law is ignored for a political aim.

(continued)

Table 4.2 *continued*

Variable	Description
Bureaucratic Quality	ICRG political risk subcomponent (4 percent weight). The institutional strength and quality of the bureaucracy can act as a shock absorber that tends to minimize revisions of policy when governments change. Therefore, high points are given to countries where the bureaucracy has the strength and expertise to govern without drastic changes in policy or interruptions in government services. In these low-risk countries, the bureaucracy tends to be somewhat autonomous from political pressure and to have an established mechanism for recruitment and training. Countries that lack the cushioning effect of a strong bureaucracy receive low points because a change in government tends to be traumatic in terms of policy formulation and day-to-day administrative functions.
Socioeconomic Conditions	The sum of ICRG subcomponents: Government Stability, Socioeconomic Conditions, and Investment Profile.
Government stability	ICRG political risk subcomponent (12 percent weight). This is a measure both of the government's ability to carry out its declared program(s) and its ability to stay in office. This will depend on the type of governance, the cohesion of the government and governing party or parties, the closeness of the next election, the government's command of the legislature, and popular approval of government policies.
Socioeconomic Conditions	ICRG political risk subcomponent (12 percent weight). This is an attempt to measure general public satisfaction, or dissatisfaction, with the government's economic policies. In general terms, the greater the popular dissatisfaction with a government's policies, the greater the chances that the government will be forced to change direction, possibly to the detriment of business, or will fall. Socioeconomic conditions cover a broad spectrum of factors ranging from infant mortality and medical provision to housing and interest rates. Within this range different factors will have different weight in different societies. PRS attempts to identify those factors that are important for the society in question, that is, those with the greatest political impact, and assess the country on that basis.
Investment Profile	ICRG political risk subcomponent (12 percent weight). This is a measure of the government's attitude to inward investment. The investment profile is determined by PRS's assessment of three subcomponents: (1) risk of expropriation or contract viability; (2) payment delays; and (3) repatriation of profits. Each subcomponent is scored on a scale from zero (very high risk) to four (very low risk).
Conflict	The sum of ICRG subcomponents: Internal Conflict, External Conflict, Religious Tensions, Ethnic Tensions.

Table 4.2 *continued*

Variable	Description
Internal Conflict	ICRG political risk subcomponent (12 percent weight). This is an assessment of political violence in the country and its actual or potential impact on governance. The highest rating is given to those countries where there is no armed opposition to the government and the government does not indulge in arbitrary violence, direct or indirect, against its own people. The lowest rating is given to a country embroiled in an ongoing civil war. The intermediate ratings are awarded on the basis of whether the threat posed is to government and business or only business (e.g., kidnapping for ransom); whether acts of violence are carried out for a political objective (i.e., terrorist operations); whether such groups are composed of a few individuals with little support or are well-organized movements operating with the tacit support of the people they purport to represent; whether acts of violence are sporadic or sustained; and whether they are restricted to a particular locality or region, or are carried out nationwide.
External Conflict	ICRG political risk subcomponent (12 percent weight). The external conflict measure is an assessment of the risk to both the incumbent government and inward investment. It ranges from trade restrictions and embargoes, whether imposed by a single country, a group of countries, or the whole international community, through geopolitical disputes, armed threats, exchanges of fire on borders, border incursions, foreign-supported insurgency, and full-scale warfare.
Religion in Politics	ICRG political risk subcomponent (6 percent weight). Religious tensions may stem from the domination of society and/or governance by a single religious group that seeks to replace civil law by religious law and to exclude other religions from the political and/or social process; the desire of a single religious group to dominate governance; the suppression of religious freedom; the desire of a religious group to express its own identity, separate from the country as a whole. The risk involved in these situations ranges from inexperienced people imposing inappropriate policies through civil dissent to civil war.
Ethnic Tensions	ICRG political risk subcomponent (6 percent weight). This component measures the degree of tension within a country attributable to racial, nationality, or language divisions. Lower ratings are given to countries where racial and nationality tensions are high because opposing groups are intolerant and unwilling to compromise. Higher ratings are given to countries where tensions are minimal, even though such differences may still exist.

(continued)

Table 4.2 *continued*

Variable	Description
BERI Measures on Privatization, Credit Market, and Financial Openness	Three indices collected from Business Environment Risk Intelligence (BERI). Privatization measures the degree of privatization within each country. The Credit Market index reflects the stability and operating climate of the short-term credit, long-term loans, and venture capital markets. Finally, the Financial Openness index reflects the legal framework surrounding remittances and the repatriation of capital, with attention to both how the laws are formally written and the actual practices within each country. For each index, a larger number denotes an improvement.
Social Security Index	From Botero, Djankov, La Porta, Lopez-de-Silanes, and Shleifer (2002), measures social security benefits: (1) old age, disability, and death benefits; (2) sickness and health benefits; and (3) unemployment benefits. The first group covers the risk of old age, disability, and death: months of contributions or employment required for normal retirement by law; percentage of the worker's monthly salary deducted by law to cover old-age and disability benefits; and percentage of the pre-retirement salary covered by the old-age cash-benefit pension. The second group covers the risk of sickness: months of contributions or employment required to qualify for sickness benefits by law; percentage of the worker's monthly salary deducted by law to cover sickness and health benefits; waiting period for sickness benefits; and percentage of the salary covered by sickness cash benefits for a two-month sickness spell. The final group covers the risk of unemployment: months of contributions or employment required to qualify for unemployment benefits by law; percentage of the worker's monthly salary deducted by law to cover unemployment benefits; waiting period for unemployment benefits; and percentage of the salary covered by unemployment benefits in case of a one-year unemployment spell. Each subgroup is quantitatively scored and summed to create the overall index.
Foreign Debt Index	ICRG financial risk subcomponent. The constructed index reflects the estimated gross foreign debt in a given year as a percentage of the GDP. The risk points are then assigned so that lower levels of foreign debt denote a higher index level.
Gross FDI/GDP	Gross foreign direct investment is the sum of the absolute values of inflows and outflows of foreign direct investment recorded in the balance-of-payments financial account. It includes equity capital, reinvestment of earnings, other long-term capital, and short-term capital. The indicator is calculated as a ratio to GDP.

NOTE: All data are employed at the annual frequency.

Table 4.3 Summary Statistics

Panel A: Average (1981–2003)	Consumption Growth	Consumption Growth Standard Deviation	GDP Growth	GDP Growth Standard Deviation
Developed Countries	0.019	0.025	0.020	0.022
Developing Countries	0.009	0.079	0.009	0.050
Africa	0.003	0.090	0.003	0.057
Asia	0.029	0.046	0.030	0.037
Latin America	0.003	0.071	0.001	0.045
China	**0.070**	**0.044**	**0.078**	**0.027**

	Trade/GDP	Private Credit/GDP	MCAP/GDP	Turnover	Official Equity Liberalization	Equity Openness Intensity	Capital Account Openness (Quinn)
Developed Countries	0.600	0.864	0.599	0.509	0.954	0.929	0.855
Developing Countries	0.590	0.326	0.253	0.304	0.267	0.117	0.480
Africa	0.636	0.267	0.289	0.139	0.150	0.033	0.430
Asia	0.486	0.617	0.420	0.499	0.588	0.374	0.511
Latin America	0.418	0.284	0.179	0.225	0.312	0.233	0.564
China	**0.354**	**0.923**	**0.235**	**1.477**	**0.565**	**0.078**	**0.326**

	Political Risk (Composite)	Political Conditions	Quality of Institutions	Socio-economic Conditions	Conflict Risk	Investment Profile
Developed Countries	0.835	0.963	0.923	0.649	0.939	0.675
Developing Countries	0.550	0.520	0.491	0.482	0.699	0.533
Africa	0.532	0.478	0.485	0.480	0.656	0.518
Asia	0.628	0.629	0.610	0.556	0.746	0.583
Latin America	0.553	0.524	0.469	0.446	0.741	0.496
China	**0.658**	**0.440**	**0.571**	**0.612**	**0.815**	**0.707**

(continued)

Table 4.3 *continued*

Panel B: Most Recent Data (2000–2003)	Consumption Growth	Consumption Growth Standard Deviation	GDP Growth	GDP Growth Standard Deviation
Developed Countries	0.016	0.020	0.016	0.015
Developing Countries	0.004	0.058	0.011	0.027
Africa	−0.009	0.070	0.007	0.026
Asia	0.028	0.048	0.024	0.033
Latin America	−0.004	0.043	−0.004	0.028
China	**0.036**	**0.033**	**0.073**	**0.007**

	Trade/GDP	Private Credit/GDP	MCAP/GDP	Turnover	Official Equity Liberalization	Equity Openness Intensity	Capital Account Openness (Quinn)
Developed Countries	0.746	1.022	1.322	0.832	1.000	0.952	0.923
Developing Countries	0.765	0.366	0.332	0.480	0.493	0.252	0.650
Africa	0.757	0.267	0.316	0.161	0.342	0.123	0.534
Asia	0.716	0.760	0.479	0.996	0.875	0.585	0.617
Latin America	0.532	0.295	0.258	0.126	0.571	0.419	0.821
China	**0.546**	**1.333**	**0.457**	**1.022**	**1.000**	**0.349**	**0.375**

	Political Risk (Composite)	Political Conditions	Quality of Institutions	Socioeconomic Conditions	Conflict Risk	Investment Profile
Developed Countries	0.869	0.956	0.908	0.738	0.952	0.754
Developing Countries	0.664	0.546	0.534	0.630	0.793	0.692
Africa	0.631	0.476	0.496	0.625	0.750	0.664
Asia	0.703	0.590	0.670	0.648	0.834	0.680
Latin America	0.663	0.589	0.509	0.601	0.817	0.685
China	**0.658**	**0.281**	**0.469**	**0.688**	**0.826**	**0.917**

WE explore averages of trade/GDP, private credit/GDP, market capitalization/GDP, equity market turnover, the official liberalization indicator, Quinn's capital account liberalization indicator, and political risk index (and various subgroups). For the political risk indices, higher numbers denote better conditions. Political conditions reflect the role of the military in politics and democratic accountability. Quality of institutions reflects law and order, corruption, and bureaucratic quality. The third group reflects government stability, socioeconomic conditions, and the investment profile for the country (which we also consider separately). Finally, conflict risk reflects both internal and external conflict and religious and ethnic tensions. We also present evidence for consumption and GDP growth and standard deviations. The averages are reported for several country groups: developed, developing, Africa, Asia, and Latin America (as described by the World Bank). In panel A, we report full sample averages, whereas we report only the most recent data in panel B. We also report the associated numbers for China.

and volatility is 5 percent. Thus, China manages to grow much faster than developed markets with relatively low growth volatility (3 percent).

Trade Sector

There is a perception that foreign trade has been an important engine of Chinese economic growth. To test this conjecture, we first need a measure of trade openness. We will simply use the size of the trade sector, exports plus imports to GDP. Table 4.3 shows that the actual size of the sector compared to GDP is remarkably modest. The trade sector comprises only 35 percent of GDP on average in China compared to an average of 59 percent in all developing countries. The trade sector in China is even smaller than the African regional average. Of course the average reflects a continued upward trend in trade openness, with the trade sector standing at over 60 percent in 2003. This increase is the mirror image of significant reforms to the trade regime, taking place during the 1980s and 1990s, including accession to the World Trade Organization (WTO) in 2001, which led to a steady decrease in tariffs. Branstetter and Lardy (2007), who provide a detailed analysis of trade liberalization in China, show that tariff revenues as a fraction of imports decreased from about 12 percent in 1980 to 2.5 percent in 2002. The four-time decrease in tariffs nicely mirrors the approximately four-time increase in the trade sector documented in figure 4.5. Nevertheless, Wacziarg and Welch (2003) still view China as not having experienced trade liberalization.

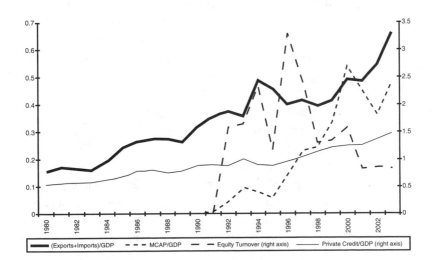

Figure 4.5   Trade and Financial Development: China

The Chinese national statistics do not reveal the large discrepancies in openness and likely its effects on economic growth within China. The major exporting and importing industries in China are located in east coastal provinces, whereas most inland provinces are still relatively isolated from world trade. A recent analysis by Jin (2005) suggests that the beneficial effects of trade openness may not extend to these inland provinces. Although it seems imperative for policymakers to address such regional divergences in economic performance, our data do not permit further analysis of this issue.

Financial Development

We consider two measures of financial development. The first is based on the size of the banking system where we measure the amount of private credit divided by GDP, which is a standard banking development indicator. For this metric, China scores high, 92 percent of GDP on average. This is higher than the average proportion for developed countries, 86 percent. Figure 4.5 shows that this measure of China's banking development has steadily improved over the sample period and that private credit to GDP is now over 100 percent. However, this statistic illustrates the tremendous measurement problem any analysis of China faces. While this ratio suggests that China's banking system is highly developed, experts have revealed a number of serious deficiencies in China's banking system. Fung, Ho, and Zhu (2005) describe how reforms to the banking system have been rather limited, with a large proportion of financial resources allocated through the state banking system and with interest rates playing little role in the resource allocation. This state of affairs was pointedly illustrated by the recent change in the official lending rate, the first in nine years! There are frequent articles in the press and in practitioner research describing serious problems with nonperforming loans (NPLs) in the banking sector. For example, table 4.1 shows that a report by Standard & Poor's in June 2003 argued that Chinese financial institutions needed a $500 billion bail-out. Apart from the formal sector, an informal credit market has emerged supplying funds to the non-state sector (see Allen, Qian, and Qian 2005), which is presumably guided by market principles. In a robustness check, we will use a financial development measure that is more correlated with the quality of the financial system.

A similar admonition holds for measures of equity market development. The turnover in the Chinese market is 148 percent per year compared to only 51 percent in developed markets on average. This does not necessarily mean that the equity market is highly developed in China. In fact, the modern Chinese stock market is very young, the two stock exchanges in Shanghai and Shenzhen having been established only in 1990 after a 49-year hiatus.[2] An important feature of the Chinese stock market is the existence of A shares for local investors and B shares for foreign investors. Until February 2001, the two markets were totally separated, with the A shares trading in local currency and the B shares, a much more limited set of companies, trading in dollars or Hong Kong dollars. Since then, Chinese residents have been allowed to purchase B shares using foreign currency. More recently, foreign qualified institutional investors have been allowed to invest on a limited basis in the A-share market.

Our turnover number is for the B shares; turnover is even higher for A shares. The huge turnover and the surprising discount on the "less liquid" B shares has generated much research into their causes. Mei, Scheinkman, and Xiong (2005) convincingly demonstrate the existence of a speculative component in Chinese share prices, which may help explain both the discount on B shares and the tremendous turnover in A shares. The increase in turnover on the B-share market after February 2001 is then viewed as due to speculation, not to an improvement in market efficiency. Other standard measures of stock market development paint a more realistic picture of the development of the Chinese stock market. For instance, the size of the equity market compared to GDP in China is only 23 percent, which is lower than the average for all developing countries and sharply lower than the 60 percent average for developed countries.

Other informal indicators suggest that Chinese stock market efficiency is still at a relatively low level (see Wang and Cheng 2004). Individual investors dominate the market, and while free float has been increasing it is still pretty limited. Short selling is impossible, and China has no futures or options markets in stocks. There are also accounts of stock price manipulation (see Aggarwal and Wu 2006) and rampant insider trading (see Du and Wei 2004). That being said, it is conceivable that the proximity of the relatively efficient Hong Kong market mitigates the adverse effects of an inefficient stock market on resource allocation. High-quality Chinese companies tend to list on the Hong Kong market rather than the domestic market, and the so-called Red Chip companies raise much more capital through the Hong Kong market than through the domestic market.

The potentially beneficial effects of further stock market development, especially with the goal of attracting foreign investors, cannot be

underestimated. We will illustrate the real benefits of equity market liberalizations below, but here we will note that the Chinese market should
be very attractive for foreign investors as returns appear to correlate very
little with world markets returns. For the period from 1993 through
2003, Lin, Menkveld, and Yang (2004) show that the correlation between returns on both A-share markets and other countries (Hong Kong,
Singapore, Taiwan, Japan, the United States, France, Germany, the
United Kingdom, and Australia) is not higher than 5 percent. For the B
shares, the correlations are higher but do not exceed 22 percent (with
Hong Kong) for countries in the East and 8 percent (with Germany) for
countries in the West. Hence, Chinese stocks are very attractive diversification vehicles for international investors.

Financial Openness

We construct three measures of financial openness, which are detailed
in table 4.2. The first indicator, denoted throughout the chapter as the
"Official Liberalization" indicator, takes a value of one when the equity
market is officially liberalized; otherwise, it takes a value of zero. Official liberalization dates are taken from the chronology presented in
Bekaert and Harvey (2005) and expanded to all the countries considered in this study in Bekaert, Harvey, and Lundblad (2006a). It is difficult to know precisely when an equity market is effectively liberalized.
That is, while regulations may change to allow foreigners to access the
local equity market, the market may be effectively open years prior to
the official date if American Depository Receipts (ADRs) and country
funds are available to foreign investors. Conversely, savvy investors may
circumvent official capital controls. Furthermore, most liberalizations
are not one-time events; rather, they are gradual and may not be comprehensive at first.

The Official Liberalization measure does not reflect the degree of
openness of the equity market. Our second equity market openness measure addresses the extent of the liberalization by taking the ratio of the
market capitalizations of the constituent members of the International Finance Corporation (IFC) investable and the IFC global indices for each
country, following Bekaert (1995) and Edison and Warnock (2003). In
this context, a ratio of one means that all of the stocks are available to foreign investors. For example, during the 1990s Korea lifted foreign ownership restrictions in a number of steps leading to an intensity indicator
that gradually moved from zero to one. For both indicators, fully segmented

countries have an indicator value of zero, and fully liberalized "open" countries have an indicator value of one.

The usual measure of capital account openness is based on the IMF's *Annual Report on Exchange Arrangements and Exchange Restrictions* (AREAER). The IMF publication details several categories of information, mostly on current account restrictions. A capital account openness dummy variable takes on a value of zero if the country has at least one restriction in the "restrictions on payments for the capital account transactions" category. However, Eichengreen (2001) has criticized the IMF capital account measure for being too coarse and therefore uninformative. Our measure of capital account openness is from Quinn (1997) and Quinn and Toyoda (2003) and is also created from the annual volume published by the IMF's AREAER. However, in contrast to the binary IMF indicator, Quinn's openness measure is scored from 0 to 4, with 4 representing a fully open economy. Quinn grades capital payments and receipts separately on a scale of 0 to 2 (0.5 increments), and then adds the two. The scale is determined as follows: 0 = approval required and rarely granted; 0.5 = approval required and sometimes granted; 1.0 = no restrictions but official approval required (and frequently granted) plus transaction is taxed; 1.5 = no official approval needed but transaction may be taxed; and 2.0 = free. The Quinn variable measures the degree to which the capital account is open and is analogous to our intensity indicator for equity market liberalization. We transform the Quinn measure into a 0 to 1 scale.

In table 4.3 we report some summary statistics on these measures for groups of countries and China. The value of 0.565 for China's Official Liberalization variable reflects the fact that the date for the official stock market liberalization is 1991, about halfway through the sample. The values for the other groups of countries show that developed countries were mostly open during the whole sample, whereas only a minority of country years (26.7 percent) for developing countries is characterized as open. Asia has been more open than Latin America. This measure ignores the fact that significant foreign ownership restrictions remain and that much of the Chinese stock market capitalization is not traded on the stock market at all. The intensity measure averages only 7.8 percent over the entire sample, which is less than the average of developing countries. By the end of the sample, only 35 percent of market capitalization is available to foreigners. This ratio (which includes H and Red Chip shares) still falls short of the averages for Asian countries as well as Latin American countries.[3]

In terms of capital account openness, China was on average less open than both the average developing country and the average Asian country. The Quinn measure stood at 0.0 in 1980 and is now 0.375. Prasad and Wei (2005) provide a detailed account of the remaining capital controls and how they evolved over time. One reason for the low value of the Quinn measure is that the Chinese government has relaxed restrictions on FDI inflows quite substantially but has only recently and cautiously started to relax restrictions on FDI outflows. Moreover, its regulations and currency inconvertibility have made foreign borrowing and portfolio inflows difficult. As a result, the composition of inflows has been very heavily tilted toward FDI. Despite this fact, Prasad and Wei debunk the myth that China has been an attractive FDI destination in terms of regulations and that FDI has been a large driver of Chinese economic growth. They show that FDI is subject to more restrictions than in other countries and that the FDI inflows in percentage of GDP are rather moderate both compared to the level of FDI in other countries and compared to the massive levels of domestic savings funneled into real investments. Finally, it is also conceivable that part of the FDI inflows reflects other forms of capitals disguised as FDI to circumvent capital controls. Nevertheless, it is worth examining whether China's reliance on FDI and reluctance to incur foreign debt has contributed to the country's growth spurt. We will do so below.

Institutions and Political Risk

Political unrest and institutional factors feature prominently in classic work on growth determinants (Barro 1997; Acemoglu, Johnson, and Robinson 2002). They may also affect risk assessments of foreign investors. That is, financial openness might not attract foreign capital if the country is viewed as risky. Therefore, these variables are also important in analyzing why countries respond differently in terms of both growth and growth volatility to financial openness. We use the International Country Risk Guide's (ICRG) ratings to measure the quality of institutions and political risk.

The ICRG provides ratings in three different categories: economic, financial, and political risk. A higher value means lower risk. Figure 4.6 shows the time series of these indices along with the composite risk measure. Over the entire period, the political risks that China faces have changed very little. The average value of this indicator in the 1990s was 65.6; in the last four years, it has averaged 66.4. There has also been only

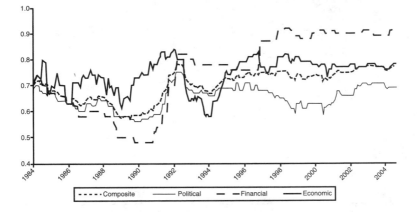

Figure 4.6 Political, Financial, and Economic Risk in China

a marginal change in the economic indicator. Most of the increase in the composite is due to the financial risk indicator.

It is important to look within these indices. Most of our study focuses on the political risk indicator and four subcategories of this indicator, reflecting political conditions, the quality of institutions, socioeconomic conditions, and conflict. Table 4.3 presents some summary statistics for these measures. We report investment profile separately as well (see table 4.2 for details).

China has on average less political risk than developing countries but substantially more risk than developed countries. The good performance relative to other developing countries is due to good scores on socioeconomic conditions and conflict risk.

Figure 4.7 shows the time-variation in four subindices that we have created. For Political Conditions (the extent of the military involvement in politics and democratic accountability), China's rating has fallen from an average value of 34.4 in the 1990s to 28.1 in the last few years. The quality of political institutions (corruption, law and order, and bureaucratic quality) has also declined. The average rating in the 1990s was 62.0, and it has fallen to 46.9 in the last four years. Socioeconomic conditions (government stability, socioeconomic conditions, and investment profile) show a substantial improvement rising from an average of 56.9 in the 1990s to 68.8 in the last four years. Looking within the subcomponents, we see that both government stability and investment profile have improved. The conflict indicator (internal conflict, external conflict, religion in politics, and ethnic tensions) has been relatively flat over the past 15 years. The substantial

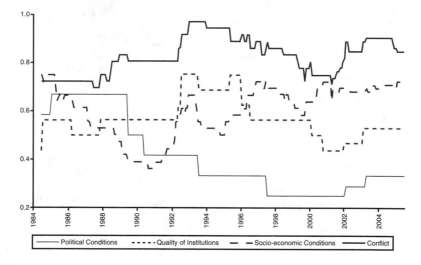

Figure 4.7   The Components of Political Risk in China

improvement from the values in the 1980s is almost entirely driven by the perceived lower probability of external conflict.

EMPIRICAL FRAMEWORK

GROWTH, GROWTH VOLATILITY, AND INTERNATIONAL RISK SHARING

There is a considerable literature on the risk-sharing benefits that may come from financial market integration. In stylized representative agent endowment models, perfect risk sharing has stark implications. Consumption growth rates across countries should be perfectly correlated, idiosyncratic consumption risk should be diversified away, and consumption growth should not react to country-specific income shocks. Early work by Backus, Kehoe, and Kydland (1992) shows that consumption correlations across countries are surprisingly low and often lower than output growth correlations. One interpretation of this result is that the benefits of risk sharing have not been realized (for example, because of home asset preference), and the literature has mostly resorted to "counterfactual" exercises within the context of parameterized general equilibrium models to compute the cost of imperfect risk sharing. A survey article by van Wincoop (1999) suggests that the benefits of perfect risk sharing are quite substantial even when only focusing on the reduction in consumption growth volatility. These benefits could be even more substantial given that open capital markets may also increase growth (see Obstfeld 1994), an implication of market integration ignored by most previous studies.

In Bekaert, Harvey, and Lundblad (2006b), we view changes in de jure international financial openness as an exogenous improvement in international risk sharing, an idea also present in Lewis's (1996) work. We then build on the framework of Athanasoulis and van Wincoop (2000) to simultaneously measure the effects of financial and trade openness on average consumption growth and idiosyncratic consumption growth volatility. Of course, opening equity markets (or opening capital markets more generally) is not likely a sufficient step to realize the theoretical benefits of perfect risk sharing. For example, markets are incomplete, and the proportion of output represented by tradable claims is probably quite small. In addition, only a minority of the population of most countries hold stocks. Nevertheless, it is likely that the benefits of risk sharing are relatively larger for emerging markets (see, for example, Lewis 1996; Obstfeld 1992; Tesar 1995).

Note that in terms of risk sharing, the benefits of equity market liberalization in emerging markets are twofold. For the world at large, emerging markets provide a great opportunity to diversify risk because of their low correlations with other global equity markets and with one another. From this perspective, any liberalization should serve to increase the total risk-sharing potential of world capital markets. Of course, the small size of many emerging markets may limit this potential. From the perspective of the emerging market, liberalization of inward investment mostly goes hand-in-hand with liberalization of outward investment (e.g., Mathieson and Rojaz-Suarez 1993). Hence, equity market liberalization provides potentially large risk-sharing opportunities for the local population as well. Consequently, for countries with asymmetric financial liberalization regimes with respect to outflows and inflows, such as China, our results must be interpreted with care.

A DIRECT MEASURE OF RISK SHARING

We use a simplified version of the specification proposed in Bekaert, Harvey, and Lundblad (2006a):

$$g_{i,t+k} - g_{w,t+k} = \alpha'(x_{i,t} - x_{w,t}) + \varepsilon_{i,t+k} \qquad (4.1)$$

$$\sigma^2_{i,t} = \gamma_k'(z_{i,t} - z_{w,t}) \qquad (4.2)$$

where i is the country, w is the world, $g_{i,t+k}$ is the logarithmic consumption growth rate for country i from time $t+1$ to $t+k$, x and z represent instrumental variables and $\sigma^2_{i,t}$ is the conditional variance of $\varepsilon_{i,t+k}$.

Equation (4.1) describes a classic Barro-type empirical growth regression, except that we formulate it in deviations from world growth. The residual in such a regression represents idiosyncratic, unpredictable growth, and its variance is the idiosyncratic growth volatility. It is also conceivable that the sensitivity of domestic growth to world growth varies with openness. We explicitly accommodate this possibility in Bekaert, Harvey, and Lundblad (2006a) but ignore it here.

The set of x instruments is largely based on Barro's (1997) work, including life expectancy, population growth, the size of the government sector, secondary school enrollment (a measure of human capital), inflation (a measure of the quality of macroeconomic policy), private credit to GDP (a financial development variable), trade to GDP and a financial openness measure. These variables should help account for steady-state GDP across countries. We also include initial per capita GDP to account for the standard conditional convergence effect in empirical growth regressions. It is well known that growth regressions suffer from a fragility problem as many variables such as human capital and life expectancy measure closely related "good" characteristics of a country. We follow the lead of Roll and Talbot (2004) in focusing primarily on variables that governments can easily modify and influence. In robustness checks, we do include investment variables as well because part of the Chinese growth experience must be related to its extraordinarily high savings rates. However, as we are interested in the growth effects of financial openness, it is problematic to directly include investment as liberalization may mainly work through the investment channel.

The system of equations in (4.1)–(4.2) defines a very large Generalized Method of Moment system with moment conditions:

$$f_t = \begin{pmatrix} \varepsilon_{i,t+k} \otimes (x_{i,t} - x_{w,t}) \\ (\varepsilon^2_{i,t+k} - \sigma^2_{i,t}) \otimes (z_{i,t} - z_{w,t}) \end{pmatrix} \qquad (4.3)$$

The system contains $N \times 2 \times L$ moment conditions (where $L = L_x + L_z$, L_x is the dimension of $x_{i,t}$, L_z is the dimension of $z_{i,t}$) and $2L(N-1)$ over-identifying conditions. Because the system is so large, it would be difficult to estimate with a general weighting matrix. We only allow for a restricted form of correlation across countries. The country mean and volatility errors are allowed to be correlated within one country but not across countries. Furthermore, the correlation is assumed to be the same across countries. The weighting matrix corrects for the induced serial correlation in the errors for overlapping growth horizons, following Bekaert, Harvey, and Lundblad (2001). We estimate the model for $k = 5$. It should be noted that our results are robust to slight variations in the weighting matrix, for example, setting the mean-volatility correlation to zero. Also note that we add a constant to both the mean and variance specifications.

RESULTS FOR AVERAGE GROWTH

BASE RESULTS ON GROWTH PREDICTABILITY

In panel A of table 4.4, we report the results of estimating (4.1)–(4.2) for our panel of, respectively, 96 countries (equity openness measures) or 77 countries (capital account openness measure). We report the regressions for both consumption and output growth. The coefficients on the size of the government sector and inflation were not significantly different from zero in any of our specifications and were therefore omitted from the regressions. The initial GDP variable is updated every five years. In all the regressions, we observe strong convergence effects. Countries that have per capita GDP below their steady states grow faster than average. Life expectancy and population growth have the expected, strongly significant effects, which are remarkably robust across the different specifications, especially for life expectancy. The effects are invariably larger for GDP growth. Secondary school enrollment makes a positive and usually significant contribution to growth. Trade has a robustly positive and significant effect on growth. The coefficients on the financial development measure are always more than one standard error from zero and are significant in the capital account openness specification. Equity market openness has a robust and significant growth effect varying between 57 basis points and 73 basis points. The effect of full capital account openness is even larger—1.33 percent for consumption and 1.88 percent for output

Table 4.4a Growth Predictability: Annual Average Real Consumption and GDP Growth in Excess of the World (five-year horizon), 1980–2003

Panel A	Official Equity Market Liberalization				Equity Market Openness			
	Consumption Growth		GDP Growth		Consumption Growth		GDP Growth	
	Estimate	Standard Error	Estimate	Standard Error	Estimate	Standard Error	Estimate	Standard Error
Constant	−0.0066	0.0020	−0.0057	0.0019	−0.0063	0.0022	−0.0060	0.0023
Initial GDP	−0.0070	0.0015	−0.0108	0.0009	−0.0072	0.0016	−0.0112	0.0009
Secondary School	0.0031	0.0037	0.0113	0.0050	0.0032	0.0038	0.0107	0.0047
Log(Life Expectancy)	0.0784	0.0123	0.0934	0.0126	0.0806	0.0127	0.0963	0.0123
Population Growth	−0.1437	0.0878	−0.2562	0.1072	−0.1623	0.0856	−0.2593	0.1068
Trade/GDP	0.0073	0.0023	0.0070	0.0017	0.0073	0.0024	0.0074	0.0017
Private Credit/GDP	0.0032	0.0027	0.0044	0.0026	0.0035	0.0028	0.0044	0.0029
Financial Openness	0.0073	0.0021	0.0063	0.0029	0.0057	0.0022	0.0067	0.0028
R^2	0.140		0.225		0.136		0.223	

Panel A	Capital Account Openness (Quinn)			
	Consumption Growth		GDP Growth	
	Estimate	Standard Error	Estimate	Standard Error
Constant	−0.0042	0.0017	−0.0064	0.0019
Initial GDP	−0.0100	0.0015	−0.0147	0.0010
Secondary School	0.0088	0.0043	0.0198	0.0043
Log(Life Expectancy)	0.0809	0.0141	0.0976	0.0133
Population Growth	−0.3107	0.0879	−0.4186	0.0913
Trade/GDP	0.0034	0.0020	0.0049	0.0015
Private Credit/GDP	0.0075	0.0025	0.0062	0.0026
Financial Openness	0.0133	0.0037	0.0188	0.0037
R^2	0.154		0.278	

The dependent variable is the overlapping five-year average growth rate of either real per capita consumption or GDP in excess of the corresponding world growth rate. Initial GDP is the log real per capita GDP level updated every five years (1980, 1985, 1990, 2000). Secondary School is the enrollment percentage for that level; Log(Life Expectancy) is the log life expectancy of the total population; Population Growth is the growth rate of total population; Trade/GDP is the ratio of export plus imports to GDP; Private Credit/GDP is the ratio of private credit to GDP. The control variables are all in excess of the world. We report the coefficient on one of three openness indicators (also in excess of the world): the Official Equity Liberalization indicator that takes a value of one when the equity market is liberalized; the Equity Liberalization Intensity measure is the ratio of IFC Investables to Global market capitalization; or the Capital Account Openness (Quinn) indicator that takes a value between 0 and 1 depending on the intensity of the reported capital account restrictions. The first two sets of regressions include 96 countries, whereas the last includes 77 countries. All standard errors provide a correction for the overlapping nature of the data.

Table 4.4b China's Experience: Decomposing the Growth Regression, Annual Average Real Consumption and GDP Growth (five-year horizon), 1980–2003

Panel B

	Excess Consumption Growth (5-year)	Initial GDP	Secondary School	Log(Life Expectancy)	Population Growth	Trade/GDP	Private Credit/GDP	Official Equity Liberalization	Predicted Excess Growth
Developed Countries	0.495%	-1.035%	0.143%	1.289%	0.132%	0.162%	0.132%	0.392%	0.555%
Developing Countries	-0.614%	0.934%	-0.034%	-0.589%	-0.090%	0.201%	-0.037%	-0.110%	-0.384%
Africa	-1.312%	1.206%	-0.065%	-1.397%	-0.163%	0.223%	-0.055%	-0.190%	-1.099%
Asia	1.300%	0.696%	0.015%	0.217%	-0.018%	0.108%	0.055%	0.131%	0.545%
Latin America	-1.050%	0.496%	-0.019%	0.200%	-0.060%	0.034%	-0.050%	-0.071%	-0.130%
China	**5.950%**	**1.742%**	**-0.017%**	**0.449%**	**0.049%**	**-0.048%**	**0.151%**	**0.108%**	**1.774%**
Temporal Dimension									
China—1980		2.203%	-0.020%	0.499%	0.069%	-0.166%	-0.085%	-0.129%	**1.710%**
China—2003		1.269%	-0.010%	0.461%	0.079%	0.052%	0.026%	0.289%	**1.505%**

	Excess Consumption Growth (5-year)	Initial GDP	Secondary School	Log(Life Expectancy)	Population Growth	Trade/GDP	Private Credit/GDP	Capital Account Openness (Quinn)	Predicted Excess Growth
Developed Countries	0.495%	-1.479%	0.403%	1.331%	0.284%	0.075%	0.317%	0.362%	0.871%
Developing Countries	-0.614%	1.335%	-0.095%	-0.608%	-0.194%	0.093%	-0.089%	-0.136%	-0.115%
Africa	-1.312%	1.723%	-0.182%	-1.442%	-0.352%	0.104%	-0.131%	-0.193%	-0.895%
Asia	1.300%	0.994%	0.042%	0.224%	-0.038%	0.050%	0.132%	-0.085%	0.899%
Latin America	-1.050%	0.709%	-0.054%	0.206%	-0.130%	0.016%	-0.118%	-0.015%	0.191%
China	**5.950%**	**2.489%**	**-0.049%**	**0.464%**	**0.106%**	**-0.022%**	**0.361%**	**-0.339%**	**2.588%**
Temporal Dimension									
China—1980		3.147%	-0.056%	0.515%	0.150%	-0.077%	-0.204%	-0.676%	**2.377%**
China—2003		1.813%	-0.030%	0.475%	0.171%	0.024%	0.062%	-0.463%	**1.631%**

This table reports the decomposition of the first and third regressions in panel A, where the dependent variable is the overlapping five-year average growth rate of real per capita consumption in excess of the corresponding world growth rate. This table shows the case for the official equity liberalization and capital account openness (Quinn) indicators. The values are reported for several country groups: Developed, Developing, Africa, Asia, and Latin America (as described by the World Bank). We also report the associated numbers for China, including the comparison of predicted growth across the sample from 1980 to 2003. Each entry shows the average for that country group multiplied by the coefficient reported in panel A.

growth. Consequently, a country with a fully open capital account grows, on average, 1.88 percent per year faster than a country with a fully closed capital account.

In panel B of table 4.4, we provide a number of different decompositions of the regression results. We consider five different groups: all developed countries, all developing countries, African countries, Asian countries, and Latin American countries. We also consider China separately. For each group we average the right-hand side variables over the sample period and compute average predicted excess consumption growth. We perform the decomposition for the official equity market liberalization (top panel) and capital account openness regressions (bottom panel). We start by discussing the top panel results.

The regression seems to capture average growth relatively well for the five groupings, although it tends to overpredict growth for Latin American and African countries, and underpredict growth for developed and Asian countries. The major contributors to growth overall seem to have been the convergence effect, life expectancy, and financial openness. Trade openness is less important quantitatively than expected. The results for GDP growth are similar.

The China experience stands out: China has the largest residual of all countries. That is, the regression fails to describe the Chinese growth experience. Financial development and equity market liberalization provide a small positive contribution to growth, but as we indicated before, these indicators are hard to interpret for China. Trade seemed to have played a relatively minor role on average. The main contributors are the convergence effect—China's per capita GDP was at least 70 percent below the world average during the sample period—and life expectancy.

These results ignore the dynamics of what China accomplished over the sample period: increased trade opening, partial financial liberalization, improvements in health care that increased life expectancy, and so on. To see the effects of these changes on growth, we repeat the experiment of panel B for 1980 and 2003. We multiply the regression coefficients by the values for China in 1980 and 2003. For 2003, we can only show predicted growth, not the actual experience. We find that the predicted excess consumption growth decreases from 1.7 to 1.5 percent from 1980 to 2003 in the equity market liberalization specification. The decrease is driven by a much higher initial GDP. In 1980, China's per capita GDP represented only 4.3 percent of the world average; in 2003, it represented 26.3 percent of the world average. The decrease in the convergence effect is partially offset by the positive impact of the equity market liberalization as well as the growing trade sector. However, again trade is shown to have played only a minor role in the Chinese growth experience.

The capital account openness regression displays similar results. Even though capital account openness provides a negative contribution to overall growth, its contribution is less negative in 2003 than in 1980 and is one of the main factors offsetting the influence of initial GDP. Later, we further explore the specific role of China's promotion of inward FDI.

Another relatively large contributor to growth in the capital account regression, both overall and in a temporal sense, is private credit to GDP. This is entirely because the private credit to GDP measures only the quantity of loans provided without taking into account the notorious poor capital allocation by Chinese state banks. La Porta, Lopez-de-Silanes, and Shleifer (2002) and Dinc (2005) correct the standard measures of banking development for state ownership of banks, viewing state control as synonymous with inefficient resource allocation. We interpolate the state ownership ratios provided by La Porta, Lopez de Silanes, and Shleifer (2002) for two years during our sample to the full sample and create a new measure of banking development as private credit to GDP × (1-ratio of state ownership). This correction drives China's private credit to GDP ratio close to zero for most of the sample, while leaving banking development in many developed countries unaffected. When we use this measure in the capital account regression (not reported), the lack of banking development now detracts 0.242 percent of China's relative growth. This suggests that one sustainable source of new growth for China may be to improve resource allocation through the banking system.

Many believe that China's embrace of trade openness (and FDI; see below) has played a significant role in its rapid economic development over the last decade or so. While we are not the first to argue that their effects are likely less important than seems generally accepted (see, e.g., Branstetter and Lardy 2006), we explore the possibility of the import plus exports measure scaled by GDP being a poor proxy to the true trade-liberalizing effects of China's trade policy. We therefore obtained the trade liberalization dates developed in Wacziarg and Welch (2003) for 75 countries. As we noted before, China is assumed to be effectively not trade liberalized. Wacziarg and Welch look at five factors: average tariff rates of 40 percent or more; nontariff barriers covering 40 percent or more of trade; a black market exchange rate that is depreciated by 20 percent or more relative to the official exchange rate, on average, during the 1970s or 1980s; a state monopoly on major exports; and a socialist economic system. If a country meets any of these five criteria, it is classified with indicator variable equal to zero and is deemed closed. Given that China is a socialist economy, it is given a closed rating. Although China undoubtedly cannot be classified as totally open, this classification seems erroneous given the account of trade liberalization in Branstetter and Lardy (2006). We therefore replaced the series for China with a series used in the Branstetter and Lardy study that captures the gradual trade liberalization in China over the last two decades: 1 minus tariff revenue as a fraction of import revenue. We view this series as providing us with an upper bound on the effects of trade liberalization in China on growth. Although we do not report the results in detail, we find that the trade liberalization variable is very significant. Because China is relatively open, trade openness now contributes significantly to excess growth, but on average never much more than 50 basis points per year.

POLITICAL RISK AND GROWTH

To examine the role of political risk for consumption and GDP growth, we reestimate our benchmark regressions, adding six different specifications for the political risk variable: overall political risk; political conditions; quality of institutions; socioeconomic conditions; conflict; and the investment profile subcomponent. A higher rating means a lower level of risk. There are 36 coefficients estimated (consumption and GDP growth for three openness measures and six political risk specifications). Although detailed results are available upon request, we note that the coefficients on the political risk measures are positive in 35 of 36 cases, more than one standard error from zero in 34 of 36 cases, and more than two standard errors from zero in 28 of 36 regressions. Overall political risk is a significant predictor of relative growth and generally diminishes the importance of the financial openness variables.

Table 4.5 reports the coefficients on the political risk variables and the growth decomposition for consumption growth. We focus on the equity market liberalization and capital account openness specifications. Examining the political risk indicators separately, we find that political conditions enter the capital account openness regressions with a coefficient that is three standard errors from zero. While the coefficient on the openness variables decreases somewhat (not reported), it is still

Table 4.5 Decomposing the Growth Predictability and Political Risk: Annual Average Real Consumption and GDP Growth in Excess of the World (five-year horizon), 1980–2003

Panel A
Official Equity Market Liberalization

	Excess Consumption Growth (5-year)	Political Risk (composite)		Political Conditions		Quality of Institutions	
				Predicted Excess Growth		Predicted Excess Growth	
		Total	Contribution	Total	Contribution	Total	Contribution
Coefficient Estimate		0.040		0.008		0.014	
Standard Error		0.012		0.006		0.007	
Developed Countries	0.495%	0.602%	0.863%	0.600%	0.258%	0.555%	0.469%
Developing Countries	-0.614%	-0.559%	-0.279%	-0.451%	-0.083%	-0.500%	-0.152%
Africa	-1.312%	-1.235%	-0.352%	-1.186%	-0.116%	-1.201%	-0.159%
Asia	1.300%	0.444%	0.036%	0.507%	0.006%	0.479%	0.020%
LatinAmerica	-1.050%	-0.389%	-0.270%	-0.191%	-0.082%	-0.300%	-0.182%
China	**5.950%**	**2.105%**	**0.165%**	**1.749%**	**-0.099%**	**1.894%**	**-0.035%**

	Socioeconomic Conditions		Conflict		Investment Profile	
	Predicted Excess Growth		Predicted Excess Growth		Predicted Excess Growth	
	Total	Contribution	Total	Contribution	Total	Contribution
Coefficient Estimate	0.051		0.013		0.046	
Standard Error	0.010		0.008		0.009	
Developed Countries	0.498%	0.644%	0.604%	0.238%	0.435%	0.488%
Developing Countries	-0.598%	-0.208%	-0.409%	-0.077%	-0.523%	-0.158%
Africa	-1.225%	-0.221%	-1.172%	-0.131%	-1.210%	-0.206%
Asia	0.444%	0.167%	0.551%	-0.011%	0.445%	0.108%
LatinAmerica	-0.574%	-0.398%	-0.111%	-0.017%	-0.448%	-0.315%
China	**2.006%**	**0.358%**	**2.048%**	**0.075%**	**2.379%**	**0.647%**

(continued)

Table 4.5 *continued*

Panel B
Capital Account Openness (Quinn)

	Excess Consumption Growth (5-year)	Political Risk (composite)		Political Conditions		Quality of Institutions	
Coefficient Estimate		0.043		0.018		0.021	
Standard Error		0.012		0.006		0.007	
		Predicted Excess Growth		Predicted Excess Growth		Predicted Excess Growth	
		Total	Contribution	Total	Contribution	Total	Contribution
Developed Countries	0.495%	1.053%	0.930%	1.194%	0.591%	1.069%	0.685%
Developing Countries	-0.614%	-0.390%	-0.301%	-0.261%	-0.191%	-0.361%	-0.221%
Africa	-1.312%	-1.161%	-0.379%	-1.116%	-0.266%	-1.158%	-0.232%
Asia	1.300%	0.986%	0.039%	1.147%	0.015%	1.051%	0.029%
Latin America	-1.050%	-0.272%	-0.291%	-0.093%	-0.188%	-0.233%	-0.266%
China	5.950%	3.317%	0.178%	3.096%	0.228%	3.193%	-0.052%

	Socioeconomic Conditions		Conflict		Investment Profile	
Coefficient Estimate	0.044		0.013		0.038	
Standard Error	0.010		0.007		0.009	
	Predicted Excess Growth		Predicted Excess Growth		Predicted Excess Growth	
	Total	Contribution	Total	Contribution	Total	Contribution
Developed Countries	0.980%	0.557%	1.191%	0.241%	0.912%	0.407%
Developing Countries	-0.453%	-0.180%	-0.223%	-0.078%	-0.366%	-0.131%
Africa	-1.225%	-0.192%	-1.138%	-0.133%	-1.185%	-0.172%
Asia	0.963%	0.145%	1.172%	-0.012%	0.961%	0.090%
Latin America	-0.419%	-0.345%	0.047%	-0.018%	-0.283%	-0.263%
China	3.086%	0.310%	3.373%	0.076%	3.383%	0.539%

This table reports the decomposition of the regressions, where the dependent variable is the overlapping five-year average growth rate of real per capita consumption in excess of the corresponding world growth rate. The regressions have the same controls as employed in table 4.4, but add separately one-by-one Political Risk, Political Conditions, Quality of Institutions, Socioeconomic Conditions, Conflict, and Investment Profile indices. For each case, we report the associated prediction for excess consumption growth and the contribution from the added variable (along with the estimate coefficient and standard error for the added variable). This table shows the case for the official equity liberalization indicator (panel A) covering 86 countries and capital account openness (Quinn) (panel B) covering 72 countries. The values are reported for several country groups: developed, developing, Africa, Asia, and Latin America (as described by the World Bank). We also report the associated numbers for China, including the comparison of predicted growth across the sample from 1980 to 2003.

large in value and highly significant. The political conditions variable does not play a significant role in the equity market liberalization/openness regressions. The quality of institutions variable plays a key role in each of the six regressions; being highly statistically significantly different from zero in every case. The magnitude of the openness variable is decreased when institutions are included in the regression. However, the equity market liberalization variable remains significant for the consumption growth specification, and capital account openness remains highly significant in both regressions. It is conceivable that the liberalization effect and the quality of institutions effect are correlated. Bekaert, Harvey, and Lundblad (2006b) document the notion that countries that liberalize their capital markets tend to be countries with high-quality institutions.

The results are stronger for socioeconomic conditions than for the quality of institutions variables. On average, the coefficients on this political risk indicator are close to 5.5 standard errors from zero. In this case, the equity market openness variables are no longer significant at standard levels. However, the capital account openness variable remains economically and statistically significant. The conflict variable is close to two standard errors from zero in each of the equity market liberalization/ openness regressions; it is almost four standard errors from zero in the GDP growth specification with capital account openness. The coefficients on the openness variable are relatively less affected when this political risk variable is used.

The final columns look at one important subcomponent of the political risk variable: investment profile. Investment profile assesses the risk of expropriation or contract viability, payment delays, and the ease with which profits can be repatriated. It is therefore a very important determinant of foreign (direct) investment and may be most closely associated with our openness measures. Moreover, China scores relatively well on this indicator. In all six regressions, the coefficient is significant, averaging 5.3 standard errors from zero.

Most of table 4.5 is devoted to the economic impact of the five subindices of political risk (as well as the composite) in explaining excess consumption growth in each region, as well as China. This table allows us to identify the political risk factors that make the largest growth contributions for China. The first panel examines equity market liberalization and suggests that socioeconomic conditions plays the most important role of all of the subcomponent measures, contributing 0.358 percent to the 2.006

percent excess growth prediction. A similar result can be found for capital account openness. Socioeconomic conditions contribute 0.310 percent of the predicted 3.086 percent excess consumption growth. The investment profile subcomponent accounts for 0.65 percent of 2.38 percent predicted growth in the case of the equity market liberalization and 0.54 percent of 3.38 percent predicted in the capital account openness regression. Poor political conditions subtract 0.23 percent of the predicted growth in the capital account specification. Thus, China's economic growth potential benefits from policies that create an attractive climate for foreign investment and good socioeconomic conditions, but its poor political conditions and relative lack of high-quality governmental institutions are growth detractors.

OTHER GROWTH DETERMINANTS

In this section, we investigate other potentially important determinants of growth, including state ownership of assets, the existence of a high-quality social security system, and stock market development. Table 4.6 contains a summary of the results.

The first panel focuses on state ownership. Although it was difficult to find a direct indicator, we obtained the political risk indicators from Business Environment Risk Intelligence (BERI). They include a measure of the degree of privatization in the 44 countries the service follows, which includes China. BERI also assesses the quality of the credit market (which includes both long- and short-term credit as well as the availability of venture capital), and we use that measure as an alternative financial development market indicator. Recall that China scores rather highly on private credit to GDP, whereas most China experts rate the Chinese banking sector as highly inefficient. In the BERI data, China's credit market score is below average. BERI also has a measure for the legal framework for remittance and repatriation that is likely very correlated with financial openness, and we use it to replace our standard financial openness measure.

The results reveal that our standard growth determinants are rather robust to the inclusion of these new variables, except for the coefficient on trade to GDP, which is no longer significantly different from zero. The coefficient on the Privatization measure is significantly different from zero for both the consumption and GDP growth regressions and provides a substantial negative contribution to Chinese excess consumption growth

Table 4.6 Other Growth Determinants: Privatization, Financial Development, and Financial Openness Annual Average Real Consumption and GDP Growth in Excess of the World (five-year horizon), 1980–2003

44 countries	Consumption Growth		GDP Growth	
	Estimate	Standard Error	Estimate	Standard Error
Constant	−0.0096	0.0024	−0.0098	0.0012
Initial GDP	−0.0161	0.0016	−0.0215	0.0010
Secondary School	0.0080	0.0044	0.0148	0.0053
Log(Life Expectancy)	0.1408	0.0162	0.1644	0.0151
Population Growth	−0.4124	0.1142	−0.5434	0.1308
Trade/GDP	−0.0028	0.0024	0.0011	0.0023
Privatization (BERI)	**0.0213**	**0.0109**	**0.0353**	**0.0062**
Credit Market (BERI)	**0.0045**	**0.0098**	**−0.0001**	**0.0081**
Openness (BERI)	**0.0196**	**0.0046**	**0.0184**	**0.0045**
R^2	0.247		0.352	

	Predicted Excess Consumption Growth				
	Actual Growth	Total	Privatization Contribution	Credit Market Contribution	Openness Contribution
Developed Countries	0.561%	0.411%	0.327%	0.081%	0.341%
Developing Countries	−0.034%	−0.647%	−0.130%	−0.040%	−0.187%
Africa	−1.147%	−1.706%	−0.082%	−0.024%	−0.183%
Asia	1.623%	1.198%	0.061%	0.013%	0.148%
Latin America	−0.729%	−0.268%	−0.170%	−0.074%	−0.330%
China	**5.950%**	**3.318%**	**0.328%**	**−0.033%**	**−0.285%**

(continued)

Table 4.6 *continued*

53 countries	Consumption Growth		GDP Growth	
	Estimate	Standard Error	Estimate	Standard Error
Constant	-0.0058	0.0021	-0.0031	0.0020
Initial GDP	-0.0165	0.0010	-0.0180	0.0010
Secondary School	0.0132	0.0039	0.0154	0.0039
Log(Life Expectancy)	0.1185	0.0108	0.1136	0.0148
Population Growth	-0.3942	0.1179	-0.3707	0.1222
Trade/GDP	-0.0031	0.0022	0.0027	0.0017
Private Credit/GDP	0.0092	0.0025	0.0118	0.0026
Financial Openness (Quinn)	0.0158	0.0033	0.0174	0.0036
Social Security	**0.0151**	**0.0032**	**0.0189**	**0.0039**
R^2	0.210		0.226	

		Predicted Excess Consumption Growth	
	Actual Growth	Total	Social Security Contribution
Developed Countries	0.522%	1.487%	0.858%
Developing Countries	0.100%	-0.446%	-0.440%
Africa	-0.866%	-1.980%	-0.933%
Asia	1.558%	1.169%	-0.252%
Latin America	-0.474%	0.798%	0.328%
China	**5.950%**	**5.041%**	0.706%

51 countries	Consumption Growth		GDP Growth	
	Estimate	Standard Error	Estimate	Standard Error
Constant	−0.0061	0.0021	−0.0049	0.0018
Initial GDP	−0.0165	0.0011	−0.0191	0.0012
Secondary School	0.0150	0.0041	0.0184	0.0045
Log(Life Expectancy)	0.1156	0.0138	0.1262	0.0139
Population Growth	−0.4488	0.1464	−0.4466	0.1348
Trade/GDP	−0.0078	0.0023	−0.0043	0.0020
Private Credit/GDP	0.0044	0.0031	0.0056	0.0030
Financial Openness (Quinn)	0.0218	0.0039	0.0259	0.0040
MCAP	**0.0027**	**0.0031**	**0.0034**	**0.0028**
R^2	0.230		0.280	

	Actual Growth	Predicted Excess Consumption Growth	
		Total	MCAP Contribution
Developed Countries	0.522%	0.475%	0.435%
Developing Countries	0.045%	−0.296%	−0.283%
Africa	−1.029%	−1.189%	−0.186%
Asia	1.435%	1.393%	0.081%
Latin America	−0.573%	0.065%	−0.401%
China	**5.950%**	**3.753%**	**−0.664%**

(continued)

Table 4.6 *continued*

51 countries	Consumption Growth		GDP Growth	
	Estimate	Standard Error	Estimate	Standard Error
Constant	-0.0062	0.0018	-0.0051	0.0015
Initial GDP	-0.0162	0.0011	-0.0188	0.0014
Secondary School	0.0150	0.0039	0.0187	0.0041
Log(Life Expectancy)	0.1110	0.0141	0.1209	0.0144
Population Growth	-0.4005	0.1250	-0.3748	0.1195
Trade/GDP	-0.0061	0.0025	-0.0022	0.0021
Private Credit/GDP	0.0041	0.0022	0.0053	0.0021
Financial Openness (Quinn)	0.0208	0.0039	0.0251	0.0043
Turnover	**0.0113**	**0.0025**	**0.0135**	**0.0030**
R^2	0.252		0.313	

	Predicted Excess Consumption Growth		
	Actual Growth	Total	Turnover Contribution
Developed Countries	0.522%	0.444%	0.228%
Developing Countries	0.045%	-0.185%	-0.147%
Africa	-1.029%	-1.520%	-0.522%
Asia	1.435%	1.473%	0.244%
Latin America	-0.573%	0.166%	-0.279%
China	**5.950%**	**4.888%**	**0.847%**

The dependent variable is the overlapping five-year average growth rate of either real per capita consumption or GDP in excess of the corresponding world growth rate. Initial GDP is the log real per capita GDP level updated every five years (1980, 1985, 1990, 2000). Secondary School is the enrollment percentage for that level; Log(Life Expectancy) is the log life expectancy of the total population; Population Growth is the growth rate of total population; Trade/GDP is the ratio of export plus imports to GDP; Private Credit/GDP is the ratio of private credit to GDP. The control variables are all in excess of the world. The first regression includes three indices reflecting the level of privatization, credit market quality, and financial openness provided by BERI. The second regression includes an index of the quality of the social security system. The last two regressions also include the Quinn capital account openness indicator. Finally, for a collection of geographical regions and China, we report the contribution toward predicted excess consumption growth provided by each of these additional explanatory variables, total predicted excess growth from the regression, and actual excess growth.

(−0.33 percent). The Credit Market variable is economically and statistically unimportant. The Openness measure has a highly significant effect on growth. China scores relatively poorly on this measure, and its contribution to excess growth is negative (0.29 percent). At first glance, this seems inconsistent with the effect Investment Profile had in the previous section, but the set of countries is different here and China's record on financial openness is indeed mixed.

All of the other panels use the standard regression (with private credit to GDP and capital account openness), but the number of countries is reduced substantially. The second panel includes a social security measure due to Botero et al. (2004). While China scores relatively high on this measure, Allen, Qian, and Qian (2005) point out some important caveats. Clearly, social security is a very important growth determinant, and according to the official numbers, having a high-quality social security system contributes 0.71 percent to Chinese excess growth. Financial openness remains important, but the significance of trade openness is severely diminished. In this regression, the predicted Chinese excess growth reaches 5.04 percent, significantly reducing unexplained growth.

Panels 3 and 4 of table 4.6 focus on stock market development, reducing our set of countries to 51. As we indicated before, measuring China's stock market development is problematic. It scores very high on the standard turnover measure but rather low on the size of the equity market (market capitalization to GDP measure). The latter number may be closer to the truth. Unfortunately, for our panel of countries the turnover measure is a much more significant predictor of growth. The regression with turnover leads to a very high-predicted excess growth for China (4.89 percent) with turnover contributing 0.85 percent. For the other regions, relative stock market development is important as well. The financial openness measure remains a very important predictor of growth.

While the results in table 4.6 suggest that the growth regressions capture the Chinese experience much better than our previous specifications, it is important to note two important caveats. First, a substantial part of the increase in China's predicted economic growth arises from a stronger convergence effect. It is well known that convergence effects are stronger among more homogeneous sets of countries and our smaller data sets here cause the convergence coefficients to more than double in magnitude. Second, although the tables show impressive growth contributions of

China's social security system and stock market turnover rates, we stress again that measurement issues suggest another interpretation. Table 4.6 shows that privatization, financial openness, a good social security system, and stock market development are all important sustainable sources of economic growth; in all these areas, China needs to catch up with the developed world.

THE CHINA PUZZLE

In the previous sections, standard growth regressions substantially under-predicted the Chinese growth numbers. Once we included institutional features such as social security or turnover (stock market development), China's excess growth was considerably reduced but still close to 1 percent. Unfortunately, China's relative outperformance on these measures is rather suspect, so that the puzzle remains. How can China achieve such extraordinary growth that is not explained by the usual predictors of GDP growth that explain other countries' growth experiences relatively well?

In this section, we explore three possibilities. First, China's asymmetric attitude toward foreign investment, promoting FDI and shunning foreign debt, may have been particularly beneficial. Second, partial state control of investments has led to investment rates that are extraordinarily high (see figure 4.3), and these may not be properly accounted for in our analysis. Third, Chinese economic statistics have met with some serious criticism, and measurement error may drive the Chinese growth puzzle.

FDI AND FOREIGN DEBT

Table 4.7 includes measures of FDI and foreign debt in our benchmark specification. We take the Foreign Debt Index from ICRG, so that higher values actually indicate less foreign debt. China's foreign debt index is 0.711 over the full sample, which is sharply higher than the 0.519 level for developing countries. Over the last four years, the debt index has climbed to 0.900, while the same measure for developing countries has slightly deteriorated to 0.510. The FDI measure is the sum of inflows and outflows over GDP. We have already noted that relative FDI levels for China are not as elevated as many may suspect and, in fact, are dwarfed by the FDI ratios in developed markets. Table 4.7 shows that the ratio of FDI to GDP

Table 4-7 The Impact of FDI and Foreign Debt: Annual Average Real Consumption and GDP Growth (five-year horizon), 1980–2003

Capital Account Openness (Quinn, 72 countries)

	Consumption Growth		GDP Growth	
	Estimate	Standard Error	Estimate	Standard Error
Constant	-0.007861	0.002087	-0.010309	0.001787
Initial GDP	-0.0109	0.0015	-0.0156	0.0010
Secondary School	0.0016	0.0041	0.0149	0.0046
Log(Life Expectancy)	0.0785	0.0140	0.0986	0.0122
Population Growth	-0.4177	0.1052	-0.4311	0.0865
Trade/GDP	0.0022	0.0024	0.0046	0.0020
Private Credit/GDP	0.0018	0.0031	0.0009	0.0023
Foreign Debt Index	**0.0381**	**0.0091**	**0.0382**	**0.0077**
Financial Openness	**0.0053**	**0.0044**	**0.0089**	**0.0040**
R^2	0.197		0.330	

Average	Foreign Debt Index (1981–2003)	Foreign Debt Index (2000–2003)
Developed Countries	0.850	0.787
Developing Countries	0.519	0.510
Africa	0.490	0.458
Asia	0.657	0.592
Latin America	0.501	0.545
China	**0.711**	**0.900**

Capital Account Openness (Quinn, 49 countries)

	Consumption Growth		GDP Growth	
	Estimate	Standard Error	Estimate	Standard Error
Constant	-0.009448	0.00245	-0.007559	0.001886
Initial GDP	-0.0164	0.0011	-0.0191	0.0012
Secondary School	0.0107	0.0040	0.0160	0.0044
Log(Life Expectancy)	0.1079	0.0146	0.1201	0.0146
Population Growth	-0.4439	0.1373	-0.4061	0.1213
Private Credit/GDP	0.0023	0.0028	0.0041	0.0024
Gross FDI/GDP	**0.0541**	**0.0255**	**0.0487**	**0.0199**
Foreign Debt Index	**0.0256**	**0.0097**	**0.0236**	**0.0085**
Financial Openness	**0.0136**	**0.0048**	**0.0186**	**0.0051**
R^2	0.239		0.293	

Average	Gross FDI/GDP (1981–2003)	Gross FDI/GDP (2000–2003)
Developed Countries	0.060	0.134
Developing Countries	0.022	0.036
Africa	0.016	0.030
Asia	0.031	0.043
Latin America	0.026	0.052
China	**0.030**	**0.046**

(continued)

Table 4.7 *continued*

	Excess Consumption Growth (5-year)	Initial GDP	Secondary School	Log(Life Expect)	Population Growth	Private Credit/GDP	Gross FDI/GDP	Foreign Debt Index	Capital Account Openness (Quinn)	Predicted Excess Growth
Developed Countries	0.522%	-2.402%	0.487%	1.775%	0.421%	0.096%	0.157%	0.663%	0.404%	0.655%
Developing Countries	0.045%	1.624%	-0.014%	0.014%	-0.170%	-0.027%	-0.050%	-0.091%	-0.169%	0.173%
Africa	-1.029%	2.105%	-0.084%	-0.967%	-0.490%	-0.039%	-0.072%	-0.222%	-0.252%	-0.966%
Asia	1.435%	1.386%	0.075%	0.461%	-0.049%	0.040%	0.005%	0.146%	-0.049%	1.070%
Latin America	-0.573%	0.224%	0.000%	0.854%	-0.105%	-0.036%	-0.019%	-0.039%	-0.100%	-0.166%
China	**5.950%**	**4.072%**	**-0.060%**	**0.621%**	**0.151%**	**0.109%**	**-0.005%**	**0.260%**	**0.062%**	**4.264%**
Temporal Dimension										
China—1980		**5.148%**	**-0.069%**	**0.687%**	**0.214%**	**-0.061%**	**-0.061%**	**0.211%**	**-0.694%**	**4.432%**
China—2003		**2.966%**	**-0.036%**	**0.619%**	**0.225%**	**-0.012%**	**-0.065%**	**0.834%**	**-0.475%**	**3.110%**

The dependent variable is the overlapping five-year average growth rate of either real per capita consumption or GDP in excess of the corresponding world growth rate. Initial GDP is the log real per capita GDP level updated every five years (1980, 1985, 1990, 2000). Secondary School is the enrollment percentage for that level; Log(Life Expectancy) is the log life expectancy of the total population; Population Growth is the growth rate of total population; Trade/GDP is the ratio of export plus imports to GDP; Private Credit/GDP is the ratio of private credit to GDP. The first regression includes an index reflecting the reliance on foreign debt. The second regression includes the foreign debt index and the gross level of foreign direct investment relative to GDP. These regressions also include the Quinn capital account openness indicator. We report a geographical breakdown of the Foreign Debt Index and the ratio of gross FDI to GDP. Finally, for a collection of geographical regions and China, we report the growth decomposition detailing the contribution of each variable toward predicted excess growth.

is only 0.03 in China over the full sample compared to a ratio of 0.06 for developed countries. In the last four years, the Chinese ratio has increased to 0.046. However, during the same period, the ratio for developed countries jumped to 0.134. Adding these two measures reduces our sample to 49 countries.

Table 4.7 shows that both measures have the expected effects on growth and that both coefficients are significantly different from zero. Interestingly, capital account openness remains significant by itself, even though it may have some correlation with the new variable. The growth decomposition shows that FDI was relatively unimportant for China's growth experience but the lack of foreign debt did provide a positive growth contribution of 0.265 percent on average. Total predicted excess growth increases to 4.264 percent, and most of its value is driven by the convergence effect. Hence, China's special foreign investment policy does not account for its growth miracle.

DOMESTIC INVESTMENT

Another possibility is that China has simply invested much more capital than other countries, and this is not directly reflected in our base specification. Table 4.8 reports some statistics on average GDP and consumption growth, the investment to GDP ratio, capital stock growth, and factor productivity. We will return to the analysis of factor productivity growth and the Young corrections later, but first we will focus on China's investment expenditures.

Both in terms of investment growth and investment to GDP, China is clearly an outlier. It is important to investigate how much these extraordinary levels of investment have contributed to growth because it is likely that they are not sustainable in the long run. For a country to really catch up with the developed world and increase GDP per capita levels, it is important to bring factor productivity levels up to developed country levels (see the discussion in Gourinchas and Jeanne 2004).

In Table 4.9, we attempt to measure how much the very high investment levels in China have contributed to growth by including investment/GDP as an explanatory variable in the regression (again in excess of the world average). We suspect that this component of growth will gradually disappear; instead China must improve institutions, financial development,

Table 4.8   Growth, Investment, and Total Factor Productivity

	GDP Growth	Consumption Growth	Investment/ GDP	Capital Stock Growth	Total Factor Productivity Growth
Developed Countries	0.020	0.019	0.225	0.021	0.014
Developing Countries	0.009	0.009	0.216	0.019	0.003
Africa	0.003	0.003	0.204	0.012	−0.001
Asia	0.030	0.029	0.260	0.042	0.018
Asia (Young adjusted)					0.017
Latin America	0.001	0.003	0.203	0.015	−0.004
China	**0.078**	**0.070**	**0.375**	**0.087**	**0.052**
China (Young adjusted)	**0.051**	**0.061**		**0.079**	**0.020**

We explore averages of real per capita GDP growth (U.S. $), real per capita consumption growth (U.S. $), the investment/GDP ratio, capital stock growth, and total factor productivity growth. The averages are reported for several country groups: developed, developing, Africa, Asia, and Latin America (as described by the World Bank). We also report the associated numbers for China, both official and Young (2003) adjusted data.

and the capital allocation process to enhance factor productivity and thus sustain its growth miracle. The investment/GDP coefficient is more than two standard errors away from zero in all of the excess consumption and GDP growth regressions. However, inclusion of this variable does not completely resolve the problem of a large growth residual. For instance, for the equity market liberalization regression, the predicted excess consumption growth rate increases from 1.774 to 2.084 percent. Across all three openness specifications, the investment to GDP ratio comprises approximately 40 percent of the total predicted excess consumption growth. We conclude that China's extraordinary investment levels can only explain part of the Chinese growth miracle. As an important side note, financial openness remains significant in the presence of investment to GDP. This indirectly suggests that the growth effect of capital market liberalization does not work only through an investment channel but that it may help increase factor productivity.

MEASUREMENT ERROR

In a series of papers, Young (1994, 1995) critically assessed the growth experience of the New Industrializing Countries in Southeast Asia, finding that

Table 4.9 Growth Predictability Including Investment: Annual Average Real Consumption and GDP Growth in Excess of the World (five-year horizon), 1980–2003

Panel A:

	Official Equity Market Liberalization				Equity Market Openness			
	Consumption Growth		GDP Growth		Consumption Growth		GDP Growth	
	Estimate	Standard Error	Estimate	Standard Error	Estimate	Standard Error	Estimate	Standard Error
Constant	−0.0066	0.0020	−0.0059	0.0019	−0.0065	0.0022	−0.0063	0.0023
Initial GDP	−0.0059	0.0016	−0.0102	0.0010	−0.0060	0.0017	−0.0105	0.0011
Secondary School	0.0036	0.0038	0.0120	0.0049	0.0033	0.0039	0.0113	0.0047
Log(Life Expectancy)	0.0667	0.0130	0.0875	0.0127	0.0683	0.0134	0.0899	0.0126
Population Growth	−0.1740	0.0819	−0.2561	0.1086	−0.1884	0.0807	−0.2578	0.1083
Trade/GDP	0.0037	0.0024	0.0049	0.0017	0.0036	0.0025	0.0053	0.0019
Private Credit/GDP	0.0001	0.0031	0.0026	0.0026	0.0001	0.0031	0.0024	0.0028
Investment/GDP	0.0546	0.0178	0.0334	0.0163	0.0575	0.0177	0.0358	0.0167
Financial Openness	0.0061	0.0020	0.0056	0.0027	0.0053	0.0023	0.0064	0.0028
R^2	0.154		0.233		0.152		0.233	

Panel A:

	Capital Account Openness (Quinn)			
	Consumption Growth		GDP Growth	
	Estimate	Standard Error	Estimate	Standard Error
Constant	−0.0057	0.0017	−0.0073	0.0017
Initial GDP	−0.0089	0.0014	−0.0140	0.0010
Secondary School	0.0085	0.0043	0.0197	0.0045
Log(Life Expectancy)	0.0666	0.0152	0.0882	0.0138
Population Growth	−0.3811	0.0907	−0.4679	0.0994
Trade/GDP	0.0002	0.0020	0.0029	0.0018
Private Credit/GDP	0.0020	0.0029	0.0029	0.0022
Investment/GDP	0.0803	0.0222	0.0547	0.0213
Financial Openness	0.0150	0.0035	0.0199	0.0036
R^2	0.183		0.293	

(*continued*)

Table 4.9 *continued*

Panel B:

| | Predicted Excess Growth | | Predicted Excess Growth | | Predicted Excess Growth | |
	Total	Contribution	Total	Contribution	Total	Contribution
Developed Countries	0.307%	0.000%	0.136%	0.000%	0.453%	0.000%
Developing Countries	−0.566%	−0.055%	−0.531%	−0.058%	−0.471%	−0.081%
Africa	−1.264%	−0.113%	−1.204%	−0.119%	−1.254%	−0.167%
Asia	0.455%	0.182%	0.338%	0.191%	0.698%	0.267%
Latin America	−0.335%	−0.127%	−0.276%	−0.133%	−0.218%	−0.186%
China	**2.084%**	**0.787%**	**1.950%**	**0.829%**	**2.968%**	**1.156%**

In panel A, the dependent variable is the overlapping five-year average growth rate of either real per capita consumption or GDP in excess of the corresponding world growth rate. Initial GDP is the log real per capita GDP level updated every five years (1980, 1985, 1990, 2000). Secondary School is the enrollment percentage for that level; Log(Life Expectancy) is the log life expectancy of the total population; Population Growth is the growth rate of total population; Trade/GDP is the ratio of export plus imports to GDP; Private Credit/GDP is the ratio of private credit to GDP; and Investment/GDP represented the ratio of Investment to GDP. The control variables are all in excess of the world. We report the coefficient on one of three openness indicators (also in excess of the world): the Official Equity Liberalization indicator that takes a value of one when the equity market is liberalized; the Equity Liberalization Intensity measure is the ratio of IFC Investables to Global market capitalization; or the Capital Account Liberalization (Quinn) indicator that takes a value between 0 and 1 depending on the intensity of the reported capital account restrictions. The first two sets of regressions include 96 countries, whereas the last includes 77 countries.

Panel B reports the decomposition of the consumption growth regressions in panel A, where the dependent variable is the overlapping five-year average growth rate of real per capita consumption in excess of the corresponding world growth rate. The values are reported for several country groups: developed, developing, Africa, Asia, and Latin America (as described by the World Bank). We also report the associated numbers for China. Each entry shows the average for that country group multiplied by the coefficient reported in panel A. All standard errors provide a correction for the overlapping nature of the data.

careful measurement of inputs makes their growth experience less extraordinary. It is striking that in our tables, Asia as a whole is still an outlier as well. Therefore, we estimated our benchmark specification with regional dummy variables (Africa, Asia, Europe, North America, and South America). This impacts the significance of some of our variables in the three specifications. However, many of the same results hold. For example, the openness variable is always positive but not significantly different from zero in the official liberalization or equity openness regressions. Similar to the results without regional dummies, the capital account openness variable is significant and economically large in size (137 basis points for consumption growth and 202 basis points for GDP growth). The openness indicator in the GDP regression is more than six standard errors from zero. These results are available on request. More importantly, the Asia regional dummy is plus 50 basis points, but this does little to better explain either the Asian or Chinese growth experience. However, there are very concrete indications of problems with Chinese statistics.

Young (2003) argues that the official government statistics in China have two relevant biases: a price deflation bias and growth in the labor force that outstrips population growth. We provide a robustness analysis of our standard growth regressions that implements the Young adjustment. GDP growth is scaled down by 1.8 percent to reflect the price adjustment and 0 percent to capture the growth in the labor force and increased labor participation. With data from 1980 to 2003, the official GDP growth rate averages 7.84 percent per year. The Young adjusted data show a growth rate of 5.14 percent. Such an adjustment substantially reduces excess GDP growth.

Young (2003) argues that consumption growth rates suffer substantially less from the price deflation bias. Consequently, we only adjust consumption growth by 0.9 percent, the labor force adjustment. We report the corrected numbers in table 4.8.

Table 4.10 investigates whether the Young adjustments to consumption and GDP growth affect the ability of the growth regressions to explain China's growth experience. In an effort to maximize explanatory power, we augment our benchmark specification with the composite political risk measure and investment to GDP. The private credit to GDP measure we use is adjusted for state ownership. When we run this specification, trade to GDP is no longer significant and has the wrong sign. We therefore remove it from the specification reported in table 4.10. We use capital account openness as the financial openness measure.

The results largely confirm the results in previous tables in the consumption growth regressions, but for GDP growth, private credit to GDP is now significantly positive, whereas the investment to GDP ratio no longer is. When we perform the growth decomposition for consumption growth, we still find unexplained excess growth close to 2 percent, but several variables have a nonnegligible effect on Chinese excess growth, including life expectancy, population growth, investment to GDP, and political risk. The lack of full financial openness is the largest growth detractor. Table 4.10 also reports a decomposition for GDP growth, with the surprising result that China's excess growth is now fully accounted for. Although this result undoubtedly confirms that measurement issues are of first-order importance, we must caution again that the convergence effect is the main contribution. This implies that Chinese growth is explained "on average"

Table 4.10a   Growth Predictability (Young adjusted Chinese GDP data): Annual Average Real GDP Growth in Excess of the World (five-year horizon), 63 Countries, 1980–2003

A. Benchmark regression

	Consumption Growth		GDP Growth	
	Estimate	Standard Error	Estimate	Standard Error
Constant	−0.0069	0.0015	−0.0101	0.0016
Initial GDP	−0.0100	0.0017	−0.0165	0.0016
Secondary School	0.0042	0.0048	0.0159	0.0050
Log(Life Expectancy)	0.0645	0.0173	0.0996	0.0166
Population Growth	−0.6341	0.1180	−0.5657	0.1096
Private Credit/GDP (adjusted)	0.0005	0.0026	0.0049	0.0022
Investment/GDP	0.0643	0.0208	0.0143	0.0243
Political Risk (composite)	0.0217	0.0109	0.0332	0.0089
Financial Openness (Quinn)	0.0070	0.0037	0.0119	0.0038
R^2	0.189		0.278	

The dependent variable is the overlapping five-year average growth rate of either real per capita consumption or GDP in excess of the corresponding world growth rate. Per capita consumption and GDP growth for China are adjusted following Young (2003). Initial GDP is the log real per capita GDP level updated every five years (1980, 1985, 1990, 2000). Secondary School is the enrollment percentage for that level; Log(Life Expectancy) is the log life expectancy of the total population; Population Growth is the growth rate of total population; Private Credit/GDP (adjusted) is the ratio of private credit to GDP adjusted for state ownership; Investment/GDP represented the ratio of Investment to GDP; and Political Risk is the ICRG composite political risk index. The control variables are all in excess of the world. We also report the coefficient on the Capital Account Openness (Quinn) indicator that takes a value between 0 and 1 (also in excess of the world) depending on the intensity of the reported capital account restrictions. All standard errors provide a correction for the overlapping nature of the data.

Table 4.1ob Growth Predictability (Young adjusted Chinese GDP data): Annual Average Real GDP Growth in Excess of the World (five-year horizon), 63 countries, 1980–2003

B. Growth Decomposition	Excess Growth (5-year) (Young Adjusted)	Initial GDP	Secondary School	Log(Life Expectancy)	Population Growth	Private Credit/GDP (adjusted)	Investment/GDP	Pol (Political Risk-composite)	Openness (Capital Account-Quinn)	Predicted Excess Growth
Developed Countries	0.495%	−1.479%	0.193%	1.060%	0.581%	0.017%	0.000%	0.468%	0.192%	0.345%
Developing Countries	−0.294%	1.334%	−0.046%	−0.484%	−0.397%	−0.008%	−0.065%	−0.151%	−0.072%	−0.577%
Africa	−1.292%	1.722%	−0.088%	−1.149%	−0.719%	−0.005%	−0.137%	−0.189%	−0.103%	−1.356%
Asia	1.489%	0.994%	0.020%	0.179%	−0.078%	0.005%	0.218%	0.018%	−0.045%	0.622%
Latin America	−0.813%	0.708%	−0.026%	0.164%	−0.266%	−0.012%	−0.148%	−0.144%	−0.008%	−0.420%
China	5.051%	2.594%	−0.027%	0.380%	0.187%	−0.018%	0.907%	0.090%	−0.157%	3.265%
Temporal Dimension										
China—1980		3.145%	−0.027%	0.410%	0.306%	−0.013%	0.657%	0.206%	−0.359%	3.636%
China—2003		1.812%	−0.014%	0.370%	0.321%	−0.024%	1.267%	−0.022%	−0.246%	2.797%
GDP										
Developed Countries	0.760%	−2.436%	0.728%	1.637%	0.518%	0.156%	0.000%	0.715%	0.325%	0.638%
Developing Countries	−0.180%	2.198%	−0.172%	−0.748%	−0.354%	−0.071%	−0.014%	−0.231%	−0.122%	−0.520%
Africa	−1.292%	2.837%	−0.330%	−1.774%	−0.642%	−0.050%	−0.030%	−0.289%	−0.173%	−1.456%
Asia	1.786%	1.637%	0.076%	0.276%	−0.070%	0.048%	0.048%	0.028%	−0.076%	0.962%
Latin America	−0.826%	1.167%	−0.098%	0.254%	−0.237%	−0.106%	−0.033%	−0.220%	−0.013%	−0.293%
China	3.965%	4.273%	−0.102%	0.587%	0.166%	−0.166%	0.202%	0.137%	−0.265%	3.826%
Temporal Dimension										
China—1980		5.181%	−0.102%	0.634%	0.273%	−0.115%	0.146%	0.314%	−0.607%	5.035%
China—2003		2.985%	−0.054%	0.571%	0.286%	−0.217%	0.282%	−0.033%	−0.416%	2.433%

This table reports the decomposition of the regressions in panel A, where the dependent variable is the overlapping five-year average growth rate of real per capita consumption or GDP in excess of the corresponding world growth rate. Per capita consumption and GDP growth for China are adjusted following Young (2003). The values are reported for several country groups: Developed, Developing, Africa, Asia, and Latin America (as described by the World Bank). We also report the associated numbers for China, including the comparison of predicted growth across the sample from 1980 to 2003. Each entry shows the average for that country group multiplied by the coefficient reported in panel A.

over the sample but that with initial GDP increasing over time, predicted Chinese growth in 2003 is much lower than in 1980.

FACTOR PRODUCTIVITY GROWTH

Because of its importance to long-run development, let us return to the factor productivity statistics produced in table 4.8. Factor productivity here is defined in the usual way. We build per capita physical capital stocks over the period from 1980 through 2003 using the method in King and Levine (1993). We derive an initial estimate of the capital stock for 1950, assuming each country is at its steady-state capital-output ratio at that time. Then, we use the aggregate real investment series from the Penn World Tables 6.0 and the perpetual inventory method with a depreciation rate of 7 percent to compute the capital stock in later years. Productivity growth is calculated as the difference between the GDP growth rate and 0.3 times the capital stock growth rate, assuming a capital share of 0.3.

As we can see from the table, developing countries have on average much lower factor productivity growth than developed countries. Again, China is an exception, displaying factor productivity growth in excess of 5 percent per annum. It is almost certain that this does not reflect the true state of affairs. Reports from experts typically mention the existence of a relatively efficient private sector, but a largely inefficient state sector. The factor productivity growth results may arise in a number of ways. First, the assumed capital share ratio of 0.3 may be erroneous for China. In fact, Young (2003) provides alternative (and higher) estimates for China and a number of Southeast Asian countries. Second, the GDP growth numbers may have been overstated, but some reports suggest that for some years official statistics may even understate Chinese growth. Third, investment growth might be understated in the official statistics.

We reestimated factor productivity growth using our data set but making use of the corrections in Young (2003): a decrease in GDP growth of 2.7 percent; a decrease in capital growth of 0.9 percent, reflecting the increased labor participation also reflected in GDP growth; and an increased capital share of 0.4. With these corrections, China's factor productivity growth falls to a more mundane 2 percent. Though still high, this may make China less of an outlier. In Bekaert, Harvey, and Lundblad (2006c), we explore the determinants of factor productivity growth. These regressions reveal that the same variables that explain growth also explain factor productivity growth. Interestingly, that decomposition reveals that the regression explains Chinese factor productivity growth, when the Young adjustments are taken into account. We intend to explore this issue further in future work.

RESULTS ON GROWTH VOLATILITY

Panel A of table 4.11 reports the results for idiosyncratic growth variability. We focus on consumption growth variability because that is most relevant from a welfare perspective.

The regression shows relatively few significant effects. The level of development, proxied by life expectancy and secondary school enrollment, has a negative effect on variability, and the coefficients are always more than one standard error below zero. High population growth significantly increases variability in each case. These results are consistent with those reported in Bekaert, Harvey, and Lundblad (2006b).

Trade openness significantly increases the variability of idiosyncratic consumption growth. This notion seems consistent with the Rodrik (1998a, 1998b) hypothesis, which conjectures that open countries are more buffeted by international shocks. However, Rodrik suggests that such countries would have large government sectors to help them smooth such shocks. By including the size of the government sector as an independent variable, we control for this effect. Nonetheless, the trade variable retains its significance. Moreover, the larger government sectors increase growth variability.

The equity market liberalization indicator is negative but is only 1.7 standard errors from zero. In contrast, the equity market openness variable is negative and 3.7 standard errors from zero. Although the capital account openness variable is also negative, it is not significantly different from zero. Consequently, having an open capital account does not necessarily lead to more real variability. In contrast, an open equity market is associated with significant lower real variability.

The bottom part of panel A compares actual idiosyncratic volatility (the square root of the average squared residuals) with the model. When we group over various regions, the model clearly gets the absolute and relative magnitudes about right. Because China represents such a big outlier in the regressions, we had to adapt the procedure to compute actual idiosyncratic volatility, subtracting the average residual first. Clearly, the regression slightly overpredicts the variability of Chinese

Table 4.11 Idiosyncratic Volatility Predictability: Annual Real Consumption Squared Growth Residuals, 1980–2003

Panel A: Volatility model estimates

	Official Equity Market Liberalization		Equity Market Openness		Capital Account Openness (Quinn)	
	Estimate	Standard Error	Estimate	Standard Error	Estimate	Standard Error
Constant	0.00076	0.00010	0.00085	0.00011	0.00069	0.00008
Initial GDP	0.00002	0.00006	0.00005	0.00006	0.00008	0.00007
Secondary School	−0.00061	0.00029	−0.00047	0.00030	−0.00050	0.00022
Log(Life Expectancy)	−0.00031	0.00050	−0.00052	0.00049	−0.00149	0.00063
Population Growth	0.01175	0.00510	0.01122	0.00514	0.01416	0.00512
Trade/GDP	0.00048	0.00021	0.00041	0.00022	0.00065	0.00016
Gov/GDP	0.00411	0.00165	0.00412	0.00167	0.00153	0.00126
Private Credit/GDP	0.00017	0.00013	0.00024	0.00014	0.00011	0.00014
Financial Openness	−0.00027	0.00016	−0.00052	0.00015	−0.00008	0.00018
R^2	0.071		0.074		0.088	

	Observed Growth Volatility (residual)	Predicted Growth Volatility	Observed Growth Volatility (residual)	Predicted Growth Volatility	Observed Growth Volatility (residual)	Predicted Growth Volatility
Developed Countries	1.292%	2.220%	1.296%	2.230%	1.315%	2.033%
Developing Countries	3.032%	3.114%	3.038%	3.217%	3.008%	3.143%
Africa	3.250%	3.526%	3.251%	3.614%	3.253%	3.584%
Asia	2.506%	2.413%	2.553%	2.548%	2.385%	2.485%
Latin America	2.777%	2.528%	2.766%	2.614%	2.787%	2.505%
China	**4.743%**		**4.846%**		**4.192%**	
China (mean-adjusted)	**1.752%**	**2.346%**	**1.783%**	**2.694%**	**1.780%**	**1.914%**

Panel B: Variance decomposition: What happens to growth volatility when a variable is omitted

	Secondary School	Log(Life Expectancy)	Population Growth	Trade/GDP	Gov/GDP	Private Credit/GDP	Openness (Quinn)
Developed Countries	-0.407	-0.478	-0.297	0.334	0.114	0.143	0.005
Developing Countries	0.040	0.091	0.085	0.173	-0.036	-0.017	-0.001
Africa	0.060	0.169	0.120	0.151	0.002	-0.019	-0.001
Asia	-0.027	-0.051	0.025	0.140	-0.120	0.038	-0.001
Latin America	0.036	-0.049	0.090	0.046	-0.139	-0.035	-0.000
China	0.039	-0.132	-0.088	-0.078	-0.124	0.129	-0.004

In panel A, the dependent variable is the squared residual (idiosyncratic volatility) from the associated growth regressions. Initial GDP is the log real per capita GDP level updated every five years (1980, 1985, 1990, 2000). Secondary School is the enrollment percentage for that level; Log(Life Expectancy) is the log life expectancy of the total population; Population Growth is the growth rate of total population; Trade/GDP is the ratio of export plus imports to GDP; Gov/GDP is the ratio of government consumption to GDP; and Private Credit/GDP is the ratio of private credit to GDP. The control variables are all in excess of the world. We report the co-efficient on one of three openness indicators (also in excess of the world): the Offical Equity Liberalization indicator that takes a value of one when the equity market is liberalized; the Equity Liberalization Intensity measure is the ratio of IFC Investables to Global market capitalization; or the Capital Account Liberalization (Quinn) indicator that takes a value between 0 and 1 depending on the intensity of the reported capital account restrictions. The first two sets of regressions include 96 countries, whereas the last includes 77 countries. We compare the predicted level of growth volatility with the observed residual volatility; for China, we also con-sider the volatility of the de-meaned growth residual. In panel B, we set the coefficient on the particular variable equal to zero. We then report the proportional change in the predicted variance when we set the variable back to its original value, that is, (actual predicted variance−new predicted variance)/(actual predicted variance). This exercise omits initial GDP from the regression.

consumption growth. However, the model does so for the developed countries as well and more dramatically so. Hence, although China has achieved remarkable growth with less variability than expected, the volatility of its growth experience is less puzzling given its economic, political, and financial infrastructure as captured by the regression variables.

Panel B of table 4.11 decomposes the contribution of each regressor to volatility. To do this, we set the coefficient on a particular variable to zero and compute the predicted variance.[4] The numbers reported are the change in the predicted variance from setting the variable back at its actual value relative to the actual predicted variance. For example, if setting life expectancy to zero increases the variance, as it does for developed countries, we report a negative value. The value of −0.478 means that having high life expectancy reduces the variance by 47.8 percent. Before we conduct this exercise, we actually rerun the regression, omitting the initial GDP variable. The variable is never significant and has a sign that is hard to interpret, likely because it is relatively colinear with life expectancy and secondary school enrollment. For developing countries, the table reveals that secondary school enrollment, life expectancy, and population growth significantly contribute to low real volatility. Interestingly, the effect of external risk, as proxied by the trade sector, is not only statistically but also economically significant. Both profligate governments and a well-developed banking sector still increase real volatility by 10 percent. Although the latter result seems counterintuitive, it is conceivable that countries with a better institutional framework to smooth income shocks can afford to incur more real risk and actually do so. China also receives a relative large contribution to private credit to GDP, but the use of the unadjusted measure makes this result difficult to interpret. Interestingly, what most contributed to China's relatively low variability is its high score on life expectancy. For a typical developing country, life expectancy has a small positive impact on idiosyncratic volatility. China behaves more like developed countries where life expectancy is a negative contributor to idiosyncratic growth volatility. Similarly, the contribution of population growth is negative and reasonably large, whereas the opposite is true for developing countries as a group. Financial openness has negligible effects on volatility.

HETEROGENEOUS RESPONSES TO FINANCIAL MARKET INTEGRATION

Does the growth and volatility effect from financial openness differ across countries? For example, theories of financial fragility (Furman and Stiglitz 1998) suggest that a good institutional framework is essential to prevent crises. We now consider a menu of characteristics that might affect both the growth and volatility response. We consider variables related to financial development, government-provided insurance, the quality of political institutions, and the investment environment.

Our method for table 4.12 is as follows. In panel A, we focus on the official equity market liberalization variable. In the main regression with control variables, we break up the liberalization indicator variable into three pieces. The first indicator is for countries that are fully liberalized throughout our sample. The second indicator is for liberalizing countries with a lower than median value of the particular characteristic that we are considering. The third indicator is for liberalizing countries with a higher than median value of the characteristic. We also consider the direct effect of the characteristic by adding it to the main regression. By examining the difference between the "from the low level of the variable" and the "from the high level of the variable," we can determine whether the growth and growth volatility response to a liberalization differs across key characteristics. For all characteristics, "high" is good (high development, low risk) and vice versa. Finally, we report the low versus high separating value and the average value for China.

In panel B of table 4.12, we explore the Quinn measure of capital account openness. Here a liberalizing country (and the date at which it liberalizes) is defined as a country that increases its capital account openness measure by more than 0.25. A fully liberalized country is a country with an openness measure above 0.75 for the full sample. We ignore the few reversals that are observed.

FINANCIAL DEVELOPMENT

We consider three measures of financial development: size of the banking system, equity market turnover, and size of the equity market.

Countries with more developed banking sectors experience significantly higher consumption growth and lower consumption growth volatility using both measures of openness. The coefficients for countries

Table 4.12 Do the Growth and Volatility Effects Differ Across Countries? Annual Average Real Excess Consumption Growth (five-year horizon), 1980–2003

Panel A: Official Equity Liberalization

	Mean			Volatility			# of Countries	Low Versus High Separating Value	China Average Value
	Estimate	Standard Error	Wald Test	Estimate	Standard Error	Wald Test			
Priv/GDP	0.00291	0.00261		0.00027	0.00014		96	0.36	0.92
Fully Liberalized	0.00775	0.00173		−0.00058	0.00009				
Low Value	0.00249	0.00326		0.00011	0.00022				
High Value	0.01214	0.00424	4.03**	−0.00044	0.00019	5.66**			
Priv/GDP (adjusted)	0.00129	0.00230		−0.00010	0.00016		67	0.31	0.004
Fully Liberalized	0.00964	0.00146		−0.00028	0.00009				
Low Value	0.00022	0.00235		0.00009	0.00024				
High Value	0.01489	0.00554	7.72***	−0.00030	0.00024	1.22			
Turnover	0.01107	0.00274		0.00010	0.00007		51	0.12	1.48
Fully Liberalized	0.01008	0.00210		−0.00022	0.00007				
Low Value	−0.01106	0.00574		0.00001	0.00019				
High Value	0.00479	0.000422	8.55***	−0.00006	0.00011	0.10			
MCAP/GDP	0.00325	0.00303		−0.00012	0.00009		51	0.13	0.24
Fully Liberalized	0.00968	0.00217		−0.00031	0.00007				
Low Value	−0.00842	0.00468		0.00040	0.00015				
High Value	0.00515	0.00457	8.22***	−0.00031	0.00015	10.25***			

Privatization	0.02996	0.00879		0.00015	0.00031		44	0.55	0.44
Fully Liberalized	0.00774	0.00233		-0.00033	0.00010				
Low Value	-0.00613	0.00373		-0.00001	0.00015				
High Value	0.00618	0.00565	3.83*	-0.00031	0.00019	1.39			
Social Security	0.01173	0.00445		-0.00068	0.00022		59	1.60	2.06
Fully Liberalized	0.00787	0.00268		-0.00016	0.00008				
Low Value	-0.00294	0.00533		0.00025	0.00016				
High Value	-0.00099	0.00341	0.12	-0.00008	0.00013	2.54			
Gov/GDP	0.00832	0.01577		0.00411	0.00168		96	0.13	0.13
Fully Liberalized	0.00762	0.00180		-0.00067	0.00013				
Low Value	0.00478	0.00460		0.00015	0.00013				
High Value	0.00857	0.00267	0.67	-0.00023	0.00028	2.04			
Quality of Inst.	0.01379	0.00645		-0.00157	0.00039		86	0.56	0.57
Fully Liberalized	0.00370	0.00162		-0.00021	0.00011				
Low Value	0.00782	0.00353		0.00022	0.00026				
High Value	0.00334	0.00378	1.04	-0.00021	0.00019	4.13**			
Socioeconomic Conditions	0.05110	0.01084		-0.00081	0.00044		86	0.53	0.57
Fully Liberalized	0.00225	0.00219		-0.00042	0.00011				
Low Value	-0.00045	0.00257		0.00018	0.00022				
High Value	0.01178	0.00547	3.98**	-0.00057	0.00026	10.78***			
Investment Profile	0.04528	0.00878		-0.00050	0.00034		86	0.50	0.71
Fully Liberalized	0.00204	0.00210		-0.00041	0.00010				
Low Value	0.00462	0.00322		0.00034	0.00022				
High Value	0.00314	0.00379	0.10	-0.00060	0.00023	24.06***			

(continued)

Table 4.12 continued

Panel B: Capital Account Openness (Quinn)

	Mean			Volatility			# of Countries	Low Versus High Separating Value	China Average Value
	Estimate	Standard Error	Wald Test	Estimate	Standard Error	Wald Test			
Priv/GDP	0.00899	0.00264		0.00015	0.00014		77	0.35	0.92
Fully Liberalized	0.00456	0.00129		-0.00018	0.00007				
Low Value	-0.00148	0.00540		0.00062	0.00032				
High Value	0.01464	0.00455	6.81***	-0.00013	0.00026	2.94*			
Priv/GDP (adjusted)	0.00676	0.00201		-0.00013	0.00011		63	0.30	0.004
Fully Liberalized	0.00591	0.00132		-0.00009	0.00005				
Low Value	-0.00701	0.00582		0.00080	0.00026				
High Value	0.02462	0.00430	18.09***	-0.00048	0.00013	20.11***			
Turnover	0.01108	0.00264		0.00000	0.00007		49	0.22	1.48
Fully Liberalized	0.00455	0.00162		-0.00003	0.00006				
Low Value	0.03273	0.00535		0.00049	0.00032				
High Value	0.02298	0.00418	3.02*	-0.00004	0.00012	3.51*			
MCAP/GDP	0.00226	0.00314		-0.00014	0.00008		49	0.21	0.24
Fully Liberalized	0.00740	0.00160		-0.00005	0.00006				
Low Value	0.02281	0.00476		0.00050	0.00025				
High Value	0.03077	0.00534	1.37***	-0.00021	0.00016	10.24***			
Privatization	0.03000	0.00960		0.00003	0.00031		44	0.58	0.44
Fully Liberalized	0.00132	0.00151		0.00002	0.00006				
Low Value	0.00425	0.00621		0.00035	0.00018				
High Value	0.01798	0.00410	3.06*	0.00002	0.00022	1.60			
Social Security	0.01230	0.00343		-0.00048	0.00017		59	1.98	2.06
Fully Liberalized	0.00514	0.00183		-0.00008	0.00006				
Low Value	0.02505	0.00454		0.00061	0.00025				
High Value	0.00200	0.00486	12.47***	-0.00008	0.00021	3.45*			

	A coef	A se	A Wald	B coef	B se	B Wald	N	R^2	R^2
Gov/GDP	−0.00953	0.01560		0.00185	0.00127		77	0.14	0.13
Fully Liberalized	0.00365	0.00135		−0.00008	−0.00008				
Low Value	0.00833	0.00607		0.00003	0.00029				
High Value	0.00989	0.00469	0.04	−0.00029	−0.00036	0.25			
Quality of Inst.	0.02136	0.00666		0.00140	0.00032		72	0.56	0.57
Fully Liberalized	0.00280	0.00118		−0.00012	0.00006				
Low Value	0.00032	0.00566		0.00056	0.00029				
High Value	0.01314	0.00381	4.35**	−0.00001	0.00012	3.29*			
Socio-eco Conditions	0.04590	0.00991		−0.00051	0.00035		72	0.53	0.57
Fully Liberalized	−0.00026	0.00142		−0.00010	0.00008				
Low Value	0.00302	0.00466		0.00062	0.00027				
High Value	0.00943	0.00435	1.52	−0.00044	0.00015	16.68***			
Investment Profile	0.03994	0.00833		−0.00049	0.00030		72	0.58	0.71
Fully Liberalized	0.00014	0.00163		−0.00017	0.00007				
Low Value	0.00263	0.00447		0.00066	0.00026				
High Value	0.00901	0.00552	1.05	−0.00074	0.00019	19.46***			

The dependent variable is either the overlapping five-year average growth rate of real per capita excess consumption growth or the associated squared growth residual (idiosyncratic volatility). In each regression, the standard control variables are included (as in table 4.4, but not reported for space). For each interaction variable, we separately conduct regressions. We also separate the official equity liberalization effect (panel A) and the capital account openness effect (panel B) for fully open and liberalizing countries. For capital account openness, we denote a liberalization country as one that experiences at least a 0.25 increase in the Quinn index value. For liberalizing countries, we estimate interaction effects with the financial development, legal, and investment condition variables; we report the associated impact on consumption growth and volatility for a liberalizing country for a low level (below the median of the associated interaction variable for liberalizing countries) and for a liberalizing country at a high level (above the median of the associated interaction variable for liberalizing countries).

The financial development variables we consider are the overlapping ratio of private credit to GDP, equity market turnover, market capitalization/GDP, and the degree of privatization. We also consider the social security index and the size of the government sector/GDP. Finally, we also consider the quality of institutions, socioeconomic conditions, and the investment profile. The number of countries for which the interaction variable is available is also provided. Finally, we provide the cutoff value for what is considered a below- or above-median country, and report the associated average for China. All standard errors provide a correction for the overlapping nature of the data. Wald tests are conducted for which the null hypothesis is the high and low coefficients are equal; test statistics are provided and *, **, and *** denote significance of the test at the 10, 5, and 1 percent levels, respectively.

that are lower than median private credit to GDP are not significant for either the growth or volatility regressions. However, high private credit to GDP countries experience increased growth and decreased volatility upon liberalization. The Wald tests indicate that the difference between the two coefficients is statistically significant. As noted earlier, using this standard indicator, we see that China can be placed in the "high" private credit/GDP group of countries, but in reality China's banking system is underdeveloped. We also rerun the regression using the adjusted private credit measure, which more accurately reflects China's true banking development. For the equity liberalization regression, the mean interaction effects become much stronger and the volatility effects are weaker. Nevertheless, it remains the case that only countries with a well-developed banking sector derive unambiguously beneficial effects of equity market liberalization. In the case of the capital account openness regression, the adjusted measure leads to even stronger interaction effects than were present for the unadjusted measure.

The results are more mixed for the other two measures of financial development. For the official liberalization indicator, the growth response to liberalization is positive (negative) for high (low) turnover countries and the difference in responses is statistically significant at the 1 percent level; for the capital account openness indicator, the sign is reversed. There is no significant difference in the volatility response using the official liberalization measure, whereas in the capital account openness regression, only high turnover countries experience a modest volatility decrease.

Countries with a high market capitalization to GDP measure experience significantly higher growth than low market capitalization countries after official liberalizations. However, there is no significant difference in the growth effect when we examine the capital account liberalization measure. However, for volatility, both the official equity market and the capital account liberalizations measures produce significantly lower volatility for countries with relatively large stock markets compared to countries with small stock markets.

PRIVATIZATION

There is a general perception that an inefficient state sector misallocates capital and that most of the growth in China comes from more or less private enterprises. Relaxing state control of the resource allocation process could potentially generate substantial additional growth and improve the efficiency with which foreign funds are allocated. In table 4.12, we use BERI's privatization measure to test whether there are threshold effects for the liberalization effect with respect to this measure. Not surprisingly, China ranks in the bottom half of our country set on the privatization measure. Privatization has a strong and significant direct effect on growth but does not significantly affect volatility. The growth effect of liberalizing countries with a small government sector (high levels of privatization) is 63 basis points, whereas it is minus 61 basis points for countries with low levels of privatization in panel A. The difference is significant at the 10 percent level. The volatility effect of liberalization is more negative for highly privatized countries, but the difference is not significant. The results using capital account liberalization in panel B are qualitatively similar for growth, but volatility in countries with low privatization levels actually increases upon liberalization, whereas it remains unchanged for the highly privatized countries.

THE GOVERNMENT AS A PROVIDER OF INSURANCE

Social security systems may be the most important means of smoothing income shocks in most countries, especially for low-income people. The effect of social security is significantly positive for growth and negative for growth volatility. As we discussed, China places somewhat implausibly in the "high" group of countries for social security. Note that our sample here is much smaller and that we do not have panel data on social security. In the consumption growth volatility regression, the coefficient for the higher than median countries is negative in both panels A and B, but only in the capital account openness specification is the difference with the coefficient for countries with poor social security systems statistically significant at the 10 percent level. Hence, there is only weak evidence that social security systems help in realizing the consumption insurance benefits from open capital markets. As to the effects of financial openness on average growth, social security generates adverse effects in the capital account openness regressions. Countries with low levels of social security seem to generate significantly larger liberalization effects. In the official equity market liberalization regression, there are neither significant coefficients nor significant interaction effects.

We also use the size of the government sector as a proxy for the extent of shock insurance through the government. For this variable, China places in the "low" group of countries. We find that countries with higher than median government sectors have a significantly positive consumption growth effect associated with financial openness. Countries with lower than median government sectors also have a positive growth increment, but the coefficient is not significantly different from zero. Although the direct effect of the size of the government sector on volatility remains positive, liberalizing countries with relatively large government sectors experience a decrease in volatility. However, the coefficient is not significantly different from zero. Countries with small government sectors experience small and insignificant volatility increases upon liberalization. Overall, we do not observe significant threshold effects.

QUALITY OF POLITICAL INSTITUTIONS

We focus on the components of the ICRG Political Risk Rating that are associated with the quality of political institutions (table 4.2). Acemoglu, Johnson, and Robinson (2002) stress the importance of the institutional environment in explaining cross-country differences in economic development. Our variable includes Corruption, Law and Order, and Bureaucratic Quality. China is slightly above the median value. The own effect of this variable is positive for growth and negative for growth volatility—both being statistically significant in each of the liberalization specifications. In the official equity liberalization specification, both countries with higher and lower than median quality of political institutions, experience positive growth increments associated with financial openness. However, neither coefficient is significantly different from zero. In the capital account liberalization specification, countries that liberalize and have higher quality institutions have significantly higher growth than liberalizing countries with poor institutions.

The volatility specifications provide consistent results. Although some of the coefficients are not significant, liberalizations (both definitions) are associated with higher volatility for countries with poor quality institutions and lower volatility for countries with good quality institutions.

SOCIOECONOMIC CONDITIONS

The coefficient on our indicator of socioeconomic conditions (government stability, socioeconomic conditions, and investment profile) shows a significant increment to consumption growth in both the official and capital account liberalization specification. However, the liberalization effect for low versus high socioeconomic conditions countries is only significant in the official liberalization specification. The volatility regression yields consistent results across both liberalization specifications. Higher than median socioeconomic conditions are associated with significantly lower consumption growth volatility upon liberalization versus countries with poor socioeconomic conditions which face higher consumption growth volatility. In addition, the difference between the two effects is significant.

INVESTMENT CLIMATE

Finally, we consider the investment profile (which is a subcomponent of our socioeconomic conditions index) of different countries. China places in the "high" group of countries. The own growth effect of this variable is very substantial in both specifications, being more than five standard errors above zero. In the volatility regressions, the coefficients are negative but only about 1.6 standard errors below zero.

For both lower and higher than median values of investment profile, the coefficients on the liberalization variables are positive but not significantly different from zero. Both volatility regressions indicate significantly different liberalization responses between investment-friendly and investment-unfriendly countries. The Wald statistics are higher for these tests than for any other tests in the two panels in table 4.12. Investment-friendly countries experience significantly lower consumption growth volatility after liberalizations.

Table 4.12 suggests that both the consumption growth and the consumption volatility response to financial openness depends on the particular situation within a country. We measure country heterogeneity by looking at the extent of financial development, the role of the government sector, the quality of institutions, and the investment climate. Although many of the coefficients are not significantly different from zero, viewed together the evidence is supportive of the hypothesis of heterogeneous responses depending on country characteristics. The responses are consistent with good institutions and financial development generating relatively larger growth and risk-sharing benefits.

CONCLUSIONS

For some, China has become critical to world economic growth. However, little is known about the sources of its extraordinary economic growth over the last two decades. In this chapter, we use panel data and Barro-type cross-country growth regression to see if we can learn something about the Chinese growth experience. From the perspective of a simple cross-country growth regression, China is a huge outlier with the bulk of its past growth unaccounted for by the standard variables. China also has achieved this remarkable growth with relatively low growth volatility, but this seems less of a puzzle given the experiences of countries with similar institutional, financial, and economic backgrounds. Surprisingly, its trade openness played an insignificant role, even though it continues to put China in the spotlight. Among the key variables in predicted growth for China are the simple convergence effect and life expectancy. We find that avoiding foreign debt was beneficial, but the FDI levels China experienced do not suffice to help explain much excess growth. Once we account for political risk variables, the quality of institutions, social security, and state ownership, the cross-country regressions predictions become closer to the actual growth numbers but still underpredict China's growth.

Interestingly, among the variables that seem important to growth and can be affected by policy (for instance, capital account openness, the quality of political institutions, and state ownership), China performs relatively poorly. Lack of full financial openness is an important growth detractor. Although it may appear that China need not grow any faster than it does right now, this perception is incorrect. China's GDP per capita is still only 26.3 percent of the world average. A large gap still needs to be closed. Moreover, as Young convincingly showed, past growth and factor productivity growth was probably overstated, and we find that the unusually high investment to GDP levels China ran also contributed significantly to its growth. Soon, China will also grapple with the consequences of a rapidly aging population, which will absorb significant resources. Before it does, it must find sustainable sources of growth that raise productivity levels toward those of the Western world and improve the capital allocation process. We believe that foreign capital can be rather helpful in this endeavor, but our threshold analysis suggests that full capital account convertibility should probably be preceded by a sound institutional framework of a highly financially developed system, less state ownership, attractive socioeconomic conditions, and a favorable investment profile. On the latter two measures, China appears to score favorably relative to other developing countries. On the other measures, China must still implement significant reforms.

In future work, we plan to investigate more closely what factors are most important in ensuring increased factor productivity. It is conceivable that trade and FDI indirectly provided significant contributions to factor productivity (see also Branstetter and Lardy 2007), and hence, such research may overturn our surprising finding that they played a relatively minor role in China's extraordinary growth.

NOTES

1. These data do not reflect the revisions implemented by the Chinese government at the end of 2005.

2. The Shanghai Stock Exchange was founded in the 1860s and ceased operations in December 1941.

3. If instead we confined the definition to only domestic A and B shares, foreign access to equity would be much smaller. Using the broader definition strengthens the argument that Chinese growth is hard to explain on the basis of financial factors.

4. Note that this is equivalent to setting the variable in question at the world average, since variables enter the regression in excess form.

REFERENCES

Acemoglu, Daron, Simon Johnson, and James A. Robinson. 2002. "Reversal of Fortune: Geography and Institutions in the Making of the Modern World Income Distribution." *Quarterly Journal of Economics* 117: 1231–94.

Aggarwal, Raj and GuojunWu. 2006. "Stock Market Manipulations." *Journal of Business* 79: 1915–1953.

Allen, Franklin, Jun Qian, and Meijun Qian. 2005. "Law, Finance, and Economic Growth in China." *Journal of Financial Economics* 77: 57–116.

Athanasoulis, Stefano G. and Eric van Wincoop. 2000. "Growth Uncertainty and Risk Sharing." *Journal of Monetary Economics* 45: 477–505.

Backus, David K., Patrick Kehoe, and Finn Kydland. 1992. "International Real Business Cycles." *Journal of Political Economy* 100(4): 745–75.

Barro, Robert. 1997. *Determinants of Economic Growth.* Cambridge, MA: MIT Press.

Bekaert, Geert. 1995. "Market Integration and Investment Barriers in Emerging Equity Markets." *World Bank Economic Review* 9: 75–107.

Bekaert, Geert and Campbell R. Harvey. 2000. "Foreign Speculators and Emerging Equity Markets." *Journal of Finance* 55: 565–614.

————. 2005. "A Chronology of Important Financial, Economic and Political Events in Emerging Markets." http://www.duke.edu/~charvey/Countryrisk/couindex.htm.

Bekaert, Geert, Campbell R. Harvey, and Christian Lundblad. 2001. "Emerging Equity Markets and Economic Development." *Journal of Development Economics* 66: 465–504.

————. 2005. "Does Financial Liberalization Spur Growth?" *Journal of Financial Economics* 77: 3–56.

————. 2006a. "Openness, International Risk Sharing and Growth." Unpublished Working Paper.

————. 2006b. "Growth Volatility and Financial Liberalization." *Journal of International Money and Finance* 25: 370–403.

————. 2006c. "Financial Openness and Growth: The Channels." Unpublished Working Paper.

Bhattacharya, Utpal and Hazem Daouk. 2002. "The World Price of Insider Trading." *Journal of Finance* 57(1): 75–108.

Botero, Juan, Simeon Djankov, Rafael La Porta, Florencio Lopez-de-Silanes, and Andrei Shleifer. 2004. "The Regulation of Labor." *Quarterly Journal of Economics* 119: 1339–82.

Branstetter, Lee and Nicholas Lardy. 2006. "China's Embrace of Globalization." NBER Working Paper No. 12373.

————. 2007. "Openness, International Trade and Foreign Investment." Working Paper.

Dinc, I. S. 2005. "Politicians and Banks: Political Influences on Government-Owned Banks in Emerging Markets." *Journal of Financial Economics* 77: 453–79.

Du, J. L. and S. J. Wei. 2004. "Does Insider Trading Raise Market Volatility?" *Economic Journal* 114: 916–42.

Edison, Hali and Frank Warnock. 2003. "A Simple Measure of the Intensity of Capital Controls." *Journal of Empirical Finance* 10: 81–104.

Eichengreen, Barry. 2001. "Capital Account Liberalization: What Do the Cross-Country Studies Tell Us?" *World Bank Economic Review* 15(3): 341–65.

Eichengreen, Barry, James Tobin, and Charles Wyplosz. 1995. "Two Cases for Sands in the Wheels of International Finance." *Economic Journal* 105: 162–72.

Forbes, Kristan. 2004. "The Asian Flu and Russian Virus: The International Transmission of Crises in Firm-Level Data." *Journal of International Economics* 63: 59–92.

Fung, Michael K. Y., Wai-Ming Ho, and Lujing Zhu. 2005. "Financial Liberalization and Economic Growth: A Theoretical Analysis of the Transforming Chinese Economy." *Pacific Economic Review* 10: 125–48.

Furman, Jason and Joseph E. Stiglitz. 1998. "Economic Crises: Evidence and Insights from East Asia." *Brookings Papers on Economic Activity*: 1–114.

Gao, Lei and Gerhard Kling. 2006. "Regulatory Changes and Market Liquidity in Chinese Stock Markets." *Emerging Markets Review* 7(2): 162–75.

Gourinchas, Pierre-Olivier and Olivier Jeanne. 2004. "On the Benefits of Capital Market Integration for Emerging Market Economies." Unpublished Working Paper, International Monetary Fund.

Harvey, C. R. 1995. "Predictable Risk and Returns in Emerging Markets." *Review of Financial Studies* 8(3): 773–816.

Hodrick, Robert J. 1992. "Dividend Yields and Expected Stock Returns: Alternative Procedures for Inference and Measurement." *Review of Financial Studies* 5: 357–86.

Jin Jang, C. 2005. "On the Relationship Between Openness and Growth in China: Evidence from Provincial Time Series Data." Unpublished Working Paper.

King, Robert and Ross Levine. 1993. "Finance and Growth: Schumpeter Might Be Right." *Quarterly Journal of Economics* 108: 717–37.

Kose, M. Ayhan, Eswar S. Prasad, and Marco E. Terrones. 2003. "Financial Integration and Macroeconomic Volatility." *IMF Staff Papers* 50: 119–42.

La Porta, Rafael, Florencio Lopez-de-Silanes, and Andrei Shleifer. 2002. "Government Ownership of Banks." *Journal of Finance* 57: 265–301.

Lewis, Karen K. 1996. "What Can Explain the Apparent Lack of International Consumption Risk Sharing?" *Journal of Political Economy* 104: 267–97.

Lin, Kuan-Pin, Albert J. Menkveld, and Zhishu Yang. 2004. "China and World Equity Markets: A Review of the First Decade." Working Paper.

Mathieson, Donald J. and Liliana Rojaz-Suarez. 1993. "Liberalization of the Capital Account: Experiences and Issues." International Monetary Fund Occasional Paper No. 103.

Mei, Jiangpin, Jose Scheinkman, and Wei Xiong. 2005. "Speculative Trading and Stock Prices: Evidence from Chinese A-B Share Premia." NBER Working Paper No. 11362.

Obstfeld, Maurice. 1992. "International Risk Sharing and Capital Mobility—Another Look." *Journal of International Money and Finance* 11: 115–21.

———. 1994. "Risk-Taking, Global Diversification, and Growth." *American Economic Review* 84: 1310–29.

Prasad, Eswar, Kenneth Rogoff, Shang-Jin Wei, and M. Ayhan Kose. 2003. "Effects of Financial Globalization on Developing Countries: Some Empirical Evidence." Working Paper, International Monetary Fund.

Prasad, Eswar, Thomas Rumbaugh, and Qing Wang. 2005. "Putting the Cart Before the Horse? Capital Account Liberalization and Exchange Rate Flexibility in China." Working Paper, International Monetary Fund.

Prasad, Eswar and Shang-Jin Wei. 2005. "Capital Flows into China." Working Paper.

Quinn, Dennis P. 1997. "The Correlates of Changes in International Financial Regulation." *American Political Science Review* 91: 531–51.

Quinn, Dennis P. and A. M. Toyoda. 2003. "Does Capital Account Liberalization Lead to Economic Growth? An Empirical Investigation." Unpublished Working Paper, Georgetown University.

Rodrik, Dani. 1998a. "Who Needs Capital Account Convertibility?" *Princeton Essays in International Finance* 207: 1–10.

———. 1998b. "Why Do More Open Economies Have Bigger Governments?" *Journal of Political Economy* 106: 997–1032.

Roll, Richard and John Talbot. 2001. "Political and Economic Freedoms and Prosperity." Working Paper, UCLA.

Sun, Qian, Wilson H.S. Tong, and Yuxing Yang. 2005. "Market Liberalization Within a Country." Working Paper.

Tesar, Linda L. 1995. "Evaluating the Gains from International Risk Sharing." *Carnegie-Rochester Conference Series on Public Policy* 42: 95–143.

Van Wincoop, E. 1994. "Welfare Gains from International Risk Sharing." *Journal of Monetary Economics* 34: 175–200.

———. 1999. "How Big Are Potential Welfare Gains from International Risk Sharing?" *Journal of International Economics* 47: 109–235.

Wacziarg, Romain and Karen Horn Welch. 2003. "Trade Liberalization and Growth: New Evidence." NBER Working Paper No. 10152.

Wang, C. Y. and M. S. Cheng. 2004. "Extreme Values and Expected Stock Returns: Evidence from China's Stock Market." *Pacific Basin Finance Journal* 12: 577–97.

Young, Alwyn. 1994. "Lessons from the East-Asian NICS—A Contrarian View." *European Economic Review* 38: 964–73.

———. 1995. "The Tyranny of Numbers: Confronting the Statistical Realities of the East Asian Growth Experience." *Quarterly Journal of Economics* 110: 641–80.

———. 2003. "Gold Into Base Metals: Productivity Growth in the People's Republic of China During the Reform Period." *Journal of Political Economy* 111: 1220–61.

Mary Wadsworth Darby

Bekaert, Harvey, and Lundbland use Barro-type cross-country empirical growth models[1] and build on standard regression techniques to address the question of what variables explain why China is growing so rapidly.[2] China's real GDP growth over the past 25 years measures nearly 7.8 percent per annum, and consumption growth has averaged 7.0 percent, a performance apparently unmatched by any other developing or developed economy. During a recent visit to the United States, China's premier, Hu Jintao, reportedly asked President Bush whether China should be seen as the new economic model for a developing economy. The chapter's methodology is ideally suited to answering this question, as the framework the authors employ is designed to permit factors identified as contributing to economic growth to be decomposed further into elements that can be related to policy prescriptions.

It is commonly accepted that one of the two key factors driving China's economic success has been its openness to the world economy.[3] The chapter examines the evidence for this hypothesis with great care, treating both trade openness and financial sector openness. Special emphasis is given to studying correlations of both GDP growth and consumption growth with measures of (de jure) openness and how the real effects of these policies are affected by financial developments, political risk, and the quality of institutions.[4] In addition, the contribution of the specified variables to volatility is analyzed with a view to analyzing the implications for policy choices by economic decision makers. The analysis rests on the foundation of the econometric cross-country growth model, which explains growth and volatility for the panel of countries the authors include.

For the panel of countries on which the authors' regressions are based, trade has a robustly positive and significant effect on growth; the coefficients on the financial development measure are always more than one standard deviation from zero. Capital account openness and equity market openness have robust and significant effects. The chapter uses several key measures of financial openness as regression variables, which are mainly intended to capture the openness of the equity markets to foreign investors and capital account openness. Indirectly related are measures of political unrest and institutional factors connected with the riskiness of foreign investment.

The authors' econometric models show that neither trade openness nor financial openness is a critical determinant of China's performance. A popular misconception about key variables affecting China's growth is that trade sector openness has been an essential engine of Chinese economic growth. There is, in the chapter's terminology, a very large "residual,"[5] which represents idiosyncratic, unpredictable growth. In fact, the residual for China is the largest of all countries in the panel.

The authors show that the trade sector comprises only 35 percent of GDP on average in China compared to 59 percent in all developing countries, with China's sector being even smaller in comparison to the African regional average. Trade openness is positively correlated and makes a significant contribution to excess growth, but on average never more than 50 basis points per year. The chapter also demonstrates that the measures of financial openness used do not seem to correlate particularly well with the measures of China's economic growth or its volatility. The authors seek to correlate growth with two different kinds of measures of financial openness—equity market liberalization and capital account openness. China does not score well under either measure. In terms of the equity markets, there are significant restrictions on foreign ownership of traded A shares.[6] In terms of capital account openness, China was on average less open, using virtually any measure, than both the average developing country and the average Asian country. This partially reflects the fact that the yuan is still largely inconvertible for capital account balances, and there are severe restrictions on outflows of foreign direct investment. Nevertheless, even FDI inflows in relation to GDP are rather moderate compared to those of other countries.[7]

As a practitioner, I can say that the conclusion about the relatively modest contribution of trade and financial openness to the excess growth of China's economy is very surprising. It definitely runs counter to my impressions as someone who has lived and worked in China since 1973, when I made my first trip to China to import Tsingtao beer. Since 1994 I have been working in the financial industry with Morgan Stanley, living in Hong Kong through 2004. I now travel back and forth to China on business fairly frequently. Over this period, I have had the opportunity to observe firsthand the opening of the economy generally and more recently the financial sector in China to foreign investors and foreign investment. There is no doubt in my mind that improvements in "openness" have had a dramatic positive effect on China's economic growth. Are these impressions simply wrong, or are there other reasons why the regressions of the Bekaert model indicate that openness has made, from an econometric standpoint, little positive contribution to China's economic growth?

The authors consider three possible explanations as to why the regressions seem to conflict with both the results for the country panels and anecdotal impressions such as mine. The most interesting possibility is that while the single-variable FDI may not itself contribute significantly to excess growth, China's embrace of FDI in combination with its shunning of foreign debt may have been particularly beneficial. However, decomposing the growth factor analysis showed that, while the lack of foreign debt did provide a positive contribution, most of the value was driven by the convergence effect and hence could not be an explanation of China's extraordinary performance over the long term.

A second possibility is that measurement error biases the result. Here the authors follow Young, who found significant measurement errors widespread in the assessment of the growth performance of countries in Southeast Asia, the so-called NICs or newly industrialized countries.[8] It would seem to be worthwhile to do a further study of the problems in relation to the data underlying the measures of financial openness used and the econometric model employed. However, it is hardly surprising, given the enormous changes in China's economy over the period in question, that the data may not entirely capture what is happening in China.

A third possibility is that China's large capital investment is the primary driver of China's growth and this fact was not properly reflected in the base specification underlying the econometric model. Apart from its astonishing growth rate, the authors point out that the most extraordinary economic statistic about China is the ratio of investment to GDP. Investment in China in 2003 was 44.3 percent of GDP. This compares with the U.S. investment ratio of 15.2 percent and an average for developing countries of 21.5 percent. The authors point out that this huge investment has been financed largely through domestic savings. Although China has attracted large amounts of FDI, it is by no means the primary source of funds for capital accumulation in China. It is also an inescapable conclusion that a significant portion of China's growth can be attributed to both the propensity of the Chinese to save and governmental policies favoring savings over consumption. However, even though the investment to GDP coefficient is more than two standard deviations away from zero, the authors conclude that the heavy commitment to investment can account for no more than 40 percent of China's excess growth.

One wishes that the authors had pursued this theme in greater depth, for it raises many important questions. Earlier studies of China's economic growth examined the investment to output ratio, employment growth, and output growth and concluded that, historically, during the period of central planning, up until about 1980, physical investment played the dominant role in China's economic growth and factor productivity contributed less. The heavy emphasis on investment during the period before 1980 is usually attributed to Maoist economic ideology adopted from Soviet planning in the 1950s and 1960s. Perhaps ensuing papers from Bekaert and his co-authors will address the question of why the investment to output ratio has remained so high even though there appear to be declining returns and developed countries have much lower ratios of investment to output.

The authors devote considerable attention to the issue of factor productivity growth. China is an outlier with a factor productivity growth in excess of 5 percent per annum. While the authors conclude that China's higher factor productivity makes a significant positive contribution, they leave the analysis of the determinants of this fact to another paper.

My overall impression is that although the conclusions from the chapter's methodology and its application have produced interesting and important results, it is to be hoped that the authors will further explore some of the secondary linkages between FDI and growth. It is also hoped that they will give more emphasis to the effects of technology transfer on growth, including the adoption and absorption, from and through Sino-foreign joint ventures, of corporate forms of business organization, better management techniques, and improved labor practices, as well as "hard" technology. For every firm in China—or elsewhere—both internal and external factors affect its productivity. Clearly, the manner in which these factors affect firms differs considerably according to the form of business organization and location and probably industry (apparel firms vs. insurance companies for example). As a practitioner, the impact of the policy of financial openness, which has encouraged growth in FDI, appears to be valuable in leading to new technologies, improvement in production methods, better managerial techniques, and better labor practices. The changes that have favorably influenced productivity of both capital and labor are accompaniments to investment inflows made possible by the policy of improving financial openness. Of course, it is difficult to generalize, as the impact of new financial and investment policies vary according to characteristics of the firm (size, management, place in manufacturing cycle, region, etc.), as mentioned before. In China, however, the overburden of state regulation and bureaucracy—and the fact that so many firms in the economy are state owned—has significant implications. The degree of state ownership of the firms indirectly affects competition and productivity. Competition itself would seem an important factor in growth of the economy, and it is increased by capital inflows.

In the state-owned sector, because it has been dominated by sluggish bureaucracies, new financial openness and new extant capital have had a much lower rate of absorption and hence less effect than in other non-public sectors of the economy. Where the most dramatic impact might have been expected, among Sino-foreign joint venture enterprises, where improved technology and better management techniques have been employed and enterprises are freed from the most restrictive labor practices, excess growth appears to me to be the norm. The chapter touches on this issue in its discussion of privatization. After remarking that China ranks in the bottom half of the country set in respect to the privatization measure employed, the authors note that privatization has a strong and significant direct effect on growth generally, but the growth effect of liberalizing countries with low levels of privatization is minus 61 basis points. I find it difficult to accept this conclusion and urge the authors to consider alternative measures of what effect the import of corporate forms of organization has had in China. One difficulty is that "privatization" is not necessarily coincident with the import of legal and management systems in private firms. Earlier studies claimed that "privatization" had little or even a negative effect on firm performance.[9] The better comparison, however, may be to study truly "private" firms. Allen, Jun, and Meijun (2005) find that the "private sector" grows much faster than the state sector or the listed sector. They conclude that China is a significant counterexample to the existing literature that the adoption of legal, institutional, and financial systems from Western models leads to improved economic results.[10] These apparent paradoxes simply demonstrate to me how difficult it is to capture measures of organizational improvement. It is very difficult to select the appropriate measures of change in a society and to then try to correlate these measures with economic variables. I would suggest that more work needs to be done to identify and quantify the impact on growth of improved managerial and financial practices as well as legal structure. I would also suggest that linkages to China's huge investment in education be explored. China now awards college degrees to four or five times as many students as it did in 2000. The improvements in education are surely key to more rapid absorption of improved business and financial methods.

What one observes everywhere is that China is placing important emphasis on importing foreign best practices as a means of revitalizing the financial sector. There are numerous examples; let me now mention several. China has now listed on international stock exchanges two of its four large banks—Bank of China and China Construction Bank. Prior to listing, China insisted on lining up major international banks to take minority stakes in advance of the listing—the obvious message being that they would act as watchdogs over reform efforts through their representatives' seats on the board. Indeed, the mere process of preparing for a listing involves a financial transformation and underwriters; accountants and lawyers pore over financial records to prepare the listing prospectus.

Recently, when China wanted to allow its banks, which have long been subject to a Glass Steagall–like separation of banking and securities, to enter the mutual fund distribution business, it did so by requiring that the banks partner with large foreign mutual fund complexes with improved investment management technology. Also, as everyone knows, China very much wants to improve its banking system from both a financial and a regulatory perspective. Right now, China has been strongly encouraging large foreign banks to take minority stakes in Chinese banks, in the anticipation that opening up this sector of the economy to significant foreign investment will bring benefits. Indeed, recently, some Chinese banks have complained that the large foreign banks were permitted to buy pre–initial public offering (IPO) stakes at significant discounts to IPO valuation. Another example is Ping An Insurance. Ping An was second in the life insurance sector after China Life, which held over 50 percent of the life insurance market share for a long time. The combination of restrictive investment regulations and virtual monopoly by one life insurance company meant that product innovation had been lacking. One exception was the introduction of unilinked policies by

Ping An, which reports growth in its new premium income in excess of the average of the industry. Another innovation has been group and personal pensions. Pension reform in 1997 sparked tremendous growth in the life insurance sector.

Though anecdotal, these examples appear to be convincing evidence that, at least from a policy perspective, China considers financial openness to be a linchpin of its efforts to modernize its economy. The importance of FDI and financial openness lies not just in the increase in the amount of capital available to the society; it is that the quality of the capital imported is so high because of the secondary effects that its importation brings.

The Chinese government is committed to the principle that the country's financial markets need to be modernized and their efficiency improved. Specifically, the government continues to introduce measures, regulations, and initiatives to deal with the issues of lack of transparency, poor corporate governance, the high degree of state-ownership, and other problems. One response has been to encourage the new growth of institutional players. China has the potential to build one of the largest institutional investor bases worldwide. Promoting the emergence of competent institutional investors is an important complement to an overall capital markets development strategy.

Institutional investors tend to have longer-term investment time horizons and provide an ideal source of funds for investment in longer-term government and infrastructure bonds. Many new initiatives and regulations have emerged in the last few years to encourage the growth of this new institutional investor base—insurance companies, pension funds, investment fund managers, trust and investment corporations, and securities companies. We do not have space to discuss these here. But these investors will add depth and liquidity to the equity markets and will improve prospects for the market to better absorb increased share supply resulting from the sale of the state shares. Institutional investors will also increase pressure on firms, listed and otherwise, to adopt better corporate governance structures and practices. This has not been an easy task. Let me also mention another new development that demonstrates China's commitment vividly. China has recently announced that it will allow foreign investors to purchase strategic stakes (10 percent or more equity interests) in listed companies that have been approved for the sale of state-owned shares (so-called G shares). Investors need only have $100 million in assets outside China or manage over

$500 million in such assets to be eligible to participate in the program. This is an important step in China's effort to use foreign investment to transform state-owned enterprises from the loss-making inefficiency that now plagues them.

Though admittedly an oversimplification, two kinds of theories of growth may be said to explain the "Asian Miracle" generally and China as part of that. One group is the "accumulation" theories, which attributed success in economic growth policies to very high rates of investment that push the economies "along their production functions." The other group is the "assimilation" theories, which stress entrepreneurship, innovation, and learning as the engines of economic growth.[11] Chinese policymakers have found an extraordinarily successful balance of these ingredients. Further work by Bekaert and his colleagues employing the sophisticated methodology of this chapter should place more emphasis on "assimilation" elements and may thereby help us unlock the puzzle of China's explosive economic growth.

NOTES

1. See Robert Barro, "Economic Growth in a Cross-Section of Countries," *Quarterly Journal of Economics* 106(2) (1991): 407–43.

2. The authors' model formulates the regressions in terms of relating instrumental variables to deviations from world growth, with a residual representing idiosyncratic, unpredictable growth.

3. See, for example, C. Bergsten, G. Bates, N. Lardy, and D. Mitchell, *China: The Balance Sheet* (New York: Public Affairs Press, 2006).

4. A very useful part of the chapter is the detailed chronology of important economic, political, and financial events over the past 25 years included in table 4.1.

5. Bekaert also pointed out in his research that traditional neoclassical growth factor models do not seem to explain China's explosive growth very well either. This fact has long been recognized. See Hu Zhuliu and Mohsin Khan, "Why Is China Growing So Fast?" International Monetary Fund Working Paper Series WP/96/75, 2006.

6. The authors measure the percentage of market capitalization available to foreigners at the end of the sample at 35 percent, but this mainly reflects H shares and Red Chips. Except for the limited program permitting very large foreign institutional investors to purchase "A" shares as qualified foreign institutional investors, the only traded shares available to foreigners at the time were the relatively illiquid "B" shares, which is a very much smaller market. (There are only approximately 70 companies with traded B shares, while there are about 1,200 companies with traded A shares.)

7. Citing Eswar Prasad and Shang-Jin Wei, chapter 3, this volume.

8. Alwyn Young, "The Tyranny of Numbers: Confronting the Statistical Realities of the East Asian Growth Experience," *Quarterly Journal of Economics* 110 (1995): 641–80.

9. For example, J. S. Qian, J. Tong, and T. Tong, "How Does Government Ownership Affect Private Firm Performance? Evidence from China's Privatization Experiment," *Journal of Business, Finance and Accounting* 29 (2002): 1–27.

10. F. Allen, Jun Qian, and Meijun Qian, "Law, Finance, and Economic Growth in China 2005," *Journal of Financial Economics* 77 (2005): 57–116.

11. R. Nelson and H. Pack, *The Asian Miracle and Modern Growth Theory* (Washington, DC: World Bank, 1997).

CHAPTER 5

The Effects of Stock Market Listing on the Financial Performance of Chinese Firms

Fred Hu

INTRODUCTION

Although China launched market-oriented economic reforms in 1978, privatization of state-owned enterprises (SOEs) did not emerge as a key component of the reform program until the mid-1990s. In contrast to the rapid-fire sales via auctions or voucher distribution schemes that characterize the privatization programs in Poland, Russia, and other Eastern European countries in the early 1990s, the Chinese privatization, particularly for medium- to large-size SOEs, has been undertaken primarily through initial public offerings (IPOs) in the stock markets, in some cases supplemented by pre-IPO sales of stakes to strategic investors. Since these IPOs typically end up selling minority equity stakes—ranging from 10 to 50 percent—to private investors, the vast majority of Chinese privatization accomplished through IPOs is partial privatization, which gives rise to widespread skepticism about its effectiveness in improving the financial performance of the listed firms. Such doubts have been further reinforced by the observed lackluster performance of firms listed in China's nascent domestic stock market.

Have stock market listings over the past decade failed to produce expected positive effects on Chinese firms' financial performance? If so,

The author is indebted to Shoukang Lin and Levin Zhu of China International Capital Corporation, Thomas Deng of Goldman Sachs, David Li and Chongen Bai of Tsinghua University, Jesse Wang of China SAFE Investments, Charles Calomiris of Columbia Business School, and Shang Jin Wei of the Brookings Institution for their valuable insights and comments, and to Kinger Lau, Liming Huang, and Yichi Zhang for outstanding research assistance. Thomas Deng and Kinger Lau generously compiled and provided much of the data used in this study.

then China's privatization program and SOE reform strategy that features IPOs as a centerpiece should largely be discredited, and one could also argue that the importance thus far given to domestic stock market development has been largely misplaced. This is a weighty question that has important implications for China's ongoing SOE privatization and reform program, as well as for the country's financial sector development.

In this chapter I examine a sample of 66 mainland Chinese companies listed in the Hong Kong Stock Exchange (HKSE) and other international exchanges. Using a variety of financial and operating yardsticks, I compare the pre- and post-IPO performance of these companies. The main finding that has emerged from this study is reassuring, if somewhat positively surprising—that is, a listing in a developed stock market such as the HKSE is associated with a significant improvement in the firm's performance. This finding appears to validate the government strategy to use IPOs as the primary means to accomplish privatizations and restructure underperforming SOEs. The results also highlight the importance of reforming and developing China's fledgling domestic stock market.

DATA AND METHODOLOGY

One way to assess the effects of stock market listing on a firm's performance is to simply compare unlisted firms and publicly listed firms. Using stock market listing as the main differentiator variable, one may detect any significant differences in financial performance between firms with broadly similar characteristics—for example, those in the same sector or with similar size and scale. The key obstacle facing this straightforward method is the limitation of data. Although listed companies in general have fairly comprehensive publicly disclosed financial and operating data available, financial accounts for the unlisted Chinese SOEs are usually fragmented, inaccurate, and inconsistent with U.S. generally accepted accounting principles or the international financial reporting standards (IFRS). In any case, much of the information for unlisted Chinese firms is either nonexistent or undisclosed publicly. Therefore, I look at publicly listed firms only.

The universe of publicly listed Chinese firms is comprised of both domestically listed (in the Shanghai and Shenzhen stock exchanges in the form of A shares and B shares) and firms listed overseas, primarily in Hong Kong. China's domestic stock market is still in its infancy, without well-developed listing standards, adequately enforced disclosure and corporate governance rules, or a sophisticated institutional investor base. Because of these widely recognized deficiencies in the Chinese stock market, it is difficult to isolate the effects of firm performance and stock market performance. This consideration leads me to focus on Chinese firms listed overseas only.

Since the early 1990s, mainland Chinese firms have sought listings in the New York Stock Exchange (NYSE), in the NASDAQ, and in the stock exchanges in Hong Kong, Singapore, London, and Tokyo. Hong Kong, however, has been the primary and preferred point of access for Chinese firms to international capital markets. With a market capitalization of U.S. $500 billion the HKSE ranks as the sixth largest stock market in the world and is widely recognized as one of the best regulated and most liquid stock markets globally. Owing to the international reputation and quality of the HKSE and other foreign stock exchanges, Chinese companies listed in the HKSE and other markets overseas make the perfect candidates for researchers to isolate the effects of stock market listing on a firm's performance.

In 1993 Tsingtao Beer was successfully listed in the HKSE as the first so-called H-share stock. As of July 2005 there are 167 mainland Chinese companies listed in Hong Kong, either in H shares (Chinese companies incorporated on the mainland but listed in Hong Kong) or Red Chips (Chinese companies both incorporated and listed in Hong Kong). Those 167 mainland Chinese companies have raised more than 928 billion Hong Kong dollars (U.S. $119 billion) in Hong Kong, compared to 523 billion renminbi (RMB) (U.S. $65 billion) raised by more than 1,400 listed companies in the Shanghai and Shenzhen stock exchanges. In the extraordinary year of 2000 alone, nearly 350 billion Hong Kong dollars' (U.S. $45 billion) worth of equities were raised by mainland Chinese companies through HKSE listings. In 2005 mainland Chinese companies accounted for one-third of the total market capitalization of the HKSE.

The HKSE is not the only place for mainland Chinese firms to list overseas. A number of Chinese firms, including the Red Chip China Mobile, China's largest wireless service provider, and the H-share company PetroChina, China's biggest oil and gas company, have a dual listing in the NYSE in the form of American Depository Receipts (ADRs). Several Chinese Internet and information technology companies are listed in NASDAQ. Note, however, that all these companies have most, if not all, of their assets and operations based in mainland China regardless of differences in the type of shares.

In this study I use a sample of 66 Chinese firms listed overseas. These are the firms that were under the research coverage of Goldman Sachs in China by summer 2005, which was the time this analysis was run. These firms are relatively actively traded stocks and have relatively high "visibility" in the marketplace. Moreover, this sample represents nearly 90 percent of the Morgan Stanley Capital International China Index in terms of market capitalization. It is therefore a representative sample of overseas-listed Chinese firms. Of the 66 companies in the sample, 61 are listed in Hong Kong (all but one on the main board), 4 are listed on NASDAQ, and 1 on Singapore. Some Hong Kong-listed firms in the sample also have a dual listing on the NYSE. As noted above, however, the distinction between H shares, Red Chips, or ADRs is inconsequential for the purpose of this study.

In the interest of tracking the longest possible operating history, the chapter examines a period of eight years, starting two years before the IPO and ending five years after it.

For data that were not available by the summer of 2005, Goldman Sachs research forecasts have been used. For 29 firms exclusively actual data are available. Goldman Sachs forecasts are made in real time and form part of the standard Goldman Sachs investment analyses made available to institutional investors. Forecasts have not been made specifically for the purpose of this chapter. Note that Goldman Sachs forecasts appear conservative relative to market consensus. For the 2005 earnings of Chinese companies, Goldman Sachs forecasts were about 4 percent lower than the consensus forecasts.

This chapter uses standard accounting measures to gauge firms' performance because reported accounting measures are what government regulators, tax authorities, private investors, and the general public tend to look at. Our key focus here is on the return on equity (ROE), which we believe is a useful summary indicator for firms' financial performance. The other measures we look at are earnings growth, dividend payout, debt-to-equity ratio, and asset turnover ratio. All measures are computed based on the consistent IFRS standard using information from companies' reported financial statements. As input variables we use net income, equity, dividend, sales, assets, and debt. Table 5.1 provides a summary describing which variables are used to compute which measures.

The Goldman Sachs data universe, from which the data for this analysis have been drawn, is not complete. Hence, some variables are missing for some firms for some years in the period under investigation, when neither actual data nor Goldman Sachs forecasts were available.

Table 5.1   Performance Measures and Raw Data

Performance Measures	Raw Data					
	NI	Equity	DIV	Sales	Assets	Debt
ROE	X	X				
Earnings Growth	X					
Dividend Payout	X		X			
D/E		X				X
Asset T/O				X	X	

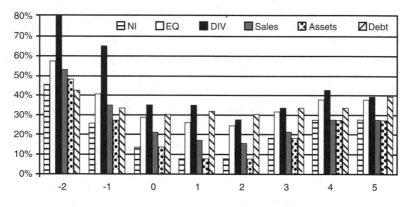

Figure 5.1   Missing Variables (percent) by Year

Consequently, the number of firms included in the actual annual computation of the accounting measures varies across the years [−2, 5], and the sample is actually truncated to below 66, with the actual sample size depending on the availability of specific variables in specific years in question. Figure 5.1 details which variables are missing in which year [−2, 5].

To check for the effects of missing variables the analysis has been rerun for subsets of firms. The results have been virtually the same as those of the original analysis.

Key financial indicators for the sample companies are summarized in table 5.2. Because of the nature of financial service firms, which render standard measures such as debt-equity ratio or net margin more difficult to interpret, the results reported in table 5.2 and in the later discussion of aggregate analyses are for the 61 nonfinancial firms only.

Table 5.2   Summary Financial Indicators

Year from IPO	−2	−1	0	1	2	3	4	5
ROE (%)	12.6	13.1	13.5	11.0	12.0	13.8	16.6	16.1
Revenue growth (%)	NA	16.5	51.5	12.8	11.7	10.5	22.9	12.1
Earnings growth (%)	NA	(3.5)	134.5	(8.6)	22.5	31.9	38.3	13.6
Net margin (%)	8.8	8.0	13.6	11.1	12.2	13.9	14.8	14.8
Dividend payout (%)	20.0	26.0	31.2	42.3	36.4	37.7	39.8	37.1
D/E (X)	2.67	0.91	0.65	0.63	0.61	0.51	0.45	0.39
Asset T/O (X)	0.47	0.51	0.54	0.52	0.54	0.57	0.67	0.66

NOTE: The summary statistics exclude the five financial companies in the sample.

Source: Goldman Sachs Strategy Research.

COMPARISON OF PRE- AND POST-IPO PERFORMANCES

The idea that a stock market listing can potentially improve an SOE's performance rests on three alternative theoretical arguments. First, a stock market listing changes the ownership structure of the SOE from pure state ownership to a more diversified, partially privatized form, thereby reducing arbitrary bureaucratic and political interference, and strengthening the firm's incentives to maximize profits and the return on capital (Allen 1993; Sachs 1992; Shleifer 1993).

Second, the pre-listing restructuring required tends to improve the firm's efficiency. In order to become listed in the international capital markets such as the HKSE and the NYSE, Chinese SOEs must undergo far-reaching restructuring exercises. Typically, these exercises involve streamlining businesses, revamping corporate structure, reducing staff and non–wage-operating costs, cleaning up balance sheets, and producing IFRS-based financial accounts (Hu and Sheng 1999; Zhu 2004). Through these restructuring efforts, stodgy and inefficient Chinese SOEs usually become leaner and more commercially oriented firms that can meet the listing requirements of the international stock exchanges and gain investor receptivity.

Third, in contrast to unlisted SOEs, or domestically listed firms, overseas listed Chinese firms are subject to far greater—and sustained—scrutiny and pressures from international investors, market regulators, and the financial media. The market discipline imposed by a stock market listing overseas likely helps improve the firm's performance (Hu and Sheng 1999).

Figure 5.2 shows the trend in the ROE for the 61 nonfinancial firms in the sample. A key result is that overseas listed Chinese firms have consistently

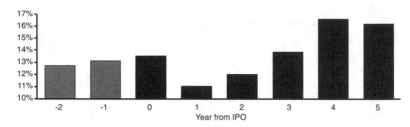

Figure 5.2   ROE Trend

Sources: Hong Kong Stock Exchange; HSI services, Global Quantum; Company data; and Goldman Sachs Strategy Research.

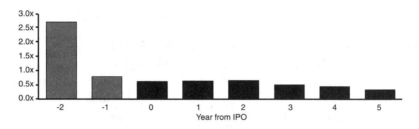

Figure 5.3   Debt-to-Equity Ratio

Sources: Hong Kong Stock Exchange; HSI services, Global Quantum; Company data; and Goldman Sachs Strategy Research.

increased their ROEs over the five-year period post-IPO, and they have generated higher ROEs post-IPO than in the pre-IPO period.

Initially, ROEs tend to decline in the immediate aftermath of the IPO. This could reflect the one-off effect of the pre-IPO restructuring—cost cutting, spin-off of noncore businesses and assets, reduction of debt, and so on—that temporarily boosted the ROE in the years immediately preceding the IPO year. Such a face-lift tends to raise the performance bar for the listed companies. As the low-hanging fruits disappear after the IPO, listed firms initially struggle to maintain their pre-IPO levels of ROE. But encouragingly, ROEs soon start to recover and improve, eventually outperforming the pre-IPO period.

This is a remarkable feat, particularly if one takes into account the effect of substantial de-leveraging taking place in the sample firms. Figure 5.3 shows the changes in the debt-to-equity ratio of the 61 nonfinancial firms in the sample. Chinese SOEs historically rely excessively on debt, primarily bank borrowing, with the average debt-to-equity ratio in the two years

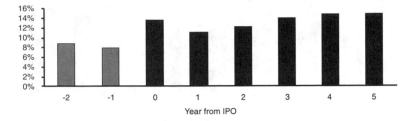

Figure 5.4   Net Margin

Sources: Hong Kong Stock Exchange; HSI services, Global Quantum; Company data; and Goldman Sachs Strategy Research.

preceding the IPO exceeding 250 percent. De-leveraging takes place from the beginning of the preparation of the stock market listing, partly by retiring old bank debt and partly by increasing the firms' equity capital base through the use of the IPO proceeds. As a result, overseas listed Chinese firms have much improved balance sheets, with average debt-to-equity ratios at less than 50 percent in the fifth year from the IPO. Despite the substantial de-leveraging, overseas listed Chinese firms have been able to increase their ROEs. In my view, this finding most powerfully demonstrates the beneficial effect of stock market listing on firms' performance.

To understand the drivers for the impressive ROE performance, figure 5.4 shows that the net margin of the 61 nonfinancial firms in the sample has improved post-IPO. This suggests that firms have done better post–stock market listing in their basic competitive strategy, pricing, product positioning, and cost control—essentially the basic operational decisions of the business.

Furthermore, the overseas listed Chinese firms have also become more efficient in the use of physical assets post-IPO, as measured by the so-called asset turnover ratios (sales relative to total assets), as shown in figure 5.5. The upward trends in net margin and operating efficiencies have been responsible for higher ROEs post–stock market listing, despite the drastic changes in the capital structure and financial policies of these firms, as evidenced by the substantial de-leveraging.

It also appears that firms have generated sustained growth post–stock market listing. Figures 5.6 and 5.7 show that overseas listed firms have shown similar or higher growth in sales and earnings in the post-IPO years compared to pre-IPO. It is important to note that earnings growth tends to outpace sales growth, which is almost a reversal from the behavioral pattern of traditional SOEs.

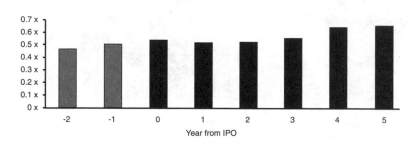

Figure 5.5   Assets Turnover

Sources: Hong Kong Stock Exchange; HSI services, Global Quantum; Company data; and Goldman Sachs Strategy Research.

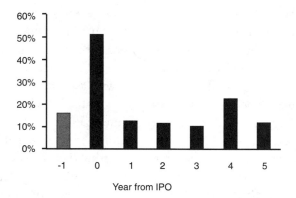

Figure 5.6   Revenue Growth

Sources: Hong Kong Stock Exchange; HSI services, Global Quantum; Company data; and Goldman Sachs Strategy Research.

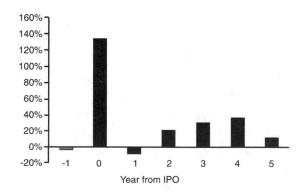

Figure 5.7   Earnings Growth

Sources: Hong Kong Stock Exchange; HSI services, Global Quantum; Company data; and Goldman Sachs Strategy Research.

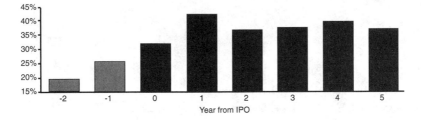

Figure 5.8   Payout Ratio

Sources: Hong Kong Stock Exchange; HSI services, Global Quantum; Company data; and Goldman Sachs Strategy Research.

Equity investors and government shareholders alike have been able to reap the rewards of improved financial performance of overseas listed Chinese firms, not only through capital gains since IPO, but also through the stream of dividend income. Dividend payout from Chinese firms is minimal pre-listing, but the payout ratio for the firms in the sample increases significantly post-IPO, as can be seen in figure 5.8.

PERFORMANCE COMPARISON BY SECTORS

The aggregate analysis in the preceding section may mask the dominance of telecom and energy companies in the financial performance of overseas listed Chinese companies. Therefore, this section goes a step further to examine the pre- and post-IPO results for a number of selected sectors, including energy (oil and gas), telecom, materials, utilities, airlines, and financials. Thirty out of the 66 firms in the sample can be broadly classified as operating in these six major sectors. The rest are scattered over consumer goods, machinery, IT electronics, property, and "conglomerates," which span across a large number of different sectors with multiple business lines but no obvious core business focus. The predominance of "conglomerates" such as Beijing Enterprises and Shanghai Industrials, which bundle unrelated assets such as highways, department stores, power stations, and beer breweries, is a rather unique but increasingly discredited phenomenon for Chinese listed companies.

The oil and gas sector produces the highest ROEs (above 20 percent), and the airline industry produces the poorest ROE performance. The oil and gas companies have the strongest balance sheet with the lowest debt-to-equity ratio at less than 20 percent, and the airlines are the most

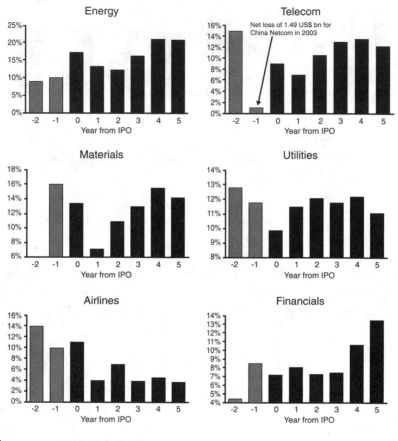

Figure 5.9   ROE Trend of Different Sectors

Sources: Hong Kong Stock Exchange; HSI services, Global Quantum; Company data; and Goldman Sachs Strategy Research.

heavily leveraged, with the highest debt-to-equity ratio at above 200 percent.

Despite these substantial sectoral differences, figure 5.9 shows that firms across nearly all these sectors have improved ROEs post-IPO, despite marked reduction in leverage. Airlines are the only disappointing exception, with declining and very low ROEs (low single-digit level).

One unexpected strong performer is the financial sector. At the time of this study, there were only four mainland-controlled banks listed in Hong Kong: the Bank of China (Hong Kong), the Industrial and Commercial Bank of China (ICBC) (Asia), Citic Industrial Financial Holdings, and the Bank of Communications. Due to well-known legacy problems in the

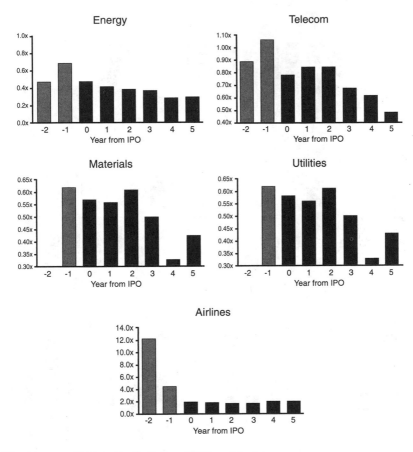

Figure 5.10   Debt-to-Equity Ratio of Different Sectors

Sources: Hong Kong Stock Exchange; HSI services, Global Quantum; Company data; and Goldman Sachs Strategy Research.

state-owned banks, Chinese banks and nonbank financial institutions all suffered in the pre-IPO period from high nonperforming loan (NPL) ratios, weak internal control and risk management, and poor ROEs. But since going public, these banks have steadily reduced their NPLs, cleaned up their balance sheets, and strengthened risk management. All these efforts have been translated into sharply increased ROEs.

In addition to the six major sectors highlighted above, the same analysis has been conducted for firms easily classifiable into other sectors, including information technology, industrials, and consumer goods, with substantially the same results. To save space and to avoid repetition, the

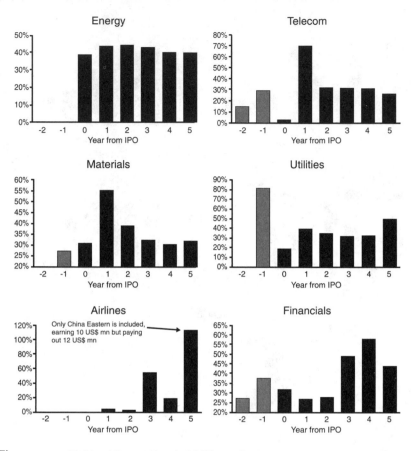

Figure 5.11   Dividend Payout Trend of Different Sectors

Sources: Hong Kong Stock Exchange; HSI services, Global Quantum; Company data; and Goldman Sachs Strategy Research.

results are not reported separately here. The results show that the steady improvement in financial performance in overseas listed companies is by no means exceptional to one particular industry but applies to a broad range of sectors.

CONCLUSIONS

In China, both academia and the media have long been skeptical about the role of stock market listings in reforming SOEs. The prevalent view is that stock market listing has done little good other than raising low-cost funds for the firms involved. The findings of this study, based on a sample

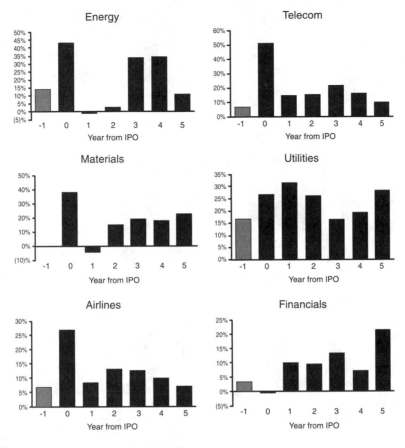

Figure 5.12   Revenue Growth of Different Sectors

Sources: Hong Kong Stock Exchange; HSI services, Global Quantum; Company data; and Goldman Sachs Strategy Research.

of 66 Chinese firms listed in overseas stock exchanges, however, provide evidence contradicting the widely held view.

According to a variety of measures, including, most importantly, the return on equity, in the period post-IPO, overseas listed Chinese firms have shown consistent and significant improvement in their financial performance compared to the pre-IPO period.

Remarkably, the improvement in ROE has been achieved despite substantial changes in the capital structure and financial policies of these firms. Since their stock market listings, these changes have sharply boosted their equity capital base and reduced reliance on bank credit, with a much stronger corporate balance sheet in place.

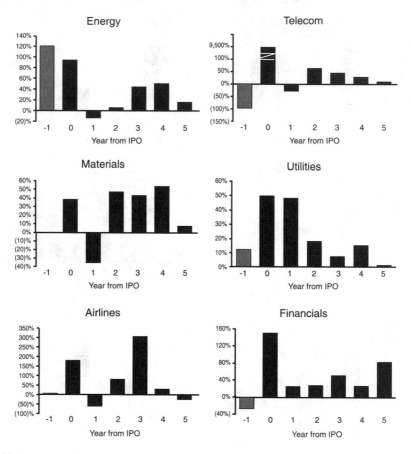

Figure 5.13   Earnings Growth of Different Sectors

Sources: Hong Kong Stock Exchange; HSI services, Global Quantum; Company data; and Goldman Sachs Strategy Research.

Improvements in financial performance are not limited to particular, favorably positioned sectors such as the oil and gas industry, which has been in a sweet spot given a sharp surge in the demand for energy and increases in global crude oil prices in recent years. Rather, firms in nearly all major sectors have shown a consistent upward trend in their ROEs. This is true, perhaps somewhat surprisingly, even for the banking sector, which has long been weighed down by massive bad loans, weak risk management, and poor ROEs. However, banks have also been able to generate much higher ROEs since they went public.

At a minimum, the widely held view that firms listed in China's domestic stock market have failed to live up to expectations should not be generalized to include overseas listed Chinese firms. This study shows that listings in well-developed capital markets such as Hong Kong have clearly produced significant efficiency gains over time across sectors and industries. The evidence uncovered here appears to validate the Chinese government's decade-long strategy of restructuring and privatizing SOEs by pushing them to list in the international capital markets. It also highlights the importance of reforming China's nascent domestic stock market so that it can play the role of efficiently allocating capital and fostering world class Chinese companies.

The stock market listing approach, as opposed to opaque, backdoor, quick asset sales witnessed in other economies in transition in Russia and parts of Eastern Europe, also has the clear advantage of being transparent and fair. Importantly, the stock market listing approach is likely more efficient as it compels the Chinese firms to undertake sweeping restructuring in order to meet the stringent listing requirements in overseas stock exchanges with higher financial, disclosure, and corporate governance standards. It also exposes them to the scrutiny and pressures from sophisticated international investors posting IPO, and it holds the boards of directors and the management team fully accountable for delivering superior performance based on international accounting standards, benchmarked by global industry peers, and market-to-market stock valuations.

REFERENCES

Allen, Franklin. 1993. "Stock Markets and Resource Allocation." In *Capital Markets and Financial Intermediation,* ed. Colin Mayer and Xavier Vives. Cambridge: Cambridge University Press.

Cha, Laura Shi Mei-lun. 2002. "Corporate Governance and Capital Markets Development in China." Speech delivered at the Goldman Sachs Investor Conference.

Deng, Thomas. 2004. *China Equity Strategy Report.* Hong Kong: Goldman Sachs Investment Research.

Hu, Fred. 2001a. *Das Kapital: The Stock Market Is Transforming China.* Goldman Sachs Global Economics Paper Series. London: Goldman Sachs.

———. 2001b. "Using Capital Markets to Deepen China's Structural Reforms." In *On the Forefront of Market Reform—Papers in Honor of Professor Wu Jinglian's 70th Birthday,* ed. Li Jiange. Shanghai: Far Eastern Publishing House.

Hu, Fred and Andrew Sheng. 1999. "Integrating Chinese Mainland and Hong Kong Equity Markets." *International Economy.*

Li, Jiange. 2001. "China's Domestic Stock Markets: Deficiencies and Promises." In *On the Forefront of Market Reform—Papers in Honor of Professor Wu Jinglian's 70th Birthday*, ed. Li Jiange. Shanghai: Far Eastern Publishing House.

Sachs, Jeffery. 1992. "Privatization in Russia: Some Lessons from Eastern Europe." Paper presented at ASSA meetings in New Orleans, January. Reprinted in *American Economic Review* (Spring).

Sachs, Jeffrey with Bozidar Djelic. 1993. "The Russian Mass Privatization Program." In *Privatization Yearbook 1993*, ed. Rodney Lord. London: Privatization International.

Shleifer, Andrei with M. Boycko and R. Vishny. 1993. "Privatizing Russia." *Brookings Papers on Economic Activity*, No. 2.

———. 1994. "Voucher Privatization." *Journal of Financial Economics* (April).

———. 1996. "A Theory of Privatization." *Economic Journal* (March). Reprinted in *Privatisation and Corporate Performance*, ed. David Parker. Cheltenham, UK: Edward Elgar, 2000.

Shleifer, Andrei with R. Vishny. 1994. "Privatization in Russia: First Steps." In *The Transition in Eastern Europe*, Vol. 2: *Restructuring*, ed. O. J. Blanchard, K. R. Froot, and J. D. Sachs. Chicago: University of Chicago Press.

Wu, Jinglian. 2001. *Shi Nian Chuang Sang Hua Gu Shi*. Beijing: n.p.

Zhu, Levin. 2004. "Capital Markets and China's SOE Reform." Paper presented at the International Finance Forum, Beijing.

Ailsa Röell

The chapter takes a contrarian stance in extolling the benefits of corporatization and stock exchange listing. The received wisdom is much more pessimistic, as surveyed by Green and Liu (2005: 30): "[T]the evidence almost all suggests that the performance of listed firms is poor, and declines after restructuring and listing." Many observers have pointed out that the ability to raise equity capital from unsophisticated investors on poorly regulated exchanges enables listed companies to waste or even divert money, and to manipulate investor sentiment so as to obtain the funds on unfairly advantageous terms. Most of the evidence concerns the impact of domestic listings on the Shanghai and Shenzhen exchanges rather than in Hong Kong. But evidence addressed specifically at H shares in the 1990s is similarly pessimistic (Aharoney, Lee et al. 2000; Huang and Song 2002). Interestingly, the chapter comes to very different conclusions, suggesting that the market discipline imposed by hardnosed international investors together with tougher international disclosure and governance standards may be responsible for the superior performance of Hong Kong–listed mainland Chinese stocks.

That Hong Kong–listed mainland shares have outperformed those listed in Shanghai and Shenzhen in terms of shareholder returns is undoubtedly true. Part of the reason is that the pent-up demand from relatively unsophisticated mainland A-share investors enabled new issues to be sold at sky-high multiples. But it stands to reason that the market discipline exerted by the Hong Kong listing has also played a role.

The effect of a foreign listing may not be quite as powerful a performance driver as the data suggest. First, companies selected for permission to list abroad have gone through a rigorous government vetting process, so that only star candidates are even allowed out of the starting gate. In some cases, such companies were forced to choose Hong Kong as the listing venue, when they would have preferred to forego the prestige of a Hong Kong listing to take advantage of the much higher multiples at which stocks listed on the Shanghai and Shenzhen exchanges were trading. Thus, the direction of causality between a Hong Kong listing and strong subsequent performance is an open issue.

Second, I do not think the distinction between H shares and Red Chips is totally inconsequential. Some of the larger Red Chip companies (those incorporated offshore and listed in Hong Kong but with Chinese controlling shareholders) have a substantial proportion of their business and assets in Hong Kong rather than the People's Republic of China (PRC)—for example, Bank of China Hong Kong (Holdings). This is basically a Hong Kong banking business and is not subject to the kinds of underperformance problems that mainland SOEs are notorious for and that corporatization and listing are meant to help resolve. It seems inappropriate to regard the performance of such a company as attributable to the exchange listing rather than to the essentially non-PRC nature of its business. Moreover, such companies are also much more answerable to Hong Kong securities regulators.

This raises an interesting issue: How long is the arm of the law? Can the Hong Kong Exchange and, more generally, international securities regulators, effectively discipline abuses taking place within the PRC? The worst sanction an exchange can impose is to suspend or delist a company or recommend the removal of its officials,[1] while securities regulators are dependent on PRC authorities for any power to sanction companies whose main business is in the PRC or to punish their officials. The limited reach of the U.S. Securities and Exchange Commission (SEC) in policing U.S.-listed foreign companies comes to mind. Foreign companies that list in the United States but subsequently violate SEC regulations are, in practice, beholden to the SEC only if they have substantive assets inside the United States that can be seized.

An interesting hypothesis explored by Pistor and Xu (2005) is that part of the disciplinary effect of a listing may be directed, not at company management itself, but at the intricate web of local and regional state agencies that tax, regulate, extract money, and otherwise exert control over the typical Chinese SOE: the "too many mothers-in-law" who negate the incentives to maximize shareholder value. Pistor and Xu have studied the quota system operating from 1993 through 2000, through which the regions obtained permission from central authorities to seek a listing for their SOEs. They show that regions whose listed firms performed badly on the stock market saw significant reductions in their quota in subsequent years (relative to other regions). Pistor and Xu argue that the system provided strong incentives for regional authorities to vet and select suitable listing candidates and to ensure their ability to perform well post-listing.

DATA ISSUES

Data problems are a matter of concern in the study at hand. The first is "look-back" or survivorship bias. The sample includes all firms that are large and attractive enough to be currently tracked by Goldman Sachs: a list of 66 internationally listed firms, of which 61 are Hong Kong listed. Naturally, any mainland Chinese firms that have gone bankrupt, delisted, or dwindled considerably in size subsequent to the initial listing would be of no interest to present international investors, and thus automatically excluded from the sample. This means that only firms that have performed reasonably well are included in the analysis.[2] The sample would not include such underperforming H shares as Shenyang Public Utility Holdings (suspended in December 2004 in the wake of a writ of summons against the company, and now still in arrears regarding financial disclosure) or Guangdong Kelon Electrical Holdings (suspended in June 2005 with the news that the executive director and other management figures were under PRC police investigation for alleged economic crime, and still in a state of considerable turmoil).

A second reason to suspect that the performance data are somewhat upward biased is that in cases where no actual financial data are available—in particular, for very recently listed firms—Goldman Sachs forecasts have been used rather than real performance histories. Even though these forecasts are, as the author notes, more conservative than those of other investment banks, we need only think of the Wall Street analyst scandals to be reminded that bullish forecasts are a great help in obtaining corporate clients.[3] Recent research finds that in the United States, relative optimism in analysts' long-term earnings growth forecasts and stock recommendations is related to potential conflicts of interest from investment banking and brokerage (Agrawal and Chen 2005). There is no reason to suppose that Hong Kong investment banks are immune to these pressures. Thus, one would expect that the forecasts of even the most conservative investment bank would not dwell too strongly on the negative. This could impart

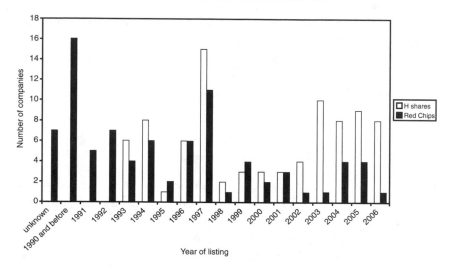

Figure 5.14   Year of Listing of Current Hong Kong Exchange Main Market Chinese Shares (August 2006)

Source: Hong Kong Stock Exchange.

a strong upward bias to the measures computed for later years, well after the listing date. As shown in figure 5.14, the number of companies with a five-year post-listing history is relatively small: of current main board-listed companies, only 41 H shares and 62 to 69 Red Chips were listed before the year 2000. Moreover, the largest companies are relatively recent listings: all 8 companies with a current (August 2006) market capitalization of over 100 billion HK dollars were listed in 2000 or later, except for China Mobile Ltd.

A final issue to be considered here is the use of accounting measures of performance. Even in the United States and Europe, despite a strong tradition of stock listings and strong established accounting standards, it is generally acknowledged that earnings and other accounting measures are not entirely free of manipulation, in particular in the run-up to an IPO (see, for example, Teoh, Welch et al. 1998). The statistics in the chapter show some worrying declines in performance in the year of the listing. Whether these declines are entirely attributable to restructuring expenses, as the chapter suggests, or to some measure of pre-IPO manipulation is an open question.

In the context of Chinese SOEs, a number of factors make it even harder to interpret the performance figures. The process of incorporating an SOE into a form that is suitable for a stock exchange listing involves the fencing off of performing assets into a listing vehicle while obligations (such as social welfare responsibilities for the existing workforce) and nonperforming assets are placed in the hands of a holding company that typically takes a controlling stake in the listed company. Moreover, post-listing, the intricate ties between the listed company and its associated holding company can make the interpretation of performance measures especially difficult. For example, take the dividend policy of Maanshan Iron & Steel, listed in 1993 and currently the thirty-seventh Hong Kong Main Board H share by market capitalization. As described by Steinfeld (1998), in the immediate aftermath of its listing Maanshan was able to declare an artificially high dividend payout by simply paying out dividends to individual investors but withholding the portion owed to the (62.5 percent majority owner) parent holding company, essentially forcing an impromptu "loan" of the unpaid dividend (as well as ore and services contracts). Thus, the true dividend payout was substantially lower than the declared one.

CONCLUSIONS

Despite all these words of caution, I would agree with Fred Hu's contention that getting listed can be an important driver of performance. The ongoing step-by-step reform process within China is, over time, creating the environment needed to ensure that these benefits will emerge. Greater management autonomy can be beneficial but only if coupled with more accountability and proper incentives, less political intervention, and, most important, more disciplined bank lending. For the latter problem, the ongoing program of privatizing and listing major banks is particularly crucial. Several other major current policy issues surround the listing of stock. One problem involves how to remove the enormous overhang of shares currently in state hands on the domestic (A-share) markets, without further depressing stock prices. A-share holders will need to vote in favor of any plan to privatize the overhang, and politically some form of compensation may be needed to sweeten the pie.[4] Another issue is the recurrent concern with misappropriation of state-owned assets that has led to the recent temporary embargo on further Red Chip listings.

NOTES

1. The current (2006) issue of the Annual Report of the Hong Kong Exchange's Listing Committee illustrates the limitations of its powers:

> Over the past year, the Listing Committee has heard a number of cases arising from serious breaches of the Listing Rules. In one such case concerning an "H" share listed company, Luoyang Glass, the Committee found the Company in breach of a number of the rules . . . including failure to comply with reporting, announcement and independent shareholder approval procedures in relation to connected transactions. The Company received a public censure and a number of its former directors received public censures or public statements involving criticisms for their breach of the Director's Undertaking.
>
> In addition to receiving public censure, the Committee took the relatively rare step of stating publicly that the retention of office by certain individuals was prejudicial to the interests of investors. This is the first time the directors of an "H" share company have received this sanction. Follow-up action to pursue and give effect to the Committee's view is continuing.

2. Even a sample containing all companies that are still listed today, or all companies that have been listed for at least a minimum time span, would automatically exclude firms that delist because they go bankrupt or they fail to comply with exchange listing standards. Selecting the sample of firms based on their current status necessarily induces look-back bias.

3. See, for example, Michael Lewis's description of how Merrill Lynch hired Henry Blodget:

> Merrill's investment bankers, theretofore incidental victims of their Internet analyst's bearish views, became incidental beneficiaries of the firm's new bullishness. They were quite open about this . . . the head of Merrill's technology banking division explained his new success to Bloomberg News. "It's difficult to take companies public when your analyst has a less-than-constructive view on some of the biggest companies out there," Ryles said. Having Blodget on board was great, he said, because Blodget "has been unabashedly bullish and has been proved right."

Michael Lewis, "In Defense of the Boom," *New York Times Magazine*, October 27, 2002.

4. Even though the role of retail investors as opposed to professional players in the A-share market is surprisingly small, as argued by Walter and Howie (2003).

REFERENCES

Agrawal, A. and M. A. Chen. 2005. "Do Analyst Conflicts Matter? Evidence from Stock Recommendations." Robert H. Smith School Research Paper No. RHS 06-38, University of Maryland.

Aharoney, J., C. W. J. Lee, et al. 2000. "Financial Packaging of IPO Firms in China." *Journal of Accounting Research* 38(1): 103–26.

Green, S. and G. S. Liu. 2005. *Exit the Dragon? Privatization and State Control in China*. London: Blackwell Publishing.

Huang, S. and F. Song. 2002. *Can a Capitalist Equity Market Help the Reform of Chinese State-Owned Enterprises?* Hong Kong: University of Hong Kong.

Pistor, K. and C. Xu. 2005. "Governing Stock Markets in Transition Economies: Lessons from China." *American Law and Economics Review* 7(1): 184–210.

Steinfeld, E. S. 1998. *Forging Reform in China: The Fate of State-Owned Industry*. Cambridge: Cambridge University Press.

Teoh, S. H., I. Welch, et al. 1998. "Earnings Management and the Long-Run Market Performance of Initial Public Offerings." *Journal of Finance* 53(6): 1935–74.

Walter, C. E. and F. J. T. Howie. 2003. *Privatizing China: The Stock Markets and Their Role in Corporate Reform*. Hoboken, NJ: John Wiley & Sons (Asia).

CHAPTER 6

China's Exchange Rate Regime:
The Long and Short of It

Barry Eichengreen

INTRODUCTION

China's exchange rate system is a work in progress. The accelerating pace of change makes efforts to analyze it much like attempting to hit a moving target.

- In July 2005, following more than a year of intense discussion, the government announced that it was revaluing the renminbi (RMB) by 2.1 percent, switching from the dollar peg to a basket and allowing the currency to float more freely.[1]
- In August, it expanded the forward market by allowing all banks, including foreign banks, with licenses to trade in the interbank foreign exchange market to transact RMB forward and swap contracts with clients as well as in the interbank market, and it allowed the banks to determine forward rates independently. The People's Bank of China (PBOC) also provided additional information on the composition of the reference basket, specifying that it includes not just the dollar, the euro, the yen, and the Korean won but also the Malaysian ringgit, the Russian ruble, the Australian dollar, the Thai baht, the Canadian dollar, and the British pound. The governor of the PBOC did not, however, reveal the weights on the constituent currencies.
- In September the authorities eliminated an inconsistency between its rules for fluctuations against the dollar and fluctuations against the basket. Under the new regime instituted in July, daily fluctuations against the dollar were supposed to be limited to 0.3 percent per day, while at the same time daily fluctuations against the basket were supposed to be limited to 1.5 percent. The problem was that if the dollar moved against other currencies by 2 percent in a day, a not

unprecedented event, it might prove impossible to respect both rules at the same time. On September 23 the PBOC therefore announced that henceforth the RMB would be allowed to fluctuate by 3 percent a day against the euro, yen, and other nondollar currencies, essentially relaxing this constraint.

- On November 25, foreign exchange regulators announced that they were going ahead with a system of market makers to trade the RMB against foreign currencies. At the same time, the PBOC enhanced the ability of the banks to hedge foreign currency exposures by conducting its first domestic currency swaps, selling $6 billion to 10 domestic banks at the current exchange rate with an agreement to buy them back in a year's time. A pair of additional currency swaps totaling $8.8 billion followed in December, suggesting that further swap operations would follow at fortnightly intervals.

- On January 3, 2006, the People's Bank of China announced that it would allow over-the-counter foreign exchange transactions to take place, effective immediately with the over-the-counter mechanism running concurrently with the existing centralized automatic price matching system.[2] This was designed to permit authorized participants in the interbank market to quote rates before the morning opening of the market, influenced by overnight moves in G7 currencies (subject, of course, to the daily fluctuation band set by the PBOC). The intent was to introduce a more market-based "price-finding" system for the establishment of daily benchmark reference rates.[3]

- Trading in RMB-denominated interest-rate swaps began in February. The PBOC published a list of 18 banks approved to deal in such swaps.[4]

- In April 2006 the PBOC accounted a further relaxation of capital controls, allowing companies and individuals to hold more foreign exchange and qualified financial institutions to invest abroad. Limits were relaxed on the conversion of RMB to foreign exchange by individuals and on the retention of foreign exchange earned abroad by companies.

Yet further changes will presumably have been introduced between the writing of this chapter and its publication.

For the analyst this creates the danger that early pronouncements on the efficacy of the country's new exchange rate system may be premature.

That system is continuing to evolve as officials ferret out inconsistencies in existing arrangements, forward foreign exchange and other financial markets continue to develop, and the authorities gain experience with managing their now more flexible rate.

The analyst's task is more challenging still because discussions of the RMB's management are laden with political overtones and rolled up with the state of U.S.-Chinese relations. Even those who approach the question from a narrowly economic point of view reach different conclusions because they start from different assumptions about the objective function that the Chinese authorities should seek to maximize. For some the issue is the regime that is most appropriate for the Chinese economy. Here the question is whether a currency arrangement entailing greater flexibility will enable the Chinese authorities to steer the economy more effectively as they continue moving in the direction of a market-based monetary policy, or whether such flexibility could be destabilizing for the country's financial system and export-led growth in the absence of prior financial reform and the further development of forward markets in foreign exchange. For others the issue is that of the exchange rate regime with which China can most effectively contribute to the orderly resolution of global imbalances. Here the question is whether Chinese authorities need to allow significant further appreciation in order to limit the expansion of the U.S. deficit and China's own surplus and to reconcile global rebalancing with continued expansion of the world economy.

That different people have different things in mind creates scope for confusion, as will be appreciated by anyone who has followed the debate. To avoid misunderstanding, I therefore start with a statement of what this chapter is and is not about. It is about the regime that is appropriate for China. It is *not* about the equilibrium level of the exchange rate and whether the RMB is 25.4 percent undervalued.[5] Economists will understand that efforts to estimate equilibrium exchange rates are problematic.[6] Over and above the methodological problems that arise when attempting to implement conventional exchange rate models, there is the question of whether the current account balance should be an argument for the Chinese authorities' objective function. (This appears to be the view of the U.S. Treasury and of others who argue that China has a responsibility for contributing to the process of global rebalancing, but not of mainstream models of inflation targeting.)[7]

A considerable amount of additional water will have passed under the bridge by the time this chapter finally appears in print. We will have learned more about the sustainability of China's rapid rates of growth. We will know more about the appetite of foreign investors for holding claims on the United States and about the validity of the global-savings-glut view of international imbalances. We will know more about how the Chinese authorities are operating the new regime in practice. Hence, this chapter is not about the appropriate level of the dollar-RMB rate but about what exchange rate *regime* is right for China over various horizons.[8]

In this context, it can be argued that the decision of July 21, 2005 was broadly correct.[9] The 2.1 percent revaluation of the RMB has symbolic value, notably in the United States. It is indicative of the recognition that China now shares responsibility for the stability of the global economy. At the same time, it is not so large as to significantly damage the profitability of Chinese exports. A more flexible exchange rate should enable the PBOC to more effectively tailor monetary conditions to local needs as it moves toward a more market-based financial system. Continued heavy management of the currency will minimize the danger of excessive volatility that could damage financial stability, exports, and economic growth.[10] Finally, switching to a basket should help to reconcile the further dollar decline needed for the readjustment of the U.S. deficit with the export-centered nature of China's growth model.

My criticisms of the new policy regime center on the ambiguity that remains about the likely degree of exchange rate flexibility. I worry that the authorities may not permit the rate to fluctuate sufficiently to create the perception of a two-way bet and encourage prudence on the part of financial market participants. Measures to suppress volatility may encourage speculators to line up on one side of the market, which at present is the side anticipating further appreciation, subjecting the economy to worrisome capital inflows and aggravating the risk of overheating. Over time, an even more flexible exchange rate will become desirable, and at that point the fluctuation band retained as part of the new regime may become binding. Repeated changes in the regime—widening the band or abandoning it entirely—will then create unnecessary questions about the consistency and credibility of policy. I will argue that from this point of view it would have been better to eliminate the band on July 21, 2001. Given the Chinese authorities' very extensive foreign exchange reserves, they have ample resources with which to manage the rate via intervention; already the band has become an unnecessary crutch. Finally, I worry that for domestic political and economic reasons the Chinese authorities may be reluctant to accept the further appreciation of the exchange rate needed over time to help smoothly resolve the problem of global imbalances.

LESSONS FROM THE THEORY OF OPTIMUM CURRENCY AREAS

The theory of optimum currency areas is the obvious jumping-off point for this analysis.[11] This theory and its empirical counterpart suggest that large countries subject to distinctive business cycle conditions ("asymmetric shocks") will want a more flexible exchange rate, since they can both afford and will wish to tailor monetary policy to domestic conditions.[12] In contrast, relatively open economies with weak financial systems will want a less flexible rate, since volatility will be corrosive to financial stability and export growth.[13] Here we immediately see the dilemma confronting the Chinese authorities and the fact that there is no simple answer to the question of what exchange rate regime is right for the country. On the one hand, China is a large economy whose exceptionally rapid development and transformation subject it to distinctive business cycle risks. These structural factors create an obvious case for a more flexible rate. On the other hand, the country has a high export/gross domestic product (GDP) ratio and a weak financial system. These considerations point toward a less flexible rate. Splitting the difference suggests a moderate increase in flexibility, which was precisely the decision taken on July 21.

This framework also suggests that China will want to move over time in the direction of greater exchange rate flexibility. Sooner or later the country will have to address the problems in its banking and financial system, and a stronger financial system will enable it to cope more easily with the consequences of a more flexible exchange rate. Moreover, China will not run savings rates of 50 percent forever. Social demands for higher consumption standards, the development of financial markets that enable households and firms to insure themselves against market risks at lower cost, and the construction of a social safety net will make this so. We know that economies more dependent on domestic demand and less dependent on export demand demonstrably prefer a more flexible rate.[14]

The question that arises is: When should China commence its movement in this direction? My argument in this chapter (as in an earlier paper, Eichengreen 2006) is that the government was right to begin moving in the summer of 2005. The appropriate regime given current conditions is a managed float in which the exchange rate is allowed to fluctuate more than in the last 10 years. Greater flexibility will allow the authorities to steer the economy more effectively. It will prevent domestic interest rates and financial conditions from being dictated by interest rates and financial conditions in the rest of the world, which becomes a growing danger as the capital account continues to open through a combination of policy action and market development. Such flexibility will become all the more important as the banks are commercialized and stakes are sold to foreign investors, rendering less effective the past practice of managing monetary conditions by issuing instructions to financial institutions.[15]

To be clear, the government is right to insist that its more flexible exchange rate should still be heavily managed. But the degree of intervention should decline over time, for the reasons described earlier. Ten years from now, the RMB might appropriately fluctuate as freely as the South Korean won or the Brazilian real today.[16]

What exchange rate regime is best for navigating this transition? We know that repeated changes in the exchange rate regime are undesirable because repeated changes inevitably encourage speculation about changes in the currency's level, complicating the conduct of monetary policy. The best way of enhancing the credibility of policy is for the authorities to follow a consistent monetary policy-operating strategy, something that will not be possible if they are repeatedly changing the exchange rate regime. This argues against moving first to a band and then later to a band-free float. It also argues against serial increases in bandwidth over time. Rather, given the exchange rate regime that will be appropriate for China 10 years from now—a moderately managed float—the government would have been better advised to eliminate all pretense of a band previously.

LESSONS FROM THE LITERATURE ON SEQUENCING

The other obvious jumping-off point for this analysis is the literature on the sequencing of international monetary and financial reforms. A one-sentence summary of that literature is that exchange rate flexibility should precede capital account convertibility. Exchange rate flexibility should come first to avoid creating one-way bets for speculators, who can force the authorities to abandon their exchange rate commitment under duress, at considerable cost to their policy credibility, or to reverse prior measures liberalizing the capital account, which will also raise questions about the consistency of policies. If, instead, the capital account is opened first, large amounts of liquidity may flow in, creating a financially-disruptive credit boom and fanning fears of a socially disruptive inflation that can only be headed off by revaluation.[17] Otherwise large amounts of liquidity may flow out, draining reserves unless the authorities devalue. Thus, capital account liberalization should be preceded by a modicum of exchange rate flexibility that creates losses in the event that expectations of revaluation or devaluation are disappointed, avoiding one-way bets and thereby preventing currency speculators from all lining up on one side of the market. This is one of the principal lessons of the Asian financial crisis of 1997–1998, which was aggravated by the fact that many countries in the region opened the capital account before moving to greater exchange rate flexibility rather than the other way around.[18]

From this point of view, many of us were alarmed by the argument frequently heard in Beijing of the need to delay the transition to greater exchange rate flexibility until more progress had been made in liberalizing the capital account. To the contrary, that China has now taken a modest step in the direction of greater flexibility is reassuring precisely in light of the significant steps taken in the last year to further liberalize the capital account.[19] The capital account is already sufficiently porous that large amounts of portfolio capital are attracted by expectations of rapid economic growth and currency appreciation. The authorities' capacity to insulate the economy from the effects of these inflows, by inter alia instructing the banks not to lend, are increasingly limited by the ability of that finance to circumvent the banking system.[20] Greater exchange rate flexibility, which forces international investors to think twice before all lining up on one side of the market, will not eliminate these risks, but it should attenuate them to some extent.

Equally, there is already scope for disruptive capital outflows in a future scenario in which there is a sharp slowdown in growth, new problems surface in the financial system, or a geopolitical dispute with the United States develops. Rather than succumbing, the authorities may then be tempted to deploy their reserves to defend the exchange rate. Both theory and evidence suggest that this would be a losing battle even for a central bank with $1 trillion of reserves. In the absence of controls, even this formidable war chest is nothing compared to the resources that can be mobilized by the markets.[21]

This observation also points to the principal lesson of the literature on exit strategies: countries should exit from a peg while the going is good. They should exit while growth is strong, capital is flowing in, and expectations are for appreciation.[22] Exiting under duress, in contrast, is almost always costly.[23] It forces the authorities to reluctantly abandon their commitment to defend the peg, contradicting previous policy statements and diminishing their credibility, something that is inevitably damaging to confidence, stability, and growth. The literature on exit strategies also suggests that growth can be supported by expanding domestic demand, most logically through implementing expansionary fiscal initiatives, at the same time the growth of external demand is being slowed by the appreciation of the currency. This fiscal expansion is most likely to be feasible—and confidence enhancing rather than threatening—when the underlying condition of the economy is strong. Recent work also suggests that a nondisruptive exit to greater flexibility is easier to engineer while at least some capital controls remain in place.[24] The authorities are better able to move at a time of their own choosing, and the disruptive financial fallout is less. Again one worries that, had the Chinese authorities waited too long to loosen the peg and if they now wait too long to allow greater flexibility, the opportunity for a smooth transition will be lost.

Chinese economists are well aware of these literatures. What then explains their emphasis on international financial liberalization as a prerequisite for greater exchange rate flexibility? The weightiest argument is that a more liberal capital account regime fosters the development of deep and liquid spot and forward foreign exchange markets, which in turn are needed for banks and firms to hedge their foreign exposures. Banks have currency mismatches on their balance sheets, which they have to be able to hedge in order to protect themselves from volatility. Similarly, foreign investment enterprises and domestic enterprises assembling imported components have foreign-currency-denominated obligations. Absent adequate hedging opportunities, an increase in exchange rate volatility could be destabilizing for both the financial and industrial sectors.

There is something to this point, although it should not be pushed too far. Hedging foreign currency exposures on financial markets is impossible, by definition, when the capital account is closed.[25] It would be ludicrous for a country with a fully closed capital account to subject banks and firms, unable to hedge the exposures created by their transactions on current account, to significant exchange rate volatility. At the same time we know, for all the reasons enumerated earlier, that a large country with a fully open capital account should embrace some degree of exchange rate flexibility. Because the degree of capital account liberalization in practice is a continuum, there must be an intermediate stage at which it is optimal to move from a peg to a more flexible exchange rate. In effect, the question boils down to the following: At precisely what point in the process of capital account liberalization should the country begin to move toward greater flexibility?

HEDGING FOREIGN EXPOSURES

It can be argued that China has now reached this point—that it can indulge in greater currency flexibility without subjecting banks and firms to significantly increased risks. For one thing, the principal banks do not have large foreign exposures. To be sure, the problems of the Chinese banking system are well known. The banks are still burdened by a legacy of nonperforming policy loans, information systems are inadequate, and internal controls are lax; fixing these problems should be an urgent priority. That said, it is not clear that these problems will be significantly aggravated by a modest increase in exchange rate variability. It is not as if the banks' foreign exposures, such as they are, will become vastly more difficult to manage. China's outward investment having been limited in the past by a combination of factors including capital controls, the banks possess limited foreign-currency-denominated assets.[26] Capital controls and financial regulations have limited the accumulation of foreign-currency-denominated liabilities even more strictly.[27] Consequently, the announced change in the exchange rate's level and a modest future increase in volatility should not have major balance-sheet implications for the financial sector. As capital account liberalization proceeds, certainly the banks will have more scope for funding themselves abroad, and these risks will become more acute. This points to the importance of tightening regulation of the banks as the process of external opening proceeds—whether or not the authorities move to a significantly more flexible exchange rate—a point that is elaborated in the following section. But it does not suggest that, in the short run, a limited increase in exchange rate volatility would significantly compound the problems of the banks.

The main risk to the banks lies in the danger that export growth and growth generally will slow sharply owing to movements in the currency. Slower growth will mean more nonperforming loans (NPLs), and slower export growth will make for more NPLs in the export sector. A substantial (double-digit) appreciation of the RMB might have had this effect, given the relatively low (single-digit) profit rates in the export sector.[28] But this was not the decision taken on July 21. In any case, the argument of this chapter is not for a substantial appreciation of the currency.[29] Rather, it is for a gradual increase in the degree of exchange rate variability. And the evidence that exchange rate volatility has a first-order impact on export growth, much less aggregate economic growth, varies from weak to nonexistent.[30] Even studies that find evidence of such an effect generally conclude that its magnitude is small.

There are also a number of reasons for thinking that the effect of exchange rate volatility on exports and growth will be even smaller in China than the country's dependence on foreign markets otherwise suggests. Export enterprises not only sell final products abroad, but they also source inputs abroad, providing them with a natural hedge. In addition, foreign investment enterprises account for a large share (by some estimates, a majority) of Chinese exports. Foreign owners and joint venture partners are in a favorable position to hedge against currency fluctuations. They can invest in a diversified portfolio of production locations or in financial assets that covary negatively with the profits of Chinese export enterprises, since they are not prevented from accumulating assets abroad by China's capital controls. This allows them to ride out temporary fluctuations in the exchange rate and to provide bridge finance to the export enterprise in question. These factors may change with time: Chinese exporters will source more inputs domestically, while foreign investment enterprises will ultimately account for a smaller share of total exports. By the time that happens, however, China will have developed alternatives, such as deeper and more liquid markets in currency forwards and other derivatives with which the risk of currency fluctuations can be hedged.

Were exchange rate volatility to rise immediately to very high levels, higher than is typical of the countries analyzed in cross-sectional studies of the correlation between export growth and currency volatility, this would be a different story. But this is not something that anyone foresees. The currency's movement will continue to be damped by the PBOC. The central bank will lean against the wind, pumping liquidity into the market if the exchange rate shows a tendency to appreciate excessively and selling foreign assets into the market if there is the danger of a currency collapse. By providing this liquidity, the central bank in effect supplies the hedging services required by the export sector. This is precisely the situation in other emerging markets that operate a managed float despite the retention of capital controls limiting the development of hedging opportunities. India is an example of a large, export-oriented emerging market that has successfully reconciled currency flexibility with the maintenance of capital controls through heavy management of the exchange rate.[31] There is no obvious reason why China cannot do what India does.[32]

As noted, there will be growing scope over time for export enterprises and others to purchase hedges on financial markets. Already the development of the foreign exchange market provides some scope for doing so. Early in the summer of 2005 the authorities agreed to let the big four state-owned commercial banks and three shareholding commercial banks offer RMB forward cover to their corporate clients, subject to tight control of the pricing of the forward contracts. In mid-August they expanded the market by allowing all banks, including foreign banks, with licenses to trade in the interbank foreign exchange market in order to transact RMB forward and swap contracts with clients as well as in the interbank market, and they allowed the banks to determine the forward rates independently. Restrictions on the duration of forward contracts were removed. The scope of legitimate transactions was extended from those arising from trade in goods and services and investment income to all current account transactions and select capital account transactions, including repayment of approved foreign borrowing, domestic companies' foreign exchange receipts from foreign listing, and so on. Qualified nonbank financial institutions and nonfinancial corporates with a "genuine need" for foreign exchange transactions are now allowed to participate in the interbank forex (foreign exchange) market.

The infrastructure for foreign exchange trading has also been strengthened by the establishment of the Shanghai-based China Foreign Exchange Trading System (CFETS), powered by a technology provided by Reuters.[33] Previously, CFETS traded only four overseas currencies—the euro, the Japanese yen, the Hong Kong dollar, and the U.S. dollar. The new system will allow for trading in four additional currencies—the pound sterling, the Swiss franc, the Australian dollar, and the Canadian dollar. Liquidity will be provided by nine global market makers: ABN Amro, HSBC, Bank of Montreal, Bank of China, CITIC Industrial Bank, ING, Royal Bank of Scotland, Deutsche Bank, and Citigroup. Banks in China will be able to place orders, request prices, and execute foreign exchange transactions, either over the Internet or via leased line circuits, with a single click. These facilities should be particularly valuable to smaller banks that have found it difficult to obtain competitive interbank rates, since CFETS will act as the trading counterparty for the foreign liquidity providers and only subsequently will settle with its domestic member banks. It will not be long before the growing volume of spot transactions on this market is supplemented by currency forwards and futures. The PBOC can help to jump-start forward market activity by providing backup cover to commercial banks, enabling the commercial banks to conduct forward sales and purchases and square their open positions, as countries such as Ireland, New Zealand, and Finland did in the 1970s and 1980s when they first emerged from heavily controlled capital account regimes.[34]

But more than infrastructure is needed to foster the development of deep and liquid foreign exchange markets. In addition, agents must have an incentive to engage in foreign currency transactions. Duttagupta, Fernandez, and Karasadag (2004) show that countries with more variable exchange rates tend to have more liquid foreign exchange markets, since it is there that banks and firms have an incentive to participate in the market. Foreign exchange market liquidity is not simply a prerequisite for greater exchange rate flexibility. In addition, greater exchange rate flexibility can promote market liquidity.[35]

PRUDENTIAL CONSIDERATIONS

I have argued that a modest increase in exchange rate flexibility like that announced on July 21 will not create major new risks for China's banking, financial, and corporate sectors. But neither are such dangers absent. In particular, the fact that China's banks are incompletely commercialized and that the big four banks are too big to fail limits the incentive for managers to internalize the relevant risks. Similarly, the weakness of corporate governance heightens the danger that industrial borrowers will not pay sufficient attention to the risks posed by their foreign exposures.

This makes it important to adapt prudential policies to the reality of greater flexibility. Duttagupta, Fernandez, and Karasadag (2004) provide a convenient taxonomy of the prudential measures that should be taken by the government of a country exiting from a peg. First, supervisors should issue guidelines for strengthening the banks' internal risk policies and procedures. Such policies may include laying down written policies on foreign exchange operations, exposure limits, risk management procedures, and the preservation of firewalls between front and back offices, while the relevant procedures should regularly include stress testing the potential impact of exchange rate movements on the performance of foreign currency loans. Given the fact that the Chinese banking system is incompletely commercialized, it is critical that such instructions be re-inforced by strict prudential regulations. These regulations should include binding limits on net open positions as a percentage of capital, on foreign currency lending as a percentage of foreign currency liabilities, and on overseas borrowing and bond issuance. They should distinguish the special risks of foreign currency lending to sectors that do not generate foreign currency revenues or that are subject to unusually volatile returns. They could include tighter reserve requirements for banks with foreign currency deposits, minimum credit-rating requirements for external borrowing by domestic corporations, and asymmetric open position limits. China already has a number of such measures in place. These now should be modernized and elaborated.

Second, effective management of exchange rate risk requires the creation of information systems capable of monitoring the current condition of the banking system. The easy part is requiring banks to report foreign currency positions in a standardized format and on a regular schedule. More difficult is ensuring that the assets and liabilities underlying those positions are valued using modern accounting rules and procedures and marked to market continuously. It is also necessary to get banks to report large exposures to individual borrowers; for the authorities to obtain information from the corporate sector on their foreign currency incomes, other foreign currency debts, and hedging operations; and for them to assemble information on the exposures of those large borrowers to the banking system as a whole. All this will become more important but at the same time more difficult as the banks are commercialized, lengthening the distance between bank managers and government bureaucrats, and as the private sector gains ground over the state sector.

Finally, the exchange rate should be allowed to fluctuate freely enough that lenders and borrowers are aware of the risks of foreign exposures. This is another lesson of the Asian crisis of the late 1990s.[36] Officially operating a managed float but in practice strictly limiting the variability of the exchange rate through intervention in the foreign exchange market, as South Korea did in the run-up to its crisis, may encourage banks and borrowers to underestimate the risk of exchange rate changes and to assume excessive foreign exposures, which can come back to bite them in the event of a sudden increase in volatility.[37] Sufficient variability in the exchange rate on a day-to-day basis can provide a constant reminder of the risks of those exposures.

AN EVALUATION OF THE JULY 2005
POLICY ANNOUNCEMENT

Only time will tell whether the new regime really entails greater exchange rate flexibility. The fact that there is no change in official bandwidth is also compatible with no increase in the degree of flexibility. We will have to see whether the authorities in fact permit the exchange rate to fluctuate more freely. There are many examples of emerging markets that officially pursue managed floats but in practice operate what amounts to a de facto peg (Calvo and Reinhart 2002; Reinhart and Rogoff 2004). If this is what China does, then domestic interest rates will become even more tightly linked to foreign interest rates as the capital account opens further. This will make it harder for those responsible for macroeconomic management to tailor money and credit conditions to domestic needs. Lack of exchange rate variability will also heighten risks in the financial sector by encouraging lenders and borrowers to underestimate the dangers of foreign exposures. If, on the other hand, the new regime really represents a shift toward greater flexibility, then it is a step in the right direction on all these grounds. In addition, if the Chinese authorities are truly prepared to see the exchange rate exhibit greater flexibility, then there will be more scope for relative price adjustments to facilitate global rebalancing.

DEGREE OF FLEXIBILITY

The current regime is still too new to definitively characterize the degree of flexibility. At the time of this writing, we have fewer than a hundred daily close-of-business observations on the realized rate. (Recall that the authorities' new rules for the exchange rate's fluctuation pertain to the change in the rate between successive trading days, quoted at the close of business.) This is a small number of observations for econometric work. Nonetheless, it may be useful to experiment with the limited data we have in an attempt to characterize the post-reform behavior and management of the rate and in an effort to recover the implicit weights placed on the major currencies in the authorities' basket peg.

I follow Benassy-Quere and Coeure (2001), who in turn follow Frankel and Wei (1993) in estimating a simple model of a basket peg. I regress the change in the exchange rate of the RMB against a numeraire (N) on the change in the exchange rates of the dollar ($), euro (E), yen (Y), and the won (W) against that same numeraire.

$$\delta[\text{RMB/N}] = a_0 + a_1\delta[\$/\text{N}] + a_2\delta[\text{E/N}] + a_3\delta[\text{Y/N}]$$
$$+ a_4\delta[\text{W/N}] \tag{6.1}$$

As more data become available, it will presumably be possible to add the other currencies that Chinese officials suggest as figuring in their intervention decisions.[38] Here I focus on the major currencies to conserve degrees of freedom. In the old (pre–July 21) regime, a_1 would presumably have been unity, while a_2, a_3, and a_4 would have been zero. In the new regime it is interesting to ask whether the weight on the dollar has declined, how close the weights on these currencies come to summing to either one (in which the four of them effectively constitute a rigid basket peg), or zero (in which case the currency is effectively floating), and whether there have been changes in these relationships over time.

The appeal of this approach is its simplicity. Its limitation is its sensitivity to the choice of numeraire, which is taken here as the Swiss franc—which Chinese officials have stated does not figure in their basket. The problem is that if the numeraire covaries with one of the currencies included in the basket, then that component of the basket will exhibit a relatively small variance, complicating estimation and conceivably causing the currency in question to be confused with the constant term. Here one might think that the Swiss franc covaries with the euro, even though the franc is officially a floating currency. If so the method may tend to understate the importance of the euro in the RMB basket. There is no perfect solution to this problem. Most any currency used as numeraire would have some tendency to covary with one of the big four.[39] Here I check the sensitivity of the results to choice of numeraire by substituting the Australian dollar for the Swiss franc, since the Australian and Swiss economies and therefore the A$ and SF are likely to possess very different cyclical properties.

I estimate these relationships on data starting immediately after July 21. Including the observation for July 21, when there was a one-time revaluation against the dollar, would bias the coefficient on that independent variable downward. It would be tantamount to estimating a relationship while ignoring the existence of a structural break or regime change. I estimate rolling regressions on 30 days of data to allow for variation over time.

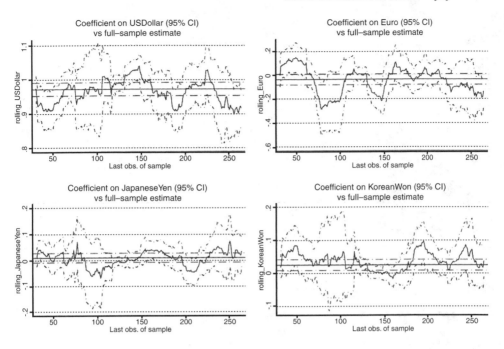

Figure 6.1   Rolling Regression Estimates for Chinese RMB

NOTES: Exchange rate data use the **Swiss franc** as the numeraire.
Period coverage: July 22, 2005 to July 26, 2006 (with gaps). Total of 264 observations.
Solid and dotted straight lines depict full-sample coefficient and 95 percent confidence intervals, respectively.
Moving-window width is fixed at 30 observations.

Source: Global Financial Database.

The results using the Swiss franc as numeraire, in figure 6.1, suggest the continued dominance of the dollar in the PBOC's intervention strategy. Over the full sample, the weight on the dollar is on the order of 0.9. None of the other currencies considered shows up with a coefficient that is significantly greater than zero at standard confidence levels. The rolling regressions, which allow for structural change over the period, suggest a somewhat lower weight on the dollar. They suggest a positive weight for the Korean won, which is presumably a proxy for other East Asian currencies around the middle of the sample period.[40] But they provide little if any evidence of a decline over time in the weight attached to the dollar.

As noted above, using the Swiss franc as numeraire may well lead to some understatement of the importance of the euro. Substituting the

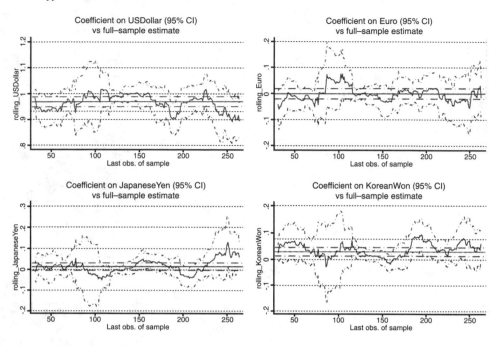

Figure 6.2   Rolling Regression Estimates for Chinese RMB

NOTES: Exchange rate data use the **Australian dollar** as the numeraire.
Period coverage: July 22, 2005 to July 26, 2006 (with gaps). Total of 264 observations.
Solid and dotted straight lines depict full-sample coefficient and 95 percent confidence intervals, respectively.
Moving-window width is fixed at 30 observations.

Source: Global Financial Database.

Australian dollar, as in figure 6.2, produces a larger point estimate of the weight on the euro in the latter part of the sample period, but not one that differs significantly from zero at standard confidence levels. Like the estimates in figure 6.1, these results suggest the continuing dominance of the dollar in the PBOC's intervention strategy. They provide no indication that the weight on the greenback is declining or that other currencies figure significantly in the PBOC's management practices.

MAINTENANCE OF THE BAND

In addition, I have reservations about the maintenance of the band. The logic laid out in the earlier section, "Lessons from the Theory of Optimum Currency Areas," suggests that as China further strengthens its financial system and diversifies its demand it will want to let the currency fluctuate more freely. As it moves toward a market-based financial system and acquires a more conventional monetary policy transmission mechanism, it will wish to adopt a form of inflation targeting, either formal or informal, as the anchor for monetary policy. It will thus have to widen its narrow band and ultimately drop it entirely.

From this point of view, retaining the 0.3 percent daily fluctuation band as part of the new regime was an opportunity missed. Repeated changes in monetary regime, including changes in foreign exchange market intervention rules, create uncertainty about the future. They raise questions about the consistency of the authorities' policy commitments. They diminish the credibility of policy. Agents need to be able to anticipate reliably how the authorities will react in the future to new information about the state of the economy. If that reaction is liable to differ over time, in uncertain ways, then the stabilizing impact of current policy will be less. A 0.3 percent daily fluctuation band is not a binding constraint now, when the problems of the financial system, the importance of export demand, the weakness of conventional mechanisms for monetary transmission, and the maintenance of residual capital controls all militate in favor of a limited increase in flexibility. But it may bind five years from now. If speculation about whether China will revalue is replaced by speculation about how quickly it will relax or abandon its fluctuation band, stability will suffer, and little will have been gained.

IMPACT ON GLOBAL IMBALANCES

A 2 percent appreciation of the RMB, even accompanied by appreciations of other Asian currencies, is too small to have much impact on the pattern of global imbalances. A 7 percent current account deficit like that which the United States is currently running is unsustainable. This deficit will have to be cut by at least half in order to stabilize net claims on the United States as a share of global wealth, and substantial exchange rate changes will be needed as part of that adjustment.[41] Mainstream models (e.g., Obstfeld and Rogoff 2004) suggest that a real effective dollar depreciation of at least 20 percent will be required to reduce the U.S. current account deficit to the requisite 3 percent of GDP.[42]

Assume that half this adjustment will have to occur in the next year, while the other half can occur the year after that. For purposes of back-of-the-envelope calculations, we can consider U.S. trade with Europe and

Asia to be of roughly equal importance. Then the 10 percent fall in the effective exchange rate of the dollar that must occur in the next 12 months can be accomplished by a 15 percent appreciation of Asian currencies against the dollar and a 5 percent appreciation of the euro against the dollar. Europe's competitiveness and growth will be hurt by the euro's further appreciation against the dollar but will be more than cushioned by its fall against the Asian currencies. (Still taking trade shares with the two regions of one half for purposes of back-of-the-envelope calculation, we see that the euro's effective rate depreciates by 2.5 percent.) The negative impact on profitability and growth in Asia is similarly moderated by the fact that the appreciation of Asian currencies is less against the euro than the dollar. (Again, with trade shares of one-half, effective appreciation is 12.5 percent.)

This simple arithmetic is just a reminder that China's 2 percent revaluation has not solved the problem of global imbalances and that further appreciation of the RMB is likely to follow as a result of the operation of market forces. Putting profit margins in the export sector at 6 percent and noting that imported content accounts for half of the value of exports suggests that Chinese exporters might just be able to tolerate a 12 percent appreciation.[43] Of course, how easily they do so will depend on how quickly they succeed in moving down the learning curve and cutting their costs. This will also be critical for whether the second part of this process of global adjustment can be smoothly reconciled with rapid Chinese (and global) growth.

Be that as it may, the unavoidable conclusion is that global rebalancing requires continued currency flexibility on China's part. But there is also a danger: hot money inflows may accelerate in anticipation of the yuan's further strengthening. This makes it all the more essential that the Chinese authorities allow the currency to exhibit greater volatility. Only the presence of a two-way bet—only the possibility that the yuan can fall as well as rise from day to day—will prevent currency traders from all lining up on one side of the market and limit speculative inflows. This is another reason why retaining the currency band was a mistake.

SOME LESSONS FROM JAPAN

Few historical precedents are available to help inform decision making by the Chinese authorities. One prior historical experience with the capacity to shed light on their dilemmas is Japan's exit from its dollar peg at the beginning of the 1970s.[44] Like China today Japan then was a high-growth economy. The rate of growth of real GDP averaged almost 10 percent per annum between 1955 and 1971, approaching current Chinese levels. As in China today, elastic supplies of labor released from rural underemployment supported the growth of the modern sector: employment in Japanese agriculture declined by 3 percent per annum throughout the 1950s. Like present-day China, Japan then was committed to export-led growth. Exports expanded by more than 17 percent per annum between 1955 and 1971. This export growth was supported by an exchange rate that was pegged to the dollar at 360 yen from April 25, 1949, in conjunction with the Dodge Line, a level that was increasingly regarded as undervalued over time.[45] As in China now, savings and investment in 1960s Japan rose to high levels—40 percent of GDP—much higher than the rates that prevailed in earlier periods. The combination of a competitively valued exchange rate and a high savings rate produced persistent current account surpluses and rapidly growing international reserves in the second half of the 1960s.

As in China today, there was strong resistance to arguments for greater exchange rate flexibility and to the idea of allowing the yen to appreciate against the dollar. Those few economists and officials who did consider the possibility of revaluation tended to dismiss it as damaging to exports, investment, and confidence.[46] An exchange-rate-centered policy was also essential because Japan did not possess a normal monetary-policy transmission mechanism. Open market operations of the normal sort did not really exist, since there was little in the way of a liquid bond market. The central bank rationed discounts and loans against bills. It gave window guidance to the large city banks in the 1950s and then to the long-term credit banks, large regional banks, and trust banks in the 1960s. A more variable exchange rate was dismissed as undesirable because strict capital controls limited corporations' ability to hedge against exchange rate fluctuations. Critics of greater flexibility observed that the volume of transactions on the forward market, where foreign exposures might have been hedged, was extremely low.

All this makes for suggestive parallels with China's position today. Thus, it is also important to acknowledge the existence of significant differences between the two cases. Industrial development had been under way in Japan for a longer period—by the end of World War II, for more than half a century. China, in contrast, had a dearth of modern industry when it embarked on reform in 1978. Compared to China today, Japan then was closer to the technological frontier defined by the United States.[47]

The system of technology transfer was different (Japan restricted inward FDI and relied on technology licensing and reverse engineering). The movement of labor from the countryside to the cities was not governed by a system of internal passports or visas. The banking system was stronger. And notwithstanding the industrial policies of the Ministry of International Trade and Industry, there was less government intervention in the economy.

Still, when U.S. President Richard Nixon suspended the convertibility of the dollar on August 15, 1971, and the greenback fell sharply against the European currencies, the Japanese authorities had little choice but to decouple their currency. Initially, the Japanese government and the Bank of Japan (BOJ) prevented the yen from rising against the dollar. For two additional weeks the central bank intervened in the foreign exchange market, buying dollars, to prevent the yen-dollar rate from changing. Over these two weeks the combined reserves of the Ministry of Finance and the BOJ rose by 50 percent. At that point, intervention was curtailed and the yen was allowed to rise, from 360 to the dollar on August 27 to 308 toward the end of the year, when intervention resumed following negotiation of the Smithsonian agreement. When the Smithsonian agreement collapsed in early 1973, the yen was allowed to fluctuate again; it floated upward toward 265, where the exchange rate's fluctuation was limited to a narrow band.

This revaluation was a large one by contemporary Chinese standards. It also bears some resemblance to the kind of two-stage adjustment suggested for the RMB by observers such as Goldstein and Lardy (2003). Thus, it is interesting to ask how the Japanese economy was affected. Econometric estimates for this period suggest relatively low passthrough from exchange rates to prices, and thus the change in the nominal exchange rate had a substantial impact on the real exchange rate, profitability, and competitiveness. In turn, the appreciation of the real rate had a substantial impact on exports and investment. Counterfactual estimates in Eichengreen and Hatase (2005) suggest that the revaluation depressed exports by 8 percent in 1972, other things being equal. The real appreciation reduced investment by 11 percent, other things being equal. These are precisely the strong negative implications for growth feared by Chinese officials today.

Yet, in fact, capital investment rose by almost 2 percent between 1971 and 1973, while export volumes rose by 12 percent. Growth was interrupted only for a quarter. The economy bottomed out in December 1971 according to the business cycle dates of the Economic Planning Agency.

Real GNP then grew by more than 10 percent on an annualized basis in the first quarter of 1972 and continued powering ahead thereafter. The explanations for this happy outcome lie in the timing of the exit and the extent of domestic demand support. The exit occurred in a period when the world economy was growing strongly, with the first OPEC oil shock not having hit and the subsequent recession yet to follow. Buoyant external demand was particularly important for the continued growth of Japanese exports. In addition, the government applied extensive fiscal stimulus to support aggregate demand as the composition of spending rotated away from net exports toward domestic demand. A supplementary budget was passed for April 1971–March 1972, and a more expansionary stance was adopted for fiscal year 1972, with expenditure on general account up by 22 percent and expenditure on public investment and lending through the Fiscal Investment and Loan Program of the Ministry of Finance up by 32 percent over the previous year. The lessons for China are clear: exit while global demand growth is still strong, and provide fiscal support.

The flaw in the Japanese authorities' exit strategy was their continued reluctance to cut the link with the dollar even in a period when the greenback was falling significantly against other currencies and when keeping a dollar peg meant a significant intensification of inflationary pressure on the Japanese economy. To prevent the yen from moving further, the BOJ was forced to cut its discount rate repeatedly, starting in December 1971 and June 1972 (by 50 basis points on both occasions). Inflation rose alarmingly as the authorities allowed accelerating money supply growth to prevent the currency from rising further. In 1974, when the first OPEC oil shock was superimposed on this inflationary environment, the inflation rate rose to 25 percent, at which point the authorities were forced to apply the brakes, precipitating a major recession. Better in retrospect would have been a more gradual shift in the direction of appreciation starting at an earlier date, which would not have forced the authorities to choose between an explosion of inflation and a major recession, or to have countenanced both. If Chinese officials, for their part, are confronted by a sharp fall in the dollar, this will be an important lesson to recall.

CONCLUSION

The 2 percent revaluation of the RMB and the commitment to greater exchange rate flexibility announced on July 21 were important first steps. Greater flexibility will help the Chinese authorities tailor monetary conditions to domestic needs. The revaluation is a modest Chinese contribution to resolving the problem of global imbalances. But definitively resolving that problem will require, together with other adjustments, considerable further appreciation of the RMB-dollar rate. Effectively tailoring monetary conditions to local needs and averting the danger that China will be overwhelmed by speculative capital flows will require accepting considerably higher levels of exchange-rate variability than officials have shown a tolerance for so far.

These arguments for greater exchange rate flexibility and further appreciation against the dollar may create discomfort among Chinese officials. The old regime of limited volatility and stability against the dollar has now delivered more than a decade of economic growth at double-digit rates. There is an understandable reluctance to tamper with success. But circumstances in China and the world are now very different from those of 1994, in turn requiring adaptations in monetary and exchange rate policies. The example of Japan in the early 1970s suggests that the transition to a new regime, involving both a higher level of volatility and trend appreciation against the dollar, can be navigated successfully, without unduly disrupting the growth process, if the Chinese authorities draw the right lessons from history.

NOTES

1. The PBOC announced that it was keeping the existing fluctuation band that limits daily changes in the exchange rate to 0.3 percent while allowing the operating range, and thus the frequency and extent of repositioning of that band, to depend more heavily on market conditions. The last part of this statement was initially interpreted as a commitment to permit an increase in flexibility, although in the week following the announcement quite a few commentators expressed second thoughts about its meaning.

2. The automatic price matching system will presumably be more attractive to smaller financial institutions that have not yet established bilateral credit lines.

3. The CFETS now asks for prices from all market makers before the market opens, removes the highest and lowest offers, and then takes a weighted average of the remaining quotes as the central rate of CNY/USD trading that day. Rates for other currencies are set using cross rates against the dollar quoted in international markets.

4. It then reported that a notional $1.2 billion of swaps had been traded through the beginning of April.

5. The precision of the figure is intended ironically. It is the difference between the 27.5 percent estimate of the extent of undervaluation cited in the bill introduced in the U.S. Congress by Senator Charles Schumer (which is in turn an average of the

10, 30, and 40 percent estimates of the extent of China's undervaluation that were offered to the relevant congressional committee) and the 2.1 percent revaluation announced on the evening of July 21, 2005.

6. This problem is even dicier than usual given disagreement over whether the Chinese economy is beginning to slow or is still at risk of overheating and the fact that there will be new information on the state of the economy between now and our publication.

7. A more systematic statement of the view that external balance should figure in the monetary-policy reaction function of central banks is Truman (2005).

8. The various-horizons part explains the "long and short" of the title.

9. The late Rudi Dornbusch once said that agreeing with the authorities is not a way for an economist to become famous, but the chips fall where they may.

10. Some, like Goldstein and Lardy (2003), will argue that such a small revaluation is apt to be destabilizing, since it will only excite expectations of further revaluation. My own view, to the contrary, is that coupling revaluation with a freer float creates a two-way bet that should prevent currency speculators from all automatically lining up on one side of the market (Eichengreen 2006).

11. See Mundell (1961), McKinnon (1963), and Kenen (1969).

12. Country size also increases the utility of the currency as a means of payment, store of value, and unit of account even when it is floating, both because financial markets are subject to strongly increasing scale economies and simply because so many agents are using the currency in day-to-day transactions.

13. These are all findings of the cross-country econometric comparisons in Bayoumi and Eichengreen (1997).

14. This, too, is a robust finding of Bayoumi and Eichengreen (1997).

15. I regard the standard objections to this advice—and in particular the notion that further steps to foster the development of forward markets on which banks and firms can hedge exchange-rate risk are a prerequisite for greater flexibility—as unconvincing, for reasons explained below.

16. Some will say that this is not a very high standard of flexibility. They should be reminded that both countries have moved in the direction of very much greater exchange rate flexibility in recent months and years.

17. So far, China has been able to avoid most of these consequences, aside from what many observers refer to as a bubble in property markets in Shanghai and elsewhere along the coast. It has been able to sterilize the effects because domestic interest rates are lower than those prevailing abroad. (The PBOC and the government can mop up capital inflows by purchasing them in exchange for domestic securities without incurring a balance-sheet or fiscal cost.) But this will not be the case forever; as savings rates normalize, interest rates will rise. And as the banks are commercialized, they will grow more reluctant to hold government bonds at artificially low interest rates. Already there are signs of this (see the discussion in the *Financial Times*, December 30, 2003, p. 10).

18. See, inter alia, the discussions of this issue in Goldstein (1998) and Eichengreen (1999). In the interest of fairness, it should be noted that the decision to open the capital account was often taken in response to external pressure from the U.S.

Treasury and the International Monetary Fund. It is gratifying to see that the International Monetary Fund (IMF) now recognizes the danger of liberalizing the capital account prior to moving to greater flexibility (see Prasad, Rumbaugh, and Wang 2005)—in contrast to its de facto position in 1997–1998.

19. In 2004, the government unified regulations affecting the ability of banks operating in China to fund themselves abroad, allowed multinational corporations operating in China more freedom to move funds in and out of the country, permitted insurance companies to invest in foreign-currency-denominated assets overseas, allowed social insurance funds to invest in overseas securities markets, allowed qualified foreign institutions to issue RMB-denominated bonds in China, and permitted emigrants as well as overseas citizens receiving inheritances to transfer their property abroad. The further steps in the direction of liberalization taken a couple of weeks following the July 21 announcement point in the same direction. The first week in August, the State Administration for Foreign Exchange announced two measures that further relaxed controls on the foreign exchange transactions of individuals and corporations. Chinese residents departing the country for less (more) than 6 months were allowed to purchase currencies with value equivalent to $5,000 ($8,000), up from $3,000 ($5,000) previously. Corporations were allowed to keep up to 80 percent of their foreign exchange earnings in their own accounts, up from 50 percent previously. The first measure was designed to offset large capital inflows and pressure for further appreciation, while the second one in principle allows firms to better hedge their exposures. But the bottom line is that these changes make it all the more imperative that the RMB now be allowed to exhibit more flexibility on a day-to-day basis in order to discourage banks, firms, and others from building up excessive foreign currency positions.

20. Everyone will be familiar with stories of foreign finance flowing directly into the Shanghai property market without first passing through the banks. And, as already noted, the power of lending directives will decline further with the commercialization of the banking system.

21. The hedge fund industry alone is sometimes estimated to have $1 trillion of capital, and with leverage its ability to take positions is considerably greater. And then there are the commercial banks, investment banks, insurance companies, and pension funds whose capital is a multiple of this figure.

22. See Eichengreen, Masson et al. (1998).

23. This finding of the 1998 study cited in the preceding footnote has been verified by the more comprehensive recent analysis of Asici, Ivanova, and Wyplosz (2005).

24. This is another finding of Asici, Ivanova, and Wyplosz (2005).

25. One might object that there is always the offshore market in nondeliverable forwards, but when the capital account is completely closed residents will have no access to that market, as a matter of definition.

26. The consolidated financial sector is a different story, of course, since the PBOC holds large amounts of U.S. Treasury and U.S. agency securities. But this is a policy problem of a different sort.

27. The net open positions of the banks are limited to 20 percent of working capital according to the latest information I have (Canales-Kriljenko 2004). All data on the Chinese banking system should be taken with multiple grains of salt. But

the figures for September 2004 suggest that foreign liabilities comprise only about 1 percent of the total liabilities of the aggregate commercial banking sector, and that they are dominated by foreign assets by a factor of 5 to 1. The source for these figures is J. P. Morgan Chase, *Global Data Watch*, February 4, 2005.

28. For more on this, see "An Evaluation of the Recent Policy Announcement" below.

29. The appropriateness of that will depend on the evolution of macroeconomic conditions in China, the behavior of the U.S. dollar, and the weight that the Chinese authorities attach to their contribution to resolving global imbalances.

30. The most recent survey and contribution to this literature of which I am aware is Tenreyro (2004).

31. See Shah and Patnaik (2005).

32. A qualification to this argument is that India has a better developed forward market, but as noted below this is at least in part a consequence of its greater exchange rate flexibility.

33. Most of the information here is drawn from Leung (2005).

34. See Quirk et al. (1988). Banks active in the interbank market typically wish to have only limited open positions in foreign exchange at the end of the trading day, so they "lay these off" (distribute them) to other banks. This is difficult when only a limited number of banks are active in the interbank market, creating a role for the central bank to assume these positions in the interim period while the market is gaining liquidity and acquiring additional participation.

35. The authors' evidence of this positive relationship between exchange rate flexibility and foreign exchange market turnover is weaker for the authors' developing countries than in their advanced-country subsample, but the very small size of their developing country subsample raises questions about what conclusions can be drawn from analyzing this category of countries separately.

36. One that is emphasized in Eichengreen (1999).

37. Exchange rate policy was only one element of the Korean crisis, of course; in addition, the country opened its capital account in precisely the wrong way, freeing bank borrowing abroad while keeping restrictions on other portfolio capital flows.

38. See the discussion in the Introduction above.

39. So would the IMF's currency unit, the SDR, which is dominated by the dollar, or a basket of G-7 currencies. Moreover, in using such a basket, it will no longer be the case that when the sum of the coefficients is zero the currency can be interpreted as floating.

40. It would appear that the difference between the full-sample estimates and the rolling regressions is attributable to data located around the fiftieth observation (in early October), when for a brief period the RMB appears to covary negatively with the yen and therefore the estimated weights on the other currencies are correspondingly higher. This was a period when the yen appreciated sharply against the dollar before giving back the ground gained. It would appear that the PBOC followed the dollar, yielding a negative covariation with the yen in this portion of the sample.

41. All this is on the optimistic assumption of 6 percent nominal income growth in the United States. In this case a deficit/GDP ratio of 3 percent produces a net international investment position for the United States of 50 percent of GDP, which in turn prevents net claims on the United States as a share of global wealth from exploding. For the underlying arithmetic, see Mann (2003) and Mussa (2005).

42. The more refinements of this analysis we see, the larger the estimates of the required real exchange rate adjustment seem to become.

43. See Buckley (2005) for reports also consistent with relatively low single-digit profit margins. In addition, Gong and Ng (2005) suggest that profit rates are narrower in the export sector than economywide. Their updated estimates of industrial enterprises' profit margins (profits as a share of sales revenues) put these at 6 percent for all industrial enterprises and 4.5 percent for export-related sectors as of early 2006; see Ng and Gong (2006).

44. This parallel is studied at length in Eichengreen and Hatase (2005), some of whose findings are summarized here.

45. The Dodge Line was the set of economic reforms advanced in the late 1940s by Joseph M. Dodge, the president of Detroit Bank, who was appointed advisor to the General Headquarters of the occupying forces.

46. The prominent exceptions were the members of the Forum for Foreign Exchange Rate Policy, who recommended revaluation and shifting to a crawling peg in their report issued on July 10, 1971. Even the members of the forum recommended limiting the yen's appreciation to 2 to 4 percent a year, reflecting widespread worries about the negative repercussions of a large step revaluation.

47. Japanese per capita GDP in 1950 expressed in 1990 international Geary-Khamis dollars was $1,926, whereas Chinese per capita GDP in 1978 was $979. Five years later the comparable figures were $2,772 and $1,265.

REFERENCES

Asici, Ahmet, Nadezhda Ivanova, and Charles Wyplosz. 2005. "How to Exit from Fixed Exchange Rate Regimes." Unpublished manuscript, Graduate Institute of International Studies, Geneva.

Bayoumi, Tamim and Barry Eichengreen. 1997. "Optimum Currency Areas and Exchange Rate Volatility: Theory and Evidence Compared." In *International Trade and Finance: New Frontiers of Research*, ed. Benjamin Cohen, 184–215. Cambridge: Cambridge University Press.

Benassy-Quere, Agnes and Benoit Coeure. 2001. "On the Identification of De Facto Currency Pegs." Unpublished manuscript, CEPII.

Buckley, Chris. 2005. "When to Float the Yuan? A Debate Erupts in China." *International Herald Tribune*. June 27, 9.

Calvo, Guillermo and Carmen Reinhart. 2002. "Fear of Floating." *Quarterly Journal of Economics* 117: 379–408.

Canales-Kriljenko, Jorge Ivan. 2004. "Foreign Exchange Market Organization in Selected Developing and Transition Economies: Evidence from a Survey." IMF Working Paper No. 04/4 (January).

Duttagupta, Rupa, Gilda Fernandez, and Cem Karasadag. 2004. "From Fixed to Float: Operational Aspects of Moving Toward Exchange Rate Flexibility." IMF Working Paper No. 04/126 (July).

Eichengreen, Barry. 1999. *Toward a New International Financial Architecture: A Practical Post-Asia Agenda.* Washington, DC: Institute of International Economics.

———. 2006. "Is a Change in the Renminbi Exchange Rate in China's Interest?" *Asian Economic Papers* 4: 41–75.

Eichengreen, Barry and Mariko Hatase. 2005. "Can a Rapidly-Growing Export-Oriented Economy Smoothly Exit a Peg? Lessons for China from Japan's High Growth Era." NBER Working Paper No. 11625 (September).

Eichengreen, Barry, Paul Masson, et al. 1998. "Exit Strategies: Policy Options for Countries Seeking Greater Exchange Rate Flexibility." IMF Occasional Paper (April).

Frankel, Jeffrey and Shang-Jin Wei. 1993. "Trade Blocs and Currency Blocs." NBER Working Paper No. 1335 (April).

Goldstein, Morris. 1998. *The Asian Financial Crisis.* Washington, DC: Institute of International Economics.

Goldstein, Morris and Nicholas Lardy. 2003. "Two-Stage Currency Reform for China." *The Asian Wall Street Journal.* September 12.

Gong, Frank and Grace Ng. 2005. "China's RMB on the Way to a Long, Gradual Appreciation." JP Morgan Global Data Watch. Economic Research Note. July 22, 9–10.

Kenen, Peter. 1969. "The Theory of Optimum Currency Areas: An Eclectic View." In *Monetary Problems of the International Economy*, ed. Robert Mundell and Alexander Swoboda, 41–60. Chicago: University of Chicago Press.

Leung, Raymond. 2005. "China Develops Further Its Interbank FX Trading System." In *Asian Bond and Currency Markets 2005.* Hong Kong: Citigroup.

Mann, Catherine. 2003. "How Long the Strong Dollar?" In *Dollar Overvaluation and the World Economy*, ed. C. Fred Bergsten and John Williamson. Washington, DC: Institute for International Economics.

McKinnon, Ronald. 1963. "Optimum Currency Areas." *American Economic Review* 53: 717–25.

Mundell, Robert. 1961. "Optimum Currency Areas." *American Economic Review* 51: 657–65.

Mussa, Michael. 2005. "Sustaining Global Growth While Reducing External Imbalances." In *The United States and the World Economy: Foreign Economic Policy for the Next Decade*, ed. C. Fred Bergsten. Washington, DC: Institute for International Economics.

Ng, Grace and Frank Gong. 2006. "China: Corporate Profits Rise, Defying the Strong CNY." JP Morgan Global Data Watch. Economic Research Note. April 13.

Obstfeld, Maurice and Kenneth Rogoff. 2004. "The Unsustainable U.S. Current Account Position Revisited." NBER Working Paper No. 10869 (November).

Prasad, Eswar, Thomas Rumbaugh, and Qing Wang. 2005. "Putting the Cart Before the Horse? Capital Account Liberalization and Exchange Rate Flexibility in

China." Policy Discussion Paper No. 05/1. Washington, DC: International Monetary Fund.

Quirk, Peter, Graham Haache, Viktor Schoofs, and Lothar Weniger. 1988. "Policies for Developing Forward Foreign Exchange Markets." International Monetary Fund Occasional Paper No. 60. Washington, DC: International Monetary Fund.

Reinhart, Carmen and Kenneth Rogoff. 2004. "The Modern History of Exchange Rate Arrangements: A Reinterpretation." *Quarterly Journal of Economics* 119: 1–48.

Shah, Ajay and Ila Patnaik. 2005. "India's Experience with Capital Flows: The Elusive Quest for a Sustainable Current Account Deficit." International Monetary Fund Working Paper no. 11387 (May).

Tenreyro, Silvana. 2004. "On the Trade Impact of Nominal Exchange Rate Volatility." Unpublished manuscript, Federal Reserve Bank of Boston.

Truman, Edwin. 2005. "Postponing Global Adjustment: An Analysis of the Pending Adjustment of Global Imbalances." Working Paper No. 05-6. Washington, DC: Institute of International Economics.

Barry Eichengreen offers an in-depth analysis of China's exchange rate regime and policy suggestions. This chapter considers the choice of the appropriate exchange rate *regime* for China over various horizons, not the
target exchange rate *level* for China at some particular horizon.[1] Eichengreen concludes that the yuan revaluation of 2.1 percent in July 2005 and
the decision to move from pegging the yuan to the U.S. dollar to pegging
it to a basket of currencies were broadly in the right direction, although he
concludes that over a longer horizon greater exchange rate flexibility
would be desirable. Eichengreen's research estimates the implicit weights
in the currency basket to which the Chinese yuan is currently pegged. Interestingly, the U.S. dollar still has a dominant, if not a 100 percent,
weight. Eichengreen further draws an interesting analogy between China's exchange rate policy today and Japan's exit from its dollar peg in the
1970s. My comments will focus on the arguments in favor of, and against,
more exchange rate flexibility, which are identified by Eichengreen. In particular, I question the importance of one part of the argument in favor of
flexible exchange rates—namely, the view that exchange rate flexibility
may be of use in China today as a means of deterring destabilizing speculative capital inflows (so-called hot money).

THE EFFECT OF EXCHANGE RATE FLEXIBILITY

Eichengreen lists three reasons for greater exchange rate flexibility. First,
flexibility provides more freedom to pursue independent domestic monetary
policy. A rigid exchange rate regime, in the absence of capital control, essentially ties down the domestic interest rate. Greater flexibility in

exchange rate allows domestic monetary policy more freedom to tailor it-self to domestic economic circumstances.

Second, greater exchange rate flexibility can be associated with in-creased short-run exchange rate volatility, as compared with exchange rate volatility in a very rigid (e.g., fixed) exchange rate regime. However, the opposite may also be true. A pegged exchange rate regime can increase vol-atility when the pegging rule is subject to change, and many economists regard jumps in exchange rates associated with changes in pegs as a greater source of exchange rate volatility. For example, if the yuan were expected to appreciate *soon*, then market participants would be encouraged to im-port capital temporarily to take advantage of the anticipated currency ap-preciation. This could produce a destabilizing "hot money" inflow. In that case, a flexible exchange rate can mitigate hot money flows by eliminating the one-sided nature of the exchange rate bet. Greater flexibility in the cur-rency regime permits the exchange rate to go both up and down, thus en-tailing short-term risks for capital inflows. The possibility of a loss from the exchange rate going against one's bet serves as a deterrent for the specu-lative capital inflow. Exchange rate volatility may be an important impedi-ment to economic performance. For example, in the standard mean-variance asset allocation framework, higher volatility of a risky asset (Chinese yuan–denominated assets in this case) implies a decrease in the demand for that asset, and consequently, a lower value of the asset. Volatility can re-duce the value of investments in China and thus reduce the amount of such investments.

Third, Eichengreen's research suggests that adopting a flexible exchange rate can boost the credibility of the monetary authority by allowing it to avoid a series of embarrassing policy retreats and attendant exchange rate adjustments. It is hard to know for sure whether the financial market's confidence in the Chinese monetary authority will be affected more by one big change or by a series of small and anticipated adjustments. Nonethe-less, the credibility issue is an important dimension to consider.

Previous research focuses on several factors that argue against moving quickly toward exchange rate flexibility. In the short run, flexibility may lead to exchange rate volatility, either mechanically from the widening of the maintained band or from the currency market's search for the "right" level of the exchange rate. The increased volatility may benefit the economy by deterring speculative capital inflows, but it also may adversely affect the banking and export sectors because it is costly for them to hedge their foreign exchange exposures. For example, in China currently there is no deep, liquid market for hedging currency fluctuations. And if currency risk affects the export and banking sectors, then it can have ripple effects on the overall economy, which is a potentially large effect in China, given the export-led growth process of the Chinese economy.

Eichengreen provides a detailed and balanced discussion of the advantages and disadvantages of greater currency regime flexibility for China today. However, it is not obvious that all the factors he considers deserve substantial weight when determining the appropriate exchange rate policy regime for China. In the remainder of this comment, I will focus on one of those factors—the issue of hot money deterrence. In particular, I will question the necessity of adopting flexible exchange rates as a means of deterring hot money by pointing out the availability of an alternative deterrence mechanism—namely, a market anticipation of a slow appreciation of the Chinese yuan. I will show that currently the market anticipates a slow rise in the value of the yuan, which implies little risk of hot money inflows under the current exchange rate regime.

HOT MONEY DETERRENCE: A SLOW APPRECIATION OF THE YUAN

Suppose someone, on July 20, 2005, knows the yuan will appreciate by 2 percent the next day. Betting on the yuan is a very good investment with an annualized return of over 500 percent.[2] It is not surprising that speculative capital will be attracted. Now suppose that the yuan is still going to appreciate by 2 percent and that the market anticipates this change, except now assume that the appreciation will happen randomly sometime during the next year instead of during the next day. The annualized return is now only 2 percent, which is lower than the yield on U.S. Treasury bonds as of March 2006, a return that would not encourage speculative capital inflows.[3]

This example suggests that the speed at which the yuan is expected to appreciate matters greatly for the potential incentives to import hot money. If the financial market anticipates that the yuan will appreciate slowly, that will deter speculative capital inflows.

How can one assess whether the financial market thinks the yuan will appreciate slowly or quickly? I will employ both historical data and forward-looking derivatives data to examine that question.

First, let us examine the investment return of someone who bet on the yuan's appreciation from a very early date. From financial news reported by LexisNexis, the earliest forecast for the yuan's appreciation came from Goldman Sachs on June 13, 2003 (reported by the London-based AFX News). Goldman Sachs forecasted that the yuan would appreciate to 8.07 yuan/U.S. dollar. For speculative investors who started betting on the yuan in June 2003, the appreciation of 2 percent came very late to be highly profitable—the yuan appreciated two years later in July 2005 (offering early speculators an annual return of only 1 percent). Afterward, the yuan appreciated from 8.11 on July 21, 2005 to 8.02 on March 28, 2006. The annualized rate of appreciation was under 2 percent.

One might argue that the slow appreciation in the past implies more room to appreciate in the future, which can possibly lead to faster appreciation under certain circumstances. To examine the forward-looking expectations of the financial market, I examine nondeliverable forward (NDF) rates traded in major offshore banks. The data are sampled by WM/Reuters and provided by Datastream International. All the data are sampled by WM/Reuters at 16:00 hours London time. The NDF contract that a client purchases from an offshore bank is the same as a forward contract except that, on the expiration day, no physical delivery of the yuan or U.S. dollar takes place. Instead, any profit (loss) is settled in cash in U.S. dollars.

Figure 6.3 plots the observed term structure of forward rates against their maturities on two different dates: January 16, 2006 and a year earlier on January 14, 2005. The term structure in January 2005 is higher because the spot exchange rate was higher. Both term structures decline monotonically, reflecting the market's anticipation of the yuan's appreciation. An obvious difference between the two term structures is that the term structure in 2006 is almost linear, while the term structure in 2005 has more curvature. In 2005, the difference between the two-year and the five-year forward rates is smaller than the difference between the one-month and the two-year forward rates.

What explains the difference? I propose two models whose implied term structures of forward rates in figure 6.4 match the observed term structures. The first model considers the scenario in which the yuan adjusts to the "right" exchange rate level quickly, assuming this will happen if greater exchange rate flexibility is allowed. The second model captures the scenario in which the yuan adjusts slowly to the "right" exchange rate level. This can plausibly happen if exchange rate flexibility is increased gradually.

Specifically, in the first model, the current spot exchange rate ($e_0 = 8.27$)

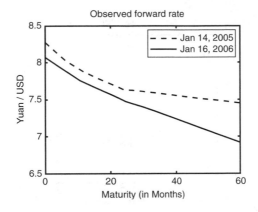

Figure 6.3   Term Structures of Observed Forward Rates

This figure plots the observed term structure of yuan/U.S. dollar forward rates. The dashed term structure is observed on January 14, 2005. The solid term structure is observed on January 16, 2006.

is assumed to equal a level that matches the observed spot rate in January 2005. The model further assumes that the changes in the exchange rate appear in a jumpy fashion,[4]

$$de_t = e_{t-} J_t dU_t \tag{6.1}$$

U_t is a Poisson process with intensity λ that characterizes the arrival of jumps. When a jump arrives, the proportional change in the exchange rate will be determined by J_t. U is further assumed to exhibit at most one jump. After a jump happens, the exchange rate will stay constant afterward. I assume the jump size $J_t = -10\%$ (the yuan appreciates by 10 percent), and the intensity λ is chosen so that the slope of the model-implied term structure matches that of the observed term structure.

In the second model, the current spot exchange rate ($e_0 = 8.27$) is derived by assuming that the yuan is expected to appreciate at the rate of 3 percent per year. The 3 percent rate of appreciation is chosen so that the slope of the model-implied term structure of forward rates matches that of the observed term structure.

Assuming no risk premium, the forward rate equals the expected spot exchange rate on the maturity date. Comparing figures 6.3 and 6.4, it is clear that the jump model (model 1) matches the observed term structure in 2005 and the model of slow appreciation (model 2) matches the

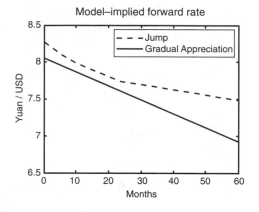

Figure 6.4   Term Structures of Model-Implied Forward Rates

This figure plots the model-implied term structure of forward rates. The dashed term structure is implied by model 1, in which the yuan/U.S. dollar exchange rate follows a jump process. The solid term structure is implied by model 2, in which the yuan appreciates gradually against the U.S. dollar at the rate of 3 percent per year.

observed term structure in 2006. The intuition of the difference between the two models is that, with the jump model, there will be no further appreciation once the yuan jumps to the "right" exchange rate and therefore future term structure becomes flatter.

These two simple models abstract from many realistic details. For example, I have assumed a zero risk premium, and I did not consider alternative models. Nonetheless, this simple calibration exercise provides suggestive evidence that the market is currently anticipating a slow and gradual appreciation of the yuan. This scenario is not conducive to hot money capital inflows.

News commentaries regarding changes in the size of hot money flows into China over time provide a similar perspective. In its January 28, 2006 issue, *The Economist* reported that: "Portfolio capital flows into the mainland—foreign currency receipts resulting from neither trade nor foreign direct investment—have dropped to $1 billion a month in the fourth quarter of last year. They averaged $8 billion a month from late 2003 until mid-2005." This observation is consistent with the interpretation of changes in the term structure of forward rates described earlier in this Comment.

CONCLUSION

Eichengreen provides a detailed and balanced discussion of the pros and cons of greater exchange rate regime flexibility for China over various horizons. This comment suggests, however, that hot money deterrence should receive a small weight in gauging the advantages of adopting a flexible exchange rate regime in China today. The evidence from forward exchange markets suggests that the one-way bet on the Chinese yuan is not an attractive investment for speculative investors. Furthermore, the risk of hot money inflows is difficult to predict. More measurable and predictable factors, such as the advantages of pursuing independent domestic monetary policy, should receive more weight when considering the appropriate foreign exchange policy regime for China.

NOTES

1. Hence the title, "The Long and Short of It."
2. Assume there are 252 business days in a year.
3. One might argue that leverage can improve the rate of return. However, after several rounds of interest rate hikes by the U.S. Federal Reserve, leverage does not significantly improve the investment return due to the cost of carry.
4. For more details on the model specification, see Yu (forthcoming), which also provides more details on the nondeliverable forward data, a more elaborate model specification, and discussions on the efficient estimation method.

REFERENCES

The Economist. 2006. "Cooling Down—China's Hot-Money Inflows Evaporate." January 28.
Yu, Jialin. Forthcoming. "Closed-Form Likelihood Approximation and Estimation of Jump-Diffusions with an Application to the Realignment Risk of the Chinese Yuan." Journal of Econometrics.

CHAPTER 7

China's Foreign Exchange Policy:
What Will China Do? What Should China Do?

Peter Garber, Robert J. Hodrick, John H. Makin, David Malpass,
Frederic S. Mishkin, and Eswar Prasad

COMMENT

Peter Garber

I will comment on China's exchange rate policy: what it has been, what it is, what it ought to be, and what it will be. There is not much dispute these days about the "what it has been" and "what it is" parts, but plenty about the "what it will be" and "what it ought to be." My colleagues, Michael Dooley and David Folkerts-Landau, and I[1] have been in the middle of this argument for three years now. We used to have to debate both academic and industry experts even about the "what it is." But now our views are rather conventional in the financial industry, if longer-term asset prices and exchange rates are any guide. Currently, the dispute is mainly with academics and policy experts about what ought to be done and about the imminence of catastrophe if nothing will be done.

WHAT IT WILL BE

Let us start at the "what it will be" dimension of these tenses. In a nutshell, we believe that the system will evolve over the longer term with no pricing discontinuities generated by the internal dynamics of its operation alone. The renminbi (RMB) will be appreciating gradually in real terms over a protracted time, sometimes via nominal appreciation, sometimes via more rapid inflation. Gradually, the underemployed labor in China will be absorbed, interventions in foreign exchange markets will slow and end, and the official sector-driven export of capital to the rest of the world will also end. Internal demand will then have to pick up to cap the end of this development process. This means that the abnormally low real interest rates in the rest of the world will converge to more normal levels.

WHAT IT HAS BEEN AND WHAT IT IS

I will touch a bit on the "what it has been" and the "what it is" of the system. Until July 2005, the exchange rate regime was simple: it had been fixed at 8.27 RMB per U.S. dollar for 11 years since the large devaluation of 1994. Backing this fixed rate regime were tight controls on inward and outward capital flows.

As part of China's development strategy, the exchange rate was undervalued to encourage the export sector. This required the accumulation of foreign exchange reserves. The reserve growth was largely unnoticed until China became a player on a global macroeconomic scale during the last six years.

Then, in July 2005, pressure mainly from the United States generated a 2.1 percent revaluation together with a statement that the currency might be allowed steadily to appreciate and that it would be tied to a basket of trading partner currencies. Since then, the RMB has appreciated slightly in as close to a textbook picture of a hard and steady crawling peg against the dollar as can be found anywhere. Drawn against time, the exchange rate is almost a perfect straight line with a slight downward slope. So a glance makes it evident that there is no basket peg.

But at the time of the revaluation, some commentators argued that this really was the end of the regime that we had observed for at least five or six years. My co-authors and I have called this regime the Revived Bretton Woods system, and it has subsequently become known as the Bretton Woods II system. In this regime China-Asia has a policy of export-driven growth that relied on undervalued exchange rates. It also has a number of other features that were designed to overcome some key distortions such as China's wealth-destroying financial system and the natural frictions that arise with trading partners when a country on a macro scale tries to implement an export-driven growth policy.

Of course, the system has generated remarkable global imbalances, and for the last three years since we wrote our initial notes about this regime, we have been arguing with just about everyone—except for participants in the financial markets—about whether or not the system was going to collapse very soon.

When the revaluation occurred, some of the more strident voices in the "it will collapse soon" camp, observing the eight basis point rise in the ten-year U.S. interest rate and the 2 percent yen appreciation that ensued (and that was reversed three days later), claimed once more that this was the beginning of the unraveling of the Bretton Woods II system. We had a more Churchillian view of things: we thought of it in terms of the unraveling of the beginning of the Bretton Woods II system. We think this system has many more years to go, a point that was made during the discussion of Barry Eichengreen's chapter in this volume.

Our general view is that the RMB's rate of appreciation is about to increase somewhat. Jun Ma, Deutsche Bank's chief economist for China, thinks (along with almost everybody else now) that the appreciation will be on the order of 3 to 5 percent per year for many years to come. Of course, he has been saying that for a couple of years now.

But we think that is about right, and we think that is the right policy. The nominal appreciation will move at that rate. But the real appreciation will be slower because nominal appreciation will reduce inflation in China. China's inflation is already below U.S. inflation, so real appreciation will be slower still.

It is clear that this change in exchange rate policy has had no discernible effect on intervention. Looking at the long-term plot of China's reserves against time, the reptilian part of any economist's brain immediately wants to hit the logarithm key to try to make sense of it. But just looking at the last year, we see that acquisition of official reserves clearly sped up. In the last six months, the reserve intervention has been on the order of magnitude of $100 billion; it was $200 billion in the last year.

"WHAT IT OUGHT TO BE" AND "WHAT IT WILL BE" AGAIN

We have heard quite a bit about the "what it ought to be's." China ought to float. China ought to appreciate the currency dramatically. China ought to encourage domestic consumption and more generally domestic demand. China ought to cooperate with the rest of the world in reducing the imbalances.

We also see these policy changes coming as a natural part of the development strategy, but China will not willingly do any of this suddenly.

China will gradually increase domestic demand as domestic real wages gradually rise. Eventually its excess labor supply will be absorbed, and only then will the world move back to a more normal system. But that involves appreciating the RMB by 4 to 5 percent per year, with further large-scale intervention. As domestic demand increases, the current account surplus will stop growing and it will then reverse, as will the current account surplus of Asia as a whole.

Then we will have returned to a more normal system as the fundamental imbalance—the excess supply of labor—will have been absorbed. Asian currencies will have appreciated against the dollar; global interest rates will return to normal levels; and the United States will service its increased debt. The "what it ought to be" will have converged with the "what it will be." But we think that all of this will be gradual—taking place over many years—barring asteroid hits on the planet like trade-killing protectionism or further Middle Eastern wars.

NOTE

1. Michael Dooley, P. Folkerts-Landau, and Peter Garber, "An Essay on the Revived Bretton Woods System," NBER Working Paper No. 9971 (September 2003). See Robert Hodrick's comment in this chapter for a review of the first Bretton Woods.

COMMENT

Robert J. Hodrick

Peter Garber has outlined what he, Michael Dooley, and David Folkerts-Landau have termed the Bretton Woods II system.[1] It is a system in which China and other Asian nations peg their currencies to the dollar at exchange rates that imply undervaluation of the RMB on foreign exchange markets. The undervaluation of the RMB makes foreign goods expensive inside of China, and the overvaluation of the dollar makes Chinese goods less expensive in the United States. The consequence of this undervaluation is export-led growth, which allows China to develop faster than it otherwise might. Dooley, Folkerts-Landau, and Garber argue that this is a deliberate policy of China and that the system works because China's goal is to rapidly absorb an underemployed labor force into an industrial system that is changing from being state controlled to privately controlled.

Let us review the first Bretton Woods system to look for some parallels and differences, and in particular to open a discussion of how the Bretton Woods II system may end. Under the original Bretton Woods system, the dollar price of gold was fixed by the United States, and other countries pegged their currencies, that is, fixed their exchange rates, to the dollar. The system required that foreign central banks hold dollar assets as international reserves, and the United States, in turn, was required to redeem its dollar liabilities for gold at the demand of foreign central banks. Initially, private capital flows were limited, and exchange rates were allowed to change only in response to fundamental disequilibrium. The Bretton Woods system worked well immediately after World War II and in the 1950s as European countries rebuilt their economies with the help of undervalued currencies.

There was one fundamental structural problem in the Bretton Woods system that contributed to its downfall. Real growth and the implied increase in the demand for money that goes along with growth were faster than the growth of gold stocks. Countries' international reserves were therefore growing more rapidly than the U.S. stock of gold, and eventually the countries' international reserves, which were the liabilities of the United States, became greater than the United States' gold stock. The credibility of the U.S. promise to redeem dollar assets for gold came into question, and foreign leaders, like Charles de Gaulle of France, began to question the desirability of the system, calling on the United States to slow down its money creation, which was exporting inflation to the rest of the world. Eventually, of course, President Richard Nixon abandoned the U.S. pledge to redeem dollars for gold in August of 1971. The breakdown of the Bretton Woods system was followed by two years of attempts to patch it up, with the eventual adoption of generalized floating exchange rates for major currencies in 1973.

The key difference between Bretton Woods I and Bretton Woods II is that the United States is no longer required to redeem U.S. Treasury bonds for anything other than U.S. dollars. The undervaluation of the RMB and consequent acquisition of dollar-denominated international reserves are totally voluntary on China's part. The Chinese know that their currency is undervalued; they know that they will be acquiring massive dollar reserves; and they know that they will face political pressure to revalue the RMB. I agree with Peter Garber that the RMB will be allowed to appreciate slowly over the next decade as the need for the undervaluation slowly unwinds.

Dooley, Folkerts-Landau, and Garber have also noted an important role that dollar-denominated international reserves play in the system. Remember, China's goal is to move its massive underemployed workforce as quickly as possible into an industrial economy that can compete on world markets. Because China's own technology and management skills are not up to the task, it needs help. The one way to ensure that the capital stock that is being employed is a world-class, competitive capital stock is to welcome foreign direct investment (FDI). Of course, the foreign owners of the capital find outsourcing attractive because of the low wages of the underemployed workers, but the big risk to someone doing FDI in China is political risk, the fear that some part or all of the profitability of the investment will be expropriated by the Chinese government. This risk is certainly real given the volatile geopolitical environment and the sometimes conflicting objectives of the leaders of the countries. What better way for China to reassure international investors than to acquire a stock of U.S. dollar paper assets that the United States can refuse to honor should the Chinese begin to systematically expropriate foreign investment. While this is an unlikely scenario, it is one that has to be taken seriously by those who would do FDI in China.

Of course, along with providing collateral for FDI, the acquisition of $200 billion per year of U.S. Treasury bonds has an additional side benefit for the United States. Interest rates are lower than they otherwise would be. My colleague, Andrew Ang, has developed a term structure model with Monica Piazzesi and Sen Dong, which I like very much.[2] The model fits the historical term structure data from the 1960s through 2000 quite well. It links long-term interest rates to the short rate, the expected rate of inflation, and the GDP growth rate. When I input in the observed short rate of 4.5 percent and use plausible values for inflation and GDP growth, the model predicts that the yield on the 10-year bond should be 6 percent. The only major macroeconomic difference between now and 10 years ago is the emergence of Bretton Woods II. I conjecture that if the yield on the 10-year bond was closer to 6 percent than to 4.5 percent as it is now, the values of U.S. real estate and equities would be considerably lower. Chinese policymakers know this, too, and they recognize that the U.S. government and U.S. consumers are benefiting while enjoying consuming the exports of the Chinese workers.

One place where I disagree with the Dooley, Folkerts-Landau, and

Garber analysis is that I think that the currency of denomination of the reserves matters. They argue that major currencies are effectively perfect substitutes, but I think risk premiums differ across countries. Put differently, the quantity of bonds outstanding matters. If the market for U.S. Treasury bonds had to absorb $200 billion more per year, the required yield on the bonds would be higher.

Let us push this fundamental idea a little further. I am arguing that acquiring additional international reserves supports more FDI. Therefore, there must be an optimal rate of acquisition of international reserves that is determined by the rate at which China can absorb new FDI. There are adjustment costs in installing plant and equipment and in moving 200 million workers into the modern industrial sector. Acquiring and installing capital must be done over time. Thus, the RMB can be allowed to appreciate slowly to keep reserve acquisition at the desired rate. Also, China has recently begun to relax its restrictions on foreign investment by its citizens. These restrictions can be relaxed to allow an increase in the demand for dollars from the Chinese private sector. Increasing the private demand for dollars lessens the excess supply of dollars that must be purchased by the People's Bank of China (PBOC) at any given exchange rate. Relaxing the restriction also provides some welfare benefits for the Chinese residents.

How will the Bretton Woods II system end? Certainly, U.S. workers who face the "unfair" competition from their undervalued Chinese counterparts have a legitimate complaint. Do they have enough political power to cause the United States to forego the gains from the current system? I do not think so. It may go quietly as Dooley, Folkerts-Landau, and Garber argue with eventual appreciation of the RMB over time. Another potential scenario is one that has a political angle. If the Chinese sour on the United States' geopolitical policies, the massive stocks of dollar reserves give them a strong bargaining chip. It is usually argued that the Chinese would not threaten to sell their U.S. assets because they hold too many and would suffer a loss of value in the massive run-up in interest rates and depreciation of the dollar that would result. But that is exactly what de Gaulle achieved. In the 1960s it was the Vietnam War and the fiscal profligacy of the Johnson administration that Europeans did not like. Tomorrow, the Chinese may object to how the United States is conducting the War on Terror. They may decide that they have gained enough in export-led growth and that they need to consolidate their internal gains while stepping forward as an alternative approach in international affairs. The economic costs of this action would be balanced against the political gain.

NOTES

1. Michael Dooley, David Folkerts-Landau, and Peter Garber, "Living with Bretton Woods II," Deutsche Bank, September 20, 2005.

2. See Andrew Ang, Monica Piazzesi, and Sen Dong, "No-Arbitrage Taylor Rules," Columbia Business School Working Paper, June 2005.

COMMENT

John H. Makin

Much of the hubbub over China's exchange rate policy is misplaced. Debating what will be or should be the chosen exchange rate level for China is far less interesting than considering the consequences for the global economy of a sustained period of Asian currency undervaluation, which appears quite likely.

What are the implications of a sustained undervaluation of Asian currencies? Note that I have broadened our discussion to include Asian economies other than China's, since many of them are following a similar policy of undervaluation. Obviously, China is the focus here, but the fact that it is not acting in isolation is important to bear in mind.

Let me begin by noting that this is likely to be a protracted period of overvaluation. The Chinese are not going to let their currency appreciate rapidly anytime soon. To understand the consequences for the global economy, one must posit an equilibrating process—that is, how the prices of goods and services, the prices of assets, trade flows, and economic activity around the world will adjust to accommodate Asian overvaluation. My emphasis will be on the ways in which Asian trade policy affects the global economy through its effects on asset prices.

The views I will express draw heavily on a speech by Mervyn King, the governor of the Bank of England, which he delivered in London on the occasion of the day when U.K. 50-year indexed gilts went to 38 basis points in yield, suggesting that there is indeed a search for yield out there.

How does this search for yield relate to what is going on in Asia's emerging markets and in China in particular? King suggests an interesting possibility that has been floating around for awhile. If globally traded goods are underpriced as a consequence of undervaluation, then inflationary pressures in traded goods around the world will be lower, holding all else constant. That implies that central banks will be able to maintain settings of monetary policy that are consistent with stable commodity price inflation but are inconsistent with stable asset prices. Industrial countries will be able to maintain inflation rates of 1 to 2 percent with monetary policies that maintain artificially low London Interbank Offered Rates and treasury interest rates. Those interest rates support artificially high asset prices.

In other words, in the past several years we have enjoyed something of an inflation buffer, particularly in globally traded manufactured goods markets (I will call them global-traded goods), thanks to heavy shipments of those goods out of Asia at bargain basement prices. Those sectors, in essence, are receiving a subsidy through the persistent maintenance of an undervalued currency. The essential policy choice for global markets is clear: You can let the currency exchange rate adjust, or you can let the level of worldwide liquidity adjust. Currently, liquidity is doing almost all of the adjusting.

The monetary policy settings used by the Federal Reserve, the Bank of England, and the Bank of Japan are consistent with an absence of inflation. There are varying experiences around the world. Japanese inflation is about zero, U.S. core Personal Consumption Expenditures inflation is about 1.9 percent, and Europe's is somewhere in that area.

Meanwhile, asset prices and, lately, commodity prices, seem to keep rising. That is, real interest rates are low, and consequently, equity prices remain high and rising, especially in Asia. The Japanese equity market is up 45 percent over the past year. The U.S. equity market is not up as much but it is still doing well, as are European equity markets. At the same time, everyone is searching for duration in the fixed income market. That is, they want the long-term guaranteed flows of payments, especially given the changes in pension fund legislation in the United Kingdom.

So what happens? Well, rising asset prices sustain rapid growth and consumption until the rapid increase in demand along with the rapid increase in the usage of commodities in the Asian economies that are producing the traded goods pushes up commodity prices. Those of you who have not noticed should take a careful look at the prices of gold, platinum, silver, and the copper commodity, which are exploding.

The next stage of adjustment will begin to bring the United States to closure as rising commodity prices, especially oil, spill into core inflation. Core inflation will go above the acceptable range for the Federal Reserve's policymakers. We are right at the top of that range now, and we will discover by midyear that the Fed has more tightening to do. Mervyn King worries about the protracted lags involved in the period over which one can maintain monetary policy settings that are consistent with ever rising asset prices, which in turn boost demand growth, and ultimately prices.

When the central banks finally get around to tightening, that will create a sharp downward adjustment in asset prices, which is putting it a little bit academically. Imagine if we had a bunch of equity analysts in here today and I said, "guess what, the Fed funds rate will be 6 percent by December." If they believed me, they would all throw up.

So that kind of adjustment—where asset prices drop rapidly as monetary policy tightens—could be part of the equilibrating mechanism that we will see here. In that situation, we probably would find a rapid slowdown in U.S. growth, since it is clear that to some extent higher asset prices are supporting aggregate demand and disposable income growth in the United States.

Once the monetary policy–induced asset price collapse takes hold, the dollar will depreciate sharply against most currencies and China will then face a very difficult dilemma with their pegging policy. It is unclear how China's exchange rate policy should react to a U.S. asset price collapse. I do not know where the Chinese currency should go in a world where the scale factor, that is, U.S. and global demand growth, is declining (implying a need to depreciate) but where the inflation substitution effect is suggesting the need for an appreciation.

In conclusion, I think that the undervaluation of Asian currency is just beginning to play out in ways that make me very uncomfortable about the so-called Bretton Woods II system and the viability of continuing it. Central bankers, such as Tim Geitner, are beginning to reflect on this troubling scenario. Much of the current debate among central bankers regarding the question of whether monetary policy should target asset prices is really a debate about whether the aforementioned asset collapse is a likely scenario.

COMMENT

David Malpass

I would like to begin by focusing on some simple facts about exchange rates. The official exchange rate for the yuan was fixed in the beginning of 1994. If we look at the gray market for the yuan prior to that time, it is interesting to note that it got all the way up to 12 in 1993. In a July 1993 *Wall Street Journal* article, I complimented the Chinese on their decision to stabilize the currency. I think a lot of China's internal demand growth since 1994 is related to the stability of its currency. If we look around the world, countries that have stable exchange rates tend to have fast internal demand growth.

So I guess I quarrel a little bit with the idea that the current stability of the yuan is the result of a desire to subsidize exports. Remember that in 1998 China declined to devalue the yuan. Should we interpret that decision as an attempt to pursue a policy to tax exports? I think it is better just to think of China's exchange rate policy throughout as a currency stability policy and one that's been very good for China's investment and consumption growth over those years.

My outlook for the future is that the yuan will appreciate to 7.8 around the end of 2006. The primary force working against a larger revaluation is China's preference for currency stability. The Chinese say that all the time, and I think they mean it. It has worked well for their economy. Of course, there are forces working toward larger revaluation, including pressure from the United States and the economic establishment. You still hear people calling for China and other Asian countries to pursue a big revaluation, but I do not see that point of view winning over the Chinese policymakers.

I also am not confident that a big revaluation by China would have its intended effects. If China revalues more than we expect, I would actually expect to see faster capital inflows, the opposite of what such a policy for China would be trying to achieve, because of the resulting increase in expectations of further revaluations.

China made it very clear in mid-2005 that small, gradual revaluation was all they have in mind, and I think that is what they really mean. So does the market. After the revaluation last summer, if one looks at the nondeliverable forwards of three different tenures, the one-year, six-month, and three-month, one sees that the expectations of a further revaluation all declined sharply after China's July 21 move.

This implies a declining risk of speculative or hot money inflows. At Bear Stearns, we tried to measure the size of hot money flows. We defined hot money as the difference between the current account surplus and the buildup of international reserves. That is not a perfect definition, but it serves to make my point. There has been a big decline in that measure, meaning that people are not putting as much money into China these days solely for the purpose of trying to capture profits from a revaluation. From this standpoint, China's exchange rate policy change seems to have been a success.

Another change that we have noted is the reduced cost of sterilization. In 2003 and 2004, China's interest rates were higher than U.S. interest rates, and so China had to accept lower yields when building up international reserves. Over the last year, that difference has reversed, making it less costly for China to continue the buildup as needed. I think they will not need to build up international reserves much more, because the United States is raising interest rates quickly.

A big factor in the buildup of China's international reserves in 2004 and 2005 was the fact that the United States was maintaining interest rates at too low a level. China was acting as a buffer to this monetary stimulus in the same way that corporations in the United States were serving that role by building up cash. The Federal Reserve had real rates very low.

We have seen the liberalization of China's capital account recently. Although the capital account is still displaying a relatively low level of outflows, that amount is increasing at a pretty rapid rate. We expect that to continue in 2006 and into 2007 as China liberalizes. That is a healthy, stabilizing development.

One concern for China is excess capacity in some industries. Indeed, we can see disinflationary price trends in various industries in China owing to excess capacity. There is too much investment going on. We expect China to maintain its current goals of trying to improve the efficiency of capital market allocation, restrain investment, and support more consumption growth. That is reflected in our outlook for 2006.

COMMENT

Frederic S. Mishkin[1]

In recent years, China has pegged its exchange rate to the U.S. dollar at a level that is substantially undervalued. The result has been that China has been running a large trade surplus with the United States and has been accumulating international reserves at an extremely rapid rate. Indeed, China had accumulated over $700 billion of international reserves by the end of 2005, and its accumulation of international reserves is expected to top $1 trillion in the near future.

Corresponding to China's trade surplus is, of course, a trade deficit in the United States. China's undervalued exchange rate has meant that U.S. goods are less competitive with cheap Chinese goods, and this has resulted in pressure on the Chinese to allow the value of their currency to rise relative to the U.S. dollar. Some politicians have even called for tariffs specifically against Chinese goods. Given that I have no particular expertise in forecasting what our policymakers and politicians will do, I would rather focus on the question of whether we should do anything to change the situation. To answer this question, we need to understand why China has kept its currency undervalued and whether this makes sense. I will argue that, despite some important disadvantages of this policy, an undervalued exchange rate may be a sensible development strategy for the Chinese. Because successful development of the Chinese economy is an important force in decreasing the number of extremely poor people in the world, there is an argument for the United States to acquiesce to China's exchange rate policy, at least for the near future.

CHINA'S DEVELOPMENT STRATEGY

A low value of its currency results in cheap prices for China's tradable goods relative to those produced in foreign countries, and thus provides a substantial boost to its exports. As a result, the United States runs a trade deficit that must be financed by capital inflows. The Chinese government has been willing to maintain its undervalued exchange rate by purchasing huge amounts of U.S. Treasury securities—thus in effect financing the shipping of their goods to us with very low interest loans. This is a costly strategy because it means that a poor country like China, with a per capita income of one-eighth that in the United States (in Purchasing Power Parity terms) and a relatively small capital stock is lending to a rich country. We usually do not see the poor lending to the rich, particularly at very low interest rates, so this strategy may seem a bit bizarre. Yet it actually makes a lot of sense. As argued by Dooley, Folkerts-Landau, and Garber (2003), China's exchange rate policy is a key element in a development strategy of export-led growth. I will argue that there may be tremendous benefits for China from pursuing this strategy.

Encouraging domestic markets to sell goods to the markets of rich countries is an important engine for growth in poorer countries. Because foreigners do not have a natural predeliction to buy your goods, you have to be supercompetitive—that is, your goods have to be even better and cheaper than goods made in the foreign country. From the standpoint of the United States, domestic firms will have to focus even more on being highly productive, boosting productivity and thereby economic growth.

China has noticed what its neighbor and rival Japan accomplished in the decades following World War II. In the immediate aftermath of World War II, Japan was a poor country. Its economic infrastructure had been destroyed by the war, and Japanese goods were considered to be shoddy ("made in Japan" was a derogatory statement about the quality of a product). Furthermore, Americans had just come out of a war with Japan, and many Americans refused to buy Japanese goods, just as many refused to buy German goods after the war.

To convince Americans to buy Japanese products, Japanese firms had to produce goods that were both cheaper and better than their American counterparts. Selling Japanese products in America, such as automobiles, meant that Japanese companies had to produce a superb product at low cost, and this is what they did. Eventually, Japanese cars took over a huge percentage of the American automobile market, and companies like Toyota and Honda grew to be household names, becoming far more profitable than the once dominant General Motors and Ford.

Given this need to become supercompetitive, the export industries in Japan became enormously productive, leading to rapid productivity growth in Japan, enabling it to become one of the richest countries in the world. Other East Asian economies, such as South Korea, Singapore, Hong Kong, and Taiwan, have followed a similar export-led strategy with great success. Indeed, all examples of successful growth stories among less developed countries have been export driven.

A second reason for promoting exports is that it generates incentives for institutional reform that produces a more efficient financial system. As I have argued in *The Next Great Globalization* (Mishkin 2006), getting the financial system to work well is critical to the success of an economy. To understand why, we need to recognize that the financial system is like the brain of the economy: it is the coordinating mechanism that allocates capital to building factories, houses, and roads. If capital goes to the wrong uses or does not flow at all, the economy will operate inefficiently and economic growth will be low. No work ethic can compensate for a misallocation of capital. Working hard will not make a country rich because hard-working workers will not be productive unless they work with the right amount of capital and in a firm that is capable of combining capital and labor efficiency. Brain is more important than brawn, and similarly an efficient financial system is more important than hard work to an economy's success.

Indeed, the evidence that financial development and economic growth are linked is quite strong.[2] A pioneering study by King and Levine (1993) using a sample of 80 countries found that the greater was financial development back in 1960, as represented by a larger financial sector (known as *financial deepening*),[3] the larger the economic growth over the subsequent 30 years.[4] Later studies using more sophisticated techniques have confirmed this finding and indicate that a doubling of the size of private credit in an average less-developed country is associated with a 2 percentage point annual increase in economic growth (e.g., Levine, Loayza, and Beck 2000). Furthermore, industries and firms that are more dependent on external sources of funds and so would benefit more from financial deepening are found to grow faster in countries that are more financially developed (Rajan and Zingales 1998; Demirguc-Kunt and Maksimovic 1998). Similarly, more new firms are created in countries with developed financial systems.[5] The evidence also suggests that the way financial development raises growth is more through improvements in the allocation of capital, which produces higher total factor productivity, rather than through higher investment (Beck, Levine, and Loayza 2000; Levine 2005). As stated by Honohan (2004), "The causal link between finance and growth is one of the most striking empirical macroeconomic relationships uncovered in the last decade."[6]

Although financial deepening improves an economy's rate of economic growth, it is possible that poverty will remain the same or increase if the resulting growth leads to greater income inequality. However, this potential outcome is not consistent with recent empirical evidence. In countries with better financial development, the income of the poorest fifth of the population actually grows faster than average GDP per capita (Hongyi, Squire, and Zou 2001; Beck, Demirguc-Kunt, and Levine 2004; Honohan 2004), indicating clearly that financial development is associated with reductions in poverty and even with reductions in the use of child labor (Dehejia and Gatti 2002). This finding is exactly what economic theory suggests; financial development increases the access of the poor to credit because in the absence of the development of an efficient financial sector, the poor have less access to credit than the rich (Aghion and Bolton 1997; Banerjee and Newman 1993; Galor and Zeira 1993).

Encouraging an export orientation of domestic markets creates a greater need for a well-functioning financial system. To compete effectively in the international arena, firms need better access to capital. If they cannot get capital, they will not be able to make the investments they need to increase productivity and to price their goods competitively. In this way, international trade creates a demand for reforms that will make the financial system more efficient.

We are seeing how the globalization of trade is driving financial reform in China. As Chinese enterprises have increasingly entered into international markets, China's hybrid system of communism with semicapitalist property rights (township and village enterprises) has worked less and less well in enabling businesses to grow.[7] The exploding export sector (China's exports have grown from $9.7 billion in 1978 when Deng Xiaoping came into power to $430 billion today)[8] now needs access to ever greater amounts of capital, and it needs a better financial system to achieve that access to capital. Although it has taken time, globalization is finally generating the demand for an improved financial system, which is driving the reform process in China.

We see this process unfolding, with the communist leadership recognizing that the old development model has to change. The government has announced that state-owned banks are being put on the path to be privatized and has allowed foreign investment in China's banking system of $20 billion in 2005 alone.[9] In addition, the government is engaged in legal reform to make financial contracts more enforceable. New bankruptcy law is being developed so that lenders have the ability to take over the assets of firms that default on their loan contracts.[10]

Thus, China's strategy of keeping its currency undervalued to promote exports may have such large benefits that the benefits outweigh the cost of providing low-interest loans to a rich country like the United States in order to finance the purchase of China's export goods. What at first may seem a bizarre policy makes good economic sense.

WHAT SHOULD WE DO ABOUT CHINA'S EXCHANGE RATE POLICY?

If China's development policy makes economic sense for them, should we insist that China abandon its exchange rate peg and allow the value of the yuan to rise? The answer may well be no.

By letting China continue an exchange rate policy that promotes export-led growth, we are assisting China's development. China's export-led growth strategy has removed hundreds of millions of Chinese from extreme poverty (those with an income of less than one to two dollars a day). If we truly care about the poor throughout the world, then letting poor countries like China price their goods cheaply and not erecting barriers to those products has a lot to say for it.

Of course, this is not the way much of the public and politicians think in rich countries like the United States. Rich countries, including the United States, impose higher barriers to imports from poor countries than from rich ones. While rich countries impose average tariffs on all manufactured goods of 3 percent, tariffs on labor-intensive manufactured imports from poor countries are far higher at 8 percent, and tariffs on agricultural products from poor countries average 14 percent.[11] The fact that rich countries make it even harder for poor countries to sell goods to them has led Oxfam, a prominent international charitable organization, to hand out awards for double standards in trade policy, with first prize going to the European Union, second to the United States, third to Canada, and fourth to Japan.[12]

I would also argue that even if we do not care about poor people in China, there are gains to the United States from letting China pursue its export-led development strategy. After all, it enables the United States to buy their goods very cheaply, financed by loans with very low interest rates. This sounds like a pretty good deal to me.

If doing this is such a good idea, why are so many people against it? The answer is that the benefits of having cheap goods enter the United States are spread widely, while the costs are often concentrated: that is, individual firms lose profitable business or individual people lose their jobs because of trade and so lobby hard against it. The workers who lose their jobs are of course worse off from allowing foreign goods to enter cheaply, but we can devise schemes to compensate displaced workers who lose directly from trade, either with direct compensation or with programs to help them retrain themselves to get better jobs.[13] This strategy can be described as "protecting people, not firms." Even if compensation schemes or retraining programs for displaced workers are not highly efficient, it still may be worthwhile putting them in place because doing so encourages political support for keeping our markets open, which improves overall economic performance.

I come to the conclusion that having a strategy of benign neglect to China's exchange rate policy may be the right thing to do. This does not mean that benign neglect is a feasible strategy, given the political forces against it. Furthermore, having an undervalued exchange rate forever is not a good idea for China, and at some point it will need to float its exchange rate and open up its capital markets. This should be an ultimate objective, but rushing into it before the Chinese are ready can only create friction with China, given that the Chinese view their current strategy as having substantial benefits.

NOTES

1. Any views expressed in this comment are those of the author only and not those of Columbia University or the National Bureau of Economic Research.

2. An excellent nontechnical survey of the extensive empirical evidence on this topic can be found in World Bank (2001). See also Levine (2004) and Schmukler (2004). For a recent paper that also finds that financial deepening is crucial to economic growth for developing countries, see Aghion, Howitt, and Mayer-Foulkes (February 2005).

3. In some research, financial deepening is characterized as an expansion of the financial sector. Here I am using the term *financial deepening* more generally to refer to financial development, which includes not only an expansion in the financial sector but an improvement in its institutions so that it can allocate capital to its more productive uses more efficiently. Abiad, Oomes, and Ueda (2005) find that financial liberalization, which improves the institutional framework of the financial sector, does lead to higher economic growth and is far more important to economic growth than just expansion of the financial sector.

4. One concern with this result is that high economic growth before 1960 could have led to high financial development and to further high economic growth, so that causality might not run from financial development to growth. To rule this out, later papers have used instrumental variables techniques in which the origin of the legal system (English, French, German, or Scandinavian), which was determined typically hundreds of years ago, well before recent growth, is used as an instrument for financial development at the beginning of the period. The result is the same; economic growth is positively related to financial development. For example, see Levine, Loayza, and Beck (2000), Levine and Zervos (1998), and Beck, Levine, and Loayza (2000).

5. This is particularly true in industries that depend more on external finance. See Rajan and Zingales (1998).

6. Honohan (2004: 2). Case studies such as Jeong and Townsend (2005) also support the importance of financial deepening to economic growth.

7. The view that a financial system that has worked well in the initial stages of development needs to move toward the model used in advanced countries is espoused by Rajan and Zingales (1998).

8. The source of this data is the International Monetary Fund, *Direction of Trade Statistics* (Washington, DC: IMF, 2005). The latest export data is for 2003.

9. The largest four state-owned banks, with 70 percent of China's bank deposits, are scheduled to be privatized in the following order: the Construction Bank, the Bank of China, the Industrial and Commercial Bank, and the Agricultural Bank.

10. See the speech by the governor of the central bank of China, Zhou Xiaochuan, "Improve Legal System and Financial Ecology," Speech presented at the "Forum of 50 Chinese Economists," December 2, 2004, Beijing, China.

11. Wolf (2004: 213).

12. Oxfam (2002). From p. 213 of Wolf (2004).

13. For a discussion of programs to assist workers who are displaced by trade liberalization, see Kletzer and Rosen (2005).

REFERENCES

Abiad, Abdul Nienke Oomes, and Kenichi Ueda. 2005. "The Quality Effect: Does Financial Liberalization Improve the Allocation of Capital?" Paper presented at the Journal of Banking and Finance/World Bank Conference on Globalization and Financial Services in Emerging Market Countries, June 20–21.

Aghion, Philippe and Patrick Bolton. 1997. "A Trickle-Down Theory of Growth and Development with Debt Overhang." *Review of Economic Studies* 64: 151–72.

Aghion, Philippe, Peter Howitt, and David Mayer-Foulkes. 2005. "The Effect of Financial Development on Convergence: Theory and Evidence." *Quarterly Journal of Economics* 120 (February): 173–222.

Banerjee, Abhijit and Andrew Newman. 1993. "Occupational Choice and the Process of Development." *Journal of Political Economy* 101: 274–98.

Beck, Thorsten, Asli Demirguc-Kunt, and Ross Levine. 2004. "Finance, Inequality and Poverty: Cross-Country Evidence." Mimeo, World Bank (April).

Beck, Thorsten, Ross Levine, and Norman Loayza. 2000. "Finance and the Sources of Growth." *Journal of Financial Economics* 58(1–2): 261–300.

Dehejia, Rajeev H. and Roberta Gatti. 2002. "Child Labor: The Role of Income Variability and Access to Credit in a Cross Section of Countries." World Bank Policy Research Paper 2767 (January).

Demirguc-Kunt, Asli and Vojislav Maksimovic. 1998. "Law. Finance and Firm Growth." *Journal of Finance* 53 (December): 2107–37.

Dooley, Michael, P. Folkerts-Landau, and Peter Garber. 2003. "An Essay on the Revived Bretton Woods System." NBER Working Paper No. 9971 (September).

Galor, Oded and J. Zeira. 1993. "Income Distribution and Macroeconomics." *Review of Economic Studies* 60 (January): 35–52.

Hongyi, Li, Lyn Squire, and Heng-fu Zou. 2001. "Explaining International and Intertemporal Variations in Income Inequality." *Economic Journal* 108(1): 26–43.

Honohan, Patrick. 2004. "Financial Development, Growth and Poverty: How Close Are the Links?" World Bank Policy Working Paper No. 3203 (February).

Jeong, Hyeok and Robert M. Townsend. 2005. "Sources of TFP Growth: Occupational Choice and Financial Deepening." Mimeo, University of Chicago (April).

King, Robert and Ross Levine. 1993. "Finance and Growth: Schumpeter Might Be Right." *Quarterly Journal of Economics* 108: 717–37.

Kletzer, Lori G. and Howard Rosen. 2005. "Easing the Adjustment on U.S. Workers." In *The United States and the World Economy: Foreign Economic Policy for the Next Decade,* ed. C. Fred Bergsten, 313–43. Washington, DC: Institute for International Economics.

Levine, Ross. 2005. "Finance and Growth." In *Handbook of Economic Growth,* ed. Philippe Aghion and Steven N. Durlauf, 865–934. Amsterdam: North Holland.

Levine, Ross, Norman Loayza, and Thorsten Beck. 2000. "Financial Intermediation and Growth: Causality and Causes." *Journal of Monetary Economics* 46(1): 31–77.

Levine, Ross and Sara Zervos. 1998. "Stock Markets, Banks, and Economic Growth." *American Economic Review* 88(3): 537–58.

Mishkin, Frederic S. 2006. *The Next Great Globalization: How Disadvantaged Nations Can Harness Their Financial Systems to Get Rich.* Princeton, NJ: Princeton University Press.

Oxfam. 2002. *Rigid Rules and Double Standards: Trade Globalization and the Fight Against Poverty.* Oxford: Oxfam International.

Rajan, Raghuram and Luigi Zingales. 1998. "Financial Dependence and Growth." *American Economic Review* 88(3): 559–86.

Schmukler, Sergio L. 2004. "Financial Globalization: Gain and Pain for Developing Countries." Federal Reserve Bank of Atlanta *Review* (Second Quarter): 39–66.

Wolf, Martin. 2004. *Why Globalization Works.* New Haven, CT: Yale University Press.

World Bank. 2001. *Finance for Growth: Policy Choices in a Volatile World.* Washington, DC: World Bank; Oxford: Oxford University Press.

COMMENT

Eswar Prasad[1]

Discussions about the Chinese exchange rate regime inevitably focus on China's large and growing current account surplus. The bilateral trade balance between China and the United States receives even more attention, raising the hackles of politicians in the United States who view China as gaining an unfair advantage through its currency policies. Indeed, many politicians in Washington, as well as some analysts, view China as a prime contributor to the growing global current account imbalances. This has led to calls for a sharp revaluation of the Chinese currency against the U.S. dollar.

Strong economic pressures have been exerted for an appreciation of the Chinese RMB, based in large part on relatively stronger productivity growth in China's tradable goods sector compared to those of its trading partners. And there are indications that the RMB is undervalued, with different analysts and academics producing a wide range of estimates of undervaluation.

In the face of all these pressures, can China continue to maintain a de facto pegged exchange rate that moves in a very tight range around the U.S. dollar? And what is the right remedy if the present regime is not sustainable?

The United States should first consider this issue from the Chinese domestic perspective, setting aside the matter of international pressures for the moment. Notwithstanding the sentiments of many observers, my view is that the issue of sustainability of the current regime, at least from a narrow domestic perspective, is a red herring. The current regime is likely to be sustainable for a long period. Indeed, if anything, the current constellation of Chinese domestic interest rates and industrial country interest rates makes sustainability even less of an issue than it was a couple of years ago. Here's why. One of the principal reasons that appreciation pressures on a currency become difficult to resist beyond a point is that the costs of sterilization become too large. The explicit costs of sterilization are related to the fact that the interest paid on sterilization instruments such as central bank bills or government securities is, in most developing countries, generally higher than the interest earned on reserves, which are typically held in industrial country government securities. As a result, the more capital that flows in and needs to be sterilized (in order to prevent this liquidity from flooding domestic markets and creating inflationary and other risks), the greater the costs to the central bank.

In China, however, the explicit costs of such sterilization have been held down simply by getting the state banks to purchase government (or central bank) bonds at low interest rates that are close to, or below, the rate of return earned by the central bank on its reserve holdings.[2] Indeed, as of April 2006, the rate of return on short-term U.S. Treasury instruments is almost two percentage points *above* the rate on Chinese central bank bills of corresponding maturity, meaning that the (PBOC) at the margin actually makes money on its sterilization operations!

Of course, even China cannot escape the basic laws of economics. In truth, the broader costs of sterilization may just not be obvious. Controls on capital outflows and domestic financial repression are required to help maintain at low levels the rate of interest paid on central bank bills. To maintain bank profits, the government must then mandate low-interest rates on deposits. The cost of these distortions is ultimately borne by depositors in the banking system—which includes most households, given the lack of alternative investment opportunities—in the form of very low real rates of return on their deposits (Prasad and Rajan 2005).

Thus, the perpetuation of the current regime is dependent on two sets of distortionary policies—financial repression and a relatively closed capital account. I see both of those as having very significant welfare costs for China. The lack of effective monetary control has meant that bank credit has continued to grow rapidly and by all accounts goes largely to state enterprises, with this lending not driven by commercial considerations. As a consequence, investment growth has remained unsustainably high, especially since much of this investment is being undertaken in a limited set of sectors where there are indications of a significant buildup of excess capacity (see Goldstein and Lardy 2004).

A greater concern related to a fixed exchange rate regime is that, over time, the capital controls could prove increasingly ineffectual as the incentives to evade them became stronger. Maintaining a fixed exchange rate system in the face of the inevitable erosion of capital controls could pose risks to the financial system, which remains weak in many respects (Eichengreen 2004; Prasad, Rumbaugh, and Wang 2005).

FLEXIBILITY

What alternative exchange rate policy would suit China best? Before answering that question, let me refer back to the calls for a revaluation of the RMB as the appropriate way to reduce China's current account surplus. My view is that a large revaluation by itself is unlikely to be a good idea. Ultimately, focusing on the current account surplus is probably not as useful as thinking through the deeper structural problems that may be contributing to this surplus. In fact, a revaluation as a quick fix to a large and growing current account surplus could, if done in isolation, be counterproductive by perpetuating some root problems.

The key point is that maintenance of a de facto fixed exchange rate regime can complicate domestic monetary management, as evidenced by the recent rapid accumulation of international reserves and its fallout in terms of faster domestic monetary expansion. Having more flexibility in the exchange rate would give China an autonomous monetary policy, a powerful tool to counter domestic and external shocks. Thus, it seems far more productive to frame the issue in terms of more exchange rate flexibility for

China rather than try to orchestrate a particular level of the exchange rate that would make all concerned parties satisfied.

Exchange rate flexibility could also be important for another major priority of Chinese policymakers—financial sector reform. The link is a subtle one. Since most Chinese saving is intermediated through the banking system, a more commercially oriented banking system would ensure a more efficient allocation of resources in the economy. And this, in turn, would require that banks respond to market-based measures to control economic activity. The instruments that are typically employed in such circumstances in market economies include the short-term interest rate. In the absence of exchange rate flexibility, however, the independence of monetary policy has been greatly constrained, even if capital controls have insulated the monetary system to some extent. This has resulted in the monetary authority having to use nonmarket measures such as moral suasion to control credit and investment growth, an outcome that may have worked in the short run but that has vitiated the process of banking reforms. The need to sterilize large waves of capital inflows has also put a heavy burden on the central bank.

Although exchange rate flexibility by itself is hardly going to be a panacea, attaining monetary policy independence through greater flexibility will eventually remove an important shackle that has hindered financial sector reforms and restrained other key aspects of the move toward a more market-oriented economy.

AN ALTERNATIVE NOMINAL ANCHOR

Having said that, the big question on the floor is: if not the fixed exchange rate regime, what could possibly serve as a reasonable nominal anchor for China? For a developing economy, indeed for any economy, having a firm and stable nominal anchor is essential not just in terms of price stability but in terms of overall macro stability.

Marvin Goodfriend and I have argued that in China a low-inflation objective would be a reasonable anchor for monetary policy (Goodfriend and Prasad 2006). We are particular not to use the term *inflation* targeting because that carries connotations of a very formalistic framework with very stringent requirements in terms of data, in terms of the monetary control mechanism, and so on. For an economy such as China that is undergoing marked transitions in a variety of dimensions, there would be numerous impediments to effectively operating a full-fledged inflation targeting regime.

Nevertheless, we think that a relatively more broad definition of inflation targeting, which could take the form of a long-run low-inflation objective, would be quite workable for China.[3]

Our approach is more practical for the foreseeable future, and it should deliver most of the benefits of formal inflation targeting. In light of the changing structure of the economy and weaknesses in the monetary transmission mechanism, our framework could accommodate a continued role for the monitoring and management of monetary (and credit) aggregates by the PBOC. But money would not constitute a good stand-alone nominal anchor since the changes in China's economic structure and financial markets imply that the rate of money growth consistent with a stable rate of inflation is likely to be difficult to measure and highly variable.

We view a low-inflation objective as being consistent with promoting sustained high employment growth, which is a key consideration for Chinese policymakers. Indeed, it is precisely by providing a firm and credible nominal anchor through a low-inflation objective that the PBOC can best contribute to overall macroeconomic stability and best provide for sustained employment growth and financial stability.

What is needed for such a nominal anchor to be put in place? We think that operational independence for the Central Bank is crucial. Not complete independence, but operational independence, and in fact, strategic guidance and support from the government for a low-inflation objective could be critical for the PBOC to be able to achieve its low-inflation objectives.

In terms of the mechanics, a prerequisite for the PBOC to run this sort of a regime well would include effective control of aggregate bank reserves. That makes exchange rate flexibility a primary requirement for this alternative nominal anchor because, if you are trying to use monetary policy to support an exchange rate objective, it makes it very difficult to have effective control of bank reserves.

Some of the infrastructure for effective control of reserves is already in place. The interbank market is functioning well, but other structural problems have to be dealt with, including the very large level of excess reserves in the banking system which the Chinese authorities are trying to deal with.

In addition, there is one critical aspect, which is the monetary transmission mechanism. In China, this will largely run through the banking sector since the rest of the financial sector remains rather underdeveloped.

Ultimately, then, these reform objectives are tied together. You need exchange rate flexibility in order to push forward financial sector reform. But the stability, the macroeconomic stability that could come from having a firm nominal anchor that does not require distortionary domestic policies to support it, would in fact be very important for financial sector reform.

Banking sector reform, however, is going to take a while. No one has any illusions that full modernization of the banking sector is going to be completed in the next couple of years. In order to put in place a low-inflation objective, however, Goodfriend and I argue that a relatively minimal set of financial sector reforms is all that is required. In particular, what is essential is the strengthening of bank balance sheets by removing legacy nonperforming loans (NPLs) from the banking system. This is necessary to make the banking system robust to interest rate fluctuations and would be very important in terms of giving the PBOC operational independence to be able to use the interest rate instrument very effectively.

A deeper issue is that of separating the financing of state-owned enterprises (SOEs) from the banking system because even if you clean all the existing NPLs off the books, the possibility that new lending could show up as fresh NPLs could be a problem. In our essay, we have a proposal for how we think new financing of SOEs (not financing of new SOEs!) could in fact be separated from the banking system.

TIMING

In principle, an orderly exit from a fixed exchange rate regime can best be accomplished during a period of relative tranquility in exchange markets. A next-best set of circumstances is when there are pressures for an appreciation amidst capital inflows since it is in general easier to deal with appreciation rather than sharp depreciation pressures. This is the situation that China is in today, with the added comfort of having a robust domestic economy, at least in terms of headline numbers showing high growth and low inflation.

Waiting longer to modify the exchange rate regime could present some risks, including the continued buildup of imbalances in the economy if monetary policy effectiveness remains restricted because of the fixed exchange rate regime (Goldstein and Lardy 2004). A more serious risk is related to the capital account. With a relatively closed capital account, the lack of exchange rate flexibility is less of a problem. On the other hand, an open capital account and a fixed exchange rate together make an economy highly vulnerable to external shocks, especially the vagaries of international capital flows. The problem for China is that, with expanding trade and the increasing sophistication of domestic and international investors, the capital account is becoming more porous over time.

It would therefore be prudent to consider an early move toward flexibility, while existing capital controls are still reasonably effective and the underlying structural problems are manageable. The current strength and stability of the economy, together with existing capital controls, have contributed to a reasonably high level of confidence in the domestic banking system despite its weak financial position. But domestic banks are likely to come under increasing competitive pressure, especially once foreign banks are allowed to enter the Chinese market in early 2007 under China's World Trade Organization accession commitments.

Another concern expressed by the authorities is that exchange rate flexibility cannot be instituted until the technical infrastructure is put in place. Although this is a legitimate concern, it definitely should not be a showstopper. The China Foreign Exchange Trading System has been enhanced in various ways in the last few months. Allowing more market participants to have access to this trading system, and taking other measures to improve the depth and liquidity of the market, can be done relatively easily. Besides, it is difficult to have instruments for hedging foreign exchange rate being developed and offered unless there is sufficient volatility in the exchange rate to justify them. The experiences of other emerging market economies suggest that markets can generate such instruments fairly quickly once there is a demand for them.

As for the shift to a new nominal anchor, we think there are significant advantages to consider making this move relatively soon. Our proposal for anchoring monetary policy with a low-inflation objective would allow for continuity in the operational approach to monetary policy. The PBOC could continue its current operations and gradually adapt its procedures to the pursuit of independent monetary policy as supporting reforms are put in place. Our proposal would mainly entail a shift in strategic focus to a well-defined inflation anchor. Many other emerging market economies that have made the transition to inflation targeting regimes have had to deal with the initial pain of bringing down high rates of inflation. China is fortunate that, under present circumstances, the shift to an inflation anchor would be seamless since it would involve merely locking in the current low rate of inflation.

We also believe that the adoption of an effective independent monetary policy would facilitate various reforms that have intrinsic benefits of their own. For instance, the resulting macroeconomic stability would facilitate the modernization of the financial system. In addition, the new policy regime would necessitate improvements in the statistical base that would enhance public sector transparency and encourage better communication about policy intentions.

In sum, present circumstances are favorable for moving more rapidly to a more flexible exchange rate regime and for putting in place a new nominal anchor. Such windows of opportunity for instituting major macroeconomic reforms without the risk of extensive disruptions tend to be rare and fleeting, and should not be missed. Furthermore, these steps would be in China's own interest for promoting stable and sustainable growth in the long run. As argued by Prasad and Rajan (2006), this may be the time to move beyond a piecemeal and incremental approach to reforms to a bolder and more comprehensive approach.

NOTES

1. At the time of this writing, Eswar Prasad was the Chief of the Financial Studies Division in IMF's Research Department. Previously he was the head of the IMF's China Division from 2002 to 2004. The views expressed in this comment are those of the author and do not necessarily represent the views of the IMF or IMF policy. At publication, he is the Tolani Senior Professor of Trade Policy at Cornell University.

2. Of course, in an environment where large savings continue to flow into the banking system and the banks are under pressure from the central bank to restrain their credit growth, they are quite eager to hold central bank bills rather than simply increase their reserves deposited at the central bank, since excess reserves carry a lower rate of return than that on central bank bills.

3. This is similar to the view that Ben Bernanke has espoused for the United States. Of course, given their different stages of financial sector and broader macroeconomic development, we have very different reasons for recommending a similar monetary framework for China.

REFERENCES

Eichengreen, Barry. 2004. "Chinese Currency Controversies." CEPR Discussion Paper No. 4375. London: Center for Economic Policy Research.

Goldstein, Morris and Nicholas R. Lardy. 2004. "What Kind of Landing for the Chinese Economy?" Policy Briefs in International Economics. No. PB04-7. Washington, DC: Institute for International Economics.

Goodfriend, Marvin and Eswar Prasad. 2006. "A Framework for Independent Monetary Policy in China." International Monetary Fund Working Paper. Washington, DC: International Monetary Fund.

Prasad, Eswar and Raghuram Rajan. 2005. "China's Financial Sector Challenge." Op-ed article in *Financial Times*. May 3.

———. 2006. "Modernizing China's Growth Paradigm." *American Economic Review* 96(2): 331–36.

Prasad, Eswar, Thomas Rumbaugh, and Qing Wang. 2005. "Putting the Cart Before the Horse? Capital Account Liberalization and Exchange Rate Flexibility in China." International Monetary Fund Policy Discussion Paper 05/1. Washington. DC: International Monetary Fund.

Regional Estimates of New Deposit and Loan Shares, and Nonperforming Loans

Loren Brandt and Xiaodong Zhu (Chapter 2)

The construction of estimates of new loans and deposits at the regional level poses several difficulties that we discuss more fully in this appendix.

First, our regional estimates draw on provincial-level estimates that each province reports in the annual *Jinrong Nianjian*. Provinces do not always report these numbers consistently. Sometimes loans (or deposit) figures are for renminbi (RMB) loans, and in other cases for the sum of RMB and $U.S. loans. Loans and deposits might also be reported differently. Occasionally, they are not explicit about the reporting basis. $U.S. loans only amount to slightly more than 5 percent of the total loan portfolio, but inconsistency in reporting on an annual basis can introduce slightly larger errors into the estimate of new loans in any given year. For 2003 and 2004, however, we were able to construct consistent estimates on the basis of RMB and $U.S. loans and deposits. For 2002, largely because of difficulties with the estimates for 2001, measurement error is more of an issue; nonetheless, estimates for all three years (2002, 2003, and 2004) are generally consistent.

Second, calculating the percentage of new loans by province runs into the same problem we discussed earlier regarding estimates of new loans by type of institution—namely, dealing with the transfer or disposal of existing loans, usually nonperforming. Differences across provinces in the percentage of the existing stock of provincial loans that are transferred as part of the larger transfer of assets will lead to a bias in our estimate of the growth in new loans at the provincial level, and thus, regional shares in new credit.

We have only been able to find data on the provincial breakdown of these transfers associated with the transfers in 1999 and 2000. Appendix table I reports these by province, with NA denoting that information was

Appendix Table 1   Transfer of NPLs in 1999 and 2000, by Province

Province	Loans Transferred in 1999 and 2000 (billion RMB)	As a % of Total Loans in National Banks in Each Province, Year-End 1998
Beijing	31.52	10.08
Tianjin	43.65	30.57
Hebei	64.93	23.23
Shanxi	31.74	22.89
Neimongoug	NA	NA
Liaoning	62.7	17.13
Jilin	45.2	21.33
Heilongjiang	45.2	17.77
Shanghai	NA	NA
Jiangsu	47.67	11.18
Zhejiang	26.78	8.93
Anhui	NA	NA
Fujian	NA	NA
Jiangxi	30.92	21.69
Shandong	58.42	16.43
Henan	42.21	13.90
Hubei	62.26	19.85
Hunan	40.69	26.54
Guangdong	139.81	23.59
Guangxi	33.24	46.54
Hainan	35.57	27.39
Sichuan	30.23	12.03
Chongqing	30.84	25.65
Guizhou	NA	NA
Yunnan	13.33	8.78
Tibet	NA	NA
Shaanxi	NA	NA
Gansu	21.40	21.38
Qinghai	NA	NA
Ningxia	1.26	4.43
Xinjiang	20.58	16.89
Average	41.73	19.49

Sources: Based on reported figures by each province in *Jinrong Nianjian*, 2000, 2001, and 2002.

not provided for that province. These estimates are interesting in their own right, both for what they may imply about the political economy of the reform, but also looking forward, the distribution of the stock of bad debt.

For the 23 provinces for which we have information, the transfer of nonperforming loans (NPLs) averaged 41.73 billion RMB, or an average of 19.4 percent of the stock of loans issued by national bank branches in each province as of the end of 1998. The weighted average is slightly lower and equal to 18.2 percent. For four of the six important coastal provinces (Shandong, Jiangsu, Zhejiang, and Guangdong—we do not have information for Shanghai and Fujian), the average was 15.0 percent, compared to 20.4 percent for the remaining 19 provinces for which we have information. There is heterogeneity within the coastal provinces, and in Guangdong, 23.5 percent of the loans in the national banks were transferred. In absolute terms, this amounted to nearly 140 billion RMB, the largest transfer in any single province and slightly less than 15 (10) percent of the total transferred by these 23 (all 31) provinces.

Differences across provinces and regions in these estimates likely reflect the quality of the underlying portfolios, as well as other distributive issues relating to the reform process. If the patterns for 1999 and 2000 hold true for later years, failure to take into account the transfer of NPLs can impart a bias in our estimates of the share of new loans in each region. In 2002 and 2003, the transfer and disposal of NPLs was relatively small compared to 1999 and 2000. In 2004, transfers were significant—nearly 600 billion RMB—and this needs to be kept in mind in interpreting more recent numbers.

Evolution of Capital Controls in China

Eswar Prasad and Shang-Jin Wei (Chapter 3)

This appendix provides an extensive chronology of controls on capital account transactions over the period from 1980 through 2005. It is drawn from the International Monetary Fund's (IMF) *Annual Report on Exchange Arrangements and Exchange Restrictions* (various issues). Following a detailed description of controls existing in 1980, changes to those restrictions in each subsequent year are then listed. The reporting format for the capital account transactions changed in 1996, the year in which China accepted the obligations of Article VIII of the IMF's Articles of Agreement. Another detailed overview of the restrictions in place at the end of 1996 is therefore provided, followed by a listing of changes to those restrictions in subsequent years.

EXISTING CONTROLS ON CAPITAL TRANSACTIONS AS OF DECEMBER 31, 1980

A policy of permitting foreign borrowing on a planned basis has been instituted. Loans for vital projects or projects that have a rapid rate of return are given priority approval. All sections and departments wishing to borrow abroad must prepare a plan showing the kinds of imports for which the loan is intended. Such plans must show the amount of foreign exchange needed and how much of this will be earned and how much will be borrowed from abroad. All such plans are submitted to the State Planning Commission, which reviews them in cooperation with the Foreign Investment Control Commission. If the imports are for new construction, the plans are also reviewed by the State Construction

We are indebted to Qing Wang for his help in preparing this appendix.

Commission (all three commissions are under the supervision of the State Council).

Approval of foreign loans is based on a consideration of the need for foreign capital, the ability of the borrowing unit to repay, and China's overall debt-service ratio. Most loans are made through the Bank of China (BOC) or, in the case of some loans to provinces or enterprises that are able to repay the loan themselves, with BOC guarantees. External borrowing plans by entities other than the BOC must be submitted to the State General Administration of Exchange Control (SGAEC) and the Foreign Investment Control Commission for approval, before loans from abroad or from the Hong Kong and Macao regions can be incurred. Resident organizations may not issue securities for foreign exchange unless approved by the State Council.

All foreign investment projects are subject to the approval of the Foreign Investment Control Commission. The policy with respect to foreign capital is designed both to make up the insufficiency of domestic capital and to facilitate the introduction of modern technology and management. All foreign exchange earned by joint ventures should be kept in a BOC account. Transfers of capital require SGAEC approval. When a joint venture is wound up, the net claims belonging to the foreign investor may be remitted with SGAEC approval through the foreign exchange account of the joint venture. Alternatively, the foreign investor may apply for repayment of his paid-in capital.

Profits of joint ventures, besides firms in special export zones and those exploiting petroleum, natural gas, and other resources, are subject to tax at 33 percent (30 percent basis rate plus a 10 percent surcharge on the assessed tax). Remitted profits are subject to an additional tax of 10 percent. A joint venture scheduled to operate for 10 years or more may be exempted from income tax in the first year of operation and be allowed a 50 percent reduction for the second and third years. Joint ventures in low-profit operations, or located in remote, economically underdeveloped outlying areas, may be allowed a further 15 to 30 percent reduction in income tax for the following 10 years. A participant in a joint venture that reinvests its share of profit in China for a period of not less than five years may obtain a refund of 40 percent of the tax paid on the reinvested amount. Some joint ventures concluded before passing of tax regulations in August 1980 are subject to taxes at different rates.

Foreign investment by Chinese enterprises is subject to approval; profits thereby earned must be sold to the BOC, except for a working balance.

Chinese diplomatic and commercial organizations abroad, as well as undertakings abroad and in Hong Kong and Macao, are required to draw up annual foreign exchange plans.

Four special economic zones are established.

CHANGES DURING 1981

None.

CHANGES DURING 1982

January 1. The Law on Income Taxes for Foreign Enterprises, which was adopted by the National People's Congress on December 13, 1981, came into force.

January 29. The State Council promulgated regulations on the exploitation of offshore petroleum resources in cooperation with foreign enterprises.

March 6. The BOC decided (a) to grant foreign currency loans at preferential interest rates to support the development of export commodities, projects of energy saving most pressing to the state, technical transformation of enterprises of light industries (including the textile and engineering industries), purchases by domestic enterprises of raw and semifinished materials in short supply, and projects of the packing industry; and (b) to finance export services relating to projects contracted with foreign countries.

CHANGES DURING 1983

January 1. The tax rate on income earned by foreign firms from interest on loans in respect of contracts signed during the period from 1983 through 1985 was reduced by 50 percent; and a similar reduction was extended to income earned from agriculture, energy development, communications and transport, education, and scientific research.

August 1. New rules (approved by the State Council on July 19, 1983) were introduced for the implementation of exchange controls in respect of enterprises with foreign and overseas Chinese capital and joint ventures.

September 2. The Standing Committee of the National People's Congress approved certain changes in the income tax law for joint ventures.

September 20. The State Council issued a body of regulations for the implementation of the law on joint ventures involving China and foreign capitals.

CHANGES DURING 1984

January 23. The State Council announced that Shanghai region would be given the authority to approve foreign direct investment (FDI) projects to a value of up to U.S. $10 million.

April 27. The State Council announced that 14 selected coastal cities would be allowed to open up further to the outside world, in order to help speed up the introduction of advanced foreign technologies, notably through FDI.

May 3. The harbor city of Beihai, one of the 14 coastal cities selected by the State Council for wider opening up to the outside world, was officially designated as an economic and technological development zone opened to FDI by small and medium-size electronics and light industry enterprises. Foreign nationals investing in Beihai would be given a preferential tax treatment similar to that prevailing in the four special economic zones.

June 6. The municipality of Shanghai announced that foreigners investing in the economic and technological development zone in Shanghai would be given preferential tax treatment in regard to local income tax, comparable to the tax treatment provided in the special economic zones.

July 14. As part of various steps announced by the State Council with the objective of speeding up a "wider opening up" of the 14 designated coastal cities to the outside world, it was decided that these cities would not have the status of the existing special economic zones, but would be allowed, at their own initiative, to offer additional tax incentives to foreign investors providing advanced technology. In addition, such cities could set up special economic and technological development areas where the 10 percent tax on profits remitted abroad by foreign investors would be waived. As in the special economic zones, the profits of joint venture established in the designated areas would be subject to a 15 percent income tax, and machinery, equipment, and other inputs imported by or for joint ventures operating in the 14 coastal cities would be exempt from customs duties as well as from the consolidated industrial and commercial tax. Exports would also be exempt from export duties; and a certain proportion of products requiring advanced manufacturing techniques would be permitted to be marketed domestically.

July 31. Joint ventures operating in the 14 coastal cities were formally made subject to an income tax of only 15 percent (instead of the standard 33 percent), with the approval of the Ministry of Finance. In addition, the 10 percent tax on onward remittances of foreign investment income would be waived if the foreign investment was undertaken in designated economic and technological development areas in these cities.

August 20. Special foreign currency lending facilities were set up by the BOC and the Industrial and Commercial Bank of China (ICBC) for domestic borrowers to help finance imports of advanced foreign technology.

September 1. Authorization was granted for the State Administration of Exchange Control and the BOC to settle payments of outstanding foreign currency debts of foreign and overseas Chinese banks in China (including branches undergoing or already in liquidation), which were contracted through 1949.

November 7. The ICBC was authorized to carry out business transactions in foreign exchange in the special economic zones.

November 19. New provisional regulations concerning the application of income taxes and the consolidated industrial and commerce tax in the special economic zones and in the new technology development zone in 14 newly opened-up coastal cities were issued by the State Council. The income taxes payable by joint ventures in the specified zones and areas would be reduced from the standard rate of 33 percent to 15 percent, with the approval of the Ministry of Finance. Income taxes for other long-term industrial, communication, transport, agricultural, and service trade undertakings in their first one or two profit-taking years would be waived with the approval of the taxation authority, and reductions of 50 percent would be allowed in the following two or three years, but profits made by the older sectors of the 14 coastal cities would be subject to taxation by up to 80 percent of the standard tax rate of 33 percent. In addition, consolidated industrial and commercial tax exemptions would be granted on imports of machinery and equipment, raw materials, building supplies, spare parts and other specified inputs, and exports other than those controlled by the state. Foreign participants in the joint ventures in these zones and areas were also allowed to remit their share of the profits overseas tax free, but a 10 percent tax was levied on income from royalties, dividends, interest, and rentals, compared with the standard rate of 20 percent elsewhere in China. The exemption and reductions of income tax were made applicable to the whole of 1984, while the exemption and reductions of industrial and commercial consolidated tax were to take effect from December 1, 1984.

December 13. In a move aimed at attracting FDI, the municipal authorities of Shanghai announced new concessions on tax and other policies, including reduced customs duties and preferential access to specified domestic markets. In addition, the income tax could, with approval from the Ministry of Finance, be decreased to 15 percent on condition that the project be operated with advanced technology or that the investment be for over U.S. $30 million, and customs duties on certain imported equipment and raw materials could be waived.

December 22. Foreign banks were allowed to accept deposits from foreign organizations, nonresidents, enterprises with foreign capital as well as capital belong to overseas Chinese, and Chinese and foreign joint ventures, and to make loans in foreign currency in Shanghai.

CHANGES DURING 1985

January 3. New plans to open four large industrial regions to foreign investment and trade were announced. The move represented the third stage in China's open-door policy, following experiments in the four special economic zones and the 14 coastal cities.

March 14. Regulations governing the establishment of foreign joint ventures in Shanghai were relaxed.

March 15. China and India signed a three-year agreement to develop economic and trade relations; the accord provided for encouraging joint ventures, creating consultancy services, exchanging economic, trade, and technical delegations, and participating in international fairs in the two countries.

March 26. The Foreign Economic Contract Law was adopted.

April 1. The Chinese Patent Law, enacted in 1984, came into effect. In addition, China joined the Paris Convention for the Protection of Industrial Property.

April 1. The Ministry of Petroleum and Industry announced that foreign oil companies would be allowed to participate in exploration and development of oil and gas reserves in nine provinces and one autonomous region.

April 2. The State Council introduced a regulation on the control of foreign banks and joint venture banks in special economic zones.

August 22. China approved establishment of the first foreign branch bank office in the country since 1949. In addition, the Hong Kong Shanghai Banking Corporation announced a plan to begin branch operations in Shenzhen, a special economic zone, in October 1985.

November 6. China and Libya signed a protocol aimed at consolidating bilateral cooperation between the two countries.

December 3. A joint venture bank, the first with foreign capital participation, was opened in Xiamen, a special economic zone, with Panin Group of Hong Kong.

CHANGES DURING 1986

None.

CHANGES DURING 1987

February 5. Provisional regulations were approved permitting financial institutions and enterprises with sources of foreign exchange income to guarantee the foreign exchange obligations of other debtors.

August 27. Provisional regulations were issued on a new system requiring the timely registration of external borrowing with the State Administration of Exchange Control (subsequently renamed the State Administration for Foreign Exchange, or SAFE).

CHANGES DURING 1988

April 13. The National People's Congress adopted a new Chinese-foreign cooperative joint ventures law.

CHANGES DURING 1989

February 14. The State Council issued regulations that all foreign commercial borrowing required the approval of the People's Bank of China (PBOC). All commercial borrowing is to be channeled through one of 10 domestic entities—the Bank of China, the Communications Bank of China, the China International Trust and Investment Corporation, the China Investment Bank, and six regional international trust and investment corporations. The short-term debt of each entity may not exceed 20 percent of the entity's total debt, and short-term borrowing is to be used only for working-capital purposes.

March 6. The SAEC announced procedures governing Chinese direct investment abroad. Such investments would require government and SAEC approval, a deposit of 5 percent of the investment to secure repatriation of dividends and other income from the investment, and repatriation of earnings within six months.

CHANGES DURING 1990

April 4. The National People's Congress adopted an amendment to the law on Chinese foreign equity joint ventures. The amendment stipulated that the state would not nationalize joint ventures, simplified the approval procedures for new foreign investment enterprise (requiring a decision by the competent government authority within three months), and extended the management rights of foreigners (including permitting foreigners to assume the chairmanship of the board of directors of joint ventures).

May 14. The Shanghai Municipal Government announced plans for the development of the Pudong New Area. The area is adjacent to Shanghai and covers 135 square miles. It is envisaged that the multibillion dollar project will take 30 to 40 years to complete. To attract foreign capital into the area, Chinese foreign joint ventures are to be offered tax incentives similar to those available in the special economic zones, and overseas business will be permitted to invest in the construction of airports, ports, railways, highways, and utilities, as well as to open foreign bank branches in Shanghai. Detailed regulations were announced in October 1990.

May 19. The State Council issued regulations for the sale and transfer of land-use rights in cities and towns to encourage foreign investors to plan long-term investment. Under these regulations, companies, enterprises, other organizations, and individuals within and outside of China would be permitted to obtain land-use rights and undertake land development. The maximum period for land-use rights ranges from 40 years for commercial, tourism, or recreational users to 50 years for industrial use and 70 years for residential use. The State Council issued provisional regulations for investment in large tracts of land to attract the investment of foreign firms in tract development. Under these regulations, tract development refers to the obtaining of land-use rights for state land and the development of infrastructure and other investments.

CHANGES DURING 1991

April 9. The National People's Congress adopted the Law Concerning the Income Tax of Foreign-Funded Enterprises and Foreign Enterprises and eliminated a 10 percent tax imposed on distributed profits remitted abroad by the foreign investors in foreign-funded enterprises. This law unified the tax rates for Chinese foreign equity joint ventures and wholly owned foreign enterprise. It also provided for more tax benefits in the priority industrial sectors, effective July 1, 1991.

September 26. "Regulations on Borrowing Overseas of Commercial Loans by Resident Institutions" and "Rules on Foreign Exchange Guarantee by Resident Institutions in China" were issued.

CHANGES DURING 1992

March 1. The policy on foreign trade and investment was further liberalized, opening a large number of inland and border areas to such activities.

CHANGES DURING 1993

None.

CHANGES DURING 1994

None.

CHANGES DURING 1995

None.

September 25. The regulation on External Guarantees Provided by Domestic Entities was passed, allowing for the provision of guarantees by authorized financial institutions and nonfinancial legal entities that have foreign exchange receipts.

EXISTING CONTROLS ON CAPITAL TRANSACTIONS AS OF DECEMBER 31, 1996

Controls on capital and money market instruments

On capital market securities

Purchase locally by nonresidents	Nonresidents may only purchase B shares. The face value of B shares is denominated in renminbi (RMB), which are listed on the Chinese Securities Exchange and can only be bought by foreign investors.
Sale or issue locally by nonresidents	These transactions are not permitted.
Purchase abroad by residents	Residents, except financial institutions permitted to engage in foreign borrowing, and authorized industrial and trade enterprises or groups are not permitted to purchase securities abroad. A qualifications review by the SAFE is required for financial institutions to purchase securities abroad.
Sale or issue abroad by residents	Prior approval by the PBOC, the SAFE, or the Securities Supervisory Board is required. Issuing bonds abroad must be integrated within the state's plan for utilizing foreign capital. Bonds can only be issued by financial institutions approved by the PBOC.

On money market instruments

Purchase locally by nonresidents	Nonresidents are not allowed to purchase money market instruments.

Sale or issue locally by nonresidents	Nonresidents are not allowed to sell or issue money market instruments.
Purchase abroad by residents	Residents, except financial institutions permitted to engage in foreign borrowing, and authorized industrial and trade enterprises or groups are not allowed to purchase money market instruments. Financial institutions must undergo a review of qualifications by the SAFE before purchasing foreign money market instruments.
Sale or issue abroad by residents	Sale or issue abroad of securities, other than stocks, requires PBOC and SAFE approval.

On collective investment securities

Purchase locally by nonresidents	These transactions are not allowed.
Sale or issue locally by nonresidents	There are no regulations, and if these instruments are traded, they must be approved by the Securities Policy Commission.
Purchase abroad by residents	Same regulations as for purchase of money market instruments apply.
Sale or issue abroad by residents	Same regulations as for sale or issue of money market instruments apply.

Controls on derivatives and other instruments

Purchase locally by nonresidents	These transactions are not allowed.
Sale or issue locally by nonresidents	These transactions are not allowed.
Purchase abroad by residents	Operations in such instruments by financial institutions are subject to prior review of qualifications and to limits on open foreign exchange positions.
Sale or issue abroad by residents	Same regulations as for purchases apply.

Controls on credit operations

Commercial credits

By residents to nonresidents	Industrial and commercial enterprises may not provide lending to nonresidents. Provision of loans to nonresidents by financial institutions is subject to review of qualifications by the SAFE and to a foreign exchange asset-liability ratio requirement.
To residents from nonresidents	Only financial institutions permitted by the SAFE to engage in external borrowing and authorized industrial and commercial enterprises or groups can engage in external borrowing of commercial credit. For credit over one-year maturity, the loan must be part of the state plan for utilizing foreign capital and must be approved by the SAFE.

Short-term commercial credit (with a maturity of one year or less) is subject to foreign exchange balance requirements. Financial institutions permitted to engage in foreign borrowing are free to conduct short-term foreign borrowing within the target balance without obtaining approval, but must register the borrowing with the SAFE.

Short-term foreign financing with maturity of three months or less provided to enterprises (excluding foreign-funded enterprises, or FFEs) is not subject to limitations, but short-term financing of longer than three months is subject to short-term foreign exchange balance requirements, and the borrowing must be registered with the SAFE.

FFEs may borrow from nonresidents without obtaining approval but must report the borrowing to the SAFE.

Financial credits	Same regulations as for commercial credits apply.

Guarantees, sureties, and financial backup facilities

By residents to nonresidents	The regulation on External Guarantees Provided by Domestic Entities of September 1996 allows the provision of guarantees by authorized financial institutions and nonfinancial legal entities that have foreign exchange receipts. Government agencies or institutions cannot provide guarantees.

Controls on direct investment

Outward direct investment	Foreign exchange is provided for the investment after a SAFE review of sources of foreign exchange assets and an assessment of the investment risk involved, approval by the Ministry of Foreign Trade and Economic Cooperation (MOFTEC), and registration with the SAFE.
Inward direct investment	As long as nonresidents meet requirements under Sino-foreign joint venture laws and other relevant regulations, and are approved by MOFTEC, nonresidents are free to invest in China. There is no restriction on the inward remittance of funds as far as exchange control is concerned. For environmental and security reasons, inward direct investment in some industries is prohibited.

Controls on liquidation of direct investment   No.

Controls on real estate transactions

Purchase abroad by residents	Same regulations as for direct investment apply.
Purchase locally by nonresidents	Same regulations as for direct investment apply.

Sale locally by nonresidents	Not applicable.

Provisions specific to commercial banks and other credit institutions

Borrowing abroad	Same regulations as for commercial credits apply.
Maintenance of accounts abroad	Prior approval by the SAFE is required for domestic entities opening foreign exchange accounts abroad.
Lending to nonresidents (financial or commercial credits)	Lending is allowed, subject to review of qualifications by the SAFE and to asset-liability ratio requirements.
Lending locally in foreign exchange	Lending is mainly subject to qualifications review by the SAFE and to asset-liability ratio requirements.
Purchase of locally issued securities denominated in foreign exchange	China does not issue securities denominated in foreign currency.

Differential treatment of nonresident deposit accounts and/or deposit accounts in foreign exchange

Reserve requirements	There are different reserve requirements for deposits in RMB and in foreign currency, and also between the latter in domestic banks and in FFEs (i.e., 13 percent for deposits in RMB, 5 percent for any foreign currency deposit in domestic banks, 3 percent for deposits in foreign currency for over three months, and 5 percent for less than three months, in FFEs).
Liquid asset requirements	Bank foreign exchange liquid assets (one year or less) should not be less than 60 percent of liquid liabilities (one year or less) and 30 percent of total foreign exchange assets. Total deposits with three-month maturities, deposits in both domestic and

foreign banks, funds used for purchasing transferable foreign-currency-denominated securities, deposits with the central bank, and cash holdings should not be less than 15 percent of total foreign exchange assets. Nonbank foreign exchange liquid assets (one year or less) should not be less than 60 percent of liquid liabilities (one year or less) and 25 percent of total assets. Total deposits with three-month maturities, deposits in both domestic and foreign banks, funds used for purchasing transferable foreign-currency-denominated securities, deposits with the central bank, and cash holdings should not be less than 10 percent of total assets.

Credit controls	Total loans, investment guarantees (calculated as 50 percent of the balance guaranteed), and other foreign exchange credits provided to a legal entity by banks or nonbank financial institutions should not exceed 30 percent of the foreign exchange capital owned by the banks or nonbank financial institutions.
Investment regulations	Bank equity investment should not exceed the difference between bank capital and mandatory paid-in capital. Nonbank financial institutions' total equity investment (excluding trust account) should not exceed the difference between their capital and mandatory paid-in capital.
Open foreign exchange position limits	For financial institutions trading foreign exchange on their own behalf, the daily total amount traded (total open foreign exchange position) should not exceed 20 percent of the foreign exchange working capital. As authorized by the highest level of management, financial institutions trading foreign

exchange on their own behalf may retain a small amount of overnight open position, but this should not exceed 1 percent of the foreign exchange working capital.

Provisions specific to institutional investors   No.

CHANGES DURING 1997

None.

CHANGES DURING 1998

Controls on capital and money market instruments

January 1. Regulations for issuing bonds denominated in foreign currency by domestic institutions were issued.

Controls on credit operations

January 1. The implementation bylaws of regulations for external guarantees by domestic institutions were issued.

January 1. Forward letters of credit with a maturity exceeding 90 days and less than 365 days have been included in the category of short-term credit, while those exceeding one year have been included in the category of medium- and long-term international commercial loans.

January 1. External borrowing regulations were changed.

August 20. Enterprises are barred from advance prepayment of debt.

CHANGES DURING 1999

Controls on credit operations

July 15. Some controls on RMB loans to FFEs under foreign exchange liens or guarantees were eased.

CHANGES DURING 2000

None.

CHANGES DURING 2001

Controls on capital
and money market
instruments

February 22. Domestic investors were
allowed to purchase B shares with existing
foreign currency deposits.
June 1. Domestic investors were allowed to
purchase B shares with new foreign currency
deposits.

Controls on credit
operations

September 19. Restrictions were liberalized
on purchases of foreign exchange for
advance repayments of domestic and foreign
currency loans, loans converted from foreign
debt, and foreign debts, as follows: if the
loan contract contains an advance repayment clause, the party may use its own
foreign exchange to make advance repayment, subject to SAFE approval; and, subject
to SAFE approval, a party may purchase
foreign exchange to make advance repayments of loans, including (1) loans made
with approval of the State Council; (2) loans
for enterprise debt restructuring, for permanent or temporary closure, or for merger or
transfer of ownership due to a change in
national policy; and (3) loans where advance
repayments are deemed necessary by a court.

Controls on direct
investment

September 19. The purchase of foreign
exchange was authorized for investments
abroad in strategic foreign projects that have
been approved by the State Council, projects
that entail importing of materials into China
for processing, and foreign aid projects.

CHANGES DURING 2002

Controls on capital
and money market
instruments

September 1. Prior approval by the China
Securities Regulatory Commission was
required for OLDCs and CHFLCs to sell
shares overseas. The foreign exchange
proceeds may not be retained overseas

without SAFE approval and must be repatriated within 30 days and kept in OLDCs' foreign exchange accounts or converted into RMB (with SAFE approval).

December 1. Qualified foreign institutional investors (QFIIs) were allowed to invest domestically in A shares, subject to restrictions.

Controls on direct investment

April 1. A new four-tier classification was introduced, defining activities in which foreign investment is encouraged, permitted, restricted, or banned. As a result, many industries that were previously closed to foreign investment, particularly in the services sector, were opened.

CHANGES DURING 2003

Provisions specific to commercial banks and other credit institutions

January 1. Registration with and permission from the SAFE to repay the principal were no longer required for residents to borrow foreign exchange from domestic Chinese financial institutions.

Controls on direct investment

November 1. In some provinces and regions, the limit on outward investment was increased to the equivalent of U.S. $3 million from U.S. $1 million.

Provisions specific to commercial banks and other credit institutions

January 1. Registration with and permission from the SAFE to repay the principal were no longer required for residents to borrow foreign exchange from domestic Chinese financial institutions.

November 19. A memorandum of understanding between the Hong Kong Monetary Authority and the China Banking Regulatory Commission to share supervisory information on banks operating in mainland China and Hong Kong SAR and to ensure that parent banks maintain effective control over their cross-border branches and subsidiaries came into effect.

CHANGES DURING 2004

Controls on capital market securities purchased locally by nonresidents

QFIIs may invest domestically in A shares, subject to the following restrictions: (1) a QFII must have minimum experience in the industry (5 years for fund managers; 30 years for insurance companies) and the equivalent of at least U.S. $10 billion in assets under management in the latest financial year and must be clear of any major irregularities in its home market over the past three years; (2) a QFII that is a bank must have assets that rank it among the top 100 internationally in the latest financial year; (3) a QFII that is an insurance or a securities company must have minimum paid-up capital of the equivalent of U.S. $1 billion; and (4) ownership of any Chinese company listed on the Shanghai or Shenzhen stock exchange by a QFII may not exceed 10 percent, and the total shares owned by QFIIs in a single Chinese company may not exceed 20 percent. QFIIs must set up special RMB accounts with domestic banks and use the services of domestic securities companies. Closed-end QFIIs may only remit capital after three years, in installments of no more than 20 percent of the total each time, at intervals of one month or more. Other QFIIs may only remit capital after one year, in installments of no more than 20 percent of the total, and at intervals of three months or longer. In addition to these limits, there is a cap on total A-share purchases by QFIIs, which has severely limited foreign holdings (to less than $20 billion as of 2007).

Provisions specific to commercial banks and other credit institutions	*January 1.* Under the Closer Economic Partnership Arrangement, (1) the asset requirement for Hong Kong SAR-incorporated banks to open branches in mainland China was reduced to U.S. $6 billion from U.S. $20 billion; (2) the requirement for setting up a representative office in mainland China before a Hong Kong SAR bank establishes a joint-venture bank or joint venture finance company in mainland China was lifted; and (3) for mainland China branches of Hong Kong SAR banks to apply to conduct RMB business, the minimum number of years of business operations on the mainland required of the banks was reduced to two years from three years.
	The official ceiling on foreign bank ownership of a Chinese bank was raised to 25 percent (from 20 percent), and the ceiling for any one bank was increased to 20 percent (from 15 percent).
	June 27. Domestic foreign-funded banks are not permitted to convert debt contracted abroad into RMB or to purchase foreign exchange for servicing such debts. Capital obtained through FDI can only be converted into RMB upon proof of a domestic payment order.
Inward direct investment	*June 27.* Capital remitted through FDI can only be converted to RMB upon proof of domestic payment order.
Controls on personal capital movements	*December 1.* Foreign heirs, including those from Hong Kong SAR and Macau SAR, are permitted to take inheritances out of the Mainland. Emigrants are allowed to take legally obtained personal assets with them; amounts up to U.S. $200,000 can be moved

without restriction, while amounts in excess of U.S. $200,000 can be transferred in stages over a minimum of two years.

CHANGES DURING 2005

Provisions specific to commercial banks and other credit institutions

January 15. The reserve requirements on accounts denominated in domestic and foreign-currencies were unified at 3 percent. Previously, different reserve requirements applied to deposits in RMB and in foreign currencies.

Controls on capital and money market instruments

February 1. The deadline for repatriation of foreign exchange proceeds raised by resident shareholders from overseas listing of foreign-funded and domestically funded enterprises is extended to "six months after the funds are collected."

Controls on direct investment

May 19. The pilot project to allow selected provincial and regional SAFE offices to authorize purchase of foreign exchange for outward investment is rolled out to all provinces and regions.

Geert Bekaert is the Leon G. Cooperman Professor of Finance and Economics at Columbia Business School and a research associate at the National Bureau of Economic Research. Before joining Columbia, he was a tenured associate professor of finance at the Graduate School of Business at Stanford University. He received his Ph.D. in 1992 from Northwestern University's Economics Department. His thesis won the 1994 Zellner Thesis Award in Business and Economic Statistics.

Loren Brandt is professor of economics at the University of Toronto, specializing in the Chinese economy. With Thomas Rawski, Brandt is contributor and co-editor of *China's Great Economic Transformation* (Cambridge University Press, forthcoming).

Lee Branstetter is associate professor of economics and public policy at Carnegie Mellon University, where he holds a joint appointment in the Heinz School of Policy and Management and the Department of Social and Decision Sciences. He is also a research associate at the National Bureau of Economic Research and an associate editor of the *Journal of International Economics*.

Charles W. Calomiris is the Henry Kaufman Professor of Financial Institutions at Columbia Business School and a professor at Columbia's School of International and Public Affairs. He also serves as the academic director of the Chazen Institute of International Business and of the Center for International Business Education and Research at Columbia University. Calomiris codirects the Project on Financial Deregulation at the

American Enterprise Institute (AEI) and is the Arthur Burns Scholar in International Economics at AEI. He is a member of the Shadow Financial Regulatory Committee and a research associate at the National Bureau of Economic Research, and was a senior fellow at the Council on Foreign Relations. He served as a congressional appointee to the International Financial Institutions Advisory Commission in 2000. He received a B.A. in economics from Yale University in 1979 and a Ph.D. in economics from Stanford University in 1985.

Mary Wadsworth Darby is a senior research scholar at the Chazen Institute of International Business at Columbia Business School. A China specialist with more than 20 years of professional executive experience in Chinese financial markets, Darby most recently worked as vice president of Morgan Stanley in Hong Kong and as China business manager of Morgan Stanley Investment Management. She was responsible for institutional sales to China as well as developing strategic relationships with Chinese entities and overseeing the strategic and marketing plan for entry into the investment management business in China. Prior to her work in Hong Kong, Darby was vice president and head of the Asia desk in New York. Before joining Morgan Stanley, Darby was executive director of the America-China Society, and previously, senior director China for Sears World Trade (SWT), Inc. Before joining SWT, she was corporate vice president of Allis-Chalmers Corporation. Darby received her B.A. from Princeton University and her M.B.A. and M.I.A. degrees from Columbia University.

Michael DeStefano is former managing director in the Financial Institutions Group of Standard & Poor's Ratings Group. He was that department's chief quality and criteria officer, in which capacity he had responsibility for broad analytical oversight of the ratings of global financial services. He was also the primary analyst on Fannie Mae and part of the team that followed the government-sponsored enterprises in the United States. He has worked in the commercial real estate and tax-exempt housing areas. Prior to 1985, DeStefano was training director and a financial institutions analyst in the equity department of Standard & Poor's, which he joined in 1981. He holds a B.A. in history from Fordham University, an M.B.A. in finance, and a Ph.D. in history from the University of Florida, and he is a chartered financial analyst.

Barry Eichengreen is the George C. Pardee and Helen N. Pardee Professor of Economics and Political Science at the University of California, Berkeley, where he has taught since 1987. He is also a research associate at the National Bureau of Economic Research (Cambridge, Massachusetts) and research fellow of the Centre for Economic Policy Research (London, England). In 1997 and 1998 he was senior policy adviser at the International Monetary Fund. He is a fellow of the American Academy of Arts and Sciences (class of 1997) and chairman of the Bellagio Group of academics and economic officials. He has held Guggenheim and Fulbright fellowships and has been a fellow of the Center for Advanced Study in the Behavioral Sciences (Palo Alto) and the Institute for Advanced Study (Berlin). He was awarded the Economic History Association's Jonathan R. T. Hughes Prize for Excellence in Teaching in 2002 and the University of California, Berkeley, Social Science Division's Distinguished Teaching Award in 2004. He received his bachelor's degree from the University of California, Santa Cruz in 1974, master's degrees in economics and history from Yale University, and a Ph.D. in economics from Yale in 1979.

Peter Garber joined Deutsche Bank in January 1998. As global strategist, Garber is part of the academic think tank and works closely with the senior economists. Prior to working for Deutsche Bank, he spent 15 years as a professor of economics at Brown University. In 1989, Garber began his long association with the International Monetary Fund as a consultant and has worked on a variety of high-level projects for them. He has received many grants and fellowships, including a Fulbright grant. He has a B.A. in economics from Princeton University, an M.A. in economics from Boston College, and a Ph.D. in economics from the University of Chicago.

Campbell R. Harvey is the J. Paul Sticht Professor of Finance at Duke University and a research associate at the National Bureau of Economic Research. Professor Harvey is editor of the *Journal of Finance,* the leading scientific journal in the field of finance.

Robert J. Hodrick is the Nomura Professor of International Finance at Columbia Business School. He has been a research associate at the National Bureau of Economics since 1982. He previously taught at Carnegie Mellon University from 1976 to 1983 and at the Kellogg Graduate School of Management of Northwestern University from 1983 to 1996. While at

Kellogg, he served as chair of the Finance Department and was awarded the Tokai Bank Professorship of International Finance. Hodrick joined Columbia Business School in July 1996. From November 1997 to July 2002 he was academic director of the School's Chazen Institute of International Business. From July 2002 to June 2004 he served as senior vice dean of the School. He received his Ph.D. in economics from the University of Chicago in 1976, having received his A.B. in international affairs from Princeton University in 1972.

Fred Hu is managing director and chief economist for Goldman Sachs (Asia) L.L.C. Previously he was chief economist and head of research at the World Economic Forum, Geneva, Switzerland. From 1991 to 1996 he was a staff member at the International Monetary Fund in Washington, D.C., where he served at the Asia-Pacific Department, Fiscal Affairs Department, and Research Department, respectively, and was engaged in economic analysis and policy advice to a variety of member countries including China. He holds a master's degree in engineering science from Tsinghua University, Beijing, and a Ph.D. in economics from Harvard University. His research interests include international trade and finance, macroeconomics, and public finance.

Xiaobo Lü is professor of political science at Barnard College, Columbia University. Lü is a member of the Council on Foreign Relations, the Committee of 100, and the National Committee on U.S.-China Relations. He was a senior visiting fellow of the Research Institute of Trade and Economy, Japan, in 2001 and 2002. From 2003 to 2004 he was a visiting professor at Tsinghua University and Jiaotong University in Shanghai and a senior research fellow at City University of Hong Kong. Lü is a former director of the Weatherhead East Asian Institute. He received a bachelor's degree in English language and literature from the Sichuan Institute of Foreign Studies in 1982, an M.A. in political science from Foreign Affairs College, Beijing, in 1985, and a Ph.D. in political science from the University of California, Berkeley, in 1994.

Christian Lundblad researches empirical asset pricing issues and international finance, with a specialization in emerging market development. His research has been published in the leading finance journals, such as the *Journal of Finance* and the *Journal of Financial Economics*. He served as a financial economist at the Federal Reserve Board in Washington, D.C., where he advised the Board of Governors on international financial market developments. He became an Assistant Professor of Finance at the Kenan-Flagler Business School at the University of North Carolina in 2006 after holding a faculty position at Indiana University for five years. He received a Ph.D. in financial economics and a master's degree in economics from Duke University. He earned his B.A. in economics and English literature from Washington University in St. Louis.

John H. Makin has been Caxton's chief economist since January 1990 and a principal in the firm since 1995. Makin is also a visiting scholar at the American Enterprise Institute in Washington, D.C., and has been a member of the panel of economic advisers of the U.S. Congressional Budget Office. He has also served as the chairman of the U.S.-Japan Friendship Commission. He is a member of the Council on Foreign Relations, the Economic Club of New York, and the Links. He previously was director of the Institute for Economic Research and professor of economics at the University of Washington in Seattle. Makin holds his M.A. and Ph.D. in economics from the University of Chicago.

David Malpass is Bear Stearns' chief economist and joined the firm in February 1993. He writes economic and financial studies and discusses financial market conditions with institutional investors. His duties include economic forecasts, Washington analysis, and global investment themes. He is a member of the Economic Club of New York and the Council on Foreign Relations and sits on the board of the Council of the Americas. Between February 1984 and January 1993 Malpass held a series of economic appointments during the Reagan and Bush administrations, including six years with Secretary James Baker at the Treasury and State departments. He was also Republican staff director of Congress's Joint Economic Committee and senior analyst for taxes and trade for the Senate Budget Committee. Malpass received a bachelor's degree in physics from Colorado College and an M.B.A. from the University of Denver.

Frederic S. Mishkin is a member of the Federal Reserve Board of Governors. He took office on September 5, 2006, to fill an unexpired term ending January 31, 2014. Before becoming a member of the Board, Dr. Mishkin was the Alfred Lerner Professor of Banking and Financial Institutions at the Graduate School of Business, Columbia University, from

1999 to 2006. Prior to that he was the A. Barton Hepburn Professor of Economics from 1991 to 1999 and professor at the Graduate School of Business from 1983 to 1991. He was also a research associate at the National Bureau of Economic Research (1980 to 2006) and a senior fellow at the Federal Deposit Insurance Corporation's Center for Banking Research (2003 to 2006). Dr. Mishkin has taught at the University of Chicago, Northwestern University, Princeton University, and Columbia University. He has also received an honorary professorship from the People's (Renmin) University of China. From 1994 to 1997 he was executive vice president and director of research at the Federal Reserve Bank of New York. He received a B.S. in economics from the Massachusetts Institute of Technology in 1973 and a Ph.D. in economics in 1976.

Eswar Prasad is the Tolani Senior Professor of Trade Policy at Cornell University. He was previously chief of the Financial Studies Division (2005 through 2006) and chief of the China Division (2002 through 2004) at the International Monetary Fund (IMF). Prasad has an extensive publication record, including articles in numerous collective volumes as well as top academic journals in economics. He is one of the lead authors of an IMF study on Financial Globalization and has edited IMF monographs on China and Hong Kong SAR. Prasad received his B.A. in economics, mathematics, and statistics from the University of Madras in 1985, an M.A. in economics from Brown in 1986, and a Ph.D. in 1992 from the University of Chicago.

Ailsa Röell is a professor of international and public affairs at the School of International and Public Affairs at Columbia University. Her academic specialty is financial economics and the regulation of financial markets. Her research and teaching span securities markets, corporate finance, and corporate governance. She has published extensively in the area of stock market microstructure, with empirical and theoretical papers on market trading architecture and its impact on liquidity and price formation; her latest work in the area concerns competition for cross-listing among European stock exchanges. More recently her work has focused on corporate governance, ranging from historical work on concentration of control, shareholder rights, and takeover defense mechanisms in the Netherlands to an empirical analysis of compensation, earnings manipulation, and class action litigation in the United States. She co-authored a major survey of corporate governance recently published in the *Handbook of the*

Economics of Finance (Elsevier). Röell holds a Ph.D. in political economy from Johns Hopkins University and an M.Sc. in economics from the University of Groningen. From 1997 to 2005 she was a senior research scholar at Princeton University's Bendheim Center for Finance, following a career on the faculties of the London School of Economics, Université Libre de Bruxelles, and Tilburg University.

Daniel H. Rosen is the principal of China Strategic Advisory, a specialized practice helping senior executives and directors analyze and understand commercial, economic, and policy trends in Greater China, and an adjunct associate professor at Columbia University. Rosen is currently a visiting fellow at the Institute for International Economics, where he served as a resident fellow until 1999. He is a member of the Council on Foreign Relations and the National Committee for U.S.-China Relations. In 2001 and 2002 Rosen directed research for an investment venture in Beijing and Shanghai focused on the value chain partners of American multinationals. From 2000 to 2001 he was senior adviser for International Economic Policy at the White House National Economic Council. Rosen was educated at the Graduate School of Foreign Service at Georgetown University and at the Department of Asian Studies at the University of Texas, Austin.

Shang-Jin Wei is assistant director and chief of the Trade and Investment Division at the International Monetary Fund, director of the Working Group on the Chinese Economy, a research associate at the National Bureau of Economic Research (United States), a research fellow at the Center for Economic Policy Research (Europe), and special-appointment professor of finance at Tsinghua University (China). He previously held the positions of associate professor of Public Policy at Harvard University and the New Century Chair in Trade and International Economics at the Brookings Institution. He holds a B.A. from Fudan University in 1986, an M.A. from Penn State University in 1988, and a Ph.D. in economics and an M.S. in finance from the University of California, Berkeley, in 1992.

Jialin Yu is an assistant professor of finance and economics at Columbia Business School, where he teaches the M.B.A. Capital Markets and Investments course and the Ph.D. Financial Econometrics course. He received his B.A from Fudan University in 1998 and his Ph.D. from

Princeton University in 2005. His research articles have been published or accepted for publication in the *Journal of Finance*, the *Journal of Econometrics*, and *International Economic Review*.

Xiaodong Zhu is a professor in the Department of Economics at the University of Toronto and a special-term professor at the School of Economics and Management at Tsinghua University in Beijing. Zhu received his B.S. in mathematics and his M.S. in statistics from Wuhan University, and his Ph.D. in economics from the University of Chicago in 1991.

INDEX

Note: Page numbers followed by *f* or *t* indicate figures and tables.

Acemoglu, Daron, 274
Agricultural Bank of China (ABC), 29–30, 83–84; NPLs and, 42, 88, 104, 108, 119, 128, 138
Agricultural Development Bank, 35–36
Allen, Franklin, 251, 285
American Depository Receipts (ADRs), 230, 292–93
Ang, Andrew, 355
Annual Report on Exchange Arrangements and Exchange Restrictions (AREAER), 231, 383
A-share market, 30, 54, 55, 209, 230, 311, 312n4
A shares, 53, 55, 204, 229, 282, 288n6, 291, 311, 400, 401. *See also* chronology of economic, political, and financial events in China
Asian currencies, undervaluation of, 357–59; asset and commodity prices and, 358; Bretton Woods II system and, 359; core inflation and, 358–59; inflation and, 358
Asian financial crisis of 1997, 5, 48–49, 62–63, 320; banking reforms and, 103–4; capital controls and, 203; capital flows and, 146, 149; psychological effects, 178
"Asian tigers," capital inflows, 149, 150*f*
asset management companies (AMCs), 36, 40–41, 73n71
Athanasoulis, Stefano G., 235

Backus, David K., 234
balance of payments history, 162–65
banking system, 2, 365; accounting standards, 36; administrative credit plans and, 98; assets and, 38, 91–93*t*, 132n5; bank categories, 113; "below-market" deposits and, 137–38; borrowers, 138; branch networks, 30–31, 73n67; centralization of, 104, 110–19; Communist Party and, 97; competition and complexity, 30–35, 141, 143; credit quotas and, 67; data issues, 112, 117, 119–20, 133n26, 379–81; fee income, 141; financial institutions overview, 88*t*, 89–94; financial markets and, 27–28; fixed investment and, 118–19; foreign banks and, 131–32; foreign ownership and, 139, 368n9; foreign strategic sharehold-ers and, 41; growth dynamics and, 94–98; household sector and, 139; income redistribution and, 86; interbank market reforms and, 111; interest rate regulation, 32–33; intermediation and, 90, 94, 116, 132n6; JSBs and, 115–16; lending, sector composition, 125–27; lending, state versus non-state, 95–97, 119–23, 133n10, 141–42; lending decisions, 111–12; lending restraint, 39–40; lending terms, 88*t*, 89*t*, 111, 113–14, 123–25, 133n25; loan concentration, 87, 131, 142; loan

banking system (*continued*)
distribution, geographic, 31–32; loan tenure, 142; market risk and, 142; NBFIs and, 88–94, 132n2; NPLs and, 86–87, 113, 127–30, 133n27, 134nn39–40, 228, 322–23; other financial institutions and, 90; policy banks, loans, 31, 37–38, 73n48, 104, 105*t*, 127, 138–41, 176; politics and, 33, 38–39, 72n38; pre-1995, assessment of, 103; privatization and, 68–69, 368n9; problems of, 322; RCCs and, 74n72; recapitalization of state-owned commercial banks, 36; recentralization of, 87, 130–31; redistribution and, 140–41; reform and, 5, 36–41, 86–87, 130–32, 134n40, 228, 374; reforms, post-1994, 103–12; reforms of the 1980s, 28–30; regional dimensions and, 98–103, 102*t*, 117–19; regional estimates, new loans and deposits, 379–81; regulation of, 140; roles of, 137–38; selective policy measures and, 98, 100–101*t*; shareholding banks and, 30–31, 36; SOCBs and, 89*t*, 114–15; SOEs and, 34–35, 374; state-owned banks, 88, 132n1; strengthening of, 35–36; subordinated debt and, 75n103; taxation of, 33; TICs, 88, 132n3; TVEs and, 95; transparency and governance, 140
Bank of China (BOC), 28–30, 83–84, 85n2, 128, 387; foreign loans and, 384–85; reform of, 41–42; scandals and, 42. *See also specific events and issues*
Bank of China Hong Kong (Holdings), 308
Bank of Communications, 89–90, 113, 116
Bank of Japan, 334, 335
Barro-type models, 29, 232, 236, 276, 281
Beijing Enterprises, 299
Bekaert, Geert, 10, 14–15, 202–77, 281–84
Benassy-Quere, Agnes, 327
bond markets, 27; corporate bonds, 58; functioning of, 57–58; necessity of reform of, 59–60; risks and rewards, 58
Botero, Juan, 251
Boyreau-Debray, Genevieve, 32, 99
Brandt, Loren, 9–10, 11–12, 72n39, 86–132, 137, 140–41, 379–81
Branstetter, Lee, 9, 10–11, 14, 23–70, 79–82, 84, 137, 227, 242

Bretton Woods II system, 351–52, 353–57; Asian currencies and, 359; Bretton Woods system and, 354–56
Bretton Woods system, 20, 354–56
Brilliance China Automotive, 46
B-share market, 54, 209, 210
B shares, 53, 74n91, 204, 229, 230, 288n6, 291, 392, 399. *See also* chronology of economic, political, and financial events in China
Bush, George W., 210*t*, 281
Business Environment Risk Intelligence (BERI) measures, 224*t*, 246, 247*t*, 273

Caijing, 38, 57, 66
Calomiris, Charles W., 1–22, 131
capital controls chronology, 383–403
capital flows, cross-border: Asian financial crisis of 1997 and, 146, 149; errors and omissions and, 13, 19, 63, 162–63, 165, 167–69, 186, 188n11; external debt and, 157–61, 187nn4–7; FDI and, 145, 149–57, 177–78; globalization and, 146; "hot money" and, 13, 19, 163, 165, 167, 188n11; inflows, levels and composition of, 13, 144–49; mercantilism and, 181–83; non-FDI inflows, 145, 163–65; outflows and international reserves, 161–69; renminbi valuation and, 163, 188n10; reserves accumulation and, 145, 169–72, 188n9, 188n14, 189nn20–21
Carey, Mark, 131
Central Huijin Investment, 38, 76n130, 105*t*
Chazen Institute of International Business. *See* Jerome A. Chazen Institute of International Business
China Banking Regulatory Commission (CBRC), 39, 40, 68, 82, 104; capital adequacy standards and, 41, 105*t*, 107*t*, 213*t*
China Construction Bank (CCB), 29–30, 38, 83–84, 111, 186, 286, 368n8
China Development Bank, 35–36, 104
China Economic Quarterly, 39
China Foreign Exchange Trading System (CFETS), 324–25, 375
China Insurance Regulatory Commission (CIRC), 82
China International Trust Investment Company (CITIC), 89–90
China Life Insurance Company, 65

China Minsheng Banking Corporation, 40
China Mobile Ltd., 210*t*, 292, 310
China Petroleum and Chemical Corp., 210*t*
"China's Banking Sector and Economic Growth" (Brandt and Zhu), 11–12, 86–132
China Securities Regulatory Commission (CSRC), 46, 56–57, 68, 82, 206*t*
"China's Exchange Rate Regime" (Eichengreen), 18–19, 314–36
"China's Financial Markets" (Branstetter), 10–11, 14, 23–70; themes, 79
"China's Foreign Exchange Policy" (Garber, Hodrick, Makin, Malpass, Mishkin, and Prasad), 20, 350–76
China's Trapped Transition (Pei), 6, 8–9
China Unicom Ltd., 209*t*, 210*t*
Chinese government bonds (CGBs), 24, 57
chronology of capital controls, 383–403; capital and money market instruments, 392–93; changes during 1981–1982, 385; changes during 1983, 385–86; changes during 1984, 386–88; changes during 1985, 388–89; changes during 1986–1988, 389; changes during 1989, 389–90; changes during 1990, 390–91; changes during 1991–1995, 391; changes during 1996, 392; changes during 1997–2000, 398; changes during 2001, 399; changes during 2002, 399–400; changes during 2003, 400–401; changes during 2004, 401–2; changes during 2005, 403; commercial banks, credit institutions, 396; credit operations, 394–95; derivatives and other instruments, 393; direct investment, 395; existing, as of December 31, 1980, 383–85; existing, as of December 31, 1996, 392–98; nonresident accounts, foreign exchange, 396–98; real estate transactions, 395–96
chronology of economic, political, and financial events in China, 205–14*t*; regulations on foreign investors, 213–14*t*
chronology of financial sector policy measures and regulations, 105–10*t*; AMCs, 107*t*; interbank market, 109–10*t*; JSBs, 108*t*; lending behavior, 106–7*t*; NBFIs, 109*t*; new regulation and regulatory authorities, 105*t*; PBOC, 105–6*t*; SOCB, 108*t*; UCC, UCB, RCC, RCB, 108–9*t*

Cinda Asset Management Company, 41–42
Coeure, Benoit, 327
Commercial Banking Law (1995), 104
Communist Party, 38–39, 67; banking system and, 97; executive appointments and, 56
Company Law, 46
conflict, ICRG subcomponents, 222–23*t*
crossroads, 3; capital allocation, investment, and growth, 3–7; foreign exchange system, 7–8; political evolution, 8–9; U.S. relations, 8

Darby, Mary Wadsworth, 15–16, 281–88
Datastream International, 346
Deng Xiaoping, 60, 80, 208*t*, 365; "journey to the south," 26, 46, 71n4
DeStefano, Michael, 11–12, 137–143
Dinc, I. S., 241
"Doing Business and Investing Worldwide" (PricewaterhouseCoopers), 179–81
Dong, Sen, 355
Dooley, Michael, 12, 350, 353, 355–56, 362
dual-track (*shuanggui zhi*), 81
Duttagupta, Rupa, 325

economic growth. *See* growth
Economist, The, 348
"Effects of Stock Market Listing on the Financial Performance of Chinese Firms, The" (Hu), 16–17, 290–305
Eichengreen, Barry, 10, 18–19, 231, 314–36, 343–45
equity markets, 51*f*, 67, 80–81, 116; efficiency, 229–30; equity issuance, 51*f*; experimentation, 43; growth of, in 1990s, 45–49; institutional investors, 287; liberalization, 222*t*, 245–46, 267; performance, 49–57, 50*f*, 51*f*, 70; Shanghai exchange and, 45–46, 229; share transfer and, 55–56; share types, 53, 74n91, 74–75n93, 81, 85n1, 229, 291; Shenzhen exchange and, 45–46, 229; SOEs and, 43–45, 56, 80; state holdings and, 55; turnover, 228–29; valuation and, 53–54
errors and omissions, capital flows and, 13, 19, 63, 162–63, 165, 167–69, 186, 188n11
"Evolution of Capital Controls in China" (Prasad and Wei), 383–403

exchange rate regime, 316; ambiguity and,
317–18; asymmetric shocks and, 318,
337n12; band maintenance and, 330–
31; basket peg model estimation and,
327–30; capital account convertibility
and, 319–20, 338n19; capital controls
and, 315; CFETS and, 324–25, 336n3;
degree of flexibility and, 327–30,
337n16; Dodge Line and, 333, 340n45;
dollar and, 314–15; equilibrium
exchange rates and, 316, 337n6; exiting
a peg and, 320–21, 325; fluctuation
band and, 317–18, 336n1; foreign
currencies and, 315, 328–30, 336n2,
339n40; foreign exposures and, 326,
339n39; forward market and, 314;
global imbalances and, 331–32,
340n41; hedging foreign exposures and,
322–25, 338n21; India and, 323–24,
339n32; inflation and, 320, 337n17;
information systems and, 326; interest-
rate swaps and, 315; Japan and,
332–35; market makers and, 324,
339n34; NDF rates and, 346–48;
policy announcement of July 2005, 314,
327–32, 336n1, 343; prudential
considerations and, 325–26; rate
flexibility and, 318–19, 343–45; recent
changes, 314–18, 343; renminbi
valuation and, 314, 317, 331–32,
335–36, 337n10; risk policies and
procedures and, 325–26; sequencing
literature and, 319–22; Swiss franc and,
328–30; theory of optimum currency
areas and, 318–19; U.S.-China relations
and, 316; volatility and, 321–22
Export-Import Bank, 36

Fernandez, Gilda, 325
financial integration: external borrowing
and, 176; financial development and,
267, 272; financial openness and,
275–76; growth and, 173; inflow
composition and, 175–76; investment
climate and, 268–71t, 275–76; political
institutions and, 274; privatization and,
268–71t, 272–73; social security systems
and, 273–74; socioeconomic conditions
and, 275; volatility and, 174–75, 189n26
financial markets, access to global, 174,
200; macroeconomic instability and,
25–27

"Financial Openness and the Chinese
Growth Experience" (Bekaert, Harvey,
and Lundblad), 14–15, 202–77
financial policy choices, 2
financial sector reforms, post-1994,
chronology, 105–10t
financial services sector, 65–66; de-
statization and, 83–84; gradualism and,
80–82; state-led reforms and, 82–83
Folkerts-Landau, David, 12, 350, 353,
355–56, 362
foreign direct investment (FDI), 2, 62–63;
capital markets, domestic and, 183–85,
186; capital stock and, 355; governance
and, 184; incentives and distortions for,
178–81; inflow destinations, 153–56;
legal regimes and, 179–81; outflows,
156t, 157, 187n3, 383–403; property
rights and, 186; round-tripping and,
149, 153, 179, 187n1, 187n3; sources of,
149, 153; "strategic investors" and, 186
foreign exchange policy, 350; alternative
nominal anchor and, 372–74; Bretton
Woods II and, 351–52; capital account
and, 361; closed capital account and,
371; development strategy and, 362–65;
disinflationary price trends and, 361;
domestic demand and, 353; exports and,
362–64, 366; financial repression and,
371; flexibility and, 371–72; inflation
and, 372–73; intervention and, 352;
labor supply and, 353; modification
timing, 374–76; other countries and,
365–67; renminbi valuation and, 350–
51; sterilization costs and, 361, 370–71;
trade surplus and, 362; United States
and, 370; U.S. dollar and, 361
foreign exchange system, 2–3, 61–63;
controls and, 61–62; reserves and, 7
"Four No" rule, 207t
Frankel, Jeffrey, 327
Fu Jun, 178–79
Fung, Michael K. Y., 228

Garber, Peter, 10, 12, 20, 350–53, 354–56,
362
Gaulle, Charles de, 354, 356
globalization: financial reform and, 365;
growth and, 172–76. See also financial
integration
Goldman Sachs, 76n123, 293, 309–10,
346

Goldstein, Morris, 26, 334
Goodfriend, Marvin, 372, 374
Green, S., 307
gross domestic product (GDP), 90, 132n4, 187n5, 202, 204, 215f, 216f; measurement of, 3–4, 49, 71n5. *See also* growth
growth, 79; capital account openness and, 241; chronology of, 205–14t; convergence effect and, 251; domestic investment and, 255–56, 256t, 257t; domestic savings and, 283–84; education and, 286; equity markets, volatility and, 263; exports and, 351; factor productivity and, 256t, 262–63, 284; FDI, foreign debt and, 252–55, 253–54t, 283–85; financial deepening and, 364, 367n3; financial development and, 228–30, 362–63; financial integration and, 286; financial openness and, 218–20t, 230–32, 282–83, 286–87; foreign debt and, 276–77; foreign strategic shareholders and, 286–88, 288n6; globalization and, 172–76; institutional quality and, 221–22t, 245; institutions, political risk and, 232–34; investment profile and, 222t, 245, 283–84; joint ventures and, 285; labor force and, 259; life expectancy and, 266; macroeconomic instability and, 216, 217f; measurement error and, 256–62, 283; multicountry comparisons, 216f, 217, 225–26t, 227; non-state sector and, 95–97; Openness measure and, 251; other determinants, 247–50t; policy and, 276; political conditions and, 220t, 233; political risk and, 220t, 242–46; predictability, base results for, 237–42, 238t; private credit to GDP and, 241, 259–61; privatization and, 246, 251, 285; reforms and, 240–41; risk sharing and, 234–37; social security measure and, 251; socioeconomic conditions and, 22t, 222t, 233–34, 245; SOEs and, 285; state ownership and, 246; stock market development, 249–50t, 251; summary analysis, 204, 215–17; theories of, 288; trade and, 227–28, 241–42, 281–82; volatility and, 263–71, 276; volatility and, across countries, 268–71t. *See also under* gross domestic product (GDP)
Guangdong Kelon Electrical Holdings, 309
Guo Shuping, 38–39

Harvey, Campbell R., 10, 14–15, 202–77, 281–84
Hatase, Mariko, 334
Ho, Wai-Ming, 228
Hodrick, Robert J., 10, 12, 20, 353–56
Hong Kong Stock Exchange (HKSE), 291–92, 307; mainland-controlled banks and, 300–301, 304; Listing Committee powers, 312n1
Honohan, Patrick, 364
"hot money," 13, 19, 163, 167, 343–44, 360–61; deterence of, 345–48, 349
Howie, Fraser, 46
H shares, 53, 74n91, 74–75n93, 292–93, 307–8, 309, 311
Hu, Fred, 10, 16–17, 290–305
Huang, Yasheng, 183, 184
Hu Jintao, 211t, 281
Hu Shuli, 66

India, 195–96, 205t, 212t, 323–24
Industrial and Commercial Bank of China (ICBC), 29–30, 73n66, 83–84
initial public offerings (IPOs), 308–9; asset turnover ratios and, 297, 298f; company selectivity and, 307–8; conglomerates and, 299; data and methodology and, 291–94, 309–11; de-leveraging and, 297; key financial indicators, 294, 295t; payout ratios and, 299; performance by sectors, 299–302; performance measure variables, 293–94, 310–11; Red Chips and, 308; regional quota system and, 308–9; ROE performance and, 295–99; sales and earnings and, 297, 298f; sample bias and, 309–10, 312n2; sector earnings growth and, 304f; sector payout trends and, 302f; sector revenue growth and, 303f; SOEs and, 290
institutional quality, ICRG subcomponents, 221–22t
"institution first, rules second" approach, 81–82
insurance industry, 60, 64–65, 76n118
intermediation of capital, state's role in, 24, 70n1
International Country Risk Guide (ICRG) subcomponents, 220–23t, 232–34, 274; Foreign Debt Index, 252, 255; investment profile, 222t; political conditions, 220t, 233; socioeconomic conditions, 22t, 233–34; summary analysis, 225–26t

International Finance Corporation (IFC), 212t, 230
International Monetary Fund (IMF), 62; *Annual Report on Exchange Arrangements and Exchange Restrictions* (AREAER), 231, 383

Japan: discount rates, 335; dollar peg, 332–33; exchange rate flexibility, 333; financial market liberalization, 58–59; Fiscal Investment and Loan Program, 335; loan concentration, 87, 131; Ministry of Finance, 334–35; Ministry of International Trade and Industry, 334; OPEC and, 335; post–World War II, 363; Smithsonian agreement and, 334
Jerome A. Chazen Institute of International Business, 1, 9
Jiang Zemin, 47
Jingji Ribao, 44
Jin Jang, C., 228
Jin Linzuo, 44
Jinrong Nianjian, 111, 379
Johnson, Simon, 274
joint-stock banks (JSBs), 39, 40, 59, 107t, 108t, 111, 113, 115, 116, 118, 125, 127, 141
Jun Ma, 352

Karasadag, Cem, 325
Kehoe, Patrick, 234
King, Mervyn, 357–59
King, Robert, 262, 364
Kose, M. Ayhan, 203
Kydland, Finn, 234

LaPorta, Rafael, 241
Lardy, Nicholas, 26, 33–34, 40–41, 227, 242, 334
Leckie, Stuart, 60
Lee Teng Hui, 209t
Legal person shares, 53, 54, 55, 67, 70, 74n91
Levine, Ross, 262, 364
Lewis, Karen K., 235
LexisNexis, 346
liberalization, definitions of, 22n1
Li Ka-Shing Foundation, 42
Liu, G. S., 307
Liu Mingkang, 39, 41
loans and deposits, regional estimates, 379–81
London Interbank Offered Rate, 358

Lopez-de-Silanes, Florencio, 241
Lü, Xiaobo, 11, 79–85
Lundblad, Christian, 10, 14–15, 202–77, 281–84

Maanshan Iron & Steel, 311
Makin, John H., 10, 20, 357–59
Malpass, David, 10, 12, 20–21, 359–61
market pricing, 24
Ma Weihua, 39
Mei, Jiangpin, 229
Merrill Lynch, 42
Mishkin, Frederic S., 10, 21, 361–67; *The Next Great Mobilization*, 363
Morgan Stanley, 8; Capital International (MSCI) China Index, 16, 293
multicountry macroeconomic and financial data, 218–24t

NASDAQ, 292
National Social Security Fund, 55
Naughton, Barry, 62–63
Newbridge Capital Management, 40, 54
Next Great Mobilization, The (Mishkin), 363
Nixon, Richard, 334, 354
nonbank financial institutions (NBFIs), 31, 88–89
nondeliverable forward (NDF) rates, term structures and, 346–48
nonperforming loans (NPLs), 33–34, 36–37, 74n73, 84, 85n2, 171–72, 189n19

official equity market liberalization indicator, 218t, 230–31

Pei, Minxin, *China's Trapped Transition*, 6, 8–9
Penn World Tables, 262
pension system, 60–61
People's Bank of China (PBOC), 28–29; central banking functions of, 29; reorganization of, 110–11; securities firms and, 55; state-owned banks and, 97. *See also specific activities and issues*
PetroChina, 292
Piazzesi, Monica, 355
Ping An Insurance Group, 65, 286–87
Pistor, K., 308–9
policy-based lending, 31, 37–38, 73n48, 104, 105t, 127, 138–41, 176

population, age of, 60
Prasad, Eswar, 10, 12–13, 21, 144–87, 193–98, 200, 203, 204, 232, 369–76, 383–403
PricewaterhouseCoopers (PwC), "Doing Business and Investing Worldwide," 179–81
property rights, 44

Qian, Jun, 251, 285
Qian, Meijun, 251, 285
qualified foreign institutional investors (QFIIs), 214, 400, 401; regulation and, 211*t*
Quinn, Dennis P., 202
Quinn capital account openness indicator, 218*t*, 231–32, 267

Rajan, Raghuram, 376
Rawski, Thomas, 26, 49
Red Chips, 48, 50, 51*f*, 292, 308, 311
regional banks: loans and deposits, 99, 102*t*; NBFIs and, 99, 102*f*, 133n16
"Regional Estimates of New Deposit and Loan Shares, and Nonperforming Loans" (Brandt and Zhu), 379–81
reserves, international: adequacy indicators, 171; external shocks and, 171–72; insurance value of, 170–71; sterilization costs, 169–72, 188n15
residential real estate, 35; restrictions on, 75n106
return on equity (ROE), 293, 295–301, 303, 304
risk sharing: direct measure of, 235–37; equity market liberalization and, 235. *See also under* growth
Robinson, James A., 274
Röell, Ailsa, 17–18, 307–11
Roll, Richard, 236
Rosen, Daniel H., 13, 193–201
Royal Bank of Scotland, 42
rural commercial banks (RCBs), 108–9*t*, 113
rural credit cooperatives (RCCs), 41, 42, 74n72, 88, 108–9*t*, 113
Rural Credit Cooperative Unions, 104

Scheinkman, Jose, 229
Securities Law, 46
securities markets, reform necessity, 6–7
Seht, Kaja, 111

Shang Fulin, 56
Shanghai Feile Acoustics, 43
Shanghai Industrials, 299
Shanghai stock exchange, 6, 16, 43, 45, 49, 55, 206, 207, 209, 213, 214, 229, 277n2, 291, 292, 307, 308, 401
Shenyang Public Utility Holdings, 309
Shenzhen Development Bank (SDB), 40, 45, 54
Shenzhen Provisions, 45
Shenzhen stock exchange, 6, 16, 43, 45, 49, 55, 206, 207, 209, 213, 214, 229, 291, 292, 307, 308, 401
Shleifer, Andrei, 241
socioeconomic conditions, ICRG subcomponents, 222*t*
State Committee for the Reform of Economic Structure (SCRES), "Standard Opinion," 46, 53
State-owned Asset Supervision and Administration Commission (SASAC), 68
state-owned commercial banks (SOCBs), 86–87, 108*t*, 114, 115, 128, 129, 130
state-owned enterprises (SOEs), 4; banking reform and, 34–35; capital allocation and, 32; de-statization of, 44–45; equity markets and, 43–45, 80; financial market reform and, 24–25; IPOs and, 290; privatization and, 68–69; reform and, 7, 67, 72–73n46; state control versus efficiency, 25; value-destroying expenditures and, 4, 6
State Planning Commission, 31
Steinfeld, E. S., 311
stock market listings. *See* initial public offerings (IPOs)

Talbot, John, 236
Tax Reform (1994), 104
"Third Front," 99, 133n17
Torrones, Marco E., 203
township and village enterprises (TVEs), 31–32
Toyoda, A. M., 202
Tracker Fund, 209*t*
trade openness, and idiosyncratic consumption growth, 263
trust and investment corporations (TICs), 88, 132n3
Tsai, Kellee, 33
Tsingtao Beer, 47, 292

"Understanding the Structure of Cross-Border Capital Flows" (Prasad and Wei), 12–13, 144–87
United States: relations with China, 8, 212t, 316–17; U.S. dollar valuation, 145, 167; U.S. Treasury bonds, 7, 20, 355
urban commercial banks (UCBs), 104, 108–9t, 113
urban credit cooperatives (UCCs), 31, 88, 104, 108–9t, 113

value-added tax (VAT), 35
value-destroying expenditures, 4–5; aggregate capital investment and, 4–5; SOEs and, 4, 6
van Wincoop, E., 235

Wacziarg, Romain, 227, 241–42
Wald tests, 272, 275
Walter, Karly, 46
Wei, Shang-Jin, 10, 12–13, 32, 99, 144–87, 193–98, 200, 204, 232, 327, 383–403
Welch, Karen Horn, 227, 241–42
WM/Reuters, 346

World Trade Organization (WTO), 2, 8, 210t, 212t; accession commitments, 63–64, 69, 80, 227, 375; United States and, 212t
Wu Bangguo, 212t
Wu Jiaxiang, 44

Xie Ping, 38–39
Xinghualian ("New China Union") conglomerate, 178–79
Xiong, Wei, 229
Xu, C., 308–9

Young, Alwyn, 256–57, 262, 283
Yu, Jialin, 19, 343–49
yuan, valuation of, 7, 13, 282, 332, 359–60, 365; "hot money" and, 332, 343–49; stabilization and, 359–60

Zhao Xiyou, 47
Zhou Xiaochuan, 39
Zhu, Lujing, 228
Zhu, Xiaodong, 9–10, 11–12, 72n39, 86–132, 137, 140–41, 379–81
Zhu Rongji, 33, 45